SHAKING MY BRIEFCASE

SHAKING MY BRIEFCASE

DIPLOMATIC STORIES

Alan Charlton

Matador
9 Priory Business Park,
Wistow Road, Kibworth Beauchamp,
Leicestershire. LE8 0RX
Tel: 0116 279 2299
Email: books@troubador.co.uk
Web: www.troubador.co.uk/matador
Twitter: @matadorbooks

ISBN 978 1785890 222

British Library Cataloguing in Publication Data.
A catalogue record for this book is available from the British Library.

Printed and bound by CPI Group (UK) Ltd, Croydon, CR0 4YY
Typeset in 11pt Aldine401BT by Troubador Publishing Ltd, Leicester, UK

Matador is an imprint of Troubador Publishing Ltd

Dedicated to my wife Judy
children James, Katy and Tim
grandchildren Theo Charlton and Elizabeth Lucas

Contents

Contents

Introduction

Thanks for looking at this book!

I wrote it from late 2014 to mid-2015, working from episodes outlined between diplomatic postings and on my memories, backed up by diaries mostly from 1990 onwards. The book is what I remember and reflects my opinions. If there are errors they are mine.

Youngsters around the world have asked me what it takes to become a diplomat. I think a key quality is curiosity. You have to want to see and understand new people and places and issues, again and again. I never lost wanting to do that. It was a fine decision to quit at 61 after being Ambassador to Brazil when I might have been selected as Ambassador elsewhere for a final tour. I have since asked myself whether that was the right step. On balance it was. I love the variety of things I have time to do now, mostly lecturing and work on boards in Education, and pursuing my passion for family history research - a field for other book projects. Most of all I love having more time for family...and living in the UK after many years overseas.

Other colleagues have said this before. I feel lucky to have been part of Her Majesty's Diplomatic Service for 35 years. The Service is fantastic. But not perfect - it could do more to use the talents of the retired! But I think of all those youngsters interested in Diplomacy and am amazed that I was one of the few to have lived the dream.

Preface

How to balance work and family? A diplomat moves every few years between UK and various parts of the world. Great variety, new impressions, but poor continuity.

We made some compromises. My wife Judy and James, Katy and Tim did not come with me on my mid-career posting to Bonn (and then Berlin) in the 1990s, so that the children could continue at the local schools. They all did well - helped by that continuity. They were able to enjoy earlier postings in Jordan and Berlin. They visited us in Washington once they were past the school stage. I was on my own in my final posting - in Brasilia - because wonderful though the capital of Brazil is there is not much for spouse without young children or a job to do there.

I wasn't successful at trying to explain what I did at work when the children were young. They noticed I took my briefcase to work every day. Somehow the mantra became that I went to the Embassy "to shake my briefcase".

These stories are things I shook my briefcase at.

1.

MIDDLE EAST

I AM <u>NOT</u> A GREEK TERRORIST

It was 7 March 1981. I had just arrived in Tartous in Syria on a ferry from Koper, then in Yugoslavia and now Slovenia. Passengers had given their passports to the purser on the ship. They had disembarked with their vehicles; I had a new orange Vauxhall Chevette, our first new car. The next stage was the port immigration office to have passports stamped before setting out for my next stop, Damascus. I used my Arabic to find the office ahead of the crowd with the idea of making a fast getaway.

The Syrian official compared my name with a blue index card, conferred out of my hearing with colleagues and then told me I would have to wait until there was clearance from Damascus. He told me there was another choice – to go back to Yugoslavia on the ferry.

I had no idea what the problem might be. My passport bore a stamp to say that I was a member of the British Diplomatic Service. We did not have diplomatic passports in those days. British Governments did not like the idea of special treatment for their diplomats. This caused problems because foreign immigration officials were used to seeing distinctive passports carried by diplomats from other countries; the stamp in ours did not impress. My first overseas travel as a British diplomat had been to Chad in 1979: Chadian immigration looked puzzled and politely asked why it was that a diplomat did not have a diplomatic passport.

I wondered if this was a case of a name similar to mine being on the Syrian immigration stop-list. The fact that I was free to return on the ferry was reassuring to a degree. Or perhaps it was something to do with my previous visits to Syria as a Foreign Office language student?

The situation in Syria then was bleak. The country was going through a period of brutal repression. Hundreds of people had been imprisoned, for example in the notorious centre at Palmyra in the desert. Others had been killed, thousands in the city of Hama alone. In the summer of 1980 there had been doubts about the future of the regime of Hafez Al-Asad. Foreign Office files for 1980 – I leafed through them in the National Archives in 2014 – reveal hesitation in London in meeting the understandable wish from our Ambassador in Damascus for Ministerial visits to the region not just to cover the more like-minded countries such as Jordan but also Syria.

We needed a dialogue with Syria in 1981. It was not a regime we liked. But it was key to the Arab/Israel dispute and tackling that was a high priority in our foreign policy. Diplomacy requires talking to those you don't like as well as to those you do. The UK then still had the reputation of understanding the Arab world and was seen as a bridge to the US, which had become an indispensable power in the region. Yet, in Arab eyes, we were not regarded as on the right side of history on Palestine – whether going back to the World War I Balfour Declaration supporting a Jewish homeland in Palestine or more recently on the Arab/Israel peace process. The impact of the Arab/Israel Wars of 1967 and 1973 was still fresh at that time; the issue of Palestinian rights unresolved (as it still is); and most importantly for Syria the Golan Heights still occupied by Israel.

Syria was aligning itself with the Soviet Union, not least as a way of gaining leverage over the US, which alone had strong influence with Israel. The UK never deviated from seeing the territory seized by Israel in 1967 as occupied and not annexed and Israeli settlements there as illegal.

Staying in Tartous and waiting seemed the only sensible option. I made myself useful interpreting for Bill, a fellow passenger on the ferry. He was a lorry driver from Nottingham with a consignment of cakes for Kuwait in his refrigerated container. He too had been stopped by immigration. Bill told me he had heard they had a tip-off that his lorry was carrying 1800 concealed guns. The Syrians unloaded the cakes and searched thoroughly, opening the insulation space between the cargo hold and the exterior. They found nothing. Bill finally got away on 9 March, with his cakes not in the best condition. He was convinced that a competitor from whom he had taken business had sent a bogus message to the Syrians in order to mess him about.

I slept overnight in my car on the quayside as I had been told not to leave the port area. In the morning, 8 March, I went back to the immigration office. There was no change in the situation. I did not know whether they had had a reply from Damascus telling them to wait or simply had not heard at all. They would say no more.

There was evidently going to be no action the rest of the day since it was a public holiday.

At least I was allowed out of the port area, albeit without my car. I trudged along the seafront about a mile to the Grand Hotel and checked in. So grand it was not.

There had been a lot of rain, which for some reason made the vulnerable telephone system even more unreliable. Using the phone in my room, I eventually managed to raise Vincent Fean at the Embassy in Damascus, although I could hardly

hear him and he could hardly hear me. It was enough for me
to be confident that he understood I was stuck and awaiting
the pleasure of the Syrian authorities.

At least I could spend the night in a bed. Surely there would
be news the following day. Not a bit of it. Back at the port
immigration office early on 9 March I was told they had heard
nothing from Damascus. I rang the Embassy in Damascus
again from the hotel. I learned from the Head of Chancery
Mark Marshall that they were trying to sort it out.

I tried to see the funny side of it. Sheer incompetence and
impenetrable bureaucracy have a funny side. But I felt low. I
could not raise a smile when I fell into a ditch walking back
from the port to the Grand Hotel!

Doubts began to creep into my mind. The Embassy in
Damascus would be in touch with the Syrian Foreign Ministry.
The Syrians might feel a little embarrassment about the way
a diplomat was being treated. But maybe that was just my
wishful thinking. In any case, they would not be in a position,
even if they wanted, to force the Syrian police or intelligence
services to tell them why they were stopping me. I was in an
unpredictable police state whose government had no love for
ours. Why should they worry if I was left to stew in Tartous
until I gave up and went back home?

The next day, 10 March, the Embassy in Damascus told me
on the phone that Patrick Wright, the British Ambassador (later
to become FCO Permanent Under Secretary and Head of the
Diplomatic Service), had spoken to the Chief of Protocol at the
Syrian Foreign Ministry. I don't think I ever really understood
the meaning of Protocol. But every Foreign Ministry had a
Chief of it and they were important on issues connected with
diplomatic status. They also tended to be pretty senior. Patrick
Wright had also spoken to the Deputy Foreign Minister Farouq
Sharaa, a man who was later Syrian Foreign Minister for many

years. Vincent Fean speculated on the phone that my name could have been confused with a British language student who had been at Damascus University the previous year. I hoped Syrian Intelligence were listening to this conversation.

I also had a few words on the phone with the British Embassy in Amman, both with my future boss, Head of Chancery Adrian Sindall, and Andrew Heath, whom I was about to replace. Bless them – they tried to raise my spirits.

Danger is always around the corner in the Middle East. When I was the Desk Officer for Lebanon and Israel in FCO from 1984-86, I saw this repeatedly. In September 1984 the US Embassy was attacked by a car bomb killing a lot of people. The British Ambassador David Miers was visiting the US Embassy at the time. I was in close touch with the British Embassy in Beirut: they had no news of what had happened to him for quite some time. I was doing what Desk Officers do and producing sitreps for Ministers every hour. Eventually we heard that David Miers had escaped the worst but had some minor injuries to a hand and his face.

The bomb was the work of the Shia fundamentalist Hizbollah. They and others posed a threat to any western target, especially in West Beirut. All Britons were advised to keep away. Ministers frequently asked us to review the presence of UK-based Embassy staff, generally on a Friday as they felt nervous about something happening over the weekend. The Embassy in West Beirut was left in the hands of local staff. The few Brits supporting David Miers were relocated to East Beirut and the Maronite hinterland.

I went to look at Beirut for myself in January 1985. I was one of the last British officials allowed to fly to the airport in West Beirut, where there was a risk of kidnapping or worse. I stayed in a hotel in East Beirut. In many ways life there seemed normal. There were good restaurants and bars serving food and drink well above the standard I had experienced in Jordan and Syria.

Yet it did not take long to experience the abnormality of Lebanon. Waiting outside my hotel in the morning, I heard a distant explosion. The driver who arrived shortly afterwards to collect me tuned in his car radio for news. It was an everyday hazard in the city.

British officials were still allowed at that time to visit West Beirut with the protection of the Royal Military Police detachment (there were such small RMP groups in a number of missions around the world at heightened risk to give the Ambassador in particular protection at home and travelling around). The area around the Green Line separating West and East Beirut was totally wrecked by years of intermittent fighting and uninhabited except by armed personnel. Yet along the seafront the atmosphere was deceptively calm. I had lunch in an apartment overlooking the sea and I could imagine how Beirut had been in the happier days of which I had heard from my Arabic teachers.

I was also one of the last British officials around this time to risk the overland journey from Beirut to Damascus. Together with a Lebanese fixer and a driver I went through a dozen or so militia checkpoints before the reaching the border. Passing through the town of Shtoura I was reminded of the ability of Lebanese entrepreneurs in just about any place in the world to keep going: just about anything you could want was in the shops.

Hostages

Lebanon was dangerous then, for the Lebanese and foreign visitors. FCO travel advice strongly discouraged Brits from travelling to many parts of the country. The impact on entirely blameless individuals was the most distressing dimension, especially those taken hostage.

Alec Collett worked for the UN with Palestinian refugees in Sidon. He was kidnapped on his way to Beirut in 1985. I was in touch with his daughter Suzy, a young journalist who worked for a London radio station. She showed amazing courage. There was no hard information about what had become of him. News agencies had received statements about him from the Revolutionary Organisation of Socialist Muslims (ROSM). Our best guess was that these were people associated with the terrorist Abu Nidhal, known for his attacks on westerners but not hitherto for kidnapping. Most likely this was just one of many groups in the badlands of Lebanon who had deliberately or by chance come across Alec Collett or taken him off the hands of others who had captured him.

UK government policy ever since the release from their custody of Leila Khalaf in the 1970s has been not to pay ransoms or do exchanges of detainees with terrorists. This policy comes under scrutiny as it emerges that other countries do get their kidnap victims released by paying up. But, as we have seen with ISIL in Syria/Iraq, the payment of ransoms helps bankroll terrorist groups to do yet more harm.

That does not mean not wanting to talk to hostage-takers. We would have done so if an interlocutor from ROSM had presented themselves. We sent a retired Ambassador on a confidential mission to Cyprus to follow up a mysterious call for negotiations to be held in Cyprus. But no contact was established.

In April 1986, the Americans bombed Tripoli. Soon afterwards there was a claim to the press that Alec Collett had been executed. A video was sent to a news agency. I passed the video to Suzy – her view was that it did indeed show her father's death. It was of someone hanging – no face was shown – with chanting in the background. Alec Collett's second wife in New York was not convinced. We concluded it probably was Alec Collett and as far as I know no information since then has suggested otherwise.

John McCarthy remained as a journalist in Beirut in the worsening situation. He was kidnapped by Hizbollah also in the aftermath of the US bombing of Libya. I had a couple of conversations with his girlfriend Jill Morrell on the phone and then left this liaison function to our Consular Department who had been developing expertise on how best to work with people so affected. We were concerned that Terry Waite, envoy of the Archbishop of Canterbury, who tried to help kidnap victims, might himself be taken in Lebanon. He was indeed kidnapped after I had left the Department.

The Way Prepared

So how did I get to being stranded in a drab port in Syria in turbulent times in 1981 in my third year in the Diplomatic Service?

I was born in Stapleford, six miles from Nottingham on the road to Derby. I enjoyed childhood on a street which rarely saw a car when I was small and an area where children could roam freely.

I benefited from the post-war direct-grant system making it possible for bright kids from unfashionable parts to be sent from an ordinary primary school to a high-achieving secondary school on a full County Council scholarship and then to university. It would be much more difficult to do that now from the primary school I attended. Social mobility has in this respect declined considerably over the last 30 years. My

Author dressed as Hopalong Cassidy, 1956-7

parents left school at 14 and lived in a rented house. No-one in our family had ever had a university degree.

On advice from my German teacher at school I applied to do Modern Languages, German and French, at Gonville and Caius College Cambridge. I was accepted. I enjoyed three golden years there, oblivious to most things around me. Talking to a college friend recently he was surprised I hadn't been aware of Stephen Hawking living on Tree Court Quad. With a group of others, who became lifelong friends, we lived on Grange Road in a house acquired for the eventual retirement of the Master of the College Joseph Needham, a great scientist and sinologist.

Judy and I met early on in Cambridge and married in 1974. After graduation, I decided to train as a languages teacher, took a PGCE at Leicester University, and taught for a couple of years at a Comprehensive School in Gelsenkirchen in the Ruhr on a contract with the state government of North-Rhine Westphalia.

I couldn't see myself teaching for a lifetime. Seeing the

42 Grange Road Cambridge, 1970s

Friends with 1970s hair

results of your work in pupils' progress was wonderful. But everything else – keeping order, bureaucracy of schools – was not so great, nor did I think I was good at it. So after a year doing a Bachelor of Linguistics at Manchester University, kindly part-financed by the organisation – the Centre for British Teachers – which had arranged my teaching job in Germany, I applied again to the Diplomatic Service; I had done so previously in my last undergraduate year in Cambridge and then decided against continuing after passing the first stage.

That first stage consisted of two days of intelligence tests used for all applicants to the fast stream of the Civil Service. The second stage was a day of committee exercises and interviews. I remember being asked by a psychologist about being privileged. That set me thinking. We had had no car or telephone during my childhood. Our holidays had been at Skegness or Mablethorpe. But I had indeed been privileged having hard-working parents who encouraged their children to learn.

The final stage was an interview at a round table in the Old Admiralty Building with people from the Diplomatic Service, Civil Service, business and the unions. I had a stinking cold and felt severely under the weather, but perked up when a grandee from the Foreign Office with the delightful name of Leonard Figg asked me when we were "going to kick the Reds out of the Horn of Africa". I didn't have a ready answer but found something to say – I don't remember what. It was a great question. I wish I'd adopted a similar approach in the hundreds of interviews I've conducted since, asking a question to get the interviewee into the mode of thinking on their feet, which is so important in our work.

I was accepted into the Diplomatic Service. I found out later how proud my father was when I read his journal after he died later that year.

This diplomatic career might have ended even before it

began. With a group of friends, Judy and I visited Spain and Portugal during the summer of 1978. On the drive back from Dover I began to feel unwell. I struggled into London for my first few days at the Foreign Office in King Charles Street. I was alternately hot and cold, fell over in the street, had difficulty driving. Finally, the night fevers were so severe that I kept to bed; we were staying with friends in Kenley. I had seen a local GP earlier but this had not led to further investigation. Now Judy insisted on a house visit. I was taken to Crawley Hospital, diagnosed with typhoid and kept in isolation for over three weeks, with visitors communicating by phone and waving through the glass. I was unwell for a few more days, until the antibiotics started to do their work. After that it was a case of recovery. I had lost two stone so I added boxes of chocolates to the hospital diet to regain some weight. I missed the fortnight of induction training into the FCO. Others on the course were told I was suffering from a virus, nothing more. So my fellow neophytes learned the Foreign Office's principle of disseminating information only on a "need-to-know" basis.

After a year in the West Africa Department in the Foreign and Commonwealth Office in London, I was among those selected to study a "hard" language in 1979. I asked to do Chinese as everyone then was fascinated by the new direction being ushered in by Deng Xiaoping and the prospect of China opening up after the end of the Cultural Revolution.

I expressed a negative preference for Arabic as I was not attracted by the prospect of a career in restrictive Arab societies. A phone call congratulated me on being selected to learn Arabic! This was before the days when staff applied for jobs and were considered only for those unless they could be persuaded otherwise. In 1979, you would have a conversation with your Personnel Officer about your career. Your preferences would be noted. You would later be told you had been allocated a position through a process entirely unseen, and for reasons unknown. Some people preferred it that way, and certainly the organisation was better able to plan use of its staff. But even in 1979 this was beginning to feel anachronistic. Deference had not entirely died, and it was still the Cold War; but we were after all children of the rebellious Sixties.

MECAS, the Middle Centre for Arabic Studies, the FCO Arabic School in Shemlan near Beirut, had a long and proud reputation since its inception after the Second World War, originally in Jerusalem but already for many years in Lebanon. To this day, people who learned Arabic there keep in touch, meet up, go on excursions together, even lobby the government on regional issues. There is a MECAS tie, instantly recognised by the initiated and some non-Arabists too. Its students were not only British diplomats. People from other Foreign Ministries such as the Japanese and New Zealanders and also from companies went there. It had a reputation for good results.

It was widely known as madrasat-al-jawasees, the School of Spies, which irritated some but to my mind added a not unwelcome dash of glamour. Yes, it did teach a few people from the intelligence services but most were regular diplomats. We were bound at that time by the Official Secrets Act not only not to reveal names but not even the admit existence of the Secret Intelligence Service (MI6), the Security Service (MI5) and Government Communications Headquarters (GCHQ). I would not have been able to write this paragraph then.

The School had been evacuated, not for the first time, some months previously in 1979 as the Lebanese Civil War came ever closer to its location. It had set up temporarily pending its return, which sadly never happened, in London. Its ramshackle home was Palace Chambers. This was a government building opposite the Houses of Parliament above Westminster Tube

Station, now the site of Portcullis House providing offices for MPs and deserving its name, as it is one of the most difficult places I have known to get past security.

Palace Chambers was bound to be temporary as it was barely safe to use. There had long been a plan to redevelop the site but decisions were repeatedly delayed. Meanwhile, the building deteriorated. It housed a few small bits of the Civil Service but much of it was empty. We were warned against having heavy furniture in the rooms. The Tube trains below shook the building as they passed. It looked like the kind of semi-abandoned location which would have been a good set for a film of the School of Spies.

The School had a group of teachers who had come to London from Shemlan for this "temporary" period. The Director was the irrepressible Doug Galloway, an Arabist from St Andrew's University. He commuted from there and from his family. He loved what he was doing and was never happier than when disputing with Arabs in their language. But he had signed up to be Director in Shemlan and London had not been part of the deal. He dedicated himself to the task nonetheless. He had enormous energy and always a twinkle in his eye. He rightly expected a lot from us. His crash course on Arabic grammar was brilliant in my view, though would even then be regarded as an old-fashioned approach. He combined it with an expectation that we would converse as far as possible in Arabic in our classes.

There were two MECAS courses. I was in a group embarking on the Long Course, the first 12 months up to Intermediate Standard and then 6 further months to Higher Standard. John Sawers, later Head of SIS, was one of us; Robert Gibson, later High Commissioner in Dhaka another; Doug Scrafton yet another. Sharing Palace Chambers with us was a group who had completed Intermediate and were starting their Higher Course. They had started at Shemlan and been evacuated, as described by Sherard Cowper-Coles in his memoir "Ever The Diplomat". There were no students from either course from other countries.

We used the materials prepared for the school in Shemlan, including the "The Way Prepared". To start we used " A Course in Colloquial Arabic" written by former MECAS Director Leslie McLoughlin. Using this, we found ourselves in role play asking for and giving directions from Shemlan to Beirut, and talking about surrounding villages such as Souq-el-Gharb, which had become a battlefield of the Lebanese Civil War – places none of us had visited and, as it turned out,

Chapter II
ORIENTATIONS
Dialogue 3

'in-naas fi-D-Day9a mawaarina?	Are the people in the village Maronites?
naas	people
maaroonee pl. mawaarina	Maronite
na9am, shimlaan Day9a maarooniyya	Yes, Shemlan is a Maronite village
ya9nee, maa fee 'illaa mawaarina?	That is, there are only Maronites?
'illaa	except
kallaa, fee room kamaan, laakin 'aktar 'an-naas mawaarina	No, there are Greek Orthodox as well, but most of the people are Maronites
room	(Byzantium) Greek Orthodox
laakin	but
'aktar (from "'ikteer")	most (of)
Tayyib, laakin 'aktar an-naas fee sooq-al-gharb room, mush hayk?	Good, but most of the people in Souq-el-Gharb are Greek Orthodox, aren't they?
mush hayk	(is it) not so? Equivalent to "n'est ce pas?".
SaHH, oo 'aktar 'an-naas fee 9aytaat durooz	Correct, and most of the people of Aitat are Druze
durzee pl. durooz	Druze
Tayyib, oo 'il-'inkleez 'aktarhum kaatooleek?	Good, and are most of the English Catholics?
'aktar-hum	most of them
kaatooleekee pl. kaatooleek	Catholic
kallaa, fee kaatooleek 'ikteer laakin 'aktar 'al-'inkleez brotestaant	No, there are many Catholics but most of the English are Protestants

A Colloquial course in Arabic

never would during the course. I could have done with a map of the area.

Not all students enjoyed the experience. For me, it was wonderful. I had learned a lot of useful stuff in my post-graduate course in Linguistics at Manchester. That had been a great help when I did the FCO test for language aptitude, a variation of which applicants take to this day. I had been able to write down and match unknown sounds by using phonetic script. Before that, in our two years in Gelsenkirchen, my German became ingrained. Foreign languages bore no terror and are still a delight.

Arabic was a new challenge, a non-European language with a completely different structure and very different new sounds. We were required to reach a standard at Higher level enabling us to interpret for visiting Ministers as well as read the newspapers with ease and understand the TV etc. Being a full-time student of this beautiful language while on full pay and with a job abroad in prospect was more than pretty good. I was still close enough to student days to be practised in the daily accumulative grind of study.

Doug Galloway's enthusiasm was infectious. The teachers, notably the delightfully old-school Lebanese Ahmed Moumneh, were set in their ways and could be pedantic, but all celebrated the students' progress. The arguments about the wrongs inflicted on the Palestinians, particularly with our Palestinian teacher Faisal Shana'a, were invigorating and great preparation for young diplomats who needed to understand that in many countries there are issues where you will never see fully eye to eye with your hosts (this even applies in Europe where the Germans, for example, don't get our EU-scepticism). The other teachers were Daoud and Mrs Dallal and Mrs Moumneh, wife of Ahmed. The Dallals, on the right of the photo, kindly invited us to their house.

The Dallals, 1980

Language breaks in Syria

The routine of lessons was broken up by language breaks. With Lebanon off-limits, we went to Syria. The first trip was in April 1980. Together with another student, Steve Martin, I spent a few days in Suwayda in southern Syria with the Greek Catholic bishop, a fearsome-looking character who prized his relationship with the British Embassy. We arrived on Maundy Thursday. It was still Lent. We had to subsist on unappetising long-dead cold vegetables.

Suwayda was a mix of Sunni Muslims, Christians and Druze. We were invited by some young men to visit their Druze family one evening. It was an event for them to host foreigners. What Arabs of all denominations have in common is their tradition of hospitality. We learned early on in our course the saying "beitee beitak" "my house is your house". The family proudly presented a bottle of Scotch. Asked if I liked whisky (which I then rarely drank) I said yes. They poured me a large tumbler-full and watched in great anticipation. When after a while I had barely disturbed the surface of it, I was asked with concern if it was all right. I took a gulp. Their faces brightened. They had probably never drunk it in their lives but had heard that this was the drink to offer westerners. Its cost was a demonstration of their hospitality. I somehow left without causing too much offence but also without consigning the rest of my stay in Suwayda to be overshadowed by a hangover.

We attended the Good Friday service at the Bishop's church. It lasted over three hours, including several processions through the church and plenty of incense. There was a general hubbub throughout as life seemed to go on accompanying the service. People talked. Children ran around. There were Druze and Muslims there or dropping in, just as the Christians went to their high and holy days. We joined in where we could. In response to the periodic declaration from a priest " Al-maseeh qam" "The Messiah arose", we chanted "wa haqqan qam" "Indeed he arose".

With the Mutran in Suwayda, 1980

We had time to travel around the country. The inter-city buses worked well. They were crowded and uncomfortable, and not timely, but they tended to arrive on the same day. I went to Palmyra to see the fabulous ruins linked with Queen Zenobia – some destroyed by ISIL in 2015. We are fascinated by Roman and Greek ruins in Europe. In Palmyra it was a different scale, a whole city spread across the plain, since time immemorial a key stop on a trading route through the desert. I went to Aleppo, the second city. I was struck by the strong military presence on the streets. I stayed in the traditional Baron Hotel, in better days the resting pace of travellers from West and East, and wondered which famous visitors of the past had also trodden upon the now very faded carpets.

We had a second language break in Damascus in January 1981, just weeks before our Higher exam. The idea was to immerse ourselves as much as possible. I stayed at the faded Orient Palace hotel and frequented bars and restaurants.

Damascus was lively. These were days before the Islamic conservatism which spread following the Iranian Revolution had had much of an effect in the Levant. In any case Syria was ruled by a sect which mainstream Muslims might not see as truly Muslim and there were large numbers of Druze and also Christians. Their bars and restaurants sold more than passable local Barida beer accompanied by salty pistachios. The Damascenes were talkative, as long as it wasn't about national politics. They enjoyed a foreigner trying to converse with them in their language.

The city's architecture was a mix of Eastern-European style ugly concrete with large banners bearing the smiling countenance of Hafez Al-Asad contrasting with the atmospheric ancient Souq al-Hamadiyeh where people had walked from the early days of Christianity. Knowing

Al-Yarmouk refugee camp.

the awfulness of the regime and the internal troubles of the time, as a foreigner I felt the need to be on guard. But there was knockabout Mediterranean-style banter in bars. Doug Galloway was regularly to be found in the Rayess restaurant. He held court there in his flowing Arabic. We also liked a bar called Abu George's for the chat, nuts and beer.

In the spirit of Arab hospitality we were invited to events and homes. Especially memorable was a visit to the Al-Yarmouk Palestinian refugee camp on the outskirts of Damascus. We were received in a friendly way and given what hospitality these poor people could manage. It was my first of several visits to such camps on the periphery of pre-1948 Palestine. I was struck by the determination of people to return, even those who had been born long after the exile had begun. The Palestine issue was not going away. One young man (see photo) insisted I took with me his school Arabic poetry book. I treasured it, but somehow no longer have it.

This trip to the region was an opportunity to visit for the

first time my future place of work – the British Embassy in Amman. I had been telephoned by Personnel some weeks before to be told where I would be serving in the Arab world. I actually misheard and told people for a few days I would be going to Morocco before a letter told me it was to be Jordan.

Crossing the border by bus from Syria into Jordan took hours. Relations between the two countries were tense. Jordan believed the Syrians had tried to assassinate their King Hussein and might even invade their country. The Syrians suspected that the Jordanian regime was not as solidly as it claimed against the separate peace treaty agreed with Israel by the Egyptians. It took many more years but Jordan was indeed the second of the so-called front-line Arab states to agree a peace with Israel.

Amman was such a contrast to Damascus. It had functional modern buildings and little of the charm of the ancient Damascus. It felt safer, though.

The Higher exams were held in Palace Chambers on 12-13 February. I passed well enough. I was raring to go and use my Arabic in earnest in Jordan. But first I would have a little adventure driving out there, also for the good practical reason that I wanted to have a car at hand for when Judy and young son James arrived by air a couple of weeks after me. The advice I had been given was that cars could take months to be imported into Jordan and take ages to clear the port of Aqaba. I didn't want to risk being without one.

So I set out on 27 February 1981, as winter was drawing to an end in UK. After a stop at Besançon, I drove over the Alps in snow without snow tyres or chains. It was stupid really not to think of the risk of wintry weather. I arrived in Koper to discover that the ferry had sailed that morning although I had been told it was an evening departure. Phone calls to London and the ferry company in Sweden got me on to the next ship, scheduled to leave the following afternoon. I found a hotel and watched the carnival in the streets that evening. The next day I was at the port first thing, in case this ship too left early, and only relaxed once I was on board.

The ferry voyage was easy enough. It was a modern Swedish-operated ship and the passengers were largely lorry drivers going to various parts of the Middle East. So I was pretty relaxed when I arrived in Tartous. I intended to stop in Damascus with Embassy diplomat Vincent Fean and his family, whom I had met when on language break there, and then make my way in a day to Amman.

…Will the Syrians Let Me Go?

An enduring legacy from Tartous I could have done without was amoebic dysentery. I was pretty careful about what I ate but did have a salad at a restaurant and I suspect that is what did it. Fortunately, the worst and recurring effects did not appear until I had eventually reached Amman. But they continued for months, often laying me low at weekends.

I ended up spending three days in Tartous waiting for permission to move on. On the third day, a young mukhabaraat (intelligence) national serviceman called at the hotel and said he had instructions to escort me to Damascus in my car the following morning. We did this. Unfortunately, it was raining and this slowed down the traffic already hampered by road blocks and poor driving surfaces. As a result we arrived in Damascus after 2 o'clock, went into the mukhabaraat HQ but found that the senior officer I was apparently supposed to meet had already gone home and could not be disturbed. I had to await his further orders. I was not allowed to contact the British Embassy nor to leave the building. This was disconcerting, to say the least, given the fearsome reputation of the mukhabaraat. But I was beginning to think that the situation was more cock-up than threatening.

After a couple of hours, the decision came through that I was to travel to Suwayda with another mukhabaraat man in the car with me. Asking why did not get me anywhere. The people I was dealing with did not seem to know and were used to obeying orders, the reason for which may not have been vouchsafed to them. So to Suwayda we went, where I was taken to the Chief of Police – it was by now early evening. We had a pleasant chat about the Greek Catholic bishop and my stay in the city the previous Easter. The police chief said he didn't know why I had been sent to him. He decided (or was instructed – I don't know which) that I should be escorted to the border with Jordan at Deraa. This time I was allowed to drive my car with another police car leading the way. We arrived at the border. I drove on to Amman.

What Was It All About?

Once I had a chance to talk to the Embassy in Jordan I learned that our colleagues in Damascus had been busy asking the Syrian Foreign Ministry what was happening. But they did not have any more joy than I had in eliciting an explanation. The situation was complicated by all this happening over a holiday weekend – an Eid – and in rainy weather, which messed up the road traffic and the telephone connections between cities.

During my three years in Amman I went back to Syria a few times, and each occasion asked our Embassy in Syria to speak to the Foreign Ministry so that I would not have a problem at the border. I had no further difficulties beyond the usual chaos there.

Thirty-three years later I asked Sir Vincent Fean, who

had gone on to a distinguished career in the region, why he thought I had been detained. He said the only clue came from a Duty Officer at the Syrian MFA over that weekend who had said he understood I had been identified as a Greek terrorist. I wonder. There was concern in the West about Greek terrorism at the time, but not particularly that they were visiting Syria as far as I knew. What did the Syrians have to fear from them anyway? It's an explanation which doesn't ring true as I had a British passport and showed no signs of being Greek. Vincent did comment correctly that I then had a moustache! A lot of Arabs as well as Greeks did at that time, though.

As I write in 2015, this Syria of religious tolerance seems far away. The regime of Hafez Al-Asad, father of the current President Bashar, was undemocratic and unscrupulous. It was run by a clique of people from the minority Alawites and the army. It brooked no opposition. Syria of 1981 was a forbidding place. There were elections; but the votes, if even counted, did not affect the predetermined result. There were laws; but the regime was a law unto itself.

Yet the regime did ensure there was no religious strife, allowing Christians and Druze freedom to practise their religion as long as they did not get involved in the politics of opposition. By and large they were allowed freedom to run a business and travel abroad. For minorities this was not the worst imaginable situation in a troubled region. The UK had by no means given up on the Asad regime. We had to deal with worse around the world and even in the region. Looking at the Foreign and Commonwealth (FCO) files for 1980 I found that the Young Conservatives were invited to a Youth Congress in Syria then. The Syrians certainly wanted a relationship with the UK.

Hafez Al-Asad was ruthless. Yet the West felt there could be a deal to be done with him. That's why Henry Kissinger made such an effort in shuttle diplomacy after the 1973 war and generations of American diplomats would keep on trying. Asad wanted above all else untrammelled restoration of Syrian territory on the Golan Heights, lost to Israel in the 1967 war. He may have been prepared for an arrangement for the Palestinians around the idea of a state in the West Bank, East Jerusalem and Gaza, and accepting Israel's right to exist within pre-1967 borders. From his viewpoint the separate peace concluded by Egypt with Israel was a disaster. It may be that Asad missed an opportunity in these years. Since then Israel's strength as a state and in the US domestic body politic has grown and encouraged them to be even tougher.

The domestic opposition to Hafez's son President Bashar Al-Asad of the 2010s was rightly supported by the West. But, with the emergence of the so-called Islamic State, the Asads started to appear as not the worst scenario. We are in a struggle with Islamic fundamentalism where the Asad regime shares some values and enemies with us. The situation in Syria in 2015 is much worse now than ever. A British diplomat simply would not nowadays try to drive through Syria as I did in 1981 and later in 1984. The FCO would also be much more alarmed if one of theirs was detained in Syria!

Diplomats have unpredictable lives in which odd things happen – just read some of the stories in the book "The Spanish Ambassador's suitcase". These episodes can be instructive and useful in the exchange of information and ideas which is at the heart of the work of a bilateral Embassy. So, during my time as Ambassador in Brazil 30 years later, I spoke several times to senior players in the Brazilian Foreign Ministry about the situation in Syria, underlining the awfulness of the Asad regime but also its hard-headedness and durability.

The Brazilians warned that we might make the situation in Syria worse. "Do no harm" we heard from them. They had strong support for this approach from the influential Syrian-Lebanese community in Brazil, a considerable portion of whom were Christians who felt the Asads were protection for Christian Syrians against Islamic fundamentalism. Our reply was that we could not stand by as Bashar and his cronies killed people.

The Arab Spring looked for a while like the big change in the region's politics which had been so long in coming. I suppose the hope was that that people power would lead to democracy being established as in Central and Eastern Europe after the Fall of the Berlin Wall. From the vantage point of 2015, the situation on Libya is chaotic, Egypt has reverted to authoritarian rule, Tunisia is shaky, Syria and Iraq are in turmoil. There is ISIL terrorism in Europe. The West is not prepared to risk its soldiers and treasure without being sure of achieving something palpable and having an exit strategy. What would happen if a friendly and functioning state such as Jordan needed help against Islamic state? It's a messy world.

PART II

HMQ MEETS PLK

I was sitting at my desk at the British Embassy in Amman on Saturday afternoon in March 1984 when I took a call from a British Sunday newspaper which threatened to name and shame me in the next day's London edition if I didn't give information about the impact on the imminent visit by The Queen and Duke of Edinburgh of a bomb explosion at the Intercontinental Hotel in Amman. Would the visit endanger the life of the Queen?

I had taken the call as our Press Officer was not in the building. Nor was there anyone else around apart from Security who were putting calls through to me. The Embassy was closed – our weekend was Friday and Saturday. I was finishing off work to prepare for the visit.

The caller was a well-known reporter who I imagine got carried away into trying to bully me. I was left worried. I was deeply rooted in the culture of telling outsiders only what they needed to know when security issues were involved. I was also acutely aware of the political sensitivity surrounding the visit and that press stories about the Queen's safety would not help. There was nothing about the conversation in the Sunday papers. I was relieved.

Inward visits are an opportunity for Embassies to raise the profile of their country in UK foreign policy and pursue commercial objectives. The more senior and well-known the visitor the greater the opportunity to make impact. The British Royal family have a unique attraction. The Queen is the most famous person in the world. Countries around the world want the kudos of a visit from her, preferably a formal state visit.

A Royal Visits Committee considers options for visits overseas of the Royal Family, supported by public funds. They are made to bring benefit to the UK. Of course, the Royal Family has its input. But there should not be a visit unless the government of the day judges it will help in our foreign affairs.

Jordan in 1981 was still living the aftershock of civil war with the Palestinians ten years previously, known as Black September. We had bullet impacts from the fighting, or at least I was told that was what the marks were, on inside walls in our Embassy building at Third Circle up the hill from downtown Amman. Jordan had differed with the US, such an important support for moderate Arab countries, over the separate peace concluded by Egypt with Israel at Camp David in 1979: the US Embassy was headed by a Chargé d'Affaires rather than by a full Ambassador reflecting this disagreement. In the wars of 1948 and 1967 Jordan had lost the Palestinian territory of the West Bank and East Jerusalem. Palestinian refugees were over half the population of Jordan and had questionable allegiance to their country of residence – a fact of which native East Bankers were keenly aware.

It was amazing that Jordan had survived at all. The countries in the region were created as part of the First World War settlement, or just after the Second World War in the case of Israel. Jordan, especially without the West Bank and East Jerusalem, did not have much going for it. There was no oil wealth, little in the way of minerals, little arable land. It had difficult neighbours.

The Saudi Royal Family did not like the Hashemite Royal

Family of Jordan, which claimed a strong lineage back to custodianship of the Holy Places and the Prophet. Iraq had been connected with Jordan until the Hashemite ruler there had been deposed and his body dragged through the streets in 1958; the Iraq of Saddam Hussein was not an easy neighbour. Syria was sceptical of Jordan's resolve to withstand calls for a separate peace with Israel and appeared constantly to be trying to undermine the King even to the point of being suspected of trying to kill him. There were those in Israel – including Prime Ministers Begin and Shamir – who thought the Palestine problem could be solved by declaring Jordan the Palestinian state and shunting the Palestinians of the Occupied Territories there – "The Jordan is Palestine" thesis.

Jordan had its supporters. The UK held the mandate for the whole of Palestine – now Israel, Occupied Territories, and Jordan – following the WW1 settlement until 1948. We supported the Emir of Transjordan, later King Abdullah I. Our role continued after the end of the mandate in 1948 with a military presence until the King asked British General Glubb Pasha to leave in 1956. The US then became a more important source of support. There was the beginning of some solidarity funding from the rich Arab Gulf States for Jordan after 1973 in recognition of the burden it carried as a front-line state and as an incentive not to conclude a separate peace with Israel. The Jordanian press reported payment of these instalments when they were made, no doubt encouraged by the Jordanian government. The payments were often late and some countries did not pay at all. The Jordanian public could read who was keeping to their commitments and who was not.

In fact, in 1981, compared with what had gone before in the previous 15 years, Jordan was not doing so badly. There was a construction boom, especially of new houses in Amman bought with money from the Gulf. Because of its war with

Iran, Iraq depended on supplies coming overland and by air from Jordan as access to the Gulf States was cut off: this was an economic benefit for Jordan. The souq downtown was busy.

Amman was and is very different from Damascus. It has its ancient ruins downtown, but the greater Roman legacy is at Jerash outside Amman while the more recent legacy was the desert castles of the Ottoman period. When I arrived the impact of the Iranian revolution was beginning to have its effect, not so much in the politics as Arabs supported brother Arabs in Iraq against the Persians, but in growing conservatism in Muslim society. More girls at the university started to wear black and cover up, though not so far as to obscure the face. So you could see a group of female students together some dressed colourfully and wearing short skirts and others in black and covered up.

There was more pressure on Christians over the sale in their shops of alcohol, especially during Ramadan. Pork became harder to buy locally – consequently many of us on the diplomatic staff tended to order items such as pork pies in bulk shipments from UK, and then find it on offer at all our houses for parties for the following weeks. Conservative Muslims became stronger in the only really elected bodies in Jordan, the professional associations. But none of this made life too difficult for expatriates.

We could travel outside Amman without difficulty. Negotiating the traffic was a challenge, particularly predicting the behaviour of the ancient buses and lorries and particularly during Ramadan when the drivers had nothing to drink all day. We could go out on picnics to the Dibbin pine woods, oversee the Jordan Valley from Madaba, go down to the Dead Sea, tour the desert castles, visit Petra which when we arrived had no international-class hotel, and of course the sea at Aqaba.

Amman lacked the cultural diversions of Damascus and

its lively society in restaurants and bars. Expatriates made their own entertainment. We invited each other to our houses. In the Embassy itself we had the help of local staff including the invaluable Mr Fix-it, in this case Abu Khalil, whom every Embassy in such countries needs – sorting out currency exchange, dealing with the local bureaucracy, finding you staff for parties at home etc. He even turned out for the Embassy football team though then in his mid-forties at least.

The climate varied around the country. It was baking hot in the Jordan Valley and by the Dead Sea in the summer – 45 degrees. Similarly, visits to Aqaba were best in spring and autumn and even winter. Amman was benign. Summer from April to October was blue sky with temperatures between 20-35 degrees and no rain. Winter was generally mild but occasionally cold with snowfall which caused chaos – we spent a whole night baling out the basement of our house of water from melting snow from the garden above battling to prevent our boiler being inundated.

I was Second, later First, Secretary Political. This promotion was more or less automatic for fast-streamers in their late twenties as long they had been performing reasonably. I was taught my craft by the Ambassador Alan Urwick, who regularly had me into his office to "help" with his draft telegrams – exciting for me when he had just seen the King. The first Head of Chancery Adrian Sindall taught me the basics of drafting and offered constructive criticism. I wish I had done as well by junior staff when I became senior in Embassies.

The key was to write concisely and to make busy people in London feel there was value added in a report. I developed the usual range of contacts in the Ministries and outside. I had a good trading position with the US Embassy as I could tell them about my impressions of the PLO who had re-established an office in Amman but whom my US colleagues

Our villa in Amman in the snow

were forbidden to meet. The Americans could tell me about other aspects such as the growth of Islamic conservatism: they had more people than we did to cover the waterfront.

Britain was no longer the lead foreign country in Jordan. But our reputation with many people remained as if we still were.

I received in my office a very ancient sheikh of the southern Howeitat tribe in his tribal clothes. He was bald but for a few wisps of white hair. He told me he liked to come to the British Embassy when he visited the capital. He then said with animation that he had fought together with T. E. Lawrence in World War 1. He reached over, took my hand and drew it towards him. He asked me to feel the crease in his skull where a bullet had parted his hair in the days when he had had some. I obliged, and listened to his stories of the times. He was old enough to have done what he said but I had no idea if his stories were true. They were good stories.

34

Our Ambassador was regular in taking leave in the summer and staying in Jordan most of the rest of the time. Once when he decided at short notice to leave the country for the weekend there were questions coming from Jordanians whether there was going to be a coup – the assumption was that any action of the Ambassador was very meaningful and the British knew what was going on. I was once told in flowing poetic Arabic that the British could hear the movement of a grasshopper hundreds of miles away.

King Hussein had survived assassination attempts and threats of invasion and found a policy which looked sound for the coming years – accepting Gulf support and staying aloof from efforts to bring him into a separate peace with Israel at least until circumstances were more favourable. Threats to the regime were dealt with by tough internal security forces. Yet Jordan did not have the feel of an oppressive state. People were by and large free to go about their business and say what they liked as long as it did not threaten the regime. Self-censorship was the order of the day. Parliament remained suspended as it had been ever since the 1967 war. Towards the end of our time in Jordan the King did allow elections for a new parliament and I enjoyed going round some electors with one of the candidates. This was not the King divesting himself of power. Parliament's role would be limited.

This improbable country's survival owed a lot to its leadership. First Emir, later King, Abdullah had proved a level-headed ruler first under the British mandate and then through the crisis following the 1948 war. He was assassinated in June 1951 in Jerusalem by a Palestinian who feared he would make a peace with Israel. By his side was his grandson Hussein, only 15 years old, who grappled with the assailant. A medal pinned to Hussein's chest saved his life from a gunshot which hit him. In 1953, after Hussein's father Talal was sidelined because he was not up to the job, Hussein became King, crowned exactly a month before our own Queen Elizabeth II. He left his course at Sandhurst. Not every decision Hussein went on to make turned out well, but he found his way through the complex travails of the 1950s, 1960s and 1970s to be in 1981 regarded as a benign leader and a survivor.

Hussein liked people and people liked him. There were many stories about him. A British contractor who worked at the Palace said the King would routinely stop should they meet in the corridor and ask after his family. He was the kind of man you would really like to spend time with. In his younger days he had gone around his kingdom in disguise so that he could see how people lived. Many Jordanians believed that he understood their situation.

Our own royal family had met him many times. Previously during our time in Jordan the Duke of Edinburgh visited Jordan as President of the World Wildlife Fund, to reintroduce the oryx to the Jordanian desert. The Duke and Duchess of Kent visited heading a Trade Mission. The Duke of Gloucester visited in his role with the St John's Eye Hospital in Jerusalem. There had been other royal visits before, including from Prince Charles and Princess Anne. The Queen had seen the King many times in London, where he kept a house and had – at least in his younger days – a reputation for enjoying himself: "Disco Dad" according to one of his children.

Hussein's links with Britain were important to us. He had been educated at Harrow and Sandhurst. His second wife, Toni Gardner, who became Princess Muna, was the daughter of a Defence Attaché at the British Embassy. She was the mother of four of his children, the eldest of whom was Abdullah who eventually became Hussein's successor, although there were doubts during my time in the Embassy that Hussein would risk a successor with a non-Arab mother who might not be accepted as legitimate by the population. Hussein ended the British military role in Jordan in the 1950s at a the time when Gamal Abdul Nasser and Arab nationalism were growing ever more powerful. You could see the earlier British influence in the Jordanian Armed Forces – their marching, traditions, some of their equipment and even their music, though their bagpipes music was not tuneful to western ears and one of their standard pieces sounded like "Nellie the Elephant" in Arab key. These links were assets for the British Embassy.

The King was strong in supporting our cause during the Falklands war. He saw this as the right of the Islanders to self-determination being violated by force by Argentina. He argued the parallel with the situation of the Palestinians whose right to self-determination was not being respected. His stance was particularly important for us as Jordan was then a non-permanent member of the UN Security Council when there was a vote on the Argentine invasion. Thanks to the Jordanian vote in our favour there was a majority to pass a resolution condemning the Argentine action. When news of the Argentine surrender came through on 16 June 1982 I was at an event at our Head of Chancery's house which included the Commander-in-Chief of the Jordanian Armed Forces, Zeid bin Shaker. He said: "WE have won".

The King had many admirers around the world. He was known by some (I don't know where the term originated) as PLK – Plucky Little King. That sounds disrespectful even if meant in a positive way. Little in stature he may have been. He had a strong deep voice, was powerfully built, charming and charismatic. He was one of those people who made a real positive difference to the course of history.

A State visit to Jordan had a lot to recommend it. Jordan was a moderate country. Its stability was a key building block in any effort to promote a settlement of the Arab-Israel dispute, at its heart the questions of Israel's security and Palestinian rights. The visit would be a way of showing our support for the King.

It was not politically straightforward. There had been strains in our relationship with Israel owing to the 1981 invasion of Lebanon and killing of Palestinian civilians at Sabra and Shatila. But the security of Israel remained a fundamental of British policy. The Israeli government would not like the visit, nor would some of Israel's supporters in the UK. There would also be questions whether it was wise to launch the Queen into such a controversial region.

Another issue loomed large in the run-up to the visit – the Queen's security. Palestinian terrorism threatened both Jordan and the West. This was only a few years since the terrible events at the Munich Olympics in 1972. The Abu Nidhal group had proven ability to operate in many countries. A Jordanian colleague Azmi Mufti, whom I had got on well with when he was in Amman at the Foreign Ministry, was killed by Abu Nidhal after he moved to the Jordanian Embassy in Athens. The Jordanian security authorities had found explosives in an abandoned car left for weeks on waste ground near our Embassy. Our building, rented from a Jordanian owner, was elevated on concrete pillars and had little stand-off from the roundabout Third Circle. It would have been easy enough to drive a car under the Embassy and detonate a bomb with devastating results for the building and for the people inside.

The Embassy moved after my departure to a new-build concrete fortress on the edge of the city. This improved security. But it was an inhospitable building which did not welcome visitors as had the Embassy at Third Circle. Getting the balance right between security and accessibility has been a problem ever since. For the Americans it is even more difficult as they face a greater threat and there is Congressional legislation mandating, for example, certain distances between the building and public space.

The Cabinet Office wrote several assessments in the run-up to the visit looking at just about every eventuality, without recommending cancellation. Then, on 29 March 1984, just two days before the Queen's scheduled arrival, a small bomb went off in the British Airways office at the Intercontinental hotel, just a few minutes' walk from the Embassy towards Second Circle and at that time the only hotel of international standard in Amman. No-one was hurt but the alarm bells were sounded in London.

A tabloid rang from London asking if the Queen's visit would be called off. In the absence of our Press Officer, I took the call and referred them to the FCO in London. Then it was the turn of The Sunday Times and the episode at the beginning of this section. It was reaffirmed in London that the visit would go ahead.

The preparation for major visits is hard work. My main roles were the briefing for the Queen and keeping up the political work of the Embassy while the Head of Chancery, now Peter Raftery, and others, focussed almost entirely on the visit. Perhaps my most significant contribution was to choose the dates – the end of March, when in my experience of the previous three years the weather had been mild and the rainy season had petered out. So it proved. The sun shone.

The Queen in Jordan

The Queen arrived with the Duke of Edinburgh and accompanying party in a Tristar flown by the RAF. This was the first of many formal arrival ceremonies I saw in my time as a diplomat with a band and red carpet at a military airport.

It was on another top inward visit to Jordan that a Tristar was parked with its rear facing the Royal Pavilion and blew out all the windows when it started up its powerful engines. Luckily, no-one was hurt.

The first two days of the visit were in Amman. The tradition of these occasions requires formal entertainment given by the Heads of State, in this case King Hussein and the Queen. On the first evening, the Queen hosted her dinner at the Ambassador's residence and then there was a reception at the Basman Palace at 10 pm so that more senior Jordanians could be at an event with her. The King hosted his dinner at Basman Palace with the formal speeches on the following evening; the Queen had earlier been at a garden party for the British community at the residence of the British Ambassador, just up the road from the Embassy towards Fourth Circle. Senior staff were presented. We have the photo!

On Day 3, the Queen and Duke went down the winding road to the Jordan Valley, from Amman's elevation of 2800 feet to below sea level. Jordanian soldiers lined the route, some 25 miles – a reminder of the high level of security. Crown Prince Hassan briefed them on Jordanian agriculture in this fertile and hot part of the country, which British aid and co-operation officers were helping with. Part of our preparation for this leg had been to identify suitable pit stops in this part of the world where arrangements were pretty basic.

They then visited the Dead Sea for a picnic lunch. This was at that time not such a visited part of the country. We used to go down sometimes to bathe in hot springs and float in the water. But the days of hotels down there had gone with the Israeli occupation of the West Bank in 1967 and not yet returned.

The two royal parties later separately flew from Amman to Aqaba – separately, not least for security reasons. On Day 4,

Staff being presented to the Queen, Amman 1984

Thursday, they drove up to Petra – the "rose-red city half as old as time," heart of the stunning Nabatean civilisation, which in those days was famous but not so heavily visited as now. By this time the Forum hotel had opened where the monarchs could have lunch. Back in Aqaba, they cruised in the Red Sea, no doubt looking at Israel in one direction and Saudi Arabia in another. Day 5 was departure. I enjoyed drafting Aqaba telegram no 1 to FCO with Haydon Warren-Gash, Private Secretary to Richard Luce, the accompanying Foreign Office Minister.

Ambassador Alan Urwick was knighted by the Queen at King Hussein's Palace at Aqaba. Afterwards he related that the party had one evening watched a recording of the day's activities and the Queen, noticing that the Ambassador had all but closed his eyes against the glare of the sun, declared that he had fallen asleep! It didn't do Alan Urwick any harm as he was appointed Serjeant at Arms of the House of Commons on retirement from the Diplomatic Service in 1990 until 1995.

The Jordanian media gave blanket coverage to the visit and what they thought it said about the status of their country, even though the protocol of the time and the security environment did not allow walkabouts and most of the time the royals were together in private. Other members of the Embassy received awards from the Queen. I was given by the Queen a pair of ER cufflinks which I wear to this day.

Lord Caradon

One of the great benefits of being in an Embassy is the opportunity to meet interesting people visiting from UK. One was Lord Caradon, then an elderly man and a little lame but enjoying yearly or so trips back to Palestine. I met him a couple of times at Amman airport and heard some of his stories. I felt privileged.

He told me he had arrived in Palestine in 1929 as a new member of the Palestine Civil Service. The Arab revolt was in train. He reported to HQ in Jerusalem, was asked if he could shoot, was given a gun and told to work with the police. In the Second World War he became Governor of Nablus. Later he was Governor of Cyprus as it moved towards independence and had to make decisions of life or death for convicted murderers. Perhaps he was best known in the Middle East for his role, when a Minister of the then Labour government and UK Permanent representative at New York, in creating the famous UN Security Resolution 242 of 1967 which, brief though it is, contains the basic bargain of Israel trading occupied territory for peace on which a resolution of the Arab/Israel dispute still has to be based.

We had the chance to travel to the West Bank, Jerusalem and Israel. The distances were short but there was no easy way to cross the Allenby Bridge, the only permitted route. The Israeli security made it a long and sweaty trek. It was worthwhile. We stayed at St George's Hostel in East Jerusalem where the registers listed former colleagues during the thirty previous years. Our first experience of the Old City was wonderful. On a subsequent visit, I had the honour to be shown around the Church of the Holy Sepulchre by the Keeper of the Key, a Muslim elder of the Nuseibeh family. The church was used by several Christian denominations, so who better to hold the key? This was before the days of violence in the name of Islam.

We once went on holiday to Eilat, looking over the then closed border to Aqaba – two such different societies and traditions within sight of each other but with no border crossing and no contact in those days.

George Brown

Lord George-Brown, formerly George Brown the Labour Deputy Prime Minister to Harold Wilson, was another visitor. I met him late one night at Amman airport. Fortunately, this was by then the new airport out of town in the desert. The old airport at Marka had been chaotic and served as a place to sleep for crowds of Egyptian migrant workers travelling one way or the other. Not the place to receive fragile British passengers off a plane from London.

His flight from Heathrow had been delayed for many hours and he was the worse for wear. He greeted me like an old friend, regaled me with stories as we drove to his hotel and was telling people in the bar as I left in the small hours about his belief that there was a way to end the Iran/Iraq war, that Mossad had been in touch with him and he was on his way to

Baghdad to see Saddam Hussein to help bring this about. This is something of a forgotten war in the UK because we were not involved in the fighting as we were in later conflicts in Iraq. It caused a huge death toll and was a threat to the stability of a vital region.

The next morning I heard that he had been taken ill, was in the King Hussein Medical Centre under the care of the King's personal doctor but the prognosis was uncertain. We contacted his family. I recall speaking to his brother. After a few weeks he was well enough to return back to UK. Sadly, it was no surprise when he died in June 1985.

Sporting Footnotes

The small number of British and other expats did a lot of things together. The British Embassy Club was the centre of much of this. After our first few months, we moved to a villa next door to it – a lovely place with a lemon tree and grapevine. The club was represented at an "It's a Knock-Out Competition" (known elsewhere as Jeux sans Frontières) at the Intercontinental Hotel at the end of one summer against five other teams. We took it seriously having a number of training sessions in the Embassy Club pool in the run-up. I became fitter than ever before and since. When the last event began we had a good chance of winning but things went awry and we ended up third.

The Embassy had a tradition of playing cricket against the Royal Palace. The game took place on a scrubby field near the University with an Armoured Personnel Carrier on the boundary. We hoped that the King would put in an appearance but he had apparently to see some Arab dignitary who had decided to visit Amman at short notice – not uncommon. I umpired for a while. I raised the dreaded finger to give out

It's a Knock-Out.

leg before wicket Prince Raad, the cousin of the King's father educated at Christ's Cambridge. He was of the Iraqi branch of the Hashemites, surviving the Baghdad coup of 1958 when the King of Iraq and others were killed – he was then in London with his father Zeid. Raad was a thoughtful support for King Hussein and continues to work in Amman. I should have let him carry on his innings – it was good of him to take part and he should have had more of a chance to bat!

Domesticity

As a chancery officer (doing political work), I was supposed to entertain guests as part of my role. That meant having a suitable place to live. After spending a few weeks in a hotel, we moved into the apartment of my predecessor. It was the upper floor of a fairly modern house about 10 minutes' drive from the Embassy. We had a main room suitable for a small reception or a small dinner party.

Our son James was just starting to walk as we arrived. He had some space to move around and a balcony which we fenced off. We had a view over one of the valleys between Amman's hills. We could park on waste ground next to the house. Judy had the task of schlepping the shopping upstairs and then schlepping James or vice-versa.

After a year we moved to our villa between 4th and 5th circle next to the Embassy club. This chance came about because the Regional Development Division was closing down. The house had been occupied by its Head. I was fortunate that no more senior members of the Embassy wanted it. It had a large kitchen and four bedrooms plus space around it for children to play. We had a cook, a Lebanese Abu George, who would work for us when we had an official function in the house. We had a cleaner. Our daughter Katy was born in Amman in December 1981.

It had a spacious main room. I have a photo in my head of coming back during one workday morning, quite an unusual occurrence, opening the front door and seeing this room

Amman Apartment

occupied by a sea of mothers and small children. I stepped gingerly over the bodies, collected what I needed and left feeling completely out of place.

It had vines over a carport, popular with passers-by to collect for their stuffed vine leaves, a favourite local dish. The scent of the lemons when picked from our tree was wonderful. They made unforgettable lemonade, lemon meringue etc. We also had bomolo trees, small with huge citrus fruit for which there seemed no takers.

We had help in the house, especially when we put on dinners as part of diplomatic work. One gentleman was called Abu Jameel, which became "Special Meal" for our son learning to talk.

The British Embassy Club next door had a swimming pool, tennis court and clubhouse. UK-based Embassy staff were automatically members. Some members of the expat community also joined. There was a young Filipino, Kit, who acted as barman and caretaker. He served Teem lemonade to our children. I drank the local beer, with special relish after a few sets of tennis in the sun.

Our son James had the habit of coming into our bedroom very early in the summer and saying "It's a sunny day!" It was good to see him of course, even at 5 am. But the information he imparted was not especially valuable. From April to September every day in Amman was a sunny day. The Embassy club pool had plenty of use in these months.

Orange and White Chevettes

Remember my orange Vauxhall Chevette and its troubled journey through Syria in 1981? The car sadly ended up written off by an Act of God in the snow. At least that was the opinion of the policeman who crashed into it. I learned about this in a memorable way. In the winter of 1983-84 I was at a reception at the Head of Chancery's house one winter's evening introducing some British visitors from the water industry to Jordanians. When the police called at the door early on in the event I, as the Arabic speaker, went to see what they wanted. They invited me outside to see what had happened. A police breakdown vehicle had careered across the broad road in the snow and collided with a car innocently parked outside the house. The parked car was badly damaged. It was our car!

I had a visit the next day at the Embassy from an army officer who explained that the accident was God's will, the police were not insured and the policeman would not earn enough in a lifetime to pay for the damage. Fortunately, my British insurer paid for the car to be written off. We ended up buying as a replacement a white Vauxhall Chevette estate which another member of staff had left in the Embassy back yard on his departure with an instruction to sell. I think I caught sight of the orange car again on the road a few months later!

The main exploit of Vauxhall Chevette number 2 was to get me back to UK. My wife flew back home in summer 1984 with the two children, leaving me to cover the leave of the Head of Chancery. These substitutions are important in developing the experience of young staff: I expanded my work beyond the political to become involved in personnel and admin issues too. A few weeks later I drove back to UK in six days.

I crossed through Syria, spending hours at the Jordan border because of the usual press and disorganisation there. Mindful of previous experience in Syria in 1981 – I did not stop until in Turkey. I overnighted in Adana. From there I went across poor roads to Istanbul – Turkey is a much

Two Chevettes

more modern country now but then driving through was a challenge, the roads often unmade and petrol supplies uncertain. I stopped at a wonderful old hotel in Istanbul by the railway station with iron-grilled lifts and spent a day as a tourist visiting St Sophia and considering buying a carpet. From there, it was through northern Greece into Yugoslavia, an overnight stay there, a 14-hour drive to Ulm and then another long drive all the way to Peterborough where I met up with Judy at her parents' house.

Two eventful car journeys to and from Jordan were the bookends of my three years and four months at the British Embassy Amman. The visit of HMQ to PLK was the professional highlight.

Jordan on My Mind

I went back once to Amman in 1985 when I was a desk officer in FCO. But not since. I don't think it was only because it was our first posting that it has remained on my mind. I look out for news about Jordan. I like to hear from people who have visited. We still regularly see one couple who were at the Embassy at the same time.

King Hussein died in 1999, too young. It was one of those moments, as at the time of his grandfather's death, when it was inevitable people should wonder again about the future of Jordan. Since the Six-Day War of 1967 his brother Prince Hassan had been the designated successor. Hussein changed this as he was dying, appointing instead his son Abdullah – now King Abdullah II. It was a tough decision for Hassan, who served and has continued to serve Jordan admirably. I suspect Hussein's concern was that Hassan would not connect successfully with the people and the army.

Abdullah has similarities with his father. He too has charisma, an ability to connect with people in his country and outside. I had the chance to meet him in 2008 during my posting to Washington. The similarity with his father is striking. Immediately after ISIL murdered a captured Jordanian pilot in February 2015 the outrage and determination to right a wrong came over in Abdullah's face when he spoke on TV to the nation. He decided on the execution of two convicted terrorists – not an action in line with modern western sensibilities but perhaps the kind of decisive action his father chose him for.

PART III

THE DILEMMA OF IRAQ

Anyone for Dusty Mustard?

In the generation of British diplomacy before I joined the Service in 1978 one of the most divisive episodes was Suez. It led to resignations in government and Civil Service and questions about the leadership of Prime Minister Anthony Eden. Very different though it was, the invasion of Iraq in 2003 was the closest equivalent during my time. Still today there is debate over whether the problem was one of bad execution of a reasonable plan, whether the case for involvement was fraudulently made, or whether we should become involved in intervention in other countries at all.

In one of the surprise twists not unusual in a diplomatic career, I was asked at short notice in December 1990 to switch to working on Iraq, having just spent two weeks on return from my posting in Berlin in a position in FCO working with the intelligence services. They wanted someone with experience of the Arab world. On 2 January 1991 I started in the Cabinet Office Assessments Staff.

On 14 January 1991 I was chairing a meeting, a so-called Current Intelligence Group (CIG) of people around Whitehall and experts on chemical weapons, about "dusty mustard". There was intelligence of uncertain reliability that the Iraqis were working on a form of mustard agent which could form particles capable of penetrating gas masks. It sounded a tall story; it was our job to assess whether there could be truth in it. We knew the Iraqis had a chemical weapons programme. They had used CW against Kurds in their own country. But could they be working on a substance unknown to our own UK experts at Porton Down? It turned out to be a false alarm.

The Assessments Staff was drawn from all parts of government to prepare reports on situations around the world. It had its origins in World War 2. It came into its own during periods of crisis and hostilities, co-ordinating and leading cross-government analysis and briefing the War Cabinet.

The staff at this time comprised 15 desk officers, 4 Deputy Chiefs and a Chief who reported to the Chairman of the Joint Intelligence Committee (JIC), then Sir Percy Cradock. We also worked with the Secretary of the JIC, who also functioned as an additional Deputy Chief during the crisis, and the Intelligence Co-ordinator. We were supported by a team of shift-working executive, clerical and secretarial staff. Numbers were small. Everyone knew everyone else.

My domain was North Africa, the Middle East, Asia minus the Soviet Union, Latin America, International Terrorism and International Drugs. I had four dedicated desk officers, one on North Africa, one on the Middle East, one on China/Hong Kong and one on the rest of Asia with other issues divided between them.

The Assessments Staff was on the second floor of the building and used conference rooms in the basement and elsewhere. The building is a patchwork of history, incorporating Henry VIII's tennis court. It had a connecting door to No 10, through which few people had access. It had a tunnel across Whitehall to the MOD, built for crisis during the Cold War. It had links with the Overseas and Defence

Secretariat, a foreign-policy co-ordination body whose name and initials changed subtly with each change of the British government. There were other organisations in the building with which we had no contact dealing with all manner of issues. The common factor was their position at the centre of government working with Ministries and others as necessary.

The entrance to the building had just gained a new system which resembled for us of that generation the tubes through which Scottie would beam members of the Starship Enterprise up and down from the spaceship. This was part of a steady strengthening of security in face of the terrorist threat. It's incredible now to think that the nearby Downing Street had been completely open to pedestrians when I first came to London. The Cabinet Office had been accessed earlier simply by showing a pass to a guard at the entrance. The same went for the FCO at that time.

Under Fire in London

People working in London became used to the impact of terrorism on our daily lives. The IRA conducted attacks in London and caused havoc by threatening others, for example at railway stations causing them to close and making it impossible for people to go to work or home.

On 7 February 1991, mid-morning at 10 past 10, I was in my office at 70 Whitehall when we were startled by a big bang and three reports. My windows rattled. We were told on the public address system to gather in the corridor. Air Commodore Norman Hodnett, another Deputy Chief on secondment from the RAF, and I wondered whether this was one of mine (Iraqi terrorism) or one of his (Irish). We soon heard that the Met thought PIRA responsible because it had been a mortar attack – PIRA had used this method in the Province.

Percy Cradock told a spellbound Joint Intelligence Committee that afternoon, with me sitting at the back, how some Cabinet members had dived for cover as the mortar exploded. The Cabinet had reassembled in the basement of 70 Whitehall. When the Prime Minister heard that the attack had been launched from near the MOD, he looked at the Defence Minister Tom King and asked if he were trying to stage a coup.

We later heard that the provisional IRA had fired a mortar concealed in the back of a van from the other side of Whitehall by the Old War Office of the Ministry of Defence. The shell had flown over our heads and landed in the garden of No 10. No-one was hurt. Several windows were smashed and this reinforced the move to have blast curtains at windows in government buildings as the biggest danger from such an attack was from flying glass.

Getting ready for War

In July 1990 the Iraq of Saddam Hussein had invaded Kuwait and by December it was pretty clear he was unlikely to be moved except by force. So the Assessments Staff was starting to gear up for the challenge. We had the advantage that we would know in advance when the war would begin because that would be decided by the allies involved in the action – the US, UK and France and a wider coalition including several Arab states.

We reorganised so that the whole staff, minus one hugely talented desk officer Adam Thomson handling the small matter of the disintegrating Soviet Union, would join together so that Iraq could be covered full-time. It's amazing how the rest of the world suddenly seemed less important.

Norman Hodnett took control of the timetabling so that we could work through the crisis however long it lasted. The system needed to deploy people so that we would not only not lose our edge but could keep up the service to the Government for months if necessary.

We had three sets of augmentees to manage the paper flow and telephones in an emergency room, No 213, which was manned 24 hours a day and seven days a week and always administered by one of the small team of Duty Officers, who were mostly retired members of the armed and intelligence services. The Communications Centre was only a few steps away from Room 213. This received copies of telegrams to and from the Foreign Office as well as messages specifically for the Cabinet Office. Reports from the Intelligence agencies were a vital ingredient in the information mix. We all worked five days on and two days off. Desk officers took their turn to work either days (0600-1800) or nights (2000-0800). The Deputy Chiefs would cover the crucial morning period or supervise work in the afternoons and early evenings, combining this with such of their other work as they could.

Meetings, Broadcasts and Fried Breakfasts

As a Deputy Chief, I had to get to 70 Whitehall around 4 am when on Iraq War duty. A car would collect me at home in Three Bridges as there no way I could get to the Office at that time of night/morning on public transport; the car journey at that time of night would take only 40 minutes. The routine was then to produce a draft assessment of the latest situation working with the desk officer who had been on duty overnight collecting inputs from Embassies, allies, the military and experts around government. At set times during the small hours the desk officer would be in touch with the Defence Intelligence Staff (DIS) of the MOD and the Emergency Centre of the FCO. We also used CNN – this was the first conflict to attract 24-hour TV coverage.

The task of the desk officer was to have a serviceable draft for the Deputy Chief to see at 0400. This would then be worked on and a further draft considered at a meeting starting at 0600 of the Current Intelligence Group comprising representatives from all relevant parts of government and intelligence allies. As each page was amended by the meeting it would be passed to the typists at the side of the room and then checked by the desk officer without disturbing the flow of the meeting. The paper would be 4-12 pages long. It was meant to be finalised by 0715 though sometimes it took a few minutes longer.

We then prepared a short statement to broadcast in a close-circuit TV briefing linking MOD (several parts thereof), Cabinet Office and FCO. This was to ensure we were all on the same page. The transmission began at 0800.

The daily routine for the Deputy Chief on Iraq duty continued at 0900 at a meeting with the JIC chairman, the Chief of the Assessments Staff and the Deputy Chief of Defence Intelligence. This gave impetus for the work of the next daily cycle: it could also commission separate assessments on particular issues. The day carried on from there with staff in Room 213 monitoring events and providing continuity.

After this we could enjoy a high-cholesterol breakfast from Scotland Yard. It was a moment of release, the reward for a period of intense work, and an interlude before the next phase. For the first time on my life I became a fan of black pudding.

Our assessments were short, covering the issues of most importance to the War Cabinet – battle damage assessment, attitudes of the government and people of Iraq, diplomatic moves, particular risks etc. We complemented these daily reports with assessments on individual issues completed during the rest of the day. We looked at the risk of Iraqi terrorism in Britain and around the world, the risk that the Iraqis might use their chemical weapons, try to bomb London, the situation of the Kurds and many other aspects.

As the moment drew near for the start of allied military action, there was some nervousness about international efforts to find a last-minute deal with Saddam which could put military plans on hold. It was not that the Allies were gagging to fight. On the contrary, for the Americans as for everyone else, there was a big concern about the potential for losses of their men and the reaction this could provoke in US public opinion still deeply affected by the failure and losses of the Vietnam War. But it would not be possible to keep Allied forces poised for full-scale military action if there were a long delay. Saddam had shown many times how he could string the international community along. We saw no likelihood that he would give up and retreat from Kuwait. But we did see the possibility that he might persuade mediators that he was ready to withdraw if some concessions were made.

A complicating factor was the holding of western hostages as human shields, including children. This made Saddam look even worse in international public opinion especially when he appeared on TV with them. But how much did international public opinion matter to him? He was out to annex Kuwait to which not a few Iraqis believed their country had a historical right. If the Allies could be frustrated perhaps they would have no choice but to pull back and accept the fait accompli.

On the diplomatic front, there was a lot being done to keep together the large and broad Allied coalition which even included Syria. There was also a lot to be done with potential blockers.

Russia was just emerging from the break-up of the Soviet Union. It had for a time become a less obstructive interlocutor in the UN Security Council. This facilitated the passage of UN Security Council Resolutions, though some compromises still had to be made on their provisions. The Russians did not like the West leading the world against Iraq, a country with which they had built a relationship and to which they had sold weaponry. But at this moment they were much more concerned about their domestic situation and their near abroad of countries which had just cut themselves loose from the former Soviet Union.

China was also focussing on its internal situation after the Tiananmen Square. It would not endorse the Allies' move towards military action. On the other hand, even though it had interests in Iraq, China was not overtly obstructive.

As analysts we tended to believe that Saddam would use whatever cards he had in his hand. Yet he didn't do enough with the international mediators to force the Allies to stay their hand and he ended up letting the western hostages go. We reasoned that he may have really doubted that the Allies would risk an invasion. Perhaps he saw the anger caused by his holding of hostages and reasoned that holding them might tip the Allies over the edge to fight.

Whatever the case, the fact is that Saddam's course allowed the Allies to prepare carefully and launch their military campaign at a time of their choosing.

As we moved towards the start of hostilities in December and January, we focussed on the difficulty of overcoming the Iraqi military. Saddam had large and well-equipped armed forces. They had battle experience from the earlier war with Iran. The Republican Guard, in particular, were regarded as potentially tough adversaries. The regime might well fight to the end and even use chemical weapons as it had against its own people in previous years.

The hostilities began with a period of air operations with the aim of preparing the way for as quick and decisive a land campaign as possible. Air supremacy was achieved with attacks on Iraqi aircraft and missile systems, though inevitably some remained hidden and some aircraft were also kept out of harm's way, even with some being flown to Iran.

There were moments of tension. It was not clear to us what Saddam's military plan was. The Iraqis set fire to the Kuwaiti oilfields. What else were they prepared to do? But the fighting did not last long. The big question became how and when the fighting would be concluded.

We were not involved in policy. Nor were we informed about operational planning. We did not know how the coalition would prosecute the campaign. It was nonetheless obvious to us that an element of the plan was likely to be a left hook to move round the Iraqi defensive line on the border. That proved to be the case.

The bombardment

The coalition air campaign began before midnight on 16 January. We had by then been operating our new work system for three days in anticipation of a change of gear. Whitehall was confident that overwhelming air power had by now been assembled in the area. But we wondered what tactics the Iraqis might resort to.

Terrorism was a risk on our minds. Iraq had trained agents and some appeared to have been sent abroad. The Iraqis had also encouraged Palestinian groups to attack western interests, notably the Abu Nidhal Organisation which had killed several Britons in the past.

Would the Iraqis or their surrogates try something in

London? Might they even use chemical/biological material? Iraqi intelligence had a track record of assassinations abroad, but not so far of indiscriminate attacks or use of non-conventional weapons. Was Saddam hoping that just the threat of terrorism (at which he hinted in public remarks) would help to deter us from a ground war, without him ever needing to carry out a major terrorist campaign? Or did the West's precautionary measures thwart an onslaught? There were in the event only a few unsuccessful attacks on western premises in southeast Asia.

We guessed more or less correctly about Iraq's use of Scud missiles. Attacks on Israel began on the night of 17-18 January. Saddam wanted to provoke the Israelis into retaliatory strikes against Iraq. He could then pose as the only Arab state prepared to take on the "Zionist entity". This would make it difficult for other Arab governments to support the coalition since that would look like fighting on the side of the Israelis. Fortunately, the Israeli government was able to resist this ploy, eschewing revenge at least for the time being. The Americans pressed hard for this decision: it was in the Israeli interest not to be provoked but was not a foregone conclusion since it went against the grain of Israeli policy that aggressors against Israel should be taught severe lessons.

Could Saddam have done more to push the Israelis over the edge? He could have launched even more missiles against Israel (perhaps instead of the attacks he also directed against Saudi Arabia). Could he have attacked with chemical or biological warheads? We had no evidence that he had managed to produce such warheads. But he had fired chemical shells before (in the Iran-Iraq war and against the Kurds in his own country) and it seemed likely he could fill a warhead with chemical agent. The effect on the Israeli population of such an attack, even if it caused few casualties, would have been considerable. We all saw newscasters in Israel sitting in studios wearing their gas masks. Some of the population in Tel Aviv might have panicked. The pressure for Israeli retaliation would have been enormous.

Saddam's fundamental aim was to survive the war. He probably feared that the Israelis would respond in kind to use of chemical/biological weapons against them and perhaps even with a nuclear attack – after all, Iraq under Saddam would likely have been prepared to use a nuclear option in such circumstances if it had had one. The outcome if Israel had been so provoked would have been incalculable. But – as Saddam may have worked out – one result may have been that he would himself no longer be in power. We asked ourselves during the bombardment whether Saddam would be ready to bring down the temple on the regime's head. The answer was that he intended to stick around if he could.

A third theme of our papers was the effect of Iraq's destruction of Kuwait's oilfields and deliberate spillage into Gulf waters. As occurs when there is a tanker spill, opinions on the seriousness of the impact varied wildly. The press wrote up views of "experts" who predicted the burning of the Kuwaiti oilfields would have a disastrous effect on the monsoons and therefore the climate in Asia. The more cautious prognostications – that it would probably not be too bad – were less interesting and given less weight. We tried to weigh this up as part of the daily assessments and in special papers. We relied in particular on advice from the Department of Energy, which was understandably inconclusive but was not ready to support the doom-and-gloom stories. A big concern in connection with the prosecution of the war was whether Saudi desalination plants would be affected. There were initial worries that this might happen but in fact the oil slicks proved less damaging further down the coast than we feared.

Saddam's oil vandalism was unsurprising. He wanted to gain control of Kuwait's oil: this would have removed the restrictions on Iraq's military-industrial development imposed by financial limitations. When he saw that the international community would not stand idly by, he may have hoped that the threat against Kuwait's oil would stay the West's hand. But when this did not work, he had nothing to lose by carrying out the threat. It has cost Kuwait many billions of its overseas assets to restore the oilfields and the other damage.

The attitude of Iran figured prominently in our thoughts throughout the crisis. By mid-January the Iranian leadership had evidently taken a strategic decision to stay neutral. The Iranian regime remained hostile to the West's military activity in its backyard, but stood to gain from the debilitation of Iraq. It hoped for better opportunities after the war to improve its international economic links. To cater for the expectations of its rapidly rising population, the Iranian regime needed the economic boost which co-operation with developed countries could bring.

The flight of over 100 Iraqi military aircraft to Iran seeking refuge was an intriguing phenomenon which we did not entirely fathom. We had some indications that the Iraqis may have approached the Iranian leadership about this eventuality as a way of preserving some of their better aircraft from coalition attacks on Iraqi airfields. But the Iranians clearly did not give Iraq any assurance that the aircraft would be returned – none as far as I know were returned to Iraq and a few were incorporated into the Iranian air force. The Iranian air defence system was not expecting their arrival.

As for the war itself, we wondered whether the pattern of Iraqi passivity was going to change when on 29 January the Iraqi army made a limited push into Khafji, just over the border with Saudi Arabia. On 30 January Major General John

Foley came round to the Chairman's office in the afternoon to discuss Iraqi troop movements; I was present – it was during my first day of that week's morning duties in 213. The question was whether there was a larger-scale Iraqi attack looming. I could see from the looks on faces in the room that I was not alone in feeling some consternation. I wondered how the German Ardennes offensive had looked to people in London in 1944. We pored over maps marked with the increasingly familiar symbols representing different types of military units and with various kinds of arrows depicting movement.

The Iraqis did not follow up this attack. They retreated, though still declaring Khafji a great victory. It had no effect on the course of the war. Perhaps Saddam had missed the boat by not attacking Saudi Arabia in summer 1991.

Meanwhile, PIRA were active in London. Just as they did when Britain was involved in previous overseas crises (including both World Wars) they sought to make life even more difficult for us at home. On 18 February bombs exploded at Paddington and Victoria stations during the Monday morning rush. One man was killed and 40 injured at Victoria – some 20 minutes after I had passed through the station. There were plenty of other interruptions to commuter traffic.

On Friday 15 February my wife and I were in a furniture shop in Horley when a news flash on the radio announced that Iraq had declared itself ready to withdraw from Kuwait. I was sceptical but we went home to check the coverage on TV. Excitement at a possible resolution turned to disappointment as the impossible conditions became apparent – withdrawal of foreign forces from Kuwait, withdrawal of Israeli forces from the Occupied Territories.

During the following week, we were writing assessments on Iraqi intentions as the Iraqi Foreign Minister twice visited Moscow and Gorbachev announced a "peace plan". Prime Minister John

Major was scheduled to visit us in Room 213 on 19 February but this was called off as the Cabinet considered this plan.

But it was increasingly clear that these were stalling manoeuvres. On Saturday 23 February President George H W Bush announced an ultimatum and the coalition ground operation began at 2000 that day.

Our main concerns in Room 213 during the 100 hours of ground fighting were whether Saddam Hussein, as he saw he was being overwhelmed, would resort to chemical and biological weapons. We had a report on 24 February that some US soldiers felt ill and there was speculation that anthrax had been used against them. This proved not to be case. Fears that the Iraqis were preparing to use CW in the field (based on deployments during the Iran/Iraq war of the 1980s) also turned out to be groundless. It was our task to assess them as well as we were able on the fragmentary information available.

The endgame

The Assessments Staff had a ringside seat as the coalition came to decide what to do as the fighting was drawing to an end. There were arguments that the Allied forces should carry on to Baghdad and destroy the regime of Saddam Hussein. This was not the view of President George Bush senior and John Major. Their stated objective was to reverse the invasion of Kuwait and nothing beyond that. They started with that clear in their minds and did not change.

The "turkey-shoot" of Iraqi forces at Mitla Ridge had reinforced the conclusion that the Allied forces, having already made such a big effort and needing rest, should not be involved in further hostilities. Further fighting could become a massacre killing tens of thousands more Iraqi soldiers around Basra and our own forces – in the air and on the ground – sickened by this. I had a chance in 2014 to ask General Patrick Cordingley, Commander of the British forces, and he told me he had agreed with this decision. So the Allies called a halt. The Iraqi forces were not completely destroyed.

This decision led to some suspicion in the Arab world that the West wanted Saddam to stay in power. Of course the UK and US would have preferred to see Saddam gone. But that was not the objective. Being sucked further into Iraqi territory and perhaps causing the disintegration of Iraq was too risky and beyond the remit given by the UN Security Council.

On the other hand, just 36 hours more fighting could have made a big dent in Saddam's remaining military power. It was understandable that the Kurds in the north and Shia in the south felt that the Allies had encouraged them to join in the fight and then failed to create the conditions in which they would be able to take on Saddam on their own.

We wrote in an assessment of 10 March 1991 "Saddam is not going to be overturned by the insurgents in the north or the south". Not long later we came to the view that Saddam could be around for a long time.

There followed years of frustration. The UK and US sought to keep up the pressure on Saddam to end his nuclear, chemical and biological warfare programmes and to desist from repression of the Kurds and Shia. Saddam played cat-and-mouse with UN weapons inspectors. The decision not to press on with the fighting in 1991 was understandable. To have done so would have had unforeseeable consequences. We learned that not doing so also had difficult consequences. Saddam carried on for a further decade and more. It's easy now to forget how frustrating this period was and how much the Shia and Kurds suffered.

John Major thanks Cabinet Office staff

Unfinished Business

In 1996, I was posted to Bonn as Political Counsellor and later was promoted to Deputy Head of Mission. Iraq was an issue to discuss with the German government.

The Germans had not joined in the Allied military effort against Iraq. They had remained in their post-WW2 mode of staying clear of military campaigns outside the NATO area. This was an understandable policy for many years as Germany sought to convince Europe and the world that it would never again pose a military threat. They were also constrained by the division of Germany and their need to maintain a relationship with the Soviet Union. In 1991, with the Cold War at an end, NATO Allies were making it clear that they welcomed Germany's financial support for the action to reverse the Iraqi invasion of Kuwait but also thought the time had come for Germany to share more of the military burden.

This was not a universal view. There were still those in neighbouring countries and even in the UK who had lingering doubts about the kind of country Germany would become once unified. To my embarrassment, an MP on the Foreign Affairs Committee asked Germans on a visit to Bonn whether Germany posed a threat to the UK. These concerns were absurd. Germany really had changed. The challenge was not to curb Germany but to persuade its leaders to share the international security burdens incumbent on a major western state.

I went through the arguments in my diplomatic contacts with the German Foreign Ministry, the Federal Chancellery and the Bundestag. At the very least we were looking for strong German support in the UN and other bodies against Saddam's repression of his people and infringement of UN Security Council Resolutions.

German interlocutors understood the point that more would be expected of Germany. At the same time, German foreign policy was strongly influenced, as in many countries, by commercial interest. Germany had done well in trade with Iraq. The Middle East was far away from German borders and German security concerns.

It was still early days after the end of the division of Germany. German public opinion remained cautious, in the mode it had followed since the Second World War. There had been disquiet in Germany when West Germany came to join NATO in 1955 and built up its Armed Forces. The view of many Germans then was "Ohne Uns" and that sentiment still applied. West Germany had done well by keeping its head down in international affairs and there was a reluctance to change, particularly as there was so much to do in integrating the former GDR into the new Germany and working with the newly democratic states of Central and Eastern Europe.

In the following years the feeling of unfinished business in Iraq grew stronger. Saddam Hussein sought to dodge the provisions of UN Security Resolutions passed to contain him. He suppressed the Shia in the South and Kurds in the North. Even a No-Fly Zone, patrolled by NATO aircraft, did not stop him. There was inconsistent co-operation with UN officials visiting Iraq to check he was getting rid of his weapons of mass destruction – biological and chemical (which he had used against the Kurds) and nuclear which we knew from intelligence that he had been developing.

9/11: Everything Changes

While I was in Germany up to 2000 and in London thereafter there was increasing frustration in western governments that Saddam was pulling the wool over our eyes. He was playing the game of international politics to pose as a victim of the West. He was helped by the tendency after the shock of the end of the Cold War wore away for the former non-aligned countries to be suspicious of US and western power and for Russia and China to want to keep clear blue water between themselves and the West.

Saddam could not gain much sympathy around the world. He had invaded Iraq; he had killed many of his own people; he was seen as a threat by Iran and the Arab Gulf States; there was no love lost with neighbours Syria and Turkey. So it was argued by many in the West that though it was frustrating to see Saddam behave as he did this was the consequence of the decision in 1991 not to follow up the War with toppling the regime in Baghdad and that we should pursue a policy of containment through economic sanctions and the No-Fly-Zone.

Everything was changed by the attacks on the World Trade Center in New York on 9 September 2001. George Bush, with strong international support, led a coalition of countries backed by UN Security Council Resolutions in an intervention in Afghanistan with the aim of stopping the country from being a place of refuge for terrorist groups, destroying the Taliban and helping the rebuilding of the Afghan State. This was a difficult task. The history of Afghanistan showed clearly how hard it would be to build any kind of functioning state, remove the power of the regional and ethnic warlords and gain acceptance of the presence of foreign forces. But the mood of the time was overwhelmingly can-do and the early results encouraging.

On the front foot then in Afghanistan, it was not surprising that the US Administration should consider what to do about Saddam in Iraq. This was a moment when US political and public opinion was much more open than usual to activism, including military, overseas. Should George Bush junior complete the business left over from his father's Presidency and remove Saddam by force?

There were claims, notably by Deputy Secretary Wolfowitz, an erudite and personally charming man, that Saddam had been involved in terrorism including the plotting of 9/11. He kept papers in his room at the State Department and pulled them out when I visited as Deputy Head of Mission in Washington from 2004. No-one in the UK was convinced and I suspect few in the US were either. There was no smoking gun linking Saddam with 9/11.

Intervention In The Middle East?

After the heavy losses of people and treasure suffered in Afghanistan and Iraq, and the messy outcome of intervention in Libya, UK governments are much less willing to consider commitments of forces in the Middle East. Public opinion is more cautious and this is reflected in parliamentary debate as was seen in the government's failure to secure a majority for air attacks against Syria in 2013.

Now, in 2015, the spread of Islamic fundamentalist forces in Iraq and Syria is a menace to the region. Should we care? Yes – we have interests in the fate of the people, our own security trade, investment, supply of oil. This fundamentalism could express itself in further terrorist acts in the UK, as in the case of the murder of Lee Rigby, or in more organised attacks.

It may be argued that the best way of keeping ourselves safe is to let those in the region get on with their disputes and avoid stirring up a hornet's nest. This in turn leads to the question how the UK sees itself nowadays. We are no longer a great military power. Our ability to project power and achieve outcomes in the world through deployment of our military is considerably reduced.

Yet, the UK is a truly global country and its capital London has become the world's leading global city. We still identify ourselves as a country with a strong interest in the world and its issues. We have reached the UN target of 0.7 % of GDP allocated to overseas aid. The generosity of Brits in donating money and time to causes overseas is impressive. If we want to remain a Permanent Member of the UN Security Council, and I believe that is in our interest, then we should be taking responsibility – through our alliances, exerting political and economic influence, using our well-regarded diplomatic resources and if necessary contributing to military action.

If we are to be involved again with forces on the ground in more than just a very limited way it must be as part of a big coalition as in the case of the reversal of the Iraqi invasion of Kuwait in 1991 or even wider. You will never persuade some countries of the cause – Brazil for example was not even in favour of military intervention to stop the genocide in

Rwanda. But the tent needs to be big and Russia and China, if not taking part, at the very least fully consulted and kept informed.

It is entirely understandable that the US under President Obama has focussed on completing disengagement of military forces stationed in Afghanistan and Iraq. He promised the electorate he would do that. The next US President will for sure be faced with questions of how much to engage in the Middle East. Is it good enough to eschew an overall strategy and to take piecemeal action when and where opportunities present? Or has the challenge of ISIL become too serious requiring the US in its own interest to head a coalition with a plan which requires greater engagement?

I Love Israel Too

The Foreign Office has over the years been labelled as anti-Israel because of the influence of the "camel corps", the considerable number of its staff who served in the Arab world. I suppose I'm one of that group, having learned Arabic and served in Jordan.

The FCO started up in the 1980s a scheme for young Arabists also to visit Israel as part of their development. I received groups who came through Jordan on their way to the West Bank and Israel or vice-versa. One group I hosted in Amman included Simon Fraser, later FCO Permanent Under Secretary.

I was also Israel (and Lebanon) desk officer at the FCO from 1984-86. I enjoyed liaising with the Israeli Embassy. My usual contact was the sympathetic Yehoyada Haim, an academic whose family had immigrated to Israel from Iraq. We sometimes spoke Arabic on the phone with each other.

The Israeli Ambassador Yehuda Avner was a Mancunian who delighted in his role. He and his wife Mimi, also British-born, were approachable people even for a junior diplomat like myself, and invited me to events. I got to know the Jewish organisations in UK – for example, the Board of Deputies.

The Prime Minister, Mrs Thatcher, had plenty of contact with Jewish organisations especially as several were located in her Finchley constituency. She admired the ingenuity, resilience and hard work of those she met. There were several Jewish Cabinet members.

Mrs Thatcher was keen to visit Israel and may have felt the Foreign Office camel corps was reluctant. Relations with Israel had been put in the freezer following the Israeli invasion of Lebanon in 1981 and the massacres at the Sabra and Shatila camps which, I believe, added decisive fuel to the antipathy towards Israel among student organisations in the UK. By 1984, however, we were looking again to build bridges after our own troops in Lebanon, BRITFORLEB, had pulled out. We didn't have full Israeli withdrawal from Lebanon but it was in prospect. We wanted to press for resolution of the Arab/Israel dispute, at the heart of which lay Palestine. For that, we needed a full dialogue with Israel.

As desk officer, I did a lot of spade work on inward visits. One such visitor was Yitzhak Rabin, then Defence Minister. His meeting with Foreign Secretary Geoffrey Howe stuck in my mind. The Foreign Secretary fished a crumpled package of cigarettes out of his pocket and offered one. Rabin was, let us say, not impressed. He stared with piercing blue eyes. The Foreign Secretary put over cogently the case for moving forward on Palestine. Rabin responded in a gravelly voice which reminded me of a very different man, Crown Prince Hassan of Jordan. It was hard to tell whether we were making any impression on a man who had seen so much as a soldier and statesman. But he was one of that generation, now almost gone, who had an understanding of the Arabs, their culture and language.

We then had successively Foreign Minister Shamir and Prime Minister Shimon Peres in London. Mrs Thatcher received them. The meeting with Peres was straightforward: he was then, as since, seen as one of those Israeli leaders who would like to see a resolution of the Palestine issue meeting part-way. Shamir was much more controversial. While Mrs Thatcher wanted a normalisation of our bilateral relationship, she also (so I learned from others – I was not myself present) left no doubt that she had not forgotten the killing of British Army sergeants in a booby-trap at the time of the Jewish attack on the King David hotel towards the end of the British mandate, in which the Stern gang including Shamir were suspected of being involved.

Mrs Thatcher was someone who could potentially make a difference. She had strong relationships with King Hussein and some other Arab leaders. She was Israel-friendly. Her visit to Israel went off well enough, though did not bring any breakthrough. As is the case sometimes, the desk officer had to keep an eye on what could go wrong and I was aware of concerns from our Trade Ministry about ideas from No 10 for the Prime Minister to be alongside businessman Gerald Ronson at the laying of a foundation stone at a school he was to fund. He was then under investigation by the Trade Ministry. The visit went off without a hitch. It would be much trickier in today's more transparent world.

I had a chance as desk officer to visit Tel Aviv. I was struck by the non-stop life of the city, the restless energy, the inventiveness. The Israeli Foreign Ministry had an informality about it which I found attractive. Foreign Minister Shamir ate in the staff canteen at lunchtime. It was such a contrast with the grandeur of the Foreign Office in London. Our magnificent building, then being restored from the shambles left behind by the Second World War, could be used to impress visitors; but it wasn't the best advert for modern Britain.

It's a great pity that Israel has not done more to resolve the Palestine issue (the Palestinians themselves have rarely missed the opportunity to miss an opportunity – especially Yasser Arafat). For a while in the early 1990s it looked as if there might be a comprehensive peace when Yitzhak Rabin was Prime Minister. It needed a tough man to be in charge of the process. The hope faded with his assassination.

Perhaps Ariel Sharon, the man responsible for Sabra and Shatila, might have been that person, just as the tough Menachem Begin was essential to the peace process with Egypt. Sharon decided that the Palestinians needed to live separately for the sake of the State of Israel in the long term not least given the demographic trends pointing to a risk of becoming outnumbered by Arabs within Israeli territory. In January 2006 he suffered a massive stroke. He did not recover and was relieved as Prime Minister; he died in January 2014 without regaining consciousness. Sharon was incapacitated before we could know how much he was prepared to do with the Arabs to achieve the arrangement he thought essential through negotiation, rather than through building a barrier which looked like the GDR anti-fascist protection rampart.

I recall Lord Carrington saying when he became Foreign Secretary after Mrs Thatcher's election victory in 1979 that there were three great challenges for the FCO: Rhodesia – the arrangements for an independent Zimbabwe were negotiated in 1981 at Lancaster House; Northern Ireland, which would get worse before it got better; and the Middle East Peace Process, which after looking to be on the road to some settlement in the early 1990s remains on the table and the centre of a new regional crisis.

Forces of fundamentalism destroying lives and culture are vying with forces of democratisation and forces wanting to retain authoritarian government of various kinds. How this will play out is not predictable. This matters to the region, the Islamic world, UK, Europe and North America. I wonder what my successors in the Assessments Staff make of it?

2.

GERMANY

PART I

MEETING RUDOLF
HESS

The one posting in my career I asked for and was given was Berlin, 1986-1990. I wanted to reconnect with Germany – I had spent two years as a teacher in Gelsenkirchen, 1975-1977.

For reasons I cannot now recall, but probably because of the reputation for dull bureaucracy attached to large Embassies, I preferred then to avoid the Embassy at Bonn. Berlin – that is the British Military Government in West Berlin rather than the Embassy to the GDR in East Berlin – seemed a more exciting option.

I had visited Berlin in 1971. Though I was not aware at the time, Berlin had during that year been the subject of Four-Power negotiations in the new spirit of detente between East and West. These talks led to the Quadripartite Agreement of 1971 which gave all parties a basis to carry on with the post-war status of Berlin and Germany while finding ways to live with its inconveniences. Among other things, it included a recognition of the German Democratic Republic by the West and establishment of Embassies to the GDR in East Berlin while the West maintained the view that Berlin as a whole as defined by its 1920 boundaries remained legally under Four-Power rule with Four Sectors of which East Berlin was the Soviet Sector .

Much of the way Berlin had functioned since the end

of the Second World War carried on the same. One example of this was the Allied Prison at Spandau. The War Trials at Nuremberg had sentenced seven leading Nazis to periods of imprisonment and these were incarcerated in Spandau. The diaries of Albert Speer describe how those sentenced to imprisonment in Nuremberg were separated from those condemned to death and then taken to Berlin. The Soviets were inclined to execute these people too. They certainly wanted to keep an eye on these seven. I imagine there was no choice but to locate the prison in Berlin, the one part of Germany under joint Four-Power authority after the War. Choosing the location in Berlin for the prison was, as in other such decisions, largely a practical matter of finding a suitable building not too badly damaged.

Spandau was one of the boroughs of Berlin in the British Sector. That gave the British Military Government, in which I became Deputy Political Adviser to the Commandant in 1986, a particular responsibility for its administration and for co-ordinating decisions on matters of policy between the Four Allies. Spandau Prison was one of the only two fully functioning Four-Power institutions in Berlin (the other was the Air Regime, about which more later).

After the early days of occupation, the Soviets had discarded any thought of allowing democracy to decide on the German leadership in their Zone of Germany and Sector of Berlin, which became the GDR in 1949. They tried to force the three western allies to leave Berlin and retreat to the Western Zones of Germany, connected to Berlin only by air and land corridors. Yet the Soviets also showed an interest in a measure of Four-Power co-operation to ensure Germany could not revive and become a threat once again.

By 1986, there had been only one prisoner remaining in Spandau for 20 years. That was Rudolf Hess. Born in

Spandau prison

1894, Hess had been close to Hitler from the early days of National Socialism. He became the deputy to Hitler in the party, though even in his heyday that did not mean he was the second most important man in terms of power in Nazi Germany. He was always regarded as a bit odd by other leaders and that impression grew with time. By June 1941 he was not in the forefront of decision-making. His place had effectively been taken by Martin Bormann. Hitler abolished the post of Deputy Fuehrer after Hess's flight to Scotland.

A great deal has been written about his decision in May 1941 to fly himself to Scotland and parachute down apparently to meet the Duke of Hamilton. This was a bizarre thing to do. He appears to have acted on his own, although he seemed to hint to other prisoners at Spandau that Hitler might have known.

Hitler was on the point of launching Operation Barbarossa against the Soviet Union (it began on 22 June), to this point an

Ally of Germany in World War II. He was withdrawing military assets from the West to assemble the largest force the world had ever known. Hess's motivation appears to have been to convince the UK (Pearl Harbour was still to come and the US not involved in the War) to agree a peace. The thinking behind this was that Germany's main aim was to defeat the Soviet Union and control Eastern Europe to Central Asia, both as areas for expansion of the German race and to exploit the rich resources. If the UK would agree to stop the fighting on the western front it might be allowed to keep its empire and avoid the destruction of more bombing and possible invasion.

Hess spoke some English. He had been familiar with British life during his childhood in Alexandria, where he was born and his father worked. He must have known that the Duke of Hamilton was one of the members of Archibald Ramsey's Riot Club in London, which was anti-Jewish and no doubt seen by the Germans as a group of importance to them should there be a German invasion of Britain.

A British-German peace agreement in 1940 is one of the great "What Ifs" of history. C J Sansom's novel "Dominion" unfolds in a scenario of an agreement in mid-1940 after the fall of France with Lord Halifax rather than Churchill becoming Prime Minister. In reality by mid-1941 the UK had come through the Battle of Britain, Churchill was working hard on Roosevelt to bring the US into the War, and the mindset of the country was to see the war through, however dark the prospects seemed. By turning on the Soviet Union, Germany would of course be less able to exert military pressure on the UK and force it to submission.

It seems incredible that leaders in Germany could have believed Churchill would either be persuaded to agree a peace with Germany in 1941 or that others in the UK would remove him as Prime Minister at this point in order to do so. This may have been wishful thinking – surely, the Germans may have thought, the UK could see that the common enemy of the West was the Soviet Union? Hitler had made no secret in his writings of the key goal of expansion of Germany to the East.

Hess may also not have been the only German to have had a misleading understanding of the political power of the British aristocracy. The Duke of Hamilton had visited Germany and Hess appears to have believed that he would be an influential intermediary with the British government in favour of stopping the western war. Hess was also personally under strain as he was increasingly being left out of top decision-making.

There are stories that Hess had then met Sir Samuel Hoare, former senior Cabinet Minister and the British Ambassador in Spain, and also Lord Halifax in Spain and Portugal, between February and April 1941. A member of an audience at a lecture I gave on a cruise ship in 2015 insisted that Samuel Hoare had been spotted in Geneva during this period, perhaps again seeing Hess. I can well believe that not all contact with the Hitler regime had been severed. It may be that there are papers in the National Archives yet to be released which could throw more light. But it seems highly questionable that Hess, losing ground among the Nazi elite, would have been entrusted by Hitler with a peace mission of this kind. Were Halifax and Hoare, not among Churchill's strongest supporters, likely to have been chosen by the British Prime Minister as the agents for seeking a peace deal? The idea that they were somehow working for George VI behind Churchill's back is absurd.

Hess was arrested in Scotland, after a few days brought south to the Tower of London (the last prisoner to be held there), interrogated and then kept in UK until the Nuremberg War trials in 1946-47. The newsreels of the trials show a man who looks bewildered, quite different from the others in the dock. Conspiracy theorists suggest he was drugged or brainwashed by the British. But Hess was already regarded as an oddball by his peers when he left Germany and the Speer diaries of their 20 years together in Spandau Prison indicate that his strange behaviour then was not such a surprise given what they knew of him up to 1941. Von Schirach, as he was released in 1967, advised Hess to play up further his mental aberrations as a way of achieving early release. Neurath and Raeder had been released on grounds of ill health, before completing their sentences. Hess seemed confident in 1967 that his lawyer Dr Seidl would get him out of Spandau. But the Soviets were not in the business of shortening his sentence.

Perhaps the better parallel for Hess's position was Admiral Doenitz, who had to serve every minute of his 20-year sentence in Spandau even though he was not part of the leadership of Germany until appointed as Head of State by Hitler's will when he killed himself in the Berlin Bunker on 30 April 1945. Albert Speer's diaries record that Doenitz was exercised by the decision to appoint him Head of State and believed this had been the reason for his sentence at the Nuremberg Trials.

Hess was Prisoner No 7. Speer, whose diaries capture life in the prison, was No 5. Prison regulations dictated that they could only be so addressed by Allied guards and officials, although there were lots of breaches of this in practice. The Four Allies took it in turn each month to have a detachment of soldiers guarding the prison and to conduct inspections. January, April, July and October were British months.

During a British month I accompanied Commandant General Patrick Brooking on his month's inspection. We went into Hess's cell. The Commandant referred to him as Prisoner 7 and asked if he was well and whether he had any complaints. Hess answered No in a firm voice, recognisable from his "Nein" captured in the newsreels at Nuremberg when asked how he pleaded to the charges against him. He stood slightly stooped by his bed as he spoke, used to the routine of 40 years. He wore a shirt without a collar, which reminded me of my father who also had shirts with detachable collars for work, and rather baggy trousers held up by braces around a spare frame: I was reminded that Albert Speer noted he had in the past gone without food and even been threatened with force-feeding. The furrowed brow you can see in the newsreels was still in evidence.

His cell was simple but no longer as spartan as it must have been in the early days. The Prison was austere, a solid chunk of 19th century building. But its focus was on the health of an old and odd man. Hess had access to some TV programmes, newspapers and books and seemed particularly to follow the football. He and all the others while still there had access to the garden, where Speer records several conversations with him. He was allowed to go into a summer house, a portakabin, in the garden after lunch every day. At first there had always been a guard with him, not least because of a suicide attempt in 1977 when he had cut his wrists. But over time agreement

Rudolf Hess

had been reached that he could be allowed to remain there on his own with guards checking on him every five minutes.

The Commandant's inspection also included separately speaking to the doctors about him. Not surprisingly for a man in his 90s, he had had various problems – including a hernia which required a truss. Whenever it was felt necessary he was transferred for investigation and treatment to the British Military Hospital in the neighbouring borough of Charlottenburg. A suite of rooms was kept prepared for him there, isolated from the other patients.

The procedure for this transfer, as with everything regarding the Prison and Hess, had been negotiated with the Soviets. All four Allies made up the armed guard from the Prison to the Hospital. The Guard at the Hospital, while Hess was there, similarly had to include the Soviets. It was hard to believe by 1986 that the Soviets really feared the Western Allies would abduct him for some nefarious purpose. In any event, this gave the Soviets a role in allied activity in the western sectors in Berlin which they did not want to relinquish. Hess spent several months at the BMH over the course of his captivity. The last stay had been 1-16 March 1987 after he had complained of difficulty in breathing.

In the British Military Government (BMG), which was the civilian element of the British occupation and staffed with diplomats in the senior positions, there were several people with a role at the Prison. The Commandant, also General Officer Commanding the British forces in Berlin, I have already mentioned. The Deputy Commandant and Minister, the lead diplomat, was Michael Burton. The next in line was Political Adviser Roland Smith and later Donald Lamont. Then came yours truly, the Deputy Political Adviser, and then my deputy Michael Ryder (later Paul Arkwright). As Spandau and Hess were part of the Allied responsibility we were all involved. With special roles were our Protocol Officer Tony Le Tissier, who was also Governor of the Prison, and our Legal Advisers.

A British Death Certificate for the Deputy Führer

Preparations for the eventual death of Prisoner No 7 were never far from our mind in BMG. There had always been concern to avoid Hess in death becoming the focus of Neo-Nazi sentiment in Germany. The original Four-Power agreement had been that Hess was to be cremated and his ashes committed to the four winds. With the passage of time, this became unacceptably harsh to opinion in the West.

Contrary to claims otherwise, the British government, working together with the other two western allies, sued the Soviets to allow Hess's early release. What was the point of keeping a disturbed geriatric in prison by the 1980s? The Soviets never accepted this. I heard many times from Soviet diplomats and military officers that the Soviet Union had lost over 20 million people to German aggression in the Great Patriotic War and Hess had been Deputy Führer: he should not be released. I never heard any corroboration of the claim made that Gorbachev was willing to allow his release in 1987.

But the Soviets did relent over the disposal of his remains. It was eventually agreed, years before his death, that his body could be given to his wife Ilse and son Wolf-Rüdiger for private burial in Wunsiedel Bavaria. The task of ensuring this went smoothly lay with the British Military Government in agreement with the other Allies. We had worked out that the US Air Force would fly his body from the US air base at

Berlin-Tempelhof to their base in Bavaria at Grafenwöhr and then hand it over to the family.

Having lived in Germany twice before and knowing something of German registration procedures I wondered if we might face a bureaucratic issue in securing agreement for Hess's body to be transported by air from Berlin. The Soviets might have taken the view that the Allies could do what they liked as this was not a matter for the German authorities in West Berlin or the Federal Republic. But the Western Allies worked with the Germans to make West Berlin as "normal" as possible. So this was not a trivial issue for us.

What about documentation to identify the body? Would it be possible for the Germans to issue a death certificate? All West Germans and West Berliners were required to report their address to the police so that there was a record of their whereabouts. Hess had been missing from German bureaucracy since leaving for Scotland in 1941. He was not listed by the Germans as living in Berlin or anywhere else. Our German friends would not wish to be difficult over this, or at least I hoped not. But German bureaucracy was not noted for its flexibility. Even if this problem could somehow be surmounted, would the Soviets accept the Germans issuing a death certificate? Maybe we didn't need to be so cautious. But I didn't want to have to find out whether we could rely on others on the day. It was important that the whole process should go smoothly.

The solution seemed to me to issue a British death certificate. That would ensure the issue was within our control. The British Forces On The Rhine (BAOR) had their own Registrar who was authorised to certify births, deaths and marriages in Germany. I had seen their operation when visiting BAOR HQ at Rheindalen. So we built the Registrar into our plan. He would be on notice to fly to Berlin the following day once we notified him that Hess had died in order to issue a death certificate as part of the documentation for the transfer of the body to Bavaria.

It worked! Hess had a habit of taking ill at the end of the week and ruining the weekend of those involved as he would be transported to the British Military Hospital and guarded there. We heard on Monday 17 August 1987 that he was dead. He had gone into the summerhouse in the prison garden as usual after lunch. When the guard looked in on him he was found unconscious with a weak pulse. He had tied the extension cable used for a reading lamp around his neck around his neck and to a window handle and fallen to the floor. Efforts to revive him on the spot were unsuccessful. He was taken to the BMH and, after further resuscitation attempts, he was declared dead at ten minutes past four.

The plan went into operation and worked. A Dr Cameron came out from London to perform an autopsy in the presence of medical representatives of all Four Powers. His report noted a mark on the left side of his neck consistent with a ligature. The conclusion was that death was caused by asphyxia caused by compression of the neck due to suspension.

On Friday 20 August 1987 Hess was flown by RAF Hercules to the US base at Grafenwöhr on Friday and handed over to his family.

That was by no means the end of the story. In view of the odd circumstances of his death a team from the Army Special Investigation Branch investigated. The medical advice was that he had died from asphyxiation. It appeared he had dropped to the floor and strangled himself with the cord. There was a suicide note. As was to be expected with a man with a long record of strange behaviour, it was rambling and by no means clear. It included a line "Sagt Freiberg…" We British German speakers jumped to the conclusion that it meant "Freiberg said.." but our German Legal Adviser Beate Freymuth-Brumby told us it should be read "Tell Freiberg…" That made a sort of sense. Freiberg had been his secretary.

The SIB investigation was thorough. It concluded that Hess had taken his own life. But that was not going to satisfy conspiracy theorists or those who wanted for whatever reason to maintain that all was not as it seemed.

A Hugh Thomas claimed that he had examined Hess when working at the BMH and determined that the man we had in prison was not Hess at all. This claim was one piece of his theory that we had a Double in Spandau and that the real Hess had not flown to Scotland. When Hess died, there was also the claim that the prisoner had not committed suicide but been murdered in order to prevent the truth coming out. Hess's son had no doubt that his father was Prisoner No 7 in Spandau but claimed he must have been murdered by the British to prevent his release and his revealing the content of his conversations while in Britain.

It never ceases to amaze me how much credence such stories can gain and how many books they can sell – I confess I was among the purchasers of books by both Hugh Thomas and Wolf-Rüdiger Hess.

There were a number of problems with both claims. Hess was wounded in WW1 and had scar tissue in his lung where a bullet had passed. Mr Thomas, who had by the way been dismissed from army service for reasons unconnected with his Hess stories, said he had not seen an exit wound. But he appears to have seen an entry scar – quite something to find someone as a double who not only was the spitting image of Hess but had a bullet scar too in the right place!

Hess refused for 20 years the visit per year from family he was allowed under prison rules. But when he did allow his wife Ilse to visit she never expressed any doubt about him being her husband. Nor did the other 6 inmates with whom he shared Spandau Prison. Speer's diaries record conversations with him over the 20 years they served in Spandau together. And if he had been a double why hadn't he said so at some point and spared himself 40 years in Spandau Prison!

Why should the British wait to kill him in 1987 when he was probably not so far from dying a natural death? Surely if he had had some amazing revelations about his discussions in Britain in 1941 these would have got out into the public domain long before. What could these have been? Churchill was offering the British people "blood, tears, toil and sweat". He was working on Roosevelt to increase US support. The crisis during the Battle of Britain had passed. The Blitz continued but Britain was responding with its own bomber mission. Can anyone really believe that Churchill would accept a peace deal?

The grave in Wunsiedel became a site of interest for neonazis. There was an annual pilgrimage there from 1988 on his birthday. The local community were very unhappy and the

Hess' grave at Wunsiedel (©Reuters)

Parish Council decided that the grave should be removed once the lease expired in 2011. Hess's wife and son had died in the intervening period. Some remaining relatives objected but the Council were able to come to agreement with Hess's granddaughter. Hess's remains were cremated and his ashes scattered at sea. The gravestone with the epitaph "Ich hab's gewagt" "I dared" (Hess's idea) was destroyed.

Our plan for handling his death included a longstanding intention to end the Four-Power Allied Prison Regime and demolish the prison lest it become a focus for neo-nazis. This was also agreed with the Berlin Senat; a small minority of people argued that the prison should be preserved as part of Berlin's architectural heritage. Demolition began on 21 September 1987. The rubble was guarded and then taken away and dumped in the North Sea. A new NAAFI was built on the site for the British Forces – to replace the shop, cafe and cinema in acquisitioned buildings at Theodor-Heuss-Platz in Charlottenburg. The NAAFI became immediately known on the British side as Hessco's. It was boring 1980s British utilitarian architecture and was itself demolished after the British Forces left Berlin following German unification.

Looking back, it was amazing that Hitler's erstwhile Deputy should have still been living in 1987 in an entirely different era and entirely different Germany, of which he would have limited understanding though some knowledge through television. It was hard not to feel a little sympathy for the geriatric I saw in Spandau Prison. But only a little. I can see where the Soviets were coming from in their insistence that he should not be released and that for him a life sentence should mean life. I can imagine that as his health deteriorated he must have decided enough was enough and taken his own life. He had tried to kill himself when in captivity in Britain during WW2. The Allied statement on his death mentioned the suicide attempt at Spandau in 1977. The prison regime was obviously aware of the risk. That he could kill himself in the summerhouse was not something we had foreseen.

I'm glad he was no longer with us when it came to German unification in 1990. That would have created a problem for the Four Powers and the Germans too. Would Spandau have continued under licence from the new German government until Hess died? Hard to imagine. Would he have been transferred elsewhere in Germany? Would the Soviets have given way at that point and allowed his release? We shall never know.

PART II

BERLIN FROM COLD WAR TO GERMAN UNIFICATION

I first went to West Berlin in 1971 when I was working, between school and university, at the Bayerische Hypotheken-und Wechselbank in Munich. I hitchhiked for a long weekend through the southern road corridor via Hof. My strongest memory is of going through Checkpoint Charlie on foot to East Berlin. I had difficulty in finding anything worth buying with the GDR Marks you were forced to exchange on entry for hard western currency. I had a meal in a canteen which was beneath the standards of school dinners in the 1960s in Britain – and that's saying something. I went up the Television Tower, just built and the pride of the GDR. At the top, when eventually allowed to take a seat, I was served the worst cup of coffee I have ever tasted. East Berlin was still riddled with bullet holes from the Second World War. It was grey and dirty and smelly.

I was relieved to go back to the West. For a few marks I bought some wonderful second-hand books. I went back to Munich by train. It was quite an experience for a 19-year-old to see how West Germans were mistreated by the GDR guards.

When I arrived in Berlin in October 1986 to start work as Deputy Political Adviser in the British Military Government the Cold War was still cold. It did not cross my mind as I travelled from Checkpoint Alpha on the inner-German border at Helmstedt to West Berlin entering at Checkpoint Bravo that I might be the last holder of this post.

The British Military Government (BMG) was British but was neither military nor a government by this time. It was the diplomatic staff of the British presence in West Berlin. The real government was the elected West Berlin authority and the West German government but we together with our US and French colleagues exercised the minimum of Allied authority we judged necessary to uphold the status of Berlin set up after the end of the Second World War.

BMG was housed at the Olympic Stadium complex in Charlottenburg, requisitioned on arrival of British forces in Berlin in July 1945. The main building had housed the boxing and fencing arena at the 1936 Olympic Games and had otherwise been used as the centre for sports administration of the Third Reich. There were still registers of sporting performance from the 1930s in one of my cupboards. The main building was called London Block. We in BMG, British diplomats and locally-hired staff, occupied the second floor and a few rooms on the ground floor. The British military had the rest.

The British had a military garrison of around 3000: the US had more and the French fewer. Our garrison comprised three regiments, which rotated regularly, plus special units such as the Royal Military Police. Of course there were no navy personnel given Berlin's landlocked position. I was always intrigued when visiting the US HQ in Clayallee by a door I would pass marked Office of the US Naval Advisor.

The US and French had similar diplomatic set-ups. Each had a Minister/Deputy Commandant, a Political Adviser. The three Deputy Political Advisers had weekly meetings and made most use of the dedicated secure telex system between the three Allies. We co-ordinated policy, having always a long list of items on our agenda. We were each in the chair one month of three. We were also the members of the Civil Affairs Committee of the Allied Kommandatura – the Four Power governing body for Berlin which the Soviet left in 1947 – and met at its building in Kaiserswerther Strasse from time to time in our roles as part of the governance of Berlin.

We reported back to our Embassies in Bonn through our own national chain of command. There were also regular meetings between the Western Allies and the West German government in Bonn on Berlin issues. This was called the Bonn Group. These people reported back to capitals. Berlin being such a weighty issue in the East-West relationship there were meetings of the Western Allied Foreign Ministers twice a year with the West German Foreign Minister in the so-called Berlin dinners in the margin of NATO meetings. These meetings ranged much wider than just Berlin – the label was in part a front to explain why other western

Civil Affairs Committee of the Allied Kommandatura

Foreign Ministers were not invited. I attended some of these meetings, most memorably in June 1987 in Reykjavik. There was a lot of work in Berlin and Bonn to write a Berlin report for the Foreign Ministers before these meetings.

Most of the British military officers and the diplomats lived in Charlottenburg. For some reason the Deputy Polad had a house in Fischerhüttenstrasse in Zehlendorf, in the American sector. It meant a longer journey to take the children to Charlottenburg military school and then on to the Olympic Stadium. It did not take long using the Avus motorway. In any event, the time commuting was more than compensated by having a Swiss-chalet-style house in the woods next to the lakes Krumme Lanke and Schlachtensee. I ran around these when feeling energetic. In the summer, Berliners would swim, in hot weather naked, in the lakes. In the winter, they could sometimes skate and play ice hockey.

It was, and still is, a beautiful spot. Nothing much would grow in the garden because of a collection of tall Scotch pines, an extension of the nearby woodland.

House in
Fischerhüttenstrasse Berlin

Children in the snow in Berlin winter

In the winter snow it looked especially pretty. In our first winter we had snow and ice on the ground through January–March 1987. We pulled the children along on a sled to the shops.

We employed a West African gardener, Joseph, to keep the land around the house tidy. He then also became our cleaner. A delightful man. James liked his use of English – he referred to the "study room", for example.

The forest was a joy. One cold winter's evening with the snow on the ground, I joined a ceremony of the West Berlin Foresters in a clearing. They were linked to the police and hence, in the British Sector, to the British Military Government. A boar was roasted on a spit. We ate hunks of the delicious meat together with dry grey bread. On a cord round our necks we had a small ceramic drinking vessel for schnapps. We also tried drinking schnapps from such a vessel sunk in a wooden block between deer antlers. The aim was to drink up without spilling a drop. This was part of an annual cull of the wild boar. They roamed the forests but were hemmed in by the Wall and proliferated. We would often see them in the forest. We were warned not to get between a mother and her cubs.

We travelled around West Berlin. I was fascinated by out-of-the-way places, often cut off from their natural hinterland by the Wall. I would often drive around such areas early on a Sunday morning when there was little traffic.

We could enter the East using our Allied status at Checkpoint Charlie identified by Orange Cards issued by the British Military Government. GDR border guards would check us going in and out but would not interfere. It was interesting to see the East. I went there from time to time for work purposes, to visit the Soviet Embassy where I always felt I was being watched and recorded. It always seemed to be a scene out of Smiley's Cold War – East Berlin being dark, foggy because of the fumes of their Trabant cars and knowing I would be followed by the East German Stasi!

As tourists, Allied personnel would buy a few things of quality such as crockery and glassware on visits to East Berlin. I went to Köpenick in East Berlin to buy a model train layout for the children. When I went back later to buy more track only curves were available. I was told the Plan had been fulfilled for the year and there would be no more straights available until next. I could not resist commenting to the shopkeeper that we should have to go round in circles until then.

We were not allowed by the FCO to travel into the GDR and other Soviet bloc countries. But there were a couple of occasions when I joined the British military in going to a party held by the British Mission to the Soviet Armed Forces (BRIXMIS) at their villa outside Potsdam. We could do this because the Soviets were prepared for this special annual occasion to allow us over the Glienicke Bridge nicknamed the bridge of spies under their auspices and without a visa to enter the GDR. It was always a great feeling going over the Bridge, a commonplace nowadays.

East-West in the Late 1980s

President Reagan, supported by Mrs Thatcher, had taken the view that the US was ready to build down nuclear weapons and missiles as part of an agreement with the Soviets, but was at the same ready to deploy new ones if and where the US and NATO perceived an imbalance. Chancellor Helmut Schmidt had taken a brave but politically risky decision to support the US deployment of further missiles in Germany and elsewhere in Western Europe (these were also the days of protests at Greenham Common in the UK). In the end it cost Schmidt the Chancellorship in 1982 and he was succeeded by Helmut Kohl.

The Gorbachev reforms in the Soviet Union of the mid-1980s were of huge interest to us all in the West. How far would glasnost (openness) and perestroika (restructuring) go? They were signs that the old Soviet model of a command economy and absolute refusal to tolerate internal criticism was eroding. The impact was also starting to appear in some other countries of the Warsaw Pact, notably in Poland. We were aware of the old dictum that there is never a more dangerous moment than when a government starts to reform – control can be lost. There were plenty of lessons from the past, notably Hungary in 1956 and Czechoslovakia in 1968, that the Soviets could clamp down if they felt threatened.

There was no change in the approach of the GDR leadership. I wondered at the time if this was because of the remaining huge sensitivity for the Soviets of a resurgent Germany. Perhaps this was a factor at least in not urging reform on the GDR regime. But as time wore on it was increasingly apparent that the GDR regime by Erich Honecker, most of them having experienced the Nazi period and fought for a Socialist alternative and accepting Soviet overlordship after the War, were stuck in the past and were not prepared to think about any evolution.

We overestimated the strength of the GDR regime. The economy was said by some to be in the top ten in the world. The GDR always won loads of medals at Olympic Games and European Championships. We living in West Berlin had a less rosy picture of what we saw when we visited East Berlin than people in West Germany. There were warnings even from the Russians that the GDR regime needed to inject some fresh thinking – so much so, that Soviet newspapers and periodicals were at one point not allowed in the GDR, lest the fresh winds of glasnost cause a problem! Even so, we did not see the GDR as a state on the edge of existential crisis.

The Four-Power Game of Berlin

So life went on as hitherto in Berlin. The Three Western Allies remained in occupation of the Western Sectors of the city, preserving the post-war settlement until such time as there could be agreement to end it and the division of Germany. The Three Western Allies and the Federal Republic of Germany did not accept the GDR claim that the Eastern Sector, East Berlin, was the capital of the GDR and part of their sovereign territory: the Four Allies had agreed at the end of the war that Berlin would be separate from the four zones of Germany and subject for special four-power control. The GDR did everything they could to make their claim to East Berlin stick and to cast the Western Allies as standing out against reality and not allowing the two Germanies to normalise their relationship fully as two separate independent states. The Soviets supported their GDR ally, at least up to a point. They had over the years called on us to leave West Berlin and subjected the access routes to blockade or delay. Berlin had become a touchstone in East-West relations. Every US President, British Prime Minister and

French President visited the city to show western allied resolve to defend West Berlin.

The Soviets also liked the game of Four-Power jurisdiction over Germany as a Whole. They played the Four-Power game over Spandau prison, the Air Regime (about which more below) and agreements on Military Missions operating in the Soviet case in West Germany and in the Three Allies' case in East Germany. The Soviets continued to mount the checkpoints on the three road routes and single rail route connecting West Berlin with West Germany so that the Western Allies could have access controlled by them while West Germans and West Berliners were controlled by the GDR. Their motivation was most likely maintaining military control in central Germany and a visible presence.

West Berliners made heavy use of the air routes to West Germany. Tegel had become the main airport; the pre-war Tempelhof was always threatened with closure except for US military use, because of its inner-city location and impact on the surrounding population, but remained open in the years we lived in Berlin mostly for smaller planes. Gatow was just used by the British military.

One of my roles was to supervise the British Element at the Berlin Air Safety Centre. This was a team of RAF air traffic controllers who worked with the Elements of the other three wartime Allies on the flights around Berlin and between West Germany and West Berlin. These flights were confined to three corridors – North, Centre and South – of a width of 20 miles and allowing flight up to 10,000 feet. The agreement on these corridors dated from November 1945 – at that time passenger aircraft did not have pressurised cabins and did not fly above 10,000 feet. For modern aircraft, it was inefficient in fuel terms to fly so low. It was typical of the spirit of our relations with the Soviets that they insisted on keeping to the agreements of the immediate post-war period and were not interested in modernising them.

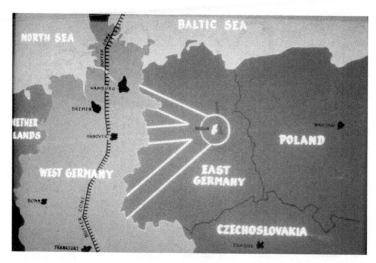

Berlin Air Regime

Originally, these flights were just military. Then the allies started putting forward flights from civilian companies from their countries – by 1986 that was British Airways, Air France and PANAM. It was understood that the Soviets would not allow flights by German companies, such as Lufthansa, or other countries. We tried to advance the boundaries where we could, for example by proposing medical emergency flights – in addition to the scheduled flights of these national carriers. These issues were hotly contested.

One of the western elements would notify the Soviet element by a written card of a flight in the corridor. Sometimes the Soviets would return the card stamped "Not Permitted", for example if some flight out of the ordinary were taking place. I would then be notified to make a political decision, if necessary with the US and French Deputy Political Advisers, on how we should respond. The Soviets would not say what action might be taken on their side. During the Berlin

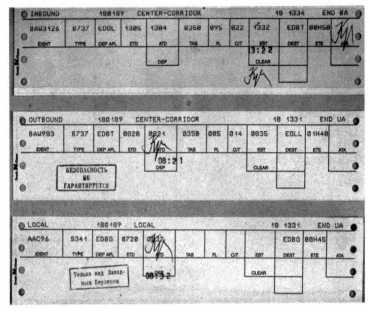

BASC flight cards

Blockade of 1948-49 Soviet fighters had buzzed allied aircraft. We did not think they would do that in the 1980s but knew it would be part of their playbook of escalation if for some reason the Soviet Bear wanted to bare his teeth to the West.

Another part of the air regime was the Berlin Air Co-ordinating Committee. This met twice a year to report on the developments of the period under review. The minutes of the meeting were written before the event – so well did we have things under control.

Working with the Soviets

I had occasional contact with the Soviet military. Their attitude was that we the western allies should look after our Germans

With Allied colleagues dealing with the air regime

and the Soviets would look after theirs. My main channel was
with the Soviet Embassy in East Berlin, some of whose staff
were dedicated to Berlin issues. The Soviet Ambassador would
have bilateral meetings with our Ambassador to Germany,
based in Bonn (and with the US and French Ambassadors).
In Berlin itself the highest level of diplomatic contact was
between our Minister and the No 2 in the Soviet Embassy
in East Berlin. Our Political Adviser also had his opposite
number – a Counsellor in the Soviet Embassy. I would have
contact with the Counsellor too and with his juniors.

On occasions, I would go over to the Soviet Embassy,
usually in a British month as the representative of all three
western allies, to deliver a protest, for example when East
Germans were killed trying to escape from East Berlin to
West. Less frequently, a Soviet diplomat would visit us in West
Berlin to make some formal complaint.

One major set piece of the year was the Soviet reception
at their monumental Embassy in East Berlin to celebrate the
anniversary of the Bolshevik takeover of power in October

1917. It was interesting that the Soviets invited representatives of the western allies to this event. They shut down that part of East Berlin, not so far from the Wall. Honecker would be on display for all to see talking to the Soviet Ambassador. It was a clear message that however strong the Soviet support for the GDR position on sovereignty in Berlin it was the Soviet Union which ultimately still called the shots.

Escapes

It was a depressing fact that over 170 people were killed trying to escape over the Berlin Wall and the frequency of escape attempts increased in 1988-89, until it became possible in summer 1989 for East Germans and others in the Soviet bloc, albeit not without difficulty, to escape to the West through Hungary. Before then, even in 1989, East Germans trying to escape the West were being killed by GDR security forces. The last was Chris Gueffroy on 5 February 1989; his companion Christopher Gaudian was led away wounded by GDR border guards and released in the autumn to the Federal Republic.

A very sad case was student Winfried Freudenberg. He died deep in West Berlin territory in the borough of Zehlendorf. Together with his wife he planned to escape from East Berlin by a balloon assembled with tent material.

A young man saw the balloon in preparation for the escape and informed the GDR police. They came to the scene. Freudenberg decided to take off quickly and decided with his wife that she should stay behind.

He took off around midnight. He was seen over Tegel on the morning of 8 March 1989. He then crashed in Zehlendorf landing in the garden of a house in Limastrasse close to where my US colleague lived and only a few hundred yards from our house. The balloon was found some distance away in a road. He died immediately. Every bone in his body was broken. He was identified from his and his wife's documents found further north of the scene.

It may be that the balloon rose too high, perhaps because there was only one person in it. He may have found himself in danger of overshooting West Berlin and reaching the GDR. He may have let the gas out of the balloon too fast. It was a terrible end. I've often wondered how the informant in East Berlin felt about his hand in Freudenberg's death.

It was uplifting when escape attempts turned out well.

Martin Notev was a 21-year-old who together with a couple of male friends sought to escape by swimming across the River Spree one Saturday afternoon in February 1989. He swam across right by the Reichstag in view of western tourists who took photos and film of the incident. He reached the bank on our side – the Reichstag was in the British sector – but was unable to climb out of the water because the bank was too steep. His two friends had crossed a little further away from the Reichstag and had managed to haul themselves out.

This attempt was emulating a successful escape on 21 August 1988 when three young men and a woman swam across the Spree, again in daylight. The men managed with some help from tourists to clamber on to the bank on the western side. The woman was some 70 yards further down the river, stuck. A group of tourists hauled her out with a GDR patrol boat nearby.

Martin Notev was not only unable to climb on to the bank but a GDR patrol boat came by and this time had two men on board, rather than just one as in the incident the previous August, and he was pulled on to the boat and taken away. He was given a prison sentence for trying to escape. It seemed that the "anti-fascist protection rampart", as the GDR called the Wall, had won again.

The media around the world published photos of Martin Notev's capture by the GDR patrol boat. We, the Western Allies, protested to the Soviet Union, first to their Embassy in East Berlin and then to the Soviet Foreign Minister in Moscow. We underlined that Notev had in fact reached the British Sector because that began at the bank on our side of the river. We called for his release. As usual, we rejected the Soviet suggestion that we should direct ourselves to the Government of the GDR. This was part of the longstanding game whereby the Soviets called Berlin the capital of the GDR and we stuck to the Four-Power agreements concerning its Four-Power status until such time as there was agreement otherwise.

We kept up the pressure on every occasion one of the Allies had a meeting with the Soviet government. And then, on 21 June 1989, Martin Notev was released and deported to West Berlin. He was received by the British Security Service. The Minister, Michael Burton, and I went to meet him at a safe house in West Berlin. He was in great spirits, a young man full of life and looking forward to living in the West. He told us he had been kept in the dark about his release right until the last moment. We toasted his release, had photos taken and he autographed the grainy photo I had of him in the Spree unable to climb out. He went off to a new life in West Germany.

There was a final part of the story. We in the British Military Government decided to install steps and ropes on our bank of the river. The Soviets protested on behalf of the GDR – and in fact not all our US and French colleagues thought this was a good idea. The BMG press spokeswoman issued a statement that the ropes and steps were to help anyone in the water. Of course, it was hardly likely that anyone would find themselves in the Spree at this point – on the border of the British and

Martin Notev

Soviet sectors – unless they were trying to escape to the West! The ropes and steps deteriorated and were removed after the Wall came down.

On 26 May, there was an eye-catchingly bold rescue mission. Two brothers who had escaped from the East some time previously flew two microlight aircraft at dawn from West Berlin over to Treptow Park in the East. One landed and picked up a third brother while the episode was filmed from the other aircraft. They flew back to the West and landed in the large space in front of the Reichstag. They sold their film and story to a magazine to pay for their project.

I was involved in the aftermath of another daring and successful escape by air. On 15 July 1987 a young GDR trainee pilot took advantage of a solo practice flight to fly to West Berlin and land at RAF Gatow. The GDR authorities were stung by this escape. They contacted the British Embassy in East Berlin to demand return of aircraft and pilot. They were given short shrift by our Ambassador there, told that this was a matter for the Powers responsible for Berlin and not an Embassy accredited to the GDR which had no legal authority for Berlin.

A few days later the Political Adviser from the Soviet Embassy in East Berlin visited me in my office at the British Military Government at the Olympic Stadium complex. He said he understood the British had some property belonging to the GDR and we should return it. I don't recall him talking about return of the pilot – who had left quickly for West Germany as a free man. I enjoyed that the GDR had felt it necessary to ask the Soviets to come to see me, thereby implicitly recognising the Four-Power status of Berlin.

The discussion of the detail took some time after this visit. The Western Allies insisted that that aircraft could only be handed back to the Soviet authorities and not the GDR. The Soviets wanted as little to do with it as possible. In the end the Soviet military agreed to receive the plane. The RAF drove it from Gatow on a flat-bed trailer with the wings dismounted to the Glienicke Bridge, staffed by the Soviet military and the scene of spy exchanges over the years, including Andrei Sakharov during my time in Berlin. The transfer took place on the bridge.

The West Berliners

Life in West Berlin was fun. Being surrounded by the GDR gave added spice. The nightlife was vibrant, particularly in the streets around the Kurfürstendamm in central West Berlin. There were plenty of young people there, a lot of students at the universities and young men who were avoiding West German military service, which did not apply to residents of West Berlin.

Some parts of West Berlin had a calmer life as time went on because of the Wall, notably those tucked away by the wall leading to the GDR: there was no through traffic!

Many West Berliners (and West Germans) were impatient for greater normalisation with East Berlin and the GDR. That was understandable. The Western Allies were not prepared to do what the GDR wanted and recognise their sovereignty over East Berlin and perhaps West Berlin as well. But working with the Senat of Berlin, the executive arm of the elected authority there, and the West German government, there was a lot which could be done to ease the situation.

There had been improvements over the years since the building of the Berlin Wall in 1961 to improve access for West Berliners and West Germans to East Berlin, particularly after the Quadripartite Agreement of 1971 which was part of the movement of East-West detente.

During my time the main negotiation between the Senat (authorised by the Western Allies) with the GDR was over an exchange of territory to iron out some of the difficulties caused by where the border between West Berlin and East Berlin and West Berlin and GDR ran, based on the borough boundaries of 1920.

One area in the package being negotiated was the Lenné Triangle. This was a triangular piece of land belonging to East Berlin close to Potsdamer Platz (then a wasteland and not the bustling modern centre of the city as it had been before the Second World War and is again now) but on the western side of where the GDR had built the Wall. This created a lawless zone since it could be used by drug dealers and prostitutes knowing that the West Berlin police were not allowed to enter it.

On 31 March 1988 agreement was reached on an Exchange of Territory including the Lenné Triangle becoming part of

West Berlin. But the entry into force of the agreement would take some time. On 30 May, a group of squatters occupied the Lenné Triangle. They erected a tented village there. This was a considerable problem for the West Berlin police. The occupation occurred before a search could be made of the area for wartime ordnance. There was a real risk to life of moving around the area before that had been done. It was also an annoyance to the GDR as some of the campers tried to scale the Wall.

The West Berlin alternative newspaper Taz had a wonderful time. It depicted the encampment as a new version of Asterix's village standing out against the Romans. The Senat pressed us to give the West Berlin police permission to enter; the Soviets expressed concerns on behalf of the GDR. Eventually, on 1 July, when the agreement came into force the West Berlin police went in and removed the squatters.

The areas belonging to the Soviet sector, East Berlin, on the western side of the wall were called the Unterbaugebiet. The GDR had decided to build the wall

Lenné Triangle, Berlin

a little way back from the actual boundary at these points, presumably for practical reasons making the wall easier to guard. Sometimes we saw GDR guards in the areas on our side of the wall. But usually these areas were simply left as No-Man's-Land.

On one occasion a West Berliner tried to commit suicide by driving his car into the wall in the Unterbaugebiet not far from the Reichstag in the British sector. The West Berlin emergency services, like the police, had no authority to enter the area. The British Royal Military Police contacted us at the British Military Government and we told them to go in to try to save a life. They extricated him; he recovered from his injuries.

As a next step the Royal Military Police called up some lifting equipment to remove the car. GDR border guards came over the Wall and refused entry to "the territory of the GDR". The RMP took their speaking lines from us and told the GDR guards that East Berlin was not part of the GDR and they should call a Soviet officer if there was to be further discussion. Meanwhile, we telephoned the Soviet Embassy in East Berlin to tell them what was happening: they told us to deal with the authorities of the GDR. Eventually a GDR officer gave an amber light to the RMP. They then went into action making clear they were doing so on British not GDR authority. The operation took several hours, recorded by West Berlin news including the conversations between the RMP and GDR border guards.

The Wall

The Wall featured all the time in my work. It had been in place for 25 years when I arrived and GDR leader Honecker made it clear it would stay for another 100 years if necessary. It was a fact of life. I explored all kinds of areas along the wall – built-up, forest, by the rivers Spree and Havel and along the canals. I came to know the geography better than I knew any other city in the world.

The most sensitive area was by the Reichstag and Brandenburg Gate, in the British Sector. We in BMG had a close relationship with the Royal Military Police who had roving patrols in the area. They also had a fixed observation point at the Reichstag. The purpose of this was also to look into West Berlin and in particular to keep an eye on the Soviet War Memorial nearby. The ceremonial Red Army Guard there had been fired upon in 1971 by a West German Ekkehard Weil who was eventually tried, convicted and sentenced to imprisonment by a special British court.

Brandenburg Gate Berlin, 1988

Will the Wall Ever Come Down?

The Western Allies were beginning by the mid-1980s to find it increasingly difficult to maintain a strong relationship with the West Berliners. I don't want to overstate this. The West Berliners had been grateful to the Western Allies ever since they had stuck it out during the Berlin Blockade of 1948-49 when the Soviets and East Germans had tried to force the Western Allies out and West Berlin to be absorbed into the GDR. Even in the mid-1980s there were large crowds at Allied military parades and other events.

But there was increasing impatience with the disadvantages which came with being a garrison city. We the British faced protests about the building of a new firing range in Gatow which residents claimed was too noisy. We had even stronger protests over our decision to cut down trees at Gatow in order to keep the Gatow airfield operational for all sizes of aircraft, in case the airstrip was needed in a time of crisis. This was seen by some West Berliners as unnecessary and a crime against the environment. There were also complaints about our tanks causing damage in their training grounds. We tried to move heavy vehicles on the roads at night and faced the music if one broke down and held up the morning traffic.

Linked to this was a growing German feeling that we ought to allow a normalisation of relations with East Berlin as capital of the GDR, accepting reality. This was the undertow of discussions I had with local political parties, particularly those of the left but also some of the conservatives too.

That was one reason why I thought the status quo in Berlin was likely to change in the next ten years. I am reminded by a Berlin friend, Professor Wolfgang Mackiewicz, that I predicted the fall of the wall within 10 years after quite a few drinks at his house in 1988.

It was a question we were always asked by official British visitors to Berlin. In answer to the question as we would gaze over the death strip from an observation platform to which I would take visitors near the Brandenburg Gate, I would say that it would come down one day but I could not say when and in what circumstances.

PART III

FALL OF THE WALL

Another reason for wondering about the future of the Wall was the changes in Central Europe and the GDR in 1988-89. Back in 1987 during the celebrations on both sides of the Wall of the 750th anniversary of Berlin, we had had visits by the leaders of the three Western Allies, including the Queen, but this had seemed more about solidarity with West Berlin than belief that the Wall would be removed any time soon.

President Reagan famously gave a speech in front of the Wall urging Mr Gorbachev to "tear down this Wall". For most West Berliners, West Germans and beyond in the West, this was seen as rhetoric in the tradition of earlier famous speeches in Berlin by US Presidents, notably Kennedy in 1963 – but in this case as much for the domestic US audience as for Mr Gorbachev. It had been a major effort by the Americans and West Berlin police to prevent graffiti artists from writing rude slogans on the Wall behind President Reagan in the run-up to the speech. In fact, I thought at the time that concerts by Pink Floyd and Genesis and others by the Wall also in the area of the Brandenburg Gate had had more impact on East Berliners and East Germans – the GDR was certainly nervous about the young people who gathered as close as they could on their side of the Wall to listen. Maybe we underestimated the force of the speech. It is seen now by many as an important moment.

In 1989, people in the GDR were protesting against their government starting in Monday evening marches in Leipzig.

I went over in October 1989 to East Berlin to see the annual GDR military parade and it was clear from the assembly of East Berliners later that day by the Palace of the Republic where Honecker was meeting Gorbachev that levels of dissent were reaching heights not seen perhaps since the uprising, brutally suppressed, of 1953. It was fascinating the crowd shouted "Gorbi, Gorbi!" – thereby criticising Honecker who was resisting Gobachev-style reform. The leather-clad Stasi were more interested in guarding the approaches to the Wall than in dealing with the crowd.

Yet the GDR regime had shown its readiness to use whatever brutality was needed to maintain control. It was a surprise when the Wall was breached on 9 November 1989.

As it happened, Judy and I and the children were at my mother's in Stapleford Nottingham during the half-term school break at the time. Judy and I went out on the Thursday evening 9 November, Judy's birthday, and when we came back my mother said there was something happening at the Wall. We watched BBC Newsnight and saw crowds of people streaming through from East Berlin to the West. On breakfast TV the next morning there was more of the same. East Berliners were not sure whether they could stay the whole night in the West or whether they might not be allowed back at all.

We planned to return by car any way on the Saturday and stuck to that. I still have the Allied movement orders for the return drive along the corridor. These, in three languages, were presented as usual to the Soviets both at the inner-German border at Marienborn/Drewitz and at the entrance to West Berlin at Drewitz/Dreilinden.

The scenes at Marienborn on Saturday 11 November 1989 were dramatic. GDR border guards had made themselves scarce as East and West Germans had a party. We

Form BTD/C

UNITED KINGDOM
ROYAUME UNI
СОЕДИНЕННОЕ КОРОЛЕВСТВО

MOVEMENT ORDERS
LAISSEZ-PASSER
ПУТЕВКА

Name Nom, Prénom Фамилия, Имя	Rank Qualité Чин	Nationality Nationalité Гражданство	Identity Document No. Pièce d'identité No. № удостоверения личности
CHARLTON A.	MR	BRITISH	0009
CHARLTON J.	MRS	BRITISH	0010
CHARLTON J.	MR	BRITISH	0011

is / are authorized to travel from est / sont autorisé(s) à se rendre de уполномочен/уполномочены следовать из **BERLIN** to à в **HELMSTEDT** and return et retour и обратно

by train or by vehicle No. par le train ou par voiture No. поездом или на автомашине № **C 316 NHK**

from (date) du (date) от (число) **27 Oct 89** to (date) au (date) по (число) **11 Nov 89** inclusive inclus включительно

by par

Commandant British Sector Berlin
Commandant du Secteur Britannique de Berlin
Комендантом Британского Сектора г. Берлин

КПП Мариенборн

ВЪЕЗД

Signature Подпись

Title Qualité Звание **COMMANDANT, BRITISH SECTOR BERLIN**

Date Число **27 Oct 89**

Berlin movement order

were fortunate that the traffic was flowing West to East. The tailback on the other side of the road as East Germans tried to enter West Germany was 35 kilometres to Marienborn. Wessis were supplying beer to Ossis. Youngsters were dancing on the roofs of their cars. I counted ourselves fortunate to make it back home to Zehlendorf that evening.

The next morning, Sunday 12 November, I tried and failed to drive to the Brandenburg Gate. The traffic, swollen by foul-smelling GDR Trabants, was jammed. Two million East Germans visited West Berlin that weekend. In the afternoon there was a free concert for East Germans at the Philharmonie with Beethoven's Ninth conducted by Daniel Barenboim. It was only later that Ode to Joy from this became the anthem of the EU. I watched the concert on TV. The Philharmonie is the most magical place for music. It was perfect for this amazing moment.

We in Berlin enjoyed weeks of pure joy. East Germans came over to the West, flooded the main streets and shops and, using the Welcome Cash (Begrüssungsgeld) provided by the Federal Government, went back with a few purchases. Bananas (always in short supply in the East except for Party bigwigs – Bonzen) were prized. So were cans of Coke. So were plastic bags – in East Germany you still had paper bags and goods were wrapped with string rather than sticky tape. East Germans had for years watched on their TVs (except for the sad people around Dresden who had poor reception of West German TV) adverts for western washing powder etc and wanted to have some. Some East Germans are said to have felt faint when they saw the cornucopia of food on display on the sixth floor of Kaufhaus des Westens (KdW).

Every day something new and historic happened – a new crossing was opened up, more of the wall was chipped away on both sides. On Thursday 16 November our Foreign Secretary Douglas Hurd came to Berlin. On that day a section of Wall was removed to allow a narrow passage for pedestrians at Potsdamer Platz. The tall, white-haired figure of our boss was carried by the crowds into the Soviet Sector. He didn't seem to mind and we retrieved him without incident. It could have been awkward if the GDR or Soviets had spotted him and decided to make a fuss.

The following Saturday there was a football match at the Olympic Stadium between West Berlin's traditional club Hertha BSC and Eisern Union, the strongest East Berlin club. It was a full house and free for East Germans. Eisern Union

Children at the
Berlin Wall

was supported by the GDR government, suffered financially after unification and fell away. It has since become again a force in Berlin football.

Looking back it seems inevitable that the events of 9 November 1989 would lead to the unification of Germany. That's the way it seemed to us in Berlin. We thought that the West German Mark would be an irresistible force for change in the GDR. What was the point of an East German state in these circumstances? In the days following we could not hazard a guess on the pace of change but we were certain that 9 November 1989 was the turning point in post-war German and European history. Michael Burton, Minister BMG, sent a report on 13 November with these thoughts.

Not everyone agreed. Our Prime Minister Margaret Thatcher, after a famous Chequers seminar about the implications of what was happening in Berlin, adopted the line that German unification was not on the agenda. There was nervousness about how the Soviets would react. Could there yet be a military clampdown to try to stop the accelerating erosion of the border between East and West? The Soviets had the forces to do this. Was this in their minds?

Not everyone in the GDR was happy with the thought that the wonderful freedom they now had to visit the West could lead to the end of their state, the GDR. They had been fed a diet of propaganda on East German TV about the social ills of drugs and violence in the West. They were glad to be rid of the police state, corrupt and sometimes brutal leaders, restrictions on freedom of expression. But capitalism was a dirty word for many conjuring up images of an uncaring society with vast disparities in wealth between citizens.

As I saw it the unification of Germany would mean Mission Accomplished for the British and other Allies in Berlin. We had held our position there for 44 years maintaining the legal position that the Germany in its 1937 borders remained legally existent until such time as there was a Four-Power Agreement on final post-war status.

What a pity then that, owing to Mrs Thatcher's concerns, the UK appeared the most reluctant of the Western Allies to embrace the idea of unification. Britain owes a lot to her leadership. Her period of office was the re-launch of the British economy which had been going backwards for a long time before. Of course, there were questions about how a united Germany would behave. I could understand the French having misgivings: would this enlarged Germany continue to bind itself in partnership with France in the European Union or would it want to assume the role as the most powerful country in Europe and have a balanced relationship with Western and Eastern Europe? But it was clear pretty soon that unification was in effect an enlargement of the existing Federal Republic of Germany rather than an FRG/GDR composite. President George Bush Senior got it right in welcoming what was happening. Mrs Thatcher got it wrong.

The right course for the UK would have been to seek a stronger partnership with Germany in 1990. There was a lot in common. We had no need to worry about the re-emergence of a German threat to the UK. The Germany of 1990 was quite different from the Germany of 1945, though the new Germany would still have work to do to convince not only the wartime allies but its neighbours, especially Poland, that it would conduct itself in an appropriate way.

Unfortunately, we persisted with this rather suspicious and grudging attitude towards Berlin and Germany for the crucial following weeks of November and December. Mrs Thatcher, a great Prime Minister, got it wrong. This was one of the factors which so weakened her support in the senior ranks of the Conservative Party that she was unable to resist a leadership challenge and ended up being replaced by John Major, who was seen as a leader with a better chance to win the next election in 1991. He did, but had a very tough time thereafter dealing with a fractious government and party.

The moment when the Brandenburg Gate opened should have been one of particular satisfaction for the UK. We had watched over this key point alongside the Reichstag since 1945. I watched from high up in the Reichstag as the pedestrian access was opened up and banners of "Come Together", a wonderful Beatles song, were memorably to the fore.

I keep writing "unification" and not "reunification". For most people the terms were interchangeable. But I and my colleagues had long been living and breathing the detailed questions of Germany's legal status. What came on to the agenda was not a turning back of the clock to boundaries before the Second World War but a new joining together of the FRG, Berlin and the GDR. We did not want to put in question boundary changes made after the Second World War. There would be no revisiting the borders of Poland or Czechoslovakia or Russia.

For the Americans the Fall of the Wall was a vindication of

their policy on Germany and towards the Soviet Union. It was hugely popular in the US itself. An American colleague told me that at that time many Americans' knowledge of Germany consisted of Berlin, Checkpoint Charlie and the Wall. The Fall of the Wall could be seen as a US victory and President Bush senior led US policy admirably, immediately seeing the moment for what it was and being the partner of Chancellor Kohl of West Germany.

A special moment for the US was the decommissioning of Checkpoint Charlie on 22 June 1990. The ceremony was a masterpiece of US dramatisation. How do you make Checkpoint Charlie into something which can be removed before the eyes of the world watching on TV? The answer was in effect to turn the hut from which the US military conducted their operation at the checkpoint into the embodiment of Charlie. Six Foreign Ministers arrived one by one in their cavalcades and took their places on a podium together with interpreters (I was one such) and the Mayors of West and East Berlin – each given a three-minute window. There were speeches which I tried to translate for Douglas Hurd but found difficult to hear and so made some of it up. Anyhow, the words didn't matter much. The moment was the lifting of the hut into the air for a photo opportunity. The hut is now in a museum.

The pace of unification quickened once Chancellor Kohl put it on the agenda in later November. The Four Allies wanted to lead the process but that was only possible with German consent. There was one meeting in Berlin of the Four Ambassadors to Germany and that was one too many for the Federal Government. After that the talks became 4 plus 2 (the two German states). As time wore on they were increasingly the FRG supported by the US with the Soviet Union.

Unification of Germany, 3 October 1990

I kept a full diary for 2 and 3 October 1990.

The first event was at the Allied Kommandatura building (owned pre-war by a fire insurance company) in Kaiserwertherstrasse in Dahlem, West Berlin. This was the Four-Power Governing Body for Berlin which the Soviets soon left for good in 1946, though the photo of their Commandant General Kotikov remained on the wall of the Soviet office from 1945 to 1990 waiting for the Soviet return which was never going to happen. We celebrated the closure of the Allied Kommandatura as three Western Allies. With October being a British month we were in the chair for the final meeting. The press were allowed in, probably for the first time, including Martin Bell of the BBC, to witness the AK's last formal act, the signature of a letter to the Governing Mayor of Berlin Walter Momper.

Then it was outside for photos. The British Commandant

The Allied Kommandatura closing ceremony

General Robert Corbett used the speech I wrote for him, which concluded "History will relate that the AK was OK". Pretty awful.

The next stop was Rathaus Schöneberg, then the seat of the Governing Mayor and the Berlin Assembly. It had been the scene of the speech by President Kennedy in 1963 "Ich bin ein Berliner", one of those seminal moments of Berlin history when West Berliners looked for reassurance that the Western Allies would not abandon them after the building of the Wall and the US difficulty with the Soviets over Cuba. There were more speeches. German Minister of State Schäfer drew loud cheers when he said that Berlin would become the capital of the united Germany. I had assumed that would be the case having lived in the city for four years and witnessing the city coming together. But it turned out not to be so straightforward. The eventual vote in the Bundestag was close. I still find it hard to believe there was any other option. The Eastern half of the city had claimed to be the capital of the GDR. Would it not be a complete betrayal of the citizens of the East to keep the capital in the old West Germany?

Then it was on to the British Officers' Club, near the Funkturm (radio tower like a minature Eiffel) and the old NAAFI, now an International Club run by Germans, for a drink in the bar and lunch in the Green Room. I moved on to the Philharmonie where Governing Mayor Momper spoke to crowds of Allied military and civilian personnel and thanked them for their work. This had been the idea of the Berlin government. It was well appreciated.

I drove back to the office at the Olympic Stadium and then later home. I set off again at 1900, this time by U-Bahn. The traffic was going to be impossible as vast numbers of people sought to be in the vicinity of the Brandenburg Gate as Germany was unified at midnight.

Last party at Berlin Air Safety Centre – Monocles and pipes de rigueur!

The first port of call was the old Berlin Supreme Court Building, the scene of show-trials during the Hitler period including of his would-be assassins in 1944. It had been requisitioned at the end of the War by the Allies and used as the seat of Four-Power Government of Germany, the Allied Control Authority. In fact, for nearly all the intervening time, it had been occupied only by the Berlin Air Safety Centre. At 2000 I was immersed in a party, the last four-power gathering at the building. It was an excited and pretty crazy event.

Then it was over to a party in Lindencorso on Unter den Linden in East Berlin. Nearby I saw the Rotes Rathaus, the home of the Mayor of East Berlin, now decked out in symbols of West Berlin and the Federal Republic. I struggled out of the party at 2330 and moved down towards the Brandenburg Gate as far as the already-assembled crowds would allow. At midnight I was around 100 metres away on the eastern side. I watched the fireworks accompanied by Handel's fireworks music. There was excitement but not wild exultation among

James and Katy with GDR border guards after fall of the wall

the crowd as there had been at the time of the Fall of the Wall.
Two women nearby were standing quite still with smiles on
their faces and tears in their eyes.

At half past midnight I walked under the Brandenburg Gate
for the first time in united Germany. I made for Tiergarten
S-Bahn station. The queues were so long that I decided to
walk on. When I reached Ernst-Reuter-Platz the crowds had
thinned out and so I took an U-Bahn home via Wittemberg
Platz. It was fitting to include Ernst Reuter in the celebration.
It was his speech of defiance in front of the Reichstag in 1948
which underlined the new relationship between Berlin and
the Western Allies. I liked to think that that relationship had
made unification in 1990 possible.

The British Military Government in West Berlin and the
British Embassy to the GDR in East Berlin had now lost their
legal basis and ceased to exist. They joined together as an

Office of the British Embassy to Germany still based in Bonn. I stayed on a few weeks until the middle of November and had the chance to travel into the former GDR and also take a train to Warsaw: the S-Bahn ticket from home to Friedrichstrasse Station in East Berlin paid in DM cost about the same as the long journey by train to Warsaw paid for in OstMark. My hotel bill in Warsaw at a western chain was about a million and a half zloty but still well in my price range.

A prized relic of my time in Berlin was a book on the Legal Status of Berlin by FCO Legal Advisers Ian Hendry and Michael Wood. After years of work this issued in 1987. The FCO were too mean to procure a copy for me so I invested the vast sum of £55 to buy one myself. It was of historical interest only after unification.

PART IV

BACK TO GERMANY

I was posted back to Germany in 1996 as Political Counsellor in the Embassy in Bonn. It hadn't been my first choice. I would have preferred the UK Mission in New York. But that went to John Sawers, then Private Secretary to the Foreign Secretary. I was perfectly happy to go back to Germany. Bonn had the great advantage of being only 6 hours drive from home – we had decided that Judy would stay in Crawley so that the children could have continuity of schooling there.

I arrived on 18 April 1996. The seat of the German government was still Bonn though the move to Berlin was now fixed for summer 1999. Bonn was a unique capital city. It was called "provisional", awaiting the resolution of the "German Question" after World War 2. Our Embassy building reflected that. When Foreign Secretary Anthony Eden had written to Prime Minister Churchill in the early 1950s about doing something to provide accommodation for our provisional Embassy, Churchill had not very helpfully suggested that we should "put up a tent".

The Embassy set up in a nondescript building on a main road on the western side of the River Rhine. John Le Carré, who worked there in the early 1960s, described it as a "biscuit factory". Having come from a place (Stapleford) whose most impressive building was a pencil factory I wondered why biscuits were so maligned.

It was next door to the HQ of the CDU, Christian

British Embassy Bonn

Democratic Union. Their large red neon sign was a helpful signpost when giving directions on how to get to the Embassy. Just up the road, six stops on the tram, was the German Foreign Ministry, in modest box-like temporary accommodation. Bonn was a town of 300,000 – a Small Town in Germany, as John Le Carré's book title dubbed it.

This modest town and its modest government accommodation fitted the Federal German narrative of a new German attitude towards its place in the world and relationship with its neighbours after the hubris of Hitler Germany and previously. It was a far cry from the old German capital in old Berlin. It was still associated with the government of Chancellor Konrad Adenauer who was at home in this part of Germany and who disliked travelling to the east. It was a Germany of the Rhine, of carnival and of proximity to Belgium, France and Luxembourg – far away from Poland and Russia. In the time since the end of the War not a few Germans had come to like this new projection of Germany and did not want the government to return to Berlin with its dark memories of a different German power projection which had brought disaster to Germany, Europe and the World. Hence the hesitation over moving the government to Berlin after unification.

Bonn was quiet, lacking the buzz of a great city. A compensation was its charm. When I became the Deputy Head of Mission in 1998 I moved into a lovely house in Bad Godesberg near the Rhine, the house I most enjoyed in my diplomatic career. It had a mature terraced garden and an area of grass at the bottom large enough for six-a-side football. I had a great cook there, a retired man in his late sixties who had earlier worked for an Ambassador and now wanted to make a comeback. He was excellent, as were the other staff such as Peter Jones and Jan Thompson, who I also worked with on Yugoslavia. The house was given up when the Embassy moved to Berlin.

Before then I had lived in a house close to some other members of staff, all requisitioned after the War. They were roomy but inelegant. My main memory was returning from UK late on a very cold night after Christmas to find that the heating had failed and the pipes frozen. I made a log fire downstairs to warm up and then slept with clothes, coat and hat on.

Bad Godesberg house

Bonn house

My favourite episode from the 3 years in Bonn was the closure of the Embassy building in summer 1999. We decided to invite John Le Carré. He agreed to come – this surprised me as he had something of a reputation as a recluse. He wrote that he thought it sporting of us to make the suggestion – he was referring, I am sure, to misgivings in the town over his book Small Town in Germany as it depicted a fictional right-wing upsurge. He had left SIS not too long later to pursue writing full-time.

We responded to Churchill's suggestion to put up a tent by so doing in front of the Embassy for our closure ceremony. John Le Carré gave a witty speech. At dinner at the Ambassador's house he told some wonderful stories. Graf Nayhaus, veteran Bild columnist, who had seen it all, told me it had been a memorable evening. It was.

Opening a New Embassy in Berlin

For me there was an awesome feeling of accompanying the flow of history when I occupied my office in the funky new British Embassy in Berlin in late 2000.

I felt it was an end point in our work following the War to achieve a peace in Europe which ended the division of Germany and marked a new hopeful chapter of European history. The British were back in Wilhelmstrasse, a name with a similar ring to Whitehall in London as the centre of government. The German Foreign Ministry did not move back to the street.

We had an empty plot of land on 70-71 Wilhelmstrasse, the site of our Embassy since 1868. We had bought the site in 1884. It had been empty during the First World War. In the Second World War it was badly damaged by Allied bombing. The GDR pulled down what was left in 1950. We had been negotiating to give up the plot in return for other land in East Berlin – and I believe had been close to concluding a deal – but were able to turn this around and retrieve the Wilhelmstrasse plot.

I was only in the new building for 6 weeks before my tour of duty in Germany came to an end. It was time enough to respond positively to a request from the mother of young Environment Minister Angela Merkel to visit the new Embassy with some friends from her church. The fact that our Embassy was in the old East meant it was somehow "their" Embassy, so I was told.

The Embassy was formally opened by the Queen and Duke of Edinburgh on 18 July 2000. The building wasn't ready for occupation but we wanted to have the visit in summer weather and this was a date suitable for the Queen. Once again the media fascination with the Queen was huge. Paul Lever

The Queen opens the British Embassy in Berlin

gave dozens of interviews and appeared on German breakfast TV. The national channel 2 ZDF broadcast the ceremony live. There were highlights on the local TV SFB in the evening.

Paul Lever decided the simplest thing was to give up his and wife Pat's house to the Royal Party for their visit which was just a single day and night. The dinner at his house the evening before was memorable. Chancellor Gerhard Schroeder, his wife Doris Schroeder-Kopf, the Foreign Minister and Culture Minister Naumann were all there. So was a German General who had been playing a leading role in Kosovo. I was standing with him before dinner when the Duke of Edinburgh came over. In what I imagine is one of his party pieces, he asked if he had met the General before, and then said one of the good things about Alzheimer's is that you meet new people every day!

British Embassy Berlin

We had more publicity when the Ambassador raised the flag when we started work at the new building on 6 November 2000. We held an Open Day on Saturday 18 November. 7000 people came in and there would have been many more if the queues had not been so long at peak times. Several of us found ourselves doing guided tours. On my last working day in the Embassy, 8 December, I hosted CSU Member of the Bundestag Christian Schmidt and 50 of his constituents.

I liked the building. Outside in the inner courtyard an oak tree had been planted in front of the reception dedicated to former FCO Minister Derek Fatchett, who had died suddenly not long after attending the topping-out ceremony. The tree reminded me of all the controversy over trees being cut down at Gatow airport in the 1980s – how things had changed. A grand stone staircase led up to a large open space, a wintergarden and a Conference Drum, on the first floor. This had British artwork, including two striking corkscrew "Dancing Columns" by Tony Cragg – these were quickly dubbed by staff as "Two Diplomats: Bitter and Twisted". The Permanent Under Secretary John Kerr once rang me late on a Friday afternoon on my mobile when I was in the gym to leave absolutely no doubt that the artwork would have to be paid for by sponsorship. The offices were on upper floors, a gallery to the public space.

It wasn't perfect. We soon discovered that it had insufficient toilets, especially as the majority of our local staff was female. The offices were not particularly spacious either. The original design had placed the Ambassador in a space overhanging the street. I had picked up on that during a visit from Bonn in the construction stage and we had moved the Ambassador to a safer location. But that left us with the issue of how to use this space.

We had to learn how to use a building which did not belong to us. Around this time Public Finance Initiative projects were high in government esteem. There was no way the Treasury would make available the money to the Foreign Office to construct a new Embassy (or for artwork as I heard from John Kerr) – I suspect Churchill at this point would have quickly seen that a tent would not be right and that we should build to impress in a capital where we would have an absolutely crucial relationship to tend with Europe's biggest economy and growing political influence.

It was decided to choose a German supplier (Atreos) to which we would lease the site. They would build the Embassy to our design (Michael Wilford was selected as the architect in a competition) and then would administer the building for us. Both sides had the right to hire out the building. There would be a substantial annual charge to cover rent, utilities, wear and tear which we expected to be around £4.5 million. We would have to pay extra to keep the lights on after working hours.

It does not take a genius to work out that the British taxpayer would end up paying much more over the long term than if the British Government had simply paid for the building outright. I was surprised that the National Audit Office, after looking into the arrangement in 2000, concluded that it was a "broadly satisfactory deal". The cost became a heavy burden on the FCO budget. There was a proposal to buy the consortium out. I don't know if this happened.

We were not the first to open a brand new Embassy building in unified Berlin. The Nordics, all five of them together, had opened in autumn 1999 in Rauchstrasse – a sea-green boat-shaped perimeter enclosing 5 separate Embassies configured with geographic accuracy around a courtyard and accessible through a common entrance building used for exhibitions. They did not always find the arrangement easy but it was impressive visually and as a statement of combining their weight.

The French rebuilt on their site at Pariser Platz by the Brandenburg Gate and opened in 2002. The Americans, also on Pariser Platz, took longer. Because of legislation requiring their missions to have considerable separation from roads and other buildings following bombings of US Embassies in Africa, they wanted the Berlin authorities to close at least part of a road and were concerned about the impact of the nearby Holocaust Memorial. This created a spat. The Mayor of Berlin did not see why Berlin should bow to US pressure. The local press were also critical. US Ambassador John Kornblum (whom I had known a little when he was Minister of the US Mission in the West Berlin in the late 1980s) was accused of high-handed behaviour. Eventually, a way forward was found and the Embassy was finally opened in July 2008 by President Bush.

We moved the British Embassy staff from Bonn to Berlin in stages in summer 1999. Our aim was to be operational in Berlin when the Bundestag held its first session there in September. We achieved that. We were open with staff about the options – making clear what positions in the new set-up in Berlin were available and offering a relocation package or severance on decent terms. A few were able to remain for a while in our small temporary Embassy office in Bonn which was to liaise with parts of the German government which had not moved to Berlin. We also had to take into account the interest in jobs in the new Berlin Embassy of local staff who had worked in our former Berlin office of the Bonn Embassy. As it happened, the whole process was fairly amicable. But it was a big wrench for local staff to leave cosy Bonn by the Rhine for the brash new Berlin hundreds of kilometres to the East. One told me her mother had been horrified by the prospect of a move half-way to Siberia!

We had always had an Ambassadorial residence in Berlin, used when the Ambassador was visiting from Bonn and now his only residence – the lovely old residence by the Rhine having been given up. As the second-in-command I moved into the house in Taubertstrasse which had been the Minister's house during the days of the British Military Government before the Wall came down. This had been built in the 1920s, I think, and owned by a Jewish family originally. I enjoyed reading the guest book from the time when I had first started working in Berlin 12 years before. I inherited with the house a large black cat called Smiley. He was certainly as inscrutable as the Smiley in John Le Carré's novels. He acted as if the house belonged to him.

The house was in Grunewald, close to the forest and close to the Ambassador's house. While the centre of Berlin, especially where the Wall had run, was changing out of all recognition, the Grunewald area remained a quiet and leafy suburb as it had been since pre-war, let alone pre-Wall, times. It was not far from the Grunewald S-Bahn station – from where Jews had been transported to camps in the Nazi era – if I wanted to use public transport rather than in the evenings and weekends.

Ambassador Paul Lever enjoyed sending the first telegram

The hall at Taubertstrasse with Smiley

in September 1999 from the new British Embassy Berlin to London 60 years to the day after Neville Henderson had sent his final telegram reporting the failure of Hitler to respond to Neville Chamberlain's ultimatum.

We had started the new Embassy in Berlin by occupying Unter den Linden 41-42, on the right-hand side of the avenue after entering the East through the Brandenburg Gate. This had been the site of our Embassy to the GDR up to German unification in 1990 and had since been the Berlin Office of the British Embassy in Bonn. We housed our overspill – the Management and Commercial Sections – temporarily on a floor of a new office development in Friedrichstrasse.

Berlin immediately felt right. It was easier for me than some others as I had lived there before. Bonners from the Ministries and Bundestag congregated in the "Permanent Representation" on Schiffbauerdamm to bewail the loss of their idyll in the Rhineland and complain about the problems of life in a big city still coming to terms with unification. But

Temporary British Embassy in Berlin, Unter den Linden

for the great majority of the new Berliners those first months were exciting. With the Bundestag, many of the Ministries and our Embassy so close together it seemed I only needed to stand on Unter den Linden or visit one of the restaurants shooting into prominence around the Gendarmenmarkt to more than meet a notional daily quota of contact-making.

The media moved heavily into Berlin. The trans-regional daily papers opened their war chests, expanded their Berlin staffs and competed for the new Berlin market. Their treatment of the scandal surrounding Helmut Kohl's illegal dealings with CDU party donations was instructive. Much sharper investigative journalism than Germany had previously experienced. Much sharper editorial comment. TV changed too. The talk show became a more important forum for political debate than the Bundestag. These shows were screened mostly from locations right in the new centre of Berlin, the borough of Mitte.

Lobbyists too flocked to Berlin. Those who had thought

they could perhaps remain based in Bonn or elsewhere quickly realised their mistake, and opened an office not just anywhere in Berlin but in the new centre.

The German government remained physically split between Berlin and Bonn. This was written into the Bonn-Berlin law governing the move to Berlin. Several Ministries – defence, environment, agriculture, international development, research and technology – had to keep most of their staff in Bonn. And some agencies were moved to Bonn as further compensation. Germany understandably wanted to keep parts of government in regions outside the new capital, in line with the German historical tradition of federalism. But this degree of compensation for Bonn was driven more by political requirements than common sense.

Privately, just about all federal politicians would admit that this situation was inefficient and wasteful. Ministers wanted to be in Berlin, where the music played. Staff in Bonn felt cut off. A senior Defence official spoke wistfully of the 90% minority of his Ministry in Bonn. Economically Bonn was doing fine. But no senior politician wanted to be the first to start off the debate about moving more people to Berlin. Votes in North-Rhine Westphalia are crucial to all 4 mainstream western parties and a state, local or federal election never seemed far away. In 2015, there are still thousands of federal German civil servants based in Bonn.

Berlin had so much to offer outside the work environment. Theatre, opera, concerts (I acquired again a season ticket for the Berlin Philharmonic), great restaurants and bars. And the city to explore and its environs too. It took a bit of time to get used to the fact that Berlin was so far to the east in Europe. Poland and the Czech Republic were much closer than Bonn. Prussian history came alive for me as I was able to travel round the city on the wonderful local transport system and by car in the new federal states. The works of my favourite writer Theodor Fontane came alive as the Berlin and Brandenburg author par excellence.

Strictly Bonn and Berlin

At one staff Christmas party at the residence of Ambassador Nigel Broomfield in Bonn, his wife Valerie Broomfield noted how few people now knew how to dance ballroom. A group of us, diplomats and local staff, organised by First Secretary Sally Axworthy went to the Lepehne-Herbst dance school in the Bonn Südstadt and learned. We took it seriously. Robert Cooper, then the Deputy Head of Mission, held a fabulous summer ball in the garden of his house in Fasanenstrasse. I repeated this at that wonderful house, when I became DHM.

The dancing continued after the move of the Embassy from Bonn to Berlin. I used the DHM's house in

Marquee at Bad Godesberg house

Our dancing instructors in the marquee at the Bad Gotesberg house

Taubertstrasse 13 in the district of Grunewald (formerly Michael Burton's house in British Military Government days) as a venue for practice of the latest steps we had learned. It was also a chance to invite German contacts for a different kind of evening. We went to some brilliant venues where people of all ages danced ballroom to all sorts of music. I and others progressed through the medal stages of the ten ballroom dances right up to Gold Star. When back in FCO I invited some of the group to dance one Saturday night in the Locarno Suite in the Foreign Office, taking a ghetto blaster for the music. I wonder if that is the only time that august venue has witnessed a Viennese Waltz?

I thought at the time that the kind of ballroom dancing being practised in Berlin and to great modern music (the Turkish samba which won the Eurovision song contest for Germany was an example) could be introduced in UK and make great TV. Why didn't I think of Strictly Come Dancing? But I would have suggested doing it differently with less shouting, more dancing and venues closer to everyday experience. So I guess it wouldn't have been such a success.

Three Ambassadors

Ambassadors need luck. The Ambassador when I arrived in Bonn, Nigel Broomfield, was an expert on Germany. He had served as a soldier on the Weser and in BRIXMIS (the British military liaison mission to the Soviet Armed Forces in Germany) and had been British Ambassador to the GDR. Bonn was a logical final post for him. He was well liked for his hard work and slightly diffident charm. Lucky he was not. His last year, which should have been the crowning glory of his diplomatic career, was soured by the disaster of BSE, with Germans asking why we were pressing them to accept our beef which had caused brain disease at home. He defended the British position robustly and never complained but we were all saddened by the tarnishing of Britain's image.

His successor, in March 1997, was Christopher Meyer. This was recognition of his achievements under fire at the FCO and No 10 as press spokesman during the last painful period of the Conservative government. He was acknowledged as the best communicator in the Service. He was also a charmer, making a remarkable impact on the people he met. Friendly, smiling, at ease yet also sharp as a razor. He proved he could do the impossible by somehow taking wicket after wicket with innocuous bowling in the annual intra-Embassy cricket match, Gentlemen against Players.

Just as he was beginning to take a grip on the Embassy, and improving his German, he was posted to Washington as Ambassador. The FCO had proposed Jeremy Greenstock for Washington; he ended up as UK Permanent Representative in New York instead. The incoming Labour Government decided they wanted Chris Meyer in Washington. He was known to Tony Blair through his work as John Major's press spokesman, and respected. I suppose Washington, and the relationship with President Clinton, was regarded as so important that the PM wanted an Ambassador whose qualities he had come to appreciate at close hand. He left Berlin in September 1998. He had real luck – to have a taste of Germany and then move to the best of all postings in Washington.

The third Ambassador also had good luck. Paul Lever was certain to lead one of the top Embassies but I doubt he had thought he would end up as Ambassador in Germany. He did so because of Chris Meyer's unexpected move and because he had made himself known as an adviser on the EU to the new Blair government. He started in Bonn in January 1998. He was immensely able, but not a Germanist and was conscious that his German (which was actually a lot better than just adequate) was not good enough at the beginning for him to say everything he wanted to say when he wanted to say it and how he wanted to say it. Nonetheless, he was highly successful in raising the Embassy's profile with the media.

The move to Berlin gave him great new opportunities. For one thing Berlin was a better location for UK diplomacy than Bonn. The past was a help. The Brits had been generally well liked as one of the three Western Allied powers before unification. There remained a good stock of goodwill towards us from West Berliners. The Ossis certainly had nothing against us. This was a comfort though not a long-term prop.

More importantly, there was no special connection between East Germany and France of the kind which existed between the Rhineland and France; the Elysée Treaty did not have the same pull in the East. This in itself was not relevant to the UK's standing. But it did mean we were not automatically relegated to a second division behind France. For their part the French were not so happy with the move to Berlin. They worried about the effect on their influence with Germany.

Britain at the heart of Europe?

History had not come to an end. The UK was then less EU-phobic than now. But we were worried about where the European project was heading. We had not joined the Euro at its recent inception. We were drifting from the centre of European decision-making at a time when the Franco-German motor, the central component of European construction for 50 years, was less automatically central. Germany was finding its feet as a unified country, incorporating some of the modesty of the Bonn years but less willing to forego its own interests for the sake of the French. In the eyes of some Germans it had made the last grand gesture of this kind by giving up the almighty D-Mark and sharing the Euro.

Still, the new Embassy gave us the chance of something of a new start in British-German relations. Not a blank sheet, but a new and more level playing field. Of course the policies of our government would be the key factor. The Euro was the key issue. But I felt we in the Embassy could do something to convey a positive image of Britain, which would make us more attractive as a political and commercial partner. We had been damaged by Mrs Thatcher's mistaken reluctance to embrace German unification in 1989. We now had a chance – not to erase that (impossible), but to start afresh.

The Labour government of Tony Blair started in 1997 with the intention of "being at the heart of Europe" and this meant a strong relationship with Germany. Writing this in

2015 gives me a curious feeling because no party in Britain would use such upbeat language about our position in the EU. The Government has to respond to the threat of UKIP which is seen as the party addressing the major public concern over the large-scale immigration to the UK over the last ten years.

The EU is now seen as part of the immigration problem as many people have come from those states which joined the EU in the last decade. This adds to the dissatisfaction with the EU for a number of other reasons – the precedence given to EU over our national law including the supremacy of European human rights law, the power given to the unelected European Commission, the sense that we are forced to contribute to an inflated Euro-bureaucracy and wasteful projects in other countries, a European Parliament which few in the UK see as a valid part of our democratic structure. We appear to have given up on the possibility of joining the Eurozone, even before the crisis caused by the 2007-8 crash.

But it looked quite different for a while after 1997. Tony Blair became Prime Minister after John Major had struggled valiantly for the length of a whole Parliament against rebels in his own party, especially over Europe. On top of this we had the "beef war" as we struggled to persuade the Germans to accept British beef and beef products even after they had been declared free of that awful disease BSE. Under the New Labour government BSE became a technical issue whereby the UK undertook to do whatever Science demanded ad co-operated with the European Commission. Tony Blair was able to show at his first EU summit at Amsterdam that the UK was not the problem. He spoke of feeling at home within the EU.

New Labour saw an opportunity to work with the social democratic SPD and Gerhard Schroeder as the candidate against Helmut Kohl in the German election of 1998. Some staff from No 10 came to visit SPD HQ; I went with them.

I was struck by the youth of the leader of the group, David Miliband. Basically, New Labour offered the benefit of their experience in winning the UK election.

Chancellor of the Exchequer Gordon Brown came up with a series of economic tests against which the case for the UK to join the Euro would be judged. Tony Blair evidently felt that there was also a political case for joining but of course he knew the British people remained to be convinced. In 1997-8 Tony Blair was in a very strong position as Prime Minister. He pushed through referenda on devolution in Scotland and Wales. Could he also have convinced people of the case for joining the Euro in another referendum? Not impossible. But with Gordon Brown sceptical and his party unlikely to be happy about putting in jeopardy Labour's grip on power so soon after 18 years in Opposition, it is not surprising that Tony Blair did not go for this.

In 1998, the senior members of the British Embassy in Bonn met up with our counterparts in Paris and I recall the then Ambassador in Paris, Christopher Mallaby, asking us for an informal show of hands on what we personally thought was best for the UK – stay out, wait and see, or join. It went without saying that as good civil servants we would help implement whatever our government decided. The majority were wait-and-sees. I was one of few in favour of joining from the beginning.

The Eurozone went through bad times after the crash of 2008 and is still not out of the woods. I recall the astonishment of a member of Bundestag in the run-up to the introduction of the Euro when I told him the news that Italy would be a founder member. He was not sure Germans would want to trust countries outside Northern Europe with their currency. We have seen how opposed Germans were to taking a soft line as Greece looked for relief from its bail-out programme. Nonetheless, I still believe the UK would have been better in the long run to join and shape the project from the beginning, make it work and cement ourselves as a part of a European triangle of UK-Germany-France. I know this view is in the minority!

Hello to New Diplomacy; Goodbye to Germany, for Good

I made a note of my penultimate Friday in the Embassy in Berlin because it struck me as the kind of day which No 2s in the British Embassy previously could scarcely have imagined.

It began with breakfast at the Adlon Hotel next door with David Marsh, in town for a seminar about consolidation of Europe's land-defence industries. With Paul Lever out of town, I then chaired the daily meeting of Embassy heads of section: main issues were BSE and the upcoming Nice European Council. Then I went downstairs to the Conference Drum to introduce a series of presentations by British entrepreneurs who had designed products for the Millennium Products exhibition in the Wintergarden. After a sandwich with the business people and visitors to the exhibition, I had an afternoon meeting with a German impresario interested in staging a musical "Eloise" based on a Noel Coward play in the new Embassy building. In the evening I gave a lecture to the Berlin Historical Association in the Conference Drum on Berlin 1986-1990 and had a drink with the 80 or so in the audience.

What Might Have Been

"The residence was just as one sees such places in films – huge rooms and butlers, chandeliers and cocktails. I met a woman from the Foreign Office and then a colleague of hers who had broken his collar bone playing football. He was an ardent Liverpool supporter and I was with Tony, an ardent Leeds supporter: result was a heated exchange of views on the strengths and weaknesses of various teams. Following this, I met the Ambassador himself who had just rushed in after an engagement in Berlin. Frau Dr Kotthof then informed us that we had to leave because there were a host of grandees invited to meet the Ambassador at 8. So we left at 7.55, some of us… much the worse for wear."

I wrote this in a diary word-for-word about the evening of Thursday 18 February 1971. I don't recall anything about the Tony mentioned above or others named in my journal. We were part of a group spending a few days in Cologne as our induction to a 6-month programme. Frau Kotthof was one of the organisers from the Carl-Duisberg-Gesellschaft, one of the party-political institutes funded out of the public purse after the War to entrench democracy and now with an active role on behalf of Germany overseas. The idea in 1971 was, just 26 years after the end of the war, to give young Britons an understanding of – and sympathy for – modern Germany. It worked. The CDG partnered with Rugby School at the UK end. How Rugby selected the participants I do not know.

I was going to a job in Munich with the Bayerische Hypotheken- und Wechselbank. I still have the reference they gave me – the only one I have as the FCO don't give them. Others on the course worked in factories, schools, as well as offices.

It was Weiberfastnacht, the wild Thursday evening before the climax of the carnival season the following Monday. After the Ambassador's reception I went downtown Cologne with the group and gazed at the weird and wonderful costumes. Unlike others, I then had an early night before things got out of hand.

On our way to the Ambassador's reception in Bonn, we had mistakenly been dumped by our taxis from the train station at the British Embassy. We then somehow found our way to the Residence by tram.

I had forgotten all about this first visit to a British Residence, and abortive visit to the Embassy, until coming across some sheets of paper in 2014. I am full of admiration for the Ambassador and his staff for bearing with a group of 18-year-old Brits and Irish who were really only there for the beer and already animated by a few drinks earlier in Cologne in the fevered atmosphere of Weiberfastnacht (I experienced being assaulted by a large group of sixth-form girls on this day when I was teaching in Gelsenkirchen 1975-77: they stole my shoelaces, which was not ideal as I had a two-mile walk home in front of me).

I was not thinking in 1971 that I would one day join the Diplomatic Service myself, nor that I too would have to manage guests who drank too much at my parties. I visited that residence many times when serving in Bonn as 1996-1999. It was a rambling old-world big house on the Rhine – you could hear the barges chugging by. The FCO sold it when we moved to Berlin in 1999.

I occasionally wondered as I became more senior in the Service if I might one day return to Germany as Ambassador. I had worked in the German private and public sectors. I had worked in Berlin and Bonn as a First Secretary, Counsellor and Minister – Ambassador would be the final step. I spoke very good German. I knew the country. I applied three times, but didn't make it and didn't think it would be productive to await a fourth opportunity after I finished in Brazil in 2013. Having lived over 10 years in Germany between 1970 and 2000, I have not spent as much as a week in total there between 2001-2015. That's not untypical of the Diplomatic Service career. You never know where it may take you. Disappointment over not being selected for one job may be followed by a new and unexpected opportunity elsewhere. That's what I always told colleagues when I was HR Director!

I enjoyed giving a lecture on Queen Mary 2 in 2015 about the potential but not inevitability for ever closer collaboration between UK and Germany. UK diplomacy has not always given Germany sufficient priority and Germany has not always listened to UK views about the EU. David Cameron and Angela Merkel are doing a better job in 2015. I am hopeful.

3.

THE HOME FRONT

PART I

IN KING CHARLES STREET

A new entrant is received on his first day in the Foreign Office in King Charles Street by his Head of Department. "Any questions?" he is asked. "Well" says the new entrant nervously "I was wondering about the hours". The Head looks him in the eye. "Well now. I generally catch the 0832 into Town: it's good to be here when the messengers bring the first telegrams at 0930-ish. Then around 1230 I walk over to the Club, have a pink gin with other members and a spot of lunch. Back in the office at 1400 and as a rule the 1737 back home". "That doesn't sound too bad at all" says a relieved new entrant. The Head regards him sternly and says: "You will find, dear boy, that it does rather eat into one's time."

I didn't know what to expect when joining the Diplomatic Service in 1978. I hadn't thought that within a few weeks I would be travelling to Cameroon by British Embassy log.

I was placed in West Africa Department on a desk dealing with a number of countries, most importantly Nigeria (with a considerable hierarchy above me) but with a special responsibility for Chad. In fact, I received a letter from my Ambassador, also the Head of the West Africa Department, appointing me Second Secretary and Vice-Consul in the British Embassy to Chad. I was informed this entitled me to no additional emoluments.

I've always since then wanted an emolument.

WAD was a typical geographical department of the FCO. The Head was Johnny Johnson, one of that generation who started his career in the old Colonial Office and who had worked in the field as District Officer in Kenya taking on a level of administrative responsibility barely imaginable today. He was a friendly, able and astute man. He did invite me to his club. He did favour cricketing terminology – sticky wickets, playing a straight bat. We did not have a pink gin.

The Assistant, a curious title then given to the Deputy to the Head of Department, was David Mackilligin. He felt issues deeply but also had a lighter side.

There were three so-called third rooms covering the geography of a region from Senegal to Congo. In mine there was a senior desk officer, who mostly handled Nigeria and was my reporting officer. There was also an archivist.

Having the Embassy to Chad within the Department was an unusual arrangement introduced in 1970 and carried on for some time after I had left West Africa Department. There have never been British Embassies in every country. Generally, countries where we do not have an Embassy are covered from neighbouring countries, with the Ambassador there accredited additionally. I don't know how this arrangement for Chad came about. We told the Chadians that it meant the Ambassador was a senior official in the FCO and would be particularly well-versed in British policy in the region. They did not seem to mind too much.

As Second Secretary I answered correspondence about Chad on Embassy-headed notepaper in English and French. Not that there was a lot of business for me. As a former French colony, landlocked and poor, there was precious little interest in the UK. The few British citizens who lived there were mostly missionaries. Our consular coverage of Chad was done from our Embassy in neighbouring Cameroon, in the capital Yaounde.

In November 1978, David Mackilligin and I went out to Chad for an Embassy visit, my first diplomatic mission. He had the title of Head of Chancery – a term which usually meant Head of the Political Section of an Embassy but in this case a rather empty designation. We travelled via Charles Gaulle airport in Paris to the capital of Chad, N'Djamena.

N'Djamena had been founded as Fort Lamy early in the 20th century. It had been, as the name suggests, a fort built by the French to help control their empire in Central West Africa. The town had developed as a small administrative centre for the French forces and so had a few whitewashed crenellated buildings for that original purpose now used by the Chadian government. These buildings were surrounded by large numbers of mud huts where the Chadians lived. It looked like a scene out of a French Foreign Legion film.

I had bought a light tropical suit at Tropiccadilly in London, with only old films about Brits in the tropics as a guide. Nothing could prepare for the blast of heat from the tarmac as we came down the steps of the aircraft from Paris at N'Djamena airport. We stayed at the Hotel Chari, one of two European hotels in the town. I rushed with relief into the air-conditioned room, shutting the door swiftly to keep out large insects in the corridor. I imagined these crowding outside my door during the night desperate to get into the cool air. Most of the guests at the hotel were French Air Force personnel who crewed the six Jaguar aircraft which helped keep President Malloum in power.

We were looked after by our Belgian Honorary Consul. The office of Honorary Consul is a good deal for Foreign Ministries. If you choose wisely, you have someone who is well connected in a place where you cannot afford to have full-time representatives. They can help with visits and consular cases and perhaps also with some business connections. In return they are paid only expenses and a small annual honorarium. They enjoy the status of being the British Honorary Consul which gives them some local prestige, special number plates and perhaps an impressive brass plaque outside their office.

Diplomatic Travel by Log

The Honorary Consul arranged for us to pay a visit to Kousseri in Cameroon on the other side of the River Chari. The river was swollen and wide at this time of year. We hired a hollowed-out log and a pilot for the crossing. I wish I had a photo of Her Majesty's representatives in this craft gliding through the hippos towards the distant Cameroonian bank!

Kousseri was not particularly interesting. There was an encampment of makeshift huts with corrugated metal roofs. I cannot recall why we went there, but am glad we did.

I learned an important lesson about food in Chad. At the hotel we had a dinner with a Nigerian diplomat in the expectation of learning more about what was going on from a representative of the largest regional power. In fact, he seemed to find the town alienating, did not speak French and could not help us with the menu. It had plenty of French dishes and I decided on a steak tartare. Mistake – having uncooked meat in N'Djamena in those days was not a wise choice. I was ill during the night and felt fragile for several days thereafter. I was much less adventurous in future with food when travelling to places I didn't know well.

I was meant to have a couple more visits to Chad in the following year 1979. But Hisseine Habré mounted a military uprising against the capital. A visit in February was called off at short notice. The airport was closed for several months. I have not returned since.

The Officer Class

I recall the first meeting I attended of the Diplomatic Service Association to which most diplomats of the so-called "fast stream" belonged – it is affiliated to the Civil Service First Division Association. It was 1979. The new Conservative Government of Margaret Thatcher appeared to think civil servants would be working in the private sector if they were any good and there was certainly no idea of restoring the link between Civil Service pay and reward in the private sector which had existed earlier in the 1970s. This was a significant financial issue in a period of high inflation.

This was a time of severe financial distress (the UK had had to appeal to the IMF for support under the previous Labour Government). We had just lived through the "winter of discontent" of strikes by public sector workers and images of refuse piling up in the streets and bodies not being buried. Mrs Thatcher had won the election because there was a feeling that things had to change, even though she was personally not as popular as Prime Minister "Sunny" Jim Callaghan.

At the meeting, some older diplomats spoke of needing to act like "commissioned officers" and set an example to the country. Deeply ingrained in the Diplomatic Service, and this has not entirely disappeared today, is the view that we give advice and work as effectively as we can but it is for the government to set policy and for diplomats/civil servants to execute it.

Other diplomats at the meeting said we should be ready to join protests and even strikes alongside other Civil Service unions and public sector workers. Otherwise, the argument ran, we should be taken for granted and find our terms and conditions becoming ever worse. I quickly came to the view that it would be futile to worry too much about pay. Either I accepted what the Government decided and enjoyed the opportunities of the Diplomatic Service uncomplainingly. Or, if it became too difficult, I would leave, go back to teaching or try something else – in those days there were not so many graduates competing for jobs.

I'm often asked whether the people in the Diplomatic Service are toffs. Yes, there are some with double-barrelled names and from well-to-do families who educated them at private school. There was something of an inner circle of people who know each other and graduated to the top jobs. But I was not alone in coming from a different background, favoured by the 11+ system to be given a scholarship to a high-achieving direct-grant school. I have no doubt it helped to know people through family connections and other networks (the old-school tie). But the Service seemed to me generally genuinely meritocratic.

Steam-Driven Comms and Gas Fires

The abiding memory of my first winter in the Foreign Office, 1978-79, was of gloomy weather, gloomy news and a gloomy building in which some former grand rooms were repositories of jumble and stuff seemed to lie around in the corridors.

Around this time the Foreign Office had just about given up hope of emulating the Home Office and having a modern office building to house it. It was fortunate that the money for this was not available or we might have ended up with a building like the Home Office (now Justice Ministry) building in Queen Anne's Gate, which had to be closed for many years later on and refurbished at huge expense to make it habitable. Prince Charles came to our rescue insisting against the spirit of the times in the 1970s that the building should be restored – and so it was between 1983-1998. Of course that wasn't the end of the building's development. Much more has been made of the space in the years since then and work goes on to create even more in 2015.

The old Foreign Office building is an amalgam of historic buildings between Downing Street and King Charles Street with connections created between them. You really had to know the route from one location to another or you could spend a lot of time wandering around. For a new entrant, going to an unknown location such as a Ministerial office and ensuring you arrived on time meant forward planning. I'm sure I wasn't the only person who often found himself completely lost, even after years of working in the building.

Rooms were heated by gas fires. You either suffered from the fug or opened the window and let in a cold blast of air. Our documents were delivered by messengers on trolleys. Some of the papers were sent by Tube, folded into canisters and propelled around by pneumatic pressure through a system of pipes; I later learned that a lot of mail in Berlin was sent using this system for many years in the early decades of the 20th century. The papers turned up slightly curled after the messengers had taken them out of the canisters. I was frequently startled by the clunk of a canister when a tube arrived just behind the wall where my desk was situated.

Drafting was then, as it is now, a core skill of the young diplomat, to be honed drawing on the experience of your seniors. We had no word processors, let alone PCs, in 1978. So drafts were either written on paper or – if you were senior – dictated to a secretary. Written drafts went to the typing pool, which was overseen with strong discipline by a lady Head.

Diplomatic skills were sorely tested when a young diplomat sought priority from Her for his work.

Every new entrant went through the process of learning on the job, especially drafting. I went through many pieces of blue draft paper, with special forms for telegrams to overseas posts, before I was ready to give a draft up for typing. You would generally ask for a handwritten manuscript to be typed in draft so that you could work on it further and then seek comments from someone more senior. It was amazing how superiors could immediately improve on it, almost – it seemed – without thinking. Experience does count. Towards the end of my career we were re-discovering its value – as well as core competences – in making decisions on appointments.

The Wonder of Paper Files

Another constant feature of the daily routine was the Registry. The third person in our room was the Archivist John Holmes, a young Liverpudlian with Liverpudlian humour just out of school and living in a hostel in London. His job was to register papers sent to him by desk officers, put them on the appropriate files according to our instructions and find the papers when we needed them. He was new at the job as I was, so it was the blind leading the blind. But we picked up without being told that record-keeping was an important part of our role, so it should have time and effort accorded to it.

The files told a story – for example, about the political relations between the UK and another country, or about a political visit by a senior UK personality to that country. The aim was that someone could pick up the file and see the story so far for that year and retrieve the files from previous years if necessary. The WAD files did not include everything about our countries. There were functional departments in the FCO who led on consular matters, energy etc. But the geographical department was generally copied into these aspects too and might sometimes lead on them with the support of the functional departments.

In the first half of the 1990s the FCO sought to embrace modernity and move to a system of electronic filing. The system for electronic record-keeping, called FOLIOS, did not work. Record-keeping started to become more haphazard. A desk officer trusted the files less and kept his/her own key papers. I don't think the FCO ever recovered from this false start on electronic record-keeping. Other initiatives following this also met with little success. Record-keeping seemed to lose the high place it had in our scale of values. I fear that the researchers of the 2020s and onwards will find much less than their predecessors in the way of fascinating material when they access files at Kew Gardens declassified after 30 years. The other factor rendering the papers over the last 10 years less interesting has been the UK experience with Freedom of Information. Ministers and officials now know that very little will be kept secret for any length of time and will tend to express themselves blandly when it comes to written communication. There is much less debating of different opinions on paper.

The most senior diplomat in our region was the British High Commissioner in Nigeria, Sir Sam Falle. He wrote in strikingly short sentences. There were few clauses. It read well. I tried for a while to imitate it. Not a bad exercise.

I made the acquaintance of several British diplomats at our posts in the region when they passed through London. One was Third Secretary in Nigeria, Martin Raven. His red hair made him unmistakeable and that may have been why he was selected by the Nigerians to be declared persona non grata (which means you are thrown out by the host government) when they wanted to show their displeasure to the UK. I knew Martin throughout my career. Thirty years later, he was my Consul General in São Paulo when I was Ambassador to Brazil.

Nigeria was the most important country we dealt with. There was – and has been since – an oscillation between democratic and military government. The UK had strong commercial interests. There were difficulties for UK companies and individuals to secure remittances, especially when oil prices were dropping as oil was the key source of Nigerian government revenue. We sought to handle all this with a country less than 20 years independent from the UK and understandably sensitive to any perceived slights from the former colonial power.

At the time Africa had a number of dictators who made headlines. Idi Amin of Uganda was the best known. His summary expulsion of Asians enriched cities like Leicester with a new wave of entrepreneurial immigrants and helped to make them the success stories they are today. Emperor Bokassa of the Central African Empire was no less appalling and an embarrassment to former colonial power France. Less well known was President Macias Nguema of Equatorial Guinea, one of the countries in my portfolio in West Africa Department.

Dear Ambassador – You May Not Become Lunch

Few people in the UK knew anything about Equatorial Guinea. These were the days before tourism was reaching lesser known parts of Africa. There was little business interest as the oil, which later was an important economic factor for the country, was then largely undeveloped. The UK had no resident Embassy in the country. Our Ambassador from Cameroon was cross-accredited there and found Equatorial Guinea especially fascinating.

What we knew about Macias Nguema and his regime was unappealing. He allowed neither free enterprise nor free speech. I received from our Embassy in Cameroon a copy of a proclamation on his behalf of which much of the first page was taken up with the titles he had awarded himself. One of these was – "The Only Miracle Of Equatorial Guinea". I have no doubt he was unique.

There were stories that President Macias Nguema was a cannibal. I do not think we had any direct evidence of this. But as the Department in charge of policy towards the country we didn't want to take any risks. When our Ambassador in Yaounde asked for permission to visit Equatorial Guinea and see the President we told him that he might accept an invitation to lunch but not become lunch.

A small country we felt could be going in the right direction was Gabon. It was another former French colony and not a part of Africa well known to the UK. The then fairly youthful President Bongo had some eccentricities too and – no fault of his – his name did provoke mirth with some of our politicians. We saw that there was oil to be developed, that he was welcoming of foreign investment and seemed to have a more stable regime than many others around him. We opened a small Embassy there.

I wouldn't claim that I became particularly expert in the affairs of these countries but I was fascinated by the reports from our Embassies around the region. My interest in these far-off places convinced me I was in a career which would always stimulate me. It did.

Reports arrived by that wonderfully traditional institution, the Diplomatic Bag. A Desk Officer was aware when the bags from a certain country would arrive and deadlines for correspondence to reach bags which would leave for a particular country. For some countries there would be a bag only every two weeks. Messages by classified telegram from and about such countries were few: we were imbued with the idea that telegrams were still under rationing, both the numbers of them and the numbers of words in them.

The Grade 5 Grind in London

Civil servants and employees in big international companies bandy around numbers and letters to signify grades in the hierarchy of the organisation. It's hard for outsiders to understand the meaning of these terms as they don't have enough knowledge of the organisation. When I came back from Amman to London I was a Grade 5, nowadays Band D (First Secretary equivalent). The important thing about this grade is that these people are the engine room and workhorses of policy advice and execution in FCO, typically Heads of Section in a Department.

The hours in those days were long and commuting into London even more of a challenge than now as you had to deal with a clapped-out rail system in which the government was just starting again to invest seriously. Victoria Street has changed. In the 1970s and 1980s it had just the Army and Navy to give it a sense of modernity. Artillery Buildings, later converted into modern smart apartments, was derelict. St James's Park was then as now a joy. The first crocuses and daffodils of the season. Deckchairs scattered around in the summer. Always ducks, geese and pelicans.

I was sent to a busy Department, the Near East and North Africa Department. In our countries, stuff was happening and Ministers were interested. The Desk Officers ground out briefs for Ministers and senior officials, policy recommendations, updates on fast-moving situations. Some of the content is in the Middle East part of this account.

So I got to see Ministers, even the Foreign Secretary, when

there were office meetings on my issues or important visitors when I would often take notes and produce a record. When I had been in West Africa Department I was a new entrant and under supervision. Now I was much more involved and much more was expected. Above all, I learned how to grind out large volumes of work.

Needle in a Haystack

A curious memory is of the days when much of the Department was helping out on the aftermath of the American bombing of Libya. Large numbers of letters from members of the public had been received. Whether these were addressed to the Foreign Secretary, the Prime Minister or even the Queen, these ended up in our Department for draft reply. We had a bit of extra help. We decided we would draw up three different standard replies to cater for the broad drift of the letters, but each would need some customisation.

We received a call from Mrs Thatcher's Constituency Secretary saying that she was expected shortly to meet someone from Finchley who they knew had written a letter to her about Libya. Could we find it and draft a reply quickly that same day? We had several thousand letters, unsorted. We emptied them on to the floor and several of us started looking. By a sheer stroke of luck we located the letter within half an hour and kept the PM – or at least her Constituency Secretary – happy.

Bullying comes back to bite you

My predecessor on the Lebanon/Israel desk had been Edward Chaplin. He was posted as the no 2 in our small Embassy in

Tehran, seeking to re-establish itself after the large British Embassy had been evacuated after the Iranian Revolution in 1979. Edward was beaten up by the Iranian intelligence service in the street for reasons unknown. He came back to London, never to return to work in the Embassy in Tehran. I enjoyed the fact that years later Edward became Director Middle East, the man senior Iranian visitors would have to meet. He was a professional and would have dealt with the issues on their merits. But the Iranians could not have been confident that he was their most positive advocate in discussions on Iran policy in London!

Thursday Morning is Joint Intelligence Committee

Working in the Assessments Staff of the Cabinet Office 1991-1992 meant joining the Intelligence Community. I was working on the inside with the Secret Intelligence Service (MI6), the Security Service (MI5), GCHQ, Defence Intelligence, and the intelligence allies (US, Canada, Australia, New Zealand). I was not privy to their operations but I did see their output of information and analysis.

The work we did in the Assessments Staff was drafted in-house, copied around Whitehall for comments, debated in a Current Intelligence Group meeting chaired by a Deputy Chief, talked through at a meeting with the Chief and the JIC chair before being considered by the Joint Intelligence Committee. During the crisis with Iraq, it met in the afternoons and at least weekly. In "normal" times it met then at 1100 on Thursday. This was the climax of the working week of the Assessments Staff.

The meetings were held in Conference Room 215.

Although a little larger than 213 which was used as the centre of our Iraq operation, it was still modest in size and much smaller than some other conference rooms in the Cabinet Office. For the JIC meeting, tables were arranged in a rectangle with further desks to one side for the Secretariat which took the minutes. Deputy Chiefs of the Assessments Staff and desk officers would be present for discussion of papers which they had prepared. Senior people, leaders in their organisations, sat rather cramped together. This lent atmosphere to the occasion and immediacy to the debate.

Until June 1992 the Chairman was Sir Percy Cradock. He held this position and concurrently was Foreign Adviser to the Prime Minister from 1984, after retiring from the Diplomatic Service. He was deeply involved in negotiations with China over the future of Hong Kong as Ambassador in Beijing and in London. He evidently caught the eye of Mrs Thatcher and it was easy to see why – he had a penetrating mind and steely resolve mixed with being a genuinely nice man who loved tending his roses at home and attending Wimbledon.

Sir Percy's command of JIC meetings was striking. Without ever browbeating he dominated the meetings. He knew how long to let a discussion run. He summed up brilliantly, often giving a clarity to confused discussion without ever twisting the outcome. He focused on the main points. He showed impatience with a line of argument or prolixity of a speaker by raising an eyebrow or grimacing. If the offender did not get the message, others did and were reminded to take their lead from the chair. This minimal gesturing was effective in disciplining very senior people in charge of the intelligence and other services – people much more used to giving orders than taking them.

Others in the Cabinet Office told me I did not see Percy in his best years. But I had the impression that the Iraq conflict presented a challenge he relished. If this wasn't his very best it was highly impressive and beat any other chairman I saw in action.

His successor was Sir Rodric Braithwaite, formerly Ambassador to the Soviet Union. He had a brilliant, inventive and restless mind. He saw the flaws in arguments in papers to be presented to the JIC. He was often absent from JIC meetings because of the requirements of being the PM's adviser and a role relating to the troubled UK Presidency of the EC in the second half of 1992.

The two deputy chairs of the JIC were the FCO Deputy Under Secretary for Defence and Intelligence and the MOD Chief of Defence Intelligence (CDI). The more senior of the two would chair JIC meetings in Rodric Braithwaite's absence.

The role of the MOD Chief of Defence Intelligence (CDI) was especially important as JIC papers often had a strong military component and the JIC judgements had implications for MOD decision-making. So, for example, pronouncements on the military threat from Russia or other security risks would be adduced to support proposals in policy papers on defence commitments. I drafted a speculative paper on the threats a European Fighter Aircraft would face up to 2030. The Assessments Staff had to ensure they factored in the views of CDI, Deputy CDI and the MOD Deputy Under Secretary Political.

The FCO representative for most of my time was Nigel Broomfield. He took a strong interest in the deliberations of the Committee. He was prepared to advance his own views even if they were at variance with the briefing he had in front of him from the FCO section concerned with the paper under discussion.

I found it illuminating to see the FCO from outside. FCO

departments were naturally primarily concerned with policy. On some issues – notably former Yugoslavia and Hong Kong – they were interested and even keen to have interdepartmentally agreed assessments. But in other areas they preferred that the Cabinet Office should keep off their turf. Some considered that judgements on foreign affairs should be left to the FCO alone.

FCO representatives would often make major contributions at CIG meetings. But thereafter the FCO often seemed to have little interest in the outcome of a paper. With the MOD, concentration on papers intensified in their final stages. CDI met his officials on Wednesday afternoon to go through the drafts for the JIC next day. That would occasionally lead to requests for major changes even at that late stage and invariably to several proposals for minor amendments.

The Heads of the three intelligence agencies were ex-officio members of the JIC. Colin McColl of SIS was the most impressive of them. He played the role of the wise old bird who would often pick up a dubious point which might otherwise have gone through unchallenged. He was always familiar with the SIS material which went into a paper and had his own views about how to interpret it.

John Adye (GCHQ) sat next to him down the table. He naturally sought to bring out the signals intelligence contribution, particularly on the former Soviet military issues with which GCHQ continued to feel most at home.

The two Security Service chiefs during my time were Patrick Walker and Stella Rimington. Neither contributed extensively to issues outside the areas of terrorism and counter-espionage. Both were listened to with special attention over PIRA.

Of the other JIC members, the Treasury representative – for most of my time Peter Sedgewick – was the strongest contributor.

Infuriatingly for the Assessments Staff the Treasury were rarely represented at CIGs and we almost never had comments before the Thursday JIC on the revised draft of a paper issued on Tuesday evening. So at the JIC meeting itself we were sometimes faced with a new line of argument. But the added value of Treasury comments at the meeting was considerable.

The Intelligence Co-ordinator usually had no axe to grind on JIC papers and so was well placed to give an independent view. This happened only occasionally but helped to season the discussion. The other committee members were the Deputy Head of PUSD in the FCO (whose main role is to support the FCO DUS and deputise in his absence) and the JIC Secretary. PUSD stood for Permanent Under Secretary's Department, an empty title for the person whose staff were a point of contact and co-ordination in the FCO for the intelligence services.

The JIC's strengths were the range of background and experience of its members, the seriousness with which the actors took their responsibilities and its interaction as a group. Nigel Broomfield said at once that JIC meetings were occasions at which "all one's favourite truths are challenged". This was as it should be. In no other forum was there such a high-level opportunity to arrive at informed inter-departmental assessments of situations relevant to UK interests. At its best the JIC told it straight when individual departments preferred not to turn over too many stones for fear of seeing something nasty underneath.

The JIC's weaknesses were that members were sometimes prepared to let others have their way with a point if this did not affect their own particular interests. This was occasionally frustrating for the Assessments Staff who might have resisted dubious judgements from one department for several days only to have these foisted on them at the meeting.

The Committee was good at seeing the wood for the trees. Most new arrivals from the FCO thought the judgements often too gloomy. It is true that committee members felt safer opting for the more pessimistic view. But only too often the downbeat forecast turned out to be right. Yugoslavia was a good example.

The Issues

At the end of 1991 the Soviet Union was dissolved. A new era of foreign relations began. This was good for people dealing with foreign affairs for a living (unless you were a Kremlinologist) because the world had become more difficult to understand. Foreign affairs could no longer be looked at through the simplifying prism of East-West relations. International co-operation against Iraq in the Gulf conflict showed the positive new possibilities. There was talk of a new world order. But the world had become more disorderly and less governable, as the conflict in Yugoslavia had had underlined.

Russia remained a potential threat to the UK over the next 20 years. We could not predict how the internal political scene would develop. The Russians would retain some nuclear weapons capability. But even if Russia became less co-operative with the West, it would not any time soon again be such a dangerous adversary as the Soviet Union either in Europe or in third-world countries.

The Assessments Staff continued to spend a great deal of time on Russia. It was vital to be as sure as we could be that we were right about the trends. However, I felt that the inevitable delay in switching resources in departments and agencies away from some of the cold-war targets meant that we gave Russia (and the other former Soviet republics) more of our time than they merited. This was despite the fact that the two major conflicts involving the UK in the previous ten years had been in the Gulf and the Falklands.

In the Middle East, Iraq continued to give us plenty to do. It was not a particularly challenging assessment task: the interest lay much more in the policy area, deciding how to handle Saddam. Iran was more of a conundrum. The Iranian regime tried to profit from neutrality during the Gulf war to forge a new relationship with the Arab Gulf states. But the Arabs generally remained wary and were certainly not prepared to keep the West at arm's length as Iran wanted. The smaller Gulf states continued to expect the western cavalry to rescue them from distress as Kuwait did in 1991-92.

Revolutions eventually moderate and then burn themselves out. How long would this process take in Iran? In 1991 we wondered whether Rafsanjani and the technocrats in the Iranian administration would continue pushing through economic reforms which might in turn affect the still extreme social and political climate in the country. When Rafsanjani appeared to consolidate his power at the Majlis elections in spring 1992, we became more hopeful about the long-term trend. But the Iranian rhetoric against the west, involvement in international terrorism and subversion continued. The JIC had to make sure there were no illusions about the Iranian regime and that we needed to watch particularly carefully the interest in developing a nuclear weapons capability. The assessment task was complicated by the US view that, even so, we were too soft on Iran. It was not always easy to separate out in discussions with some Americans on Iran (but not our main contacts at CIA) the strong urge to paint Iran as black as possible which was fed by the US experience during the Iranian revolution.

In 2015, US President Obama championed an international agreement with Iran over its nuclear programme. The aim is to ensure Iran will not develop a nuclear weapon. The agreement offers Iran a path to remove international sanctions, help develop its economy and become a more constructive member of the international community. Years of tough diplomacy have been invested in this, including in British Diplomatic Service. We shall see if Iran takes the opportunity.

The assassination of Rajiv Gandhi in May 1991 sparked press articles asking whether India's democracy and the integrity of the Indian state were in jeopardy. We tried to play down these fears and the next year and a half showed they were overdrawn.

Our concern remained more focused on the risks of an Indo-Pakistani war. The stakes were higher than before because – and this made the situation unique in the world – both sides had developed a nuclear weapons capability (Pakistan only recently). The bilateral dispute over Kashmir remained intractable. Yet we were able to give some reassurance that for the time being both sides wanted, and were able, to contain their quarrels without resorting to war.

In my last 6 months the Chinese attitude towards Hong Kong rose from an already high place on my list of priorities to the top. Policy makers wanted to know how far the Beijing leadership would go in their opposition to the constitutional reforms (a moderate extension of democracy) of new Governor Chris Patten in Hong Kong. The material we had was plentiful and not all pointing in the same direction. The conclusion had to be a pessimistic one – that the Chinese were implacable in their hostility and were prepared to make life difficult for us in Hong Kong over the last few years of our stewardship. That did not, however, mean that in due course some deal might not be worked out.

The policy background was extraordinarily sensitive. Some members of the JIC questioned whether our information could really be relied upon. Were we not being too pessimistic? There was a suspicion that the FCO Sinologists might be seeking to spread doom and gloom. All I can say is that the Assessments Staff told it like it was from the reporting we received.

Former Yugoslavia clocked up the greatest number of papers during my two years. I took only a few CIGs to cover absences but took an interest, indeed a direct one, when I was acting Chief of the Assessments Staff in Gordon Barrass's absence.

In spring 1991, Deputy Chief Gloria Craig had been disappointed by the JIC's decision to delete her conclusion to a paper that the fighting in former Yugoslavia could go on for years because there were no solutions in sight and the hatreds ran so deep. At that time it was indeed hard to contemplate that any party would have an interest in continuing the carnage for so long. Sir Percy Cradock himself commented at the JIC that "the mind recoils that people could be so stupid" when faced with the scenario that there would be war although it was in the interest of no-one. Gloria was right.

In 1992 her successor Andrew Pringle (later Major General) received some criticism from the Foreign Office for his unreservedly gloomy papers. But again, each succeeding month showed that the situation could indeed deteriorate further and there could be even worse to come. With British forces involved in the relief operation in Bosnia-Hercegovina it was right that no punches were pulled.

The Allies

The closeness of the intelligence relationship with the US, Canada and Australia took me by surprise. I saw plenty of the New Zealanders too, although they had become semi-detached from this tight-knit community in the mid-1980s owing to their refusal to allow ships to enter their ports which might be carrying nuclear weapons.

Allied liaison officers, based in Embassies/High Commissions, were regularly seen in the Assessments Staff corridor, attended some CIGs and the first part of the JIC meetings. Drafts of appropriate papers were copied to them for comment. The papers themselves were sent to allied capitals once agreed by the JIC.

The Americans were by far the biggest players. Each of our intelligence agencies has a bigger brother on the other side of the pond. GCHQ work together with NSA under the UKUSA agreement. Inevitably we received considerably more than we contributed but GCHQ nonetheless (rightly) enjoyed a large budget to enable it to pull its weight. SIS liaises with CIA; the Security Service spoke chiefly with the FBI; and the Defence Intelligence Staff had close links with the Defense Intelligence Agency of the Pentagon.

The main US interlocutor for the Assessments Staff was the analytical wing of the CIA. The personal contacts were important. CIA analysts would frequently pass through London when going out for or returning from visits to the parts of the world they covered. I would always try to see them. Similarly, we made a point of calling on our opposite numbers when visiting Washington. I saw the CIA Near East and South Asia bureau particularly often.

There were also set-piece get-togethers. I headed a

delegation at the annual conference on South Asia between the four allies. We regularly sent and received teams for wide-ranging talks.

One of the problems of working inside an intelligence community is that there are a limited number of people to whom you can speak freely. This increases the risk of uniform views. The contacts with the allies provided valuable opportunities to test our views. We could do so freely: we all operated according to the same rules, were used to dealing with each other and shared similar gut instincts.

Viewed from outside the membership of this "five-eyes" club might have seemed anachronistic, reflecting a bygone era of political relationships. While the link with the US remained fundamental to our security policy and our friendships with the Old Commonwealth remain strong, much more of our political effort was now directed towards the European Community, now European Union.

There was intelligence liaison with our European partners and with other friendly countries. European co-operation would develop further both for practical and political reasons. But there was nothing like the same sharing and close contact across the board as with the intelligence allies.

Co-operation with Europe did not strike me as a future alternative to our place in allied intelligence but rather as a second focus of activity which should not compromise the first. The allied community worked and was an enormous asset. We needed it to help understand the confusion and turbulence of the post-cold-war world. The art of diplomacy is to have the best of all worlds.

How was it?

My last working day in the Assessments Staff was Christmas Eve 1992. I remained on the books until New Year's Eve, covering as Acting Chief for some of that time. I was sorry to lose my colleagues in a small close-knit unit, although I remained in touch with some of my desk officers from the FCO such as Diane Corner, with whom I made my first visit to China and now a Head of Mission, and Greg Shapland, a Middle East researcher. It was right to move on after two years. It had been a grand time which had rekindled my enthusiasm for working on foreign affairs.

PART II

FORMER YUGOSLAVIA: DAYTON: THE EXERCISE OF A SUPERPOWER'S POWER

The US delegation packed its bags and deposited them outside their hut to demonstrate that they were about to leave the negotiation. All the other delegations could see. The idea was to increase the pressure on the Serbs. It worked. The Americans brought in their Secretary of State Warren Christopher; President Clinton was engaged on the phone. The superpower pulled out the stops. President Slobodan Milosevic gave up the Serb claim to a share of the Bosnian capital Sarajevo paving the way for a division of the country's territory into Serb, Bosniac and Croat cantons. The Dayton Agreement was initialled on 21 November 1995.

Just two years previously, the Americans had not been engaged in the diplomacy of finding a peace settlement to the Bosnia War. They had views on the immorality of Serb behaviour, especially the siege of Sarajevo. They advocated lifting the embargo mandated by the UN Security Council on arms sales to any party, arming the Bosniacs and helping them with air strikes on Serb positions. This did not align with the UK and EU policy of pressing for a negotiated settlement between the parties and meanwhile providing troops for a UN force UNPROFOR to protect aid convoys.

Let's go back to the beginning. Coming to the end of my two-year secondment to the Cabinet Office Assessments staff, I wanted a meaty job in the Foreign Office before going overseas again. The Assessments Staff had been a wonderful experience. But it was not the same as being in a policy job working closely with senior officials and Ministers.

Looking for the next posting

An advantage of a home job is proximity to the personnel people planning the next job. The usual pattern for someone given a first job at Counsellor level in London was then to be posted abroad. Personnel accepted my wish to stay at home. I had not appreciated the complications this could lead to.

I was first asked whether I would run as a candidate for Deputy Private Secretary to the Prince of Wales. I would not have thought of applying for the job. But having spoken to the incumbent, Peter Westmacott, I decide to give it a shot. The FCO occasionally throws up unexpected challenges and opportunities. Working for the heir to the throne, already then embroiled in dispute with his wife, promised something out of the ordinary.

I had my interview with Prince Charles on Wednesday 25 November 1992. I caught an afternoon train to Peterborough. I hung around at the station for 20 minutes waiting for a driver. When he belatedly identified himself we sped at alarming speed through the countryside to Sandringham. Commander Richard Aylard showed me in.

The Prince was welcoming, made typically British comments about the deficiencies of the world, sympathised with the French farmers who were defending their livelihoods so vigorously, asked about my work at the Cabinet Office showing a particular interest in Yugoslavia and spoke a little about the job (Prince of Wales' Trust etc). I did not shine. From the beginning of the interview I had the impression that I was not the lead candidate. I knew he had already seen at least one of the other two (whoever they were).

I heard the following Wednesday that I had not been selected. Deputy Head of Personnel Management Department Stephen Lamport had been chosen and I was now being asked to take his slot. I had suspected that I had been asked to run for the PS/HRH job to make up the statutory field of three. Nothing unusual or untoward in that. All part of the system. But I had not been told that it was my Grade manager who was the leading candidate! I was not overjoyed about the offer of the Deputy/ PMD position. It was time I proved myself in a frontline policy department in the FCO and was Head of something. I told Stephen the following day that I wanted to be considered for a Headship of a Department such as Near East and North Africa but was also prepared to run for the PMD job.

I telephoned him a couple of days later asking about any other jobs coming up at home and abroad. I decided on Saturday 13 December to withdraw my willingness to run for Deputy/PMD which the Administration wanted me to take. I told Edward Clay, Head of PMD, in an interview on the Monday. He pressed, but relented towards the end when he saw I was not taking the decision lightly and was already under plenty of self-imposed pressure. I rang to confirm my position the following day.

I had not crossed the Administration before. It concerned me that nothing suitable might turn up. I put it to the back of my mind over Christmas and New Year. But after that I found being at home waiting none too easy.

Stephen Lamport rang on 12 January 1993 to ask how I felt about Head/ Eastern Adriatic Unit. This was a bolt from the blue. I had thought about South Asia Department – and was not clear why I had not been given a run at it – and about the two "Arab" departments. But EAU had the profile I was looking for. I said I would run. The appointment went through on 1 February.

What were the lessons of this episode? I knew that I would never again be passive in the face of decisions about me by Personnel. EAU would be a great test. I would have a chance to show what I could do, both on policy issues and management. In short, I was fired up on my return from the Cabinet Office to the FCO.

Starting in EAU

When I first rang Charles Gray, outgoing Head of EAU, to ask when I should start he suggested I should take over the same day! There was a point to this. He had been Yugoslavia desk officer, then Assistant Head of Central European Department before promotion to lead the new independent EAU as the crisis in Yugoslavia mounted and the UK Presidency of the EC began in July 1992. He had had enough and had landed a posting as number two in Jakarta. His eagerness to move on underlined that I was about to jump on to a vehicle which would be moving very quickly indeed.

I went in fresh from a break, physically fit (having spent some of the time in the fitness centre) and thin (having dieted down to 10 ½ stone). I saw my particular strengths as strong motivation and staying power. I doubted (wrongly, as it turned out) there was any credit to be gained from policy-making on former Yugoslavia since the issues were so difficult to handle and real success on the ground unlikely. I quickly developed three pieces of general guidance to sustain myself:

a) however bad it is in former Yugoslavia it will probably get worse before it gets better;
b) never forget people are dying and suffering. However impossible it might look, we had keep pressing the parties to end the war and agree a settlement;
b) former Yugoslavia is a marathon not a sprint.

These were helpful saws in the many moments of crisis when I was asked to give advice.

The first day was a fine introduction to the harum-scarum of handling Yugoslavia policy. I was at my desk well before 0800.

The former Yugoslavia

In the absence of Under-Secretaries I had to support Douglas Hogg (Minister of State) at the daily FCO former Yugoslavia meeting at 0930. I had another meeting with him in his office at 1130. At 1730 there was a round-up meeting with the Foreign Secretary Douglas Hurd at his room in the House of Commons. He asked who could give him the overall picture. I explained that this was my first day and then had a go. This activity was made more frenetic by my poor knowledge at that stage of the location of the various offices. I used my new fitness to sprint to the House of Commons.

The policy framework

UK policy on former Yugoslavia had been set by two related developments in 1992. One was the London Conference of 25-26 August, chaired by the Prime Minister as President of the European Council together with the UN Secretary General. The International Conference on Former Yugoslavia (ICFY) was established to end the conflicts and settle all issues arising from the disintegration of the Socialist Federal Republic of Yugoslavia. Agreements were concluded on more immediate humanitarian matters. These were an early experience of how little supposedly binding commitments meant to the warring parties. The Serb agreement to allow controls on heavy weapons around Sarajevo was a distant embarrassing failure by February 1993.

The second key step was the government's decision to provide a British battalion as one of the main elements of UNPROFOR. I remember well my reaction on hearing this news. As a sceptical Cabinet Office analyst, who had been impressed by the correctly pessimistic assessments produced there by my fellow Deputy Chief Gloria Craig, I was more than mildly surprised by this deployment.

There was a strong humanitarian case for giving military support to the aid convoys in Bosnia. Public and political pressure to "do something" was high. As EC Presidency, it was for the UK to give a lead. There was a danger of "mission creep" and no obvious way of getting out. The Prime Minister said publicly that our troops would not be expected to "fight their way to hell and back". Yet it was not hard to foresee that they would be in a difficult position if atrocities were occurring and they were taking no action.

The brilliant and mercurial Glynne Evans, Head of the FCO United Nations Department, was the lead on the UNPROFOR dimension. She liaised with the British military as the concept of protected support was developed – that is, giving UNPROFOR the mission to defend aid convoys but not to intervene in the fighting between the parties.

ICFY and UNPROFOR were the basis of a policy which had international support. But this support was shallow and dependent on quick results. The Bush Administration regarded Bosnia as a dangerous tar-baby: involvement could only cause problems in the 1992 US Presidential election campaign. Some European states at that time, notably Germany and the Netherlands, hankered after a tough response to Serb aggression (but were unable to suggest how and unwilling to risk their own forces). The UK and France were seen as responsible for a policy of containment and saving lives which did not tackle "aggression". The stakes for both governments, at home and internationally, were high.

Throughout the trials of the coming years, the UK view remained that only a political settlement agreed by the parties would end the war and start the peace. That meant a restless push for agreement in the international community to create the sticks and carrots which would induce the parties to settle, in particular getting the a reluctant US Administration to engage. It meant restless engagement with the parties. It meant providing humanitarian aid. And, as things got worse – leading to the terrible massacre in Srebrenica in 1995 – it meant an ever greater readiness to use military force (which in turn led to the greater readiness in the future to intervene in other crises – Kosovo, Sierra Leone, Afghanistan, Iraq).

1993

The Vance-Owen Plan

As I started in EAU, David Owen and Cyrus Vance were in a process aimed at securing signatures from each of the three parties to each of the three elements of the Vance-Owen Plan: the map of ten cantons; the constitutional arrangements; and the military provisions. The Croats came on board fairly quickly on all three – not surprisingly since the map gave them territory beyond their 17% of the population at the 1991 census. The Muslims were brought on board through a lengthy and painful process during which they had more than half an eye on the attitude of the new Clinton Administration. By the end of April the Serbs were left holding out, having agreed only to the military arrangements.

March and April were dominated by the worsening situation in eastern Bosnia. Lady Thatcher was proclaiming that UK policy had failed and spoke of "appeasement". The Serb pressure on Srebrenica in particular was pushing the option of air strikes higher up the agenda.

The new US administration wanted tougher measures against the Serbs, but were still considering policy options and very anxious to avoid being sucked in. They were lukewarm about the peace negotiations which were widely perceived by the East Coast press as forcing the Muslims to accept an unjust deal. The Administration did not like David Owen's typically robust promotion of the peace plan to the media while the negotiations continued in New York in the early part of the year. Meanwhile, the Serbs were trying to decide how much they could get away with.

It took a lot of heavy lifting to move the Vance-Owen negotiations forward. They came to a climax at the beginning of May. As the negotiators gathered in Athens on 2 May, David Owen thought that it was going to work. Radovan Karadzic was frog-marched to the table by Milosevic and signed the map and constitutional arrangements.

Just for a while I started to worry not about whether there would be an agreement but about the practicality of implementing one. The map was too complex for the envisaged military operation to be able to guarantee success. Sarajevo was somehow to be a common city. In view of the hatreds and the at least for now irreconcilable aspirations of the three Bosnian communities arising from the break-up of Yugoslavia, there needed to be coherent boundaries within Bosnia to give some breathing space while new forms of cooperation between the parties gradually developed. In other words, I would have been more comfortable if we could have added a policy of partition to our policy of containment and saving lives. The problem was that this was internationally politically unsellable since the Muslims said they wanted a unitary state: hence the compromise of the Vance-Owen Plan.

Ministers had to back Lord Owen and were ready to do so despite misgivings about the military task and the durability of the peace agreement. The consolation was that the Americans would be on the ground too. Or would they? It seemed to me inconceivable that the Americans could back out given that NATO had developed an implementation plan with their agreement. It would severely damage NATO if they pulled the plug on implementation after the peace plan had been signed by all. How could they defend this with the Bosnian Muslims?

During its fateful debate on 15-16 May 1993 in the Bosnian Serb capital Pale, the Serb Assembly rejected the Plan despite Milosevic's support for it. Karadzic later attributed the Serb decision to US unwillingness to implement it. I wonder. David Owen certainly blamed the Americans. But I suspect Karadzic used this area of doubt as an excuse before international public opinion. The Serb hardliners believed that they could continue winning on the battlefield and achieve Greater Serbia or a separate Bosnian Serb state.

As a fallback, David Owen called for partial implementation of the plan in Muslim and Croat areas and use of air power against the Serbs. These were on the face of it, and in the light of the continuation of the war for another 2½ years thereafter, not unreasonable ideas. The Croats and Muslims were beginning to fight against each other, with the Croats determined that Mostar should be their capital. The Serbs needed to be shown that they could not flaunt the will of the international community over the peace plan. But it was never seen as a serious possibility in London that we would deploy soldiers on the ground to implement a plan which did not have the full agreement of the parties. No other government showed any readiness to do this either. The humanitarian operation was difficult and dangerous enough. Implementation of the patchwork Vance-Owen map was going to be no picnic. Intervening without Serb agreement was too risky.

So we had a policy vacuum. The new US Secretary of State, Warren Christopher, had paid his long-heralded visit to Europe to consult on Bosnia policy at the beginning of May. He met the Prime Minister and Foreign Secretary at Chevening on Sunday 3 May. I spent Saturday tidying up the brief but declined to go to the meeting itself arguing that it made more sense for me to stay behind and mind the shop.

The meeting was a disappointment. We very much wanted to unite policy across the Atlantic. We even suggested threatening air strikes to deter the Serbs as part of an effort to persuade them to accept a negotiated settlement. But Warren Christopher, although he spoke of policy options, wanted us to subscribe to a lifting of the arms embargo, with air power to be used only in the short term to prevent the Serbs from overrunning the Muslims while they were rearming. He said that air strikes were not a basis on which to unite US and UK policy.

The problem for us was that "lift" would mean abandoning our policy of containment. This would mean a volte-face for the Prime Minister and Foreign Secretary. That would have been a price worth paying if we had thought "lift" would work. We did not. Douglas Hurd later controversially described "lift" as creating a level killing field. It would not have ended the war. It might have led to a more desperate situation with even stronger pressure for western, particularly US, military intervention (some Muslims were aiming precisely for that and who could blame them?). The Americans had no answers to our questions about the practicalities of supplying arms to the Muslims (for example, the Croats controlled the land routes from the sea and would not want the Muslims to become militarily powerful).

Warren Christopher fared little better during the rest of his European tour. An opportunity had been lost. We all felt that keenly. But the need to find transatlantic agreement on the way ahead remained.

The PM's Private Secretary, Rod Lyne, telegraphed from Washington on 20 May that National Security Advisor Anthony Lake had suggested a ceasefire plus a new Balkan Conference. The next day we heard that the Americans and Russians (Foreign Minister Kozyrev was visiting Washington) had produced a draft statement by the Permanent Four of the UN Security Council. French Foreign Minister Alain Juppé was already in the US. Douglas Hurd was travelling out there. The so-called Joint Action Plan was the result. This issued in Washington on 22 May, with the Spanish Foreign Minister brought over the Atlantic (Spain was then the other main European troop contributor) to give additional EC cover.

The Joint Action Plan was a rag-bag of measures. Its main significance was that it signalled recognition of the end of the Vance-Owen Plan and a an increase in US engagement. The countries concerned had found enough common ground for the short term. But the Plan did not add up to a new policy to replace the one we had lost. It provided some breathing space – not much since the need to react to events on the ground was now exercising ever stronger influence on international policy.

Safe Areas

Historians will write reams about the UN decision in 1993 to create safe areas to deter the Serbs from attacking the Muslim civilian populations in six enclaves. This was an unhappy chapter in the story of Bosnia policy. It is not unusual in the world of international politics for risky compromises to be made. This was one on which the bluff of the international community was called, with tragic results in loss of life.

The first safe area created by the UN Security Council was the eastern town of Srebrenica. In April 1993 the Serbs increased their pressure on this small Muslim enclave. The town's normal population of 10,000 had been swollen to 65,000 by an influx of Muslim refugees forced to flee from other areas. A massacre or starvation appeared to be on the cards. UN commander Philippe Morillon managed to get through to the town. Once there he said he would stay until the crisis was resolved (the Muslims were refusing to let him leave anyway). Eventually the Serbs accepted a ceasefire, the introduction of (Canadian) UNPROFOR troops and delineation of a "safe" area. But in return the Muslims had to agree to disarm, so that no attacks could be launched from within the safe area.

This was an uneasy compromise. The Serbs were aware that a final attack on the town could be militarily costly and was likely to attract serious international reaction. They could for now tolerate the safe area as long as it was not a springboard for Muslim military operations which would tie down their increasingly thinly spread forces. The Muslim leadership, on the other hand, feared above all a ceasefire which would freeze the situation on the ground. They did not want Srebrenica to be a precedent. There was no readiness to maintain the commitment to disarm in Srebrenica.

The Joint Action Plan platform included further work to extend sanctions against the Serbs. The American sanctions negotiators headed by Vice-Presidential advisor Leon Fuerth were difficult to deal with on the detail. But the policy imperative was clear: we were keen to use the lever of sanctions to show there was an alternative to the use of force. UN Security Council Resolution 820, adopted after long preparation on 17 April 1993, had been the most far-reaching sanctions package agreed and implemented by the UN. It was now important to gear up the international community to enforce the resolution through practical action. Sanctions did not cause, and were never seriously expected to cause, the collapse of the Serb war machine. They were an important pressure point on Milosevic as the events of the second half of 1995 showed.

Encouraged by the example of the safe havens in northern Iraq, the representatives at the UN of the Non-Aligned states demanded havens to protect the Muslims in Bosnia.

A delegation of Security Council representatives led by the Venezuelan returned from Bosnia increasing the pressure for such measures. We went along with a declaratory Resolution 824 on safe areas.

Then we were faced with a proposal to provide UNPROFOR protection for these areas. The MOD were understandably opposed saying that the forces required for this task were simply not there and even if they were was any government really prepared to go to war against the Serbs? The FCO shared this worry. But we were placed in a hopeless political position by the French espousal of this idea. We were unable to resist the proposal. We concentrated on trying to reduce the risks through the drafting of what was to become Resolution 836.

The main argument centred on the mandate to be given to UNPROFOR. We tried to avoid a commitment to "defend" the areas and "protect" the population arguing that UNPROFOR would not have the legal mandate or ability to stop an all-out Serb attack. In the end the language was painfully convoluted. Yet what really counted was the impression created in public opinion that attacks on Muslim population areas would be stopped. The UN Secretariat was uneasy. They produced a report setting out options for the troop presence which pointed towards a heavy option of 36,000. We and others made it clear during the drafting of the report that they had also to include a lighter option. They did – 9,000 – which could operate on a different interpretation of the mandate.

Why did we do this, given our deep unhappiness about the whole concept and fear that it would not be sustainable? The answer is that we saw no other way. To have blocked the adoption of 836 would have meant using the UK veto in the Security Council. The resulting storm of disapproval would have ensured that was the last veto we ever cast! The further consequence would have been a loss of UK influence and probably resort to the expedient of lifting the arms embargo. As it was the Prime Minister was able at the Copenhagen European Council on 21 June with French support to head off Chancellor Kohl's suggestion that the arms embargo should be lifted.

SCR 836 was a wrong turning. No responsible western government should have voted in favour of it. But I still do not know how else we could have acted. In effect our policy was to hope that the worst would not happen and to use the breathing space to press for the elusive Bosnia peace agreement.

The situation on the ground worsened still further. There were fears that the Serbs were going for the kill. Enter NATO. It had been contracted to plan and provide a force to implement the Vance-Owen Plan. It had been contracted to enforce the No-Fly Zone imposed by the UN Security Council. At US initiative, and in response to further Serb attacks, it agreed at meetings of its Ambassadors in Brussels on 2 and 8 August to threaten air strikes if the Serbs continued to shell Sarajevo.

This was the beginning of the dual-key problem. The operation of UNPROFOR on the ground had to contend with the US wish for a campaign under different (NATO) management in the air. The UK was at the cautious end of the spectrum. The French, on the other hand, were being pressed by their public opinion to fight or withdraw (tirer ou se retirer). Without French support the UK could only try to limit the damage at NATO. Our most important objective was to ensure that the judgement of UN commanders on the ground could not be overridden by NATO. We could not defend air strikes in parliament which put the lives of UK soldiers at risk and which the UN commanders had not agreed to.

The Muslims were probably at their lowest point in the

war in June-July 1993. The Serbs were confident. The Croats were taking advantage of the Muslim weakness. You have to admire the Muslim readiness to carry on, calculating and hoping that the advantage would swing their way in the longer term. The NATO threat of air strikes was a boost for them. No wonder they held a grudge against the UK for holding NATO back. This frustration led to their attempt to take the UK government before the European Court of Justice on the ground that we were collaborating with genocide. They eventually dropped this in December, but the episode went down very badly with UK Ministers. It was unfair in view of the enormous UK effort to save lives and promote a negotiated peace. I suppose the Bosnian Government saw it as means justifying ends. But it was ill-advised.

The Invincible Plan

That brings things back to David Owen. His safest course of action after the Serb rejection of the Vance-Owen Plan and the international community's refusal to back his call for partial implementation would have been to resign (Vance had already done so and been replaced by Thorvald Stoltenberg). I salute his readiness to take the more difficult option. Instead of stepping down, he started in June to develop a new peace plan. I am reminded of the front cover of Private Eye in 1992 showing him outside No 10 following his appointment as EU negotiator with PM John Major saying "It's an impossible Job" and David Owen replying "I'm Your Man".

He went through some ideas with us at an informal evening meeting on Sunday 6 June at the Foreign Secretary's London house, 1 Carlton Gardens. We pored over big maps on the floor as he explained the scope for territorial swaps including Croatia giving up a little land north of Brcko to facilitate a Serb corridor between eastern and western Bosnia and giving Prevlaka (the small peninsula guarding access to the Bay of Kotor – a key objective for allied Montenegro and needed by the FRY navy) in exchange for the hills overlooking Dubrovnik.

David Owen was setting out to us for the first time his idea of a wider deal to solve the key problems holding up a Bosnia settlement. A glimpse of this thinking appeared at a meeting he held the following week in Geneva with Presidents Milosevic, Tudjman and Izetbegovic.

September marked the beginning of a new phase in the Bosnia political process which lasted up to the end of the year. The Owen/Stoltenberg negotiations came to decision time. The plan was built on a proposal from the Serbs and Croats which, reflecting the weak Muslim position, reduced Muslim territory to a small rump in the centre. David Owen always made it clear that his proposal had been the Vance-Owen plan: he and Stoltenberg were facilitating ideas coming from the parties.

The new proposal was an internal three-way partition of Bosnia, recognising the facts created by war with the mediators seeking adjustments to make the outcome less unpalatable to the Muslims. Some elements of the Bosnian Government at this point were considering whether they should switch from their claim to represent the whole of Bosnia to a straight advocacy of Muslim interests which could lead to the creation of a separate Muslim state.

Owen and Stoltenberg put a package on the table in Geneva on 20 August. This included temporary EC administration of Mostar to overcome the competing Muslim and Croat claims there: Tudjman would not accept UN administration as envisaged in Sarajevo. David Owen doubted that the Muslims would accept the package. The next round in Geneva broke up on 1 September without agreement. David Owen then rang to ask me if we could provide a warship for the final meeting.

This would take the leaders away from the distractions of the media in Geneva with whom they all so liked to play.

The talks in the Adriatic on HMS Invincible on 20 September 1993 must have been quite an occasion. David Owen put before the parties their responsibility to prevent the war lasting into another winter. David Owen's view when I saw him together with Assistant Under-Secretary Jeremy Greenstock in London the following day was that the Serbs would need to be worn down to give further territory to the Muslims. That proved to be right. The Bosnian Assembly rejected the proposal as it stood.

The EU Action Plan

In September it became clear that the German approach had turned around during the summer. My German opposite number Michael Steiner came to the first meeting of the EC Ad Hoc Working Group after the summer on 6 September singing a different tune. I went back to Bonn with him. He told me on the train that he had been successful in arguing for a less rhetorical and more operational policy. At the next Ad Hoc Group on 23 September Steiner dominated, taking the hitherto British line that there had to be an agreement now.

The periods after rejection of a peace plan were always particularly difficult. David Owen spoke to Foreign Ministers about his ideas for a comprehensive land deal involving the FRY and Croatia as well as Bosnia. At the following Ad Hoc Group on 6 October Steiner argued that the Invincible negotiating track should be kept going.

Out of the blue came a letter from the French and German Foreign Ministers on 8 November coupling the French proposal for an EC Joint Action on humanitarian aid to Bosnia with a political dimension on the peace negotiations. This became known as the Action Plan. The shock for the UK was that it had issued without involving or consulting us. Douglas Hurd was not pleased. Of course the French and Germans felt it necessary to do things together in order to keep their special position at the heart of Europe in good order. But it made no sense not to bring in the UK which had made so much of the running on Yugoslavia policy since mid-1992. Steiner told me he had intended to come to London to brief me and had sent a message. It was true that I had been told he wanted to come, but I had no idea why and the ball in my view had been in his court.

I imagine that the French and Germans expected that the UK would have no difficulty with the substance of their ideas. They were right. The Juppé-Kinkel letter formed the basis of policy agreed at the Foreign Ministers' meeting on 22 November. Meanwhile, David Owen had implored us not to tie his hands for future negotiations. That I found was often the problem with our European colleagues, including the Germans: too great a propensity to prescribe without the means to pull off a result. The Belgians were difficult at this point in the Working Group. We spent all day trying to negotiate a text for EC Foreign Ministers and they then ignored the discussion and circulated their preferred wording anyway.

The main addition of the Action Plan to the Invincible proposal was to say that the percentage of territory for the Muslims should be increased from 30% to 33 1/3%. As there was already at least conditional Serb agreement that the Croats should have 17.5% this meant that the perceived "goodies" would have roughly 51% and the perceived "baddies" 49%. This division would help the international saleability of an agreement. The Serbs would have to move back considerably (they held over 70%) and the Muslims and Croats would end up with over half the land.

The 12 Foreign Ministers and External Affairs Commissioner Van Den Broek chaired by Willi Claes met the leaders of the parties at the Palais des Nations in Geneva on 29 November. David Owen had the satisfaction of seeing how some Ministers were taken aback by the lack of constructive thinking among the parties. It was the first time I saw the "brigands", as Douglas Hurd called them, in the flesh. Milosevic was the most impressive at the meeting.

There was a second meeting in the same format on 22 December. I went with Douglas Hogg. The meeting came in the middle of a week travelling with him in former Yugoslavia (about which more below). So we arrived from the mud and misery of a central Bosnia wracked by a nasty Muslim/Croat war to the sight of the Foreign Ministers losing their cool, particularly with the appalling Karadzic. The talks made no progress. The Muslims were ready to fight on. The Serbs would not give up the little more territory being asked of them. The Chair Belgian Foreign Minister Willi Claes turned on Vitaly Churkin, present as a Russian observer, for suggesting that sanctions should be lifted.

This fruitless meeting contained a moment which I shall not forget. At the end of a largely nugatory occasion Willi Claes proposed that there should at least be a ceasefire over the period of the Western and Orthodox Christmases. He sought the concurrence of each head of delegation in turn. They were all seated in a line facing the Foreign Ministers. All nodded in turn. The next day the Muslims began their heaviest offensive up to that point against the Croats in Central Bosnia!

Macedonia

It was not all about Bosnia in 1993. I was also responsible for policy on the other parts of former Yugoslavia not involved in the Bosnia War. Slovenia had by now escaped the conflict.

I delighted their first Ambassador in the UK when I decided to move his country from my Unit to Central European Department. They saw this as dissociation from the Balkans!

Macedonia was much more problematic. When I became Head of EAU the question of how to secure Macedonian membership of the UN was to the fore. My first outward policy telegram to Posts abroad was on this subject. Our aim was to promote and help stabilise Macedonia as an independent state. It was right for reasons of high policy to stick with the borders of the states which emerged from the disintegration of Yugoslavia. I believe that any other approach would have been hopeless. Happily this coincided with my own sympathy for Macedonia. Gligorov was an ex-Communist like the rest of them. But I always felt he was much straighter in speaking to our Ministers than the others.

With the UK leading the way Macedonia gained membership of the UN on 8 April 1993. The price was a concession to the Greeks that it would be known internationally as "The Former Yugoslav Republic of Macedonia", not "Republic of Macedonia" as it had named itself. Macedonia remains to this day under "T" in the list of UM member states. The Greek government had whipped up the indignation of the Greek public against use of the term "Macedonia" which they claimed as purely Greek. Behind this lay Greek sensitivity over any claim that there were non-Greek minorities in their country. The Macedonians in the north were called "Slavophone Greeks".

The next campaign on Macedonia was to open diplomatic relations. We chose to regard our vote in the Security Council in favour of Macedonia's admission to the UN as meaning that we had recognised this new state. But we could not so easily finesse diplomatic relations. The EC had coordinated policy over recognition of Slovenia, Croatia and Bosnia. We could not simply open relations without consultation with European partners. The Foreign Secretary wanted to move ahead and asked regularly for news in the autumn as our campaign unwound.

It quickly transpired that some other states shared our views, notably the Danes. The Germans also wanted to move but the issue was controversial in Bonn not least since large German contracts in Greece could be at stake. We saw that if we could bring a critical mass of 4 or 5 other countries on board then more would follow and some non-EC states would join in. The French could not be counted on at an early stage. President Mitterrand was known for his pro-Greek sympathies. The Germans suspected that the French hoped to benefit from contracts the Germans might lose. Eventually we set a date of 16 December 1993 for our exchange of letters with the Macedonians. Most others, not of course including the Greeks, did the same then or later.

The timing of this step allowed us to include in Douglas Hogg's trip to the region during the week before Christmas a stop in Skopje to witness Tony Millson presenting to President Gligorov his credentials as the first British Ambassador to Macedonia. This happened on 23 December after our attendance at the Foreign Ministers' meeting with the parties on Bosnia and a short stop in Croatia. Tony Millson had memorised his speech.

We then repaired with the President and Foreign Minister Stevo Crvenkowski to our new Embassy building for a drink or two. That was a measure of Macedonian appreciation for the pioneering diplomatic work we had done and the lead we had given in having Tony Millson (previously British Government Representative) accredited as the first western Ambassador in Skopje. We did not linger too long after the opening of the

Embassy. We liked Macedonia but wanted to be away before fog could close the airport as it had on recent occasions and perhaps keep us there for Christmas.

By the end of the year, I felt well in the saddle as Head of EAU. I had travelled to all parts of my parish. I had learned to manage the physical and mental exhaustion. As I started there was a management review which had to factor in whether EAU would continue to be needed. I had no doubt about that in December 1993. My diary entry for 6 December reads: "Let me now predict we'll still have a mess in Yugoslavia this time twelvemonth".

1994

The winter was a convenient time for a ceasefire in Bosnia, just as it had been throughout the history of warfare. The weather makes military movement more difficult. The armies

President Gligorov of Macedonia

were small and stretched. They needed a chance to recuperate, regroup and resupply. So the early part of the year was generally a period of at least reduced fighting. 1994 began with a Muslim offensive against the Croats, but this died down. With the negotiating process stuck we were all uneasy. Things have a habit of happening in Bosnia when there is a gap in the political process.

Sarajevo market massacre

On 5 February 1994, 66 civilians were killed when a mortar shell landed on the crowded market-place in Sarajevo near the cathedral. The natural first assumption was that the Serbs must have been responsible for this outrage. The UN expert analysis was not so clear. Indeed there appeared a possibility that the shell had been fired from Government positions. It would not have been the first time that the Bosnian Government had tried to draw the censure of the international community down on the Serbs. But this was surely going far too far. I found it impossible to believe that the Bosnian Army would deliberately risk the lives of their own people. The Serbs had been recklessly firing on the city for so long. I doubt we shall ever be certain of the truth.

It was immediately apparent that we should again be contending with US and French demands for use of NATO air power. Number 10 quickly got out ahead talking of the need for muscular action. But Ministers were also wary about being dragged into a war without clear and achievable aims by the tide of emotion. The Ministerial Committee OPD considered instructions on 8 February for the meeting of NATO Ambassadors the following day.

Meanwhile, the UN Commander in Bosnia General Michael Rose was making progress towards agreement on a ceasefire around Sarajevo. Our line in the North Atlantic

Council was to make sure this was factored into the decision of the Allies. After a long day of discussion NATO issued an ultimatum giving the Serbs 11 days to withdraw their heavy weapons from within a 20km radius of the centre of Sarajevo or place them under UN control: if they did not, remaining weapons would be subject to air strikes. The Serbs eventually complied.

First US Political Initiative

This episode overshadowed an important development in US thinking – a sign that they were starting to dip their toes into the negotiating process. Ambassador Chuck Redman had since the previous autumn been a US observer at the Owen-Stoltenberg talks (Deputy Foreign Minister Churkin was there too for Russia). There were stories that Redman had advised the Bosnian Government against the Invincible proposal. I doubt it was like that. But it was certainly true that the deal was not regarded as fair in the East Coast press, and the Administration (as with the Vance-Owen plan) was not crazy about having to help implement it with troops on the ground.

Redman called with Deputy US Secretary Tarnoff on the Foreign Secretary on 9 February. Redman was authorised to become engaged. Douglas Hurd warmly welcomed this. He had pressed the Administration to become involved during his visit to Washington the previous month. He repeatedly said during our very frequent office meetings on Bosnia that the US detachment and the poor relationship they had with David Owen were damaging.

Redman visited Paris and Bonn too. Steiner told me that he secured agreement from Redman that the UK, France and Germany would be briefed on Redman's work in the region. This was to be kept confidential as the US did not want to have to deal with the whole EU. The three Europeans would not be able to secure agreement from EU partners that this activity could proceed in parallel to Common Foreign and Security Policy business.

So the US engagement underlined the end of the brief period in the sun of the EU as a body; a new reliance on the Close Allies' network; and further evidence of Michael Steiner's wish to become personally involved in the negotiations (he had already attached himself to the Owen-Stoltenberg effort to mediate between the Muslims and Croats early in the New Year, having failed with an earlier suggestion that all EU members should have the right to be represented in the peace talks if they so wished).

All this was bound to have implications for Owen and Stoltenberg. Since the US would not work with them they were inevitably put in the shade. Yet we were anxious that they should continue. They had a mandate from the EU and UN, and there was as yet nothing solid to replace them. David Owen had always said that governments might need to become more closely involved in the negotiations. He made it clear that he was looking for a way out, but meanwhile was prepared to stay on.

Steiner's involvement meant that I, as his UK counterpart, could be more involved. Chuck Redman called a meeting at a restaurant in Geneva on Saturday 12 February. Michael Steiner was there and my French opposite number, Christian Rouyer (whom I had known in Berlin), too. Redman was cautious but serious about exploring the scope for a political settlement. He intended to focus first on the more manageable problems between the Muslims and Croats. I dictated my report early the following morning at the UK mission in Geneva and then made my way to Athens for a meeting of the EU Ad Hoc Group (Greece now in the

Presidency). Not a word of course at the meeting about our tryst with Redman.

Our next meeting with Redman was at Frankfurt airport (a convenient rendez-vous for the Americans as they often flew into the region from the US air base on the other side of the airport). Chuck by then had the bit between his teeth and wanted to move fast. I was struck by his New-World "can-do" approach. Christian was rather sour. The French had mixed feelings about the Americans muscling in. The third meeting, again at Frankfurt airport, was on Saturday 19 February. Redman had had a tough exchange with Tudjman but felt that the Croatians were moving towards a two-nation federation in Bosnia. The three Europeans (the young Bernard Chappedelaine for the French) then saw Croatian Foreign Minister Granic elsewhere in the airport to hear it from the horse's mouth.

Somehow the process being led by Redman had to be brought into the open. An international meeting was held at Bad Godesberg near Bonn on Tuesday 22 February involving all EU states, the US, Russia, the UN, and Canada. It was well stage-managed on lines we had discussed at Frankfurt airport. Other players did not, in my experience, mind too much being organised like this as long as the hidden hand was not too obvious and they had their say. The key was to be seen domestically and internationally to be included.

Redman's work led to the agreement to form the Muslim/ Croat Federation which was signed into existence in Washington on 18 March. By this time the process was gaining a US/Russian flavour, at least in the public eye, with the Europeans (perceived as having failed in the peace process) on the sidelines. We should have done better, here and elsewhere with our public presentation.

Owen and Stoltenberg had already been working on

Michael Steiner left in Bosnia

bringing the Muslims and Croats together as one way forward after the failed EU Foreign Ministers' meetings with the parties before Christmas. But it is unlikely that the Federation would have been born without a US lead or, at the minimum, firm US backing. There was obviously tactical military advantage for both the Muslims and the Croats in ending the fighting between them and concentrating their fire on the Serbs. For Croatia, this would also enable help them to focus on gaining control of the large areas of Serb-held lands within their own borders. For the Muslims, it would mean access to supplies through Croatia and Croat-held territory in Bosnia.

Yet the two sides still played hard to get. The Croats in Bosnia feared that Muslim numbers would swamp their culture in Bosnia: Croat distrust of the Muslims is deep-rooted. The Muslims did not want to become a satellite of Croatia and insisted on retaining power in Sarajevo. The upshot was that the central government remained in place; a Federation Government was created to cover the 58% (more than the internationally agreed 51%!) of the territory of Bosnia to which it laid claim; and there would be a "confederation" between Croatia and the Federation.

More UK troops

Having brought the Americans in and with the creation of the Federation providing a vital building block towards an overall settlement in Bosnia, now was the time to invest further resources in Bosnia and to encourage others to do so as well. In March the Cabinet was persuaded that we should send a further battalion of British forces to Bosnia. These troops played a key part in underpinning the Muslim/Croat ceasefire in Central Bosnia and also supplied the numbers which made possible a UK deployment to the eastern enclave of Gorazde a little later.

We conducted a world-wide campaign to attract more troops from others. Some other Europeans came in for the first time. Islamic countries also decided to contribute: Douglas Hurd was keen on this as a way of demonstrating that Bosnia was not, as some in the Islamic World claimed, a European or a British plot to do down the Muslims in the country to the advantage of the Christians. I preached the gospel of taking risks for peace in the Ad Hoc Group. I was uneasily aware that we were being sucked in further, but that did not seem so bad now that the Americans were engaging and some other Europeans were there too. I also saw the problem that the military might start to believe that UNPROFOR could build peace from the ground up. An illusion. Only a political agreement between all three sides could provide a basis for a durable peace.

The Gorazde crisis

April 1994 was the month of the Gorazde crisis. The Serbs tightened their grip on the "safe area" and threatened to overrun it. They were calling the bluff of Security Council Resolution 836 and of NATO's threat to use air power against them. It remains unclear why the Serbs did this. Was it a reaction to the Federation Agreement? Were they bothered about attacks on them from within the safe area (unlike at Srebrenica, there had been no agreement on establishment of the other 5 safe areas that the Muslims inside them should disarm)? Were they pulled on to the punch? The Muslim defence forces on the edge of the town melted away.

Whatever the truth of the matter, the US were calling for air strikes again and we were concerned about the safety of our now larger troop contingent on the ground. The European Three had a Pol-Mil meeting with the Americans in Washington on 20-21 April, with Political Director Pauline Neville-Jones and MOD Deputy Under-Secretary David Omand leading on our side. The Americans had eventually to back down from extreme positions as this time we found a common line with the French. This paved the way for a sensible decision in the North Atlantic Council on 22 April on the triggers for air strikes, not only at Gorazde but also at the other safe areas. Lesson: the directoire of Four must prepare these things.

The Contact Group

At this time the Contact Group was born. There had been further encounters with Chuck Redman at my level, but it was apparent that he was not making headway towards a settlement including the Serbs. The Gorazde episode set back the chances still further. On top of that came the unease of the continental Europeans, particularly the French and Germans, that the US were controlling the process.

The device with the EU was to say that three Europeans – who happened to be UK, French and German – would be appointed by Lord Owen as his representatives in the Contact Group. David Owen went along with this, earning our gratitude! David Manning, then Head of Eastern Department, was chosen to be the British member. My case to be included was at that moment weakened by the appointment of my deputy, Robert Barnett, as Ambassador at Sarajevo and the resulting gap in my department.

I thought the right approach was to strengthen EAU so that I would have the spare capacity to be in the Contact Group as well as continuing as Head of EAU. David Manning had understandably insisted that he should remain as Head of Eastern Department. I was assured by the Permanent Under-Secretary, Sir David Gillmore, that I had not been considered for the job because I was needed in my present role. He was a PUS I admired. I believed him.

David Manning had all the right qualities and more. He needed only to learn the subject. I made a start by briefing him on the flight to Washington for the meeting on Gorazde. Steiner carried on as the German representative. Jacques-Alain de Sédouy (whom I had known as Ambassador in Jordan) was the French member. The excellent Alexei Nikiforov was the Russian.

I was left with the task of explaining this new arrangement to the EU in the Ad Hoc Group as Steiner could not make it and Christian Rouyer's train was delayed. They did not like it. The Dutch were particularly upset, quoting Maastricht at me. The rumblings continued. As it happened, the French were to take over the EU Presidency in July and would be followed by the Germans.

The Contact Group went on its travels again. The idea was to develop a proposal which the parties would be told to take or leave and face the consequences. The questions to be decided in the group were the precise content of the proposal (clearly it would be a development of the Action Plan and its predecessors) and the nature of the consequences of rejection. A first meeting of Contact Group Foreign Ministers in Geneva on 13 May did not bring the issues to a head. Russian Foreign Minister Kozyrev argued at length for more balanced treatment of the Serbs.

We could relax or tighten sanctions against the Serbs as one element of our incentives/disincentives. But what about air strikes and what about lifting the arms embargo? There seemed no way we could simply bomb the Serbs if they refused to accept a particular proposal. But they could be told that NATO would lower the threshold for the use of air power in relation to the safe area regime ("stricter enforcement of the NATO exclusion zones").

The UK again faced a fundamental policy decision on the arms embargo. The US pressed for agreement that we would support "lift" if the Muslims accepted the Contact Group Plan and the Serbs refused. Pauline Neville-Jones indicated at a meeting of Contact Group Political Directors in London on 16 June that we might be able to agree language on this.

The Foreign Secretary hauled this back the following day. In the end we agreed to say that "lift" could become inevitable if the Serbs rejected the plan. By this we were only recognising the fact that the current policy of containment through the agency of UNPROFOR could not continue indefinitely. Douglas Hurd wanted the Americans to understand that "lift" meant the withdrawal of UK troops. The Americans knew that this would in turn mean the withdrawal of all western troops, leaving the US exposed to Muslim cries for help if the Serbs sought to win the war in a final offensive.

The Contact Group Plan was far from perfect. It was

decided to leave the constitutional arrangements on one side, just presenting the parties with some principles. The approach was to force them to focus on the map. The Contact Group discussed this with all the parties. The teamwork was good. All realised the danger of being played off against the other. But the most important discussion was conducted by Redman alone with the Bosnian Government. He was determined to minimise the risk of arriving at a position in which the Contact Group put forward a map which the Muslims refused.

David Owen particularly disliked the absence of a Serb territorial northern corridor connecting their territory in eastern and western Bosnia. They were offered only a flyover connection just south of the town of Brcko which was to return to the Muslims. Owen's Private Secretary David Ludlow argued the case in the Contact Group. The Europeans felt they could not move the US on this and so did not support. They could not gainsay Redman's assertion (which subsequent Bosnian Government positions bore out) that this was a deal-breaker for the Muslims.

The crucial player here was Russia. Churkin complained about Brcko but did not stick on the issue. At the second Geneva Ministerial on 5 July Kozyrev said in a bilateral with Douglas Hurd that we were headed for success between ourselves and failure with the parties. That sounded right and proved to be so.

By 13 July 1994 it was apparent that the Bosnian Government would sign, confident that the Bosnian Serbs would not. It was also clear that Milosevic would support the plan and try to avoid being caught by the backwash of measures to hit the Bosnian Serbs. I visited Washington again and Moscow, for the first time, in the run-up to Geneva III, in particular to reach agreement on a sanctions package. We found ourselves in a position between the Americans and Russians on this. But we were keen to close as we wanted to focus on this disincentive and postpone, if the situation allowed, moving to stricter enforcement of the NATO exclusion zones around the safe areas and lifting the arms embargo. Either of these measures (and most certainly the second) would mean the end of our policy of containment, which we saw as the best we had as a back-up if the Contact Group Plan was not accepted.

Geneva III was held on 30 July knowing that the Bosnian Serbs had set their face against the Plan. The meeting kept the Contact Group show on the road. As ever in these processes the key was to have the next step laid out – a UN sanctions resolution to tighten sanctions against the Serbs unless they decided to accept the Contact Group Plan. Ministers could take some very much needed summer relaxation while officials worked this through.

Milosevic closes the border with the Bosnian Serbs

We had an important pointer for the future just a few days later. Milosevic began indicating that he would stop all but food and medicine across the FRY border to the Bosnian Serbs and would allow international monitoring of this decision. Milosevic had flirted with this idea after the Bosnian Serb rejection of the Vance/Owen Plan a year previously. Now he presumably calculated that he had to start taking some action to distance himself from Pale and to bolster his case for relief from sanctions. A Contact Group meeting in Berlin on 7 September agreed that Milosevic should gain some sanctions relaxation if he really sealed the border.

So on 23 September the UN Security Council adopted Resolution 942 tightening sanctions against the Bosnian Serbs and Resolution 943 suspending sanctions on international air links, culture and sport against the FRY.

The complication was the monitoring of the border closure announced by Milosevic. The ICFY took on this thankless task. The UK provided a lot of the monitors at the beginning so that the system could get off the ground. But for the next year we were continually harassed by claims, usually unsubstantiated, that the border regime was being seriously breached. Some cheating there was, but there was in our view good cooperation from the FRY authorities and the system was working.

The significance of this was not so much the economic effect on the Bosnian Serbs, which was unclear and certainly not decisive, but the political signal. It underlined that Milosevic supported the Contact Group Plan and expected the Bosnian Serbs to accept it; and it demonstrated that there was a border between the FRY and Bosnia thereby helping to undermine those saying that Greater Serbia already existed.

US Congress presses for lifting the arms embargo
Milosevic's decision to back the Contact Group Plan in this way gave our policy further breathing space. But it did not offer a clear path to a political settlement any time soon. It was not enough to prevent the US Congress from insisting that the President should lift the arms embargo against the Bosnian Government. Clinton agreed in early August that he would press for multilateral lift if the Bosnian Serbs had not accepted the CG Plan by 15 October. This led us through the summer and autumn to make crystal clear that removing the arms embargo would fly in the face of our policy on the ground and would mean our forces facing an unacceptable level of risk. So "lift" meant "leave". The Americans often criticised UNPROFOR but they did not want it to leave.

Nor did the Bosnian Government, at least for the time being. The Bosnian Army was becoming stronger and the Bosnians thought they could win in the end; the Serbs were increasingly stretched. The Bosnians needed more time while avoiding anything which would freeze the situation on the ground allowing the Serbs to hold on to their position. When he came in for a meeting on 21 September, Prime Minister Silajdzic sought a commitment from the Foreign Secretary that we would agree to lift after 6 months (following the winter) if the Serbs did not accept the Contact Group Plan.

Meanwhile, our Ministers were already concerned about the isolated position of our troops in Gorazde. They had deployed there expecting to be joined by the French. The French contingent never arrived. In September we had to persuade Ministers not to insist on withdrawing the troops from Gorazde at that point. That would have created a crisis for UNPROFOR. Even in the unhopeful position we had reached in the political process there was enough steam left in the policy to continue for a while, and the alternative of an uncontained war was even worse. The Cabinet Committee on Overseas Policy agreed in early October that we should not agree to any automaticity on "lift", and should take another look at all the options in the New Year.

Keeping the political process going – Plan B

What of the Contact Group? On the UK side, the new Permanent Under-Secretary Sir John Coles decided that he wanted David Manning as full-time Head of Policy Planning Staff. William Ehrman, hitherto Head of Near East and North Africa Department, was drafted as his replacement in September. The two of them were to operate in tandem for a couple of months while William learned the ropes. William, like David, was a top high-flyer and soon got to grips with the issues. I was again wondering why I was not chosen, but assured by John Coles that it was not a case of being overlooked. I was needed in my EAU slot. This time Political Director Pauline Neville-Jones had known nothing about the change. She was not pleased.

The Contact Group had a big problem. It had built up its plan as "take it or leave it". The Bosnian Serbs had left it. What next? A containment policy would be hollow and soon unsustainable if there were no political process. The Contact Group Plan – Plan A – was blocked. The Group looked at whether it could construct another approach which bypassed this blockage and also helped to remove it. As ever the UK did a lot of the brainwork. Enter Plan B, focussing on mutual recognition between the states of former Yugoslavia as a way to stop the war and lead to negotiations on dividing up the assets and debts of former Yugoslavia. Milosevic wanted further sanctions relief. If he would agree to recognise at least Bosnia and Croatia more could be on offer.

We were trying to work with the grain on this. The Croatians had been unhappy that there was nothing in the Contact Group Plan about their country. They had been given as a consolation prize references in the CG Ministerial statements to the requirement for mutual recognition between all the states of former Yugoslavia. Croatia attached a great deal of importance to formal FRY recognition – more, I thought, than it was worth. The Americans felt they had to help Croatia on this. The Germans continued to have a strong pro-Croatia lobby in their press and at the Auswärtiges Amt.

Plan B never took off. The American sanctions team was not prepared to put enough on the table to make an attractive package for the FRY. Nor would the Russians cooperate with this approach. Most important of all, Milosevic repeatedly said that the FRY would recognise Croatia in due course but first confidence-building measures were needed and then political agreement on the arrangements for the Serbs in Croatia.

Croatia

By this time the Croatian economy was showing an impressive degree of recovery after the 1991-1992 war. The currency had been stabilised. The Croatian army was being built up quickly. The Croatian leadership was increasingly looking to use this growing strength to resolve the impasse over the large areas of Croatian territory controlled by Serbs (the Krajina, known in UN parlance as Sectors North and South, and western and eastern Slavonia, Sectors West and East). The Croatian Serb leadership was bone-headed in its refusal to accept that there would have to be an outcome recognising the international borders of Croatia.

Efforts to resolve the situation in Croatia were stuck. The Vance Plan of November 1991 had introduced UN peacekeepers but there had been no demobilisation of the Serbs and return to normalcy as the plan had envisaged. Croatian patience with UNPROFOR was wearing ever thinner. At each of the 6-monthly debates in the UN Security Council the Croatians created a drama over the mandate.

It was high time to move the process along. This led to the work of the "Zagreb 4" on a peace plan for Croatia. The Four were the Ambassadors of the US and Russia together with the (German) EU mediator on Croatia and the UN ICFY representative on this issue. The work was delicate. I was consulted by the ICFY pair, Gerd Ahrens and Kai Eide. In the autumn, the Ad Hoc Group was briefed. The Plan provided for an autonomous Krajina, where Serbs had been in the majority for centuries, under the sovereignty of the government in Zagreb but with significant devolved powers. Western Slavonia would revert to direct Croatian administration after a short transition. Eastern Slavonia would have UN administration for a couple of years. There were to be special arrangements throughout Croatia in areas where the Serbs had been a majority before the war. Particularly sensitive was the map of the extent of the Krajina – so much so that I was never allowed to have a copy.

The plan was finally agreed among the Zagreb 4, with the backing of the EU Ad Hoc group in early January. The Croatians did not like it as it conceded far more in terms of minority rights than the strong prevailing Croat nationalist sentiment in the country would be comfortable with. But the Croatians were spared having to take a firm view by the refusal of the Croatian Serb leadership even to receive the plan. They had been told at the time of the Hague Conference in autumn 1991 that they would be well advised to settle for good arrangements within Croatia while they could. They refused now to see the writing on the wall that their position was eroding all the time.

Milosevic would also have nothing to do with it. Unlike over Bosnia, he was never prepared to take a position in the negotiating process over Croatia. He had forced the Vance Plan on the Croatian Serb leadership in early 1992 and stuck with that. I had little hope that the Zagreb 4 plan would be accepted but thought it right to develop and present it so that there was a blueprint on the table. In the end the Croatian resort to force consigned all but the ideas on eastern Slavonia to the dustbin.

David Owen was meanwhile during the autumn of 1994 trying to broker confidence-building measures as a way of breaking the ice on Croatia. His power and energy achieved more than expected. There was an agreement between the Croatian government and the Serbs on the reopening of the road through western Slavonia and on restoring energy connections. This was a real move towards normalisation, but not enough to forestall Croatian military intervention in the following spring. David Owen did not, however, have our support over tolerating shipments, notably of oil, from the FRY through Serb-held parts of Bosnia and into Croatia to supply the Serbs there. This practice fell foul of the UN sanctions resolution 820. Paragraph 12 may not have been intended for this purpose but that was its effect.

The Bihac crisis

November 1994 and the first part of December were dominated by the Bihac crisis. The Muslim Bihac pocket in northern Bosnia had generally been regarded as a sideshow in western capitals. The Bosnian Army V Corps led by General Dudakovic had performed magnificently in hanging on despite having no land connection with the rest of Bosnian Government-held territory. The Federation Agreement had helped. The Croatians were breaching the No-Fly Zone to bring in supplies by helicopter. But the situation was further complicated by the fact that the local Muslim leader, Fikret Abdic (formerly a member of the Bosnian Presidency), was at loggerheads with the Sarajevo leadership and cooperating to some degree with the Serbs.

By early November Dudakovic had gained some 250 sq. kms in a V Corps breakout from the Bihac pocket. But V Corps had overextended itself. The Serbs rolled back these gains and moved close to the safe area of Bihac around the town. The Krajina Serbs then used their airfield at Udbina, just over the border in Croatia, to launch small aircraft which dropped bombs including a napalm device which did not explode. NATO had to respond and did so by attacking Udbina airfield. The Serbs did not in the end try to take the town and Bosnian Government claims of casualties proved to be wildly exaggerated. But the crisis left me and others in

London wondering how much longer it was worth persevering with our policy of maintaining UNPROFOR which was increasingly discredited with the parties and used a whipping-boy by the Americans.

The Carter Initiative

The year 1994 ended with an extraordinary intervention by former President Jimmy Carter. He had gained headlines by dealing with the government in Haiti at a time the Administration could not. The Carter Centre in Atlanta had been following Bosnia for some time and was encouraged to become involved by Serb middle-men. Karadzic wanted to break out of the international isolation imposed on his regime after the rejection of the Contact Group Plan (one of the provisions of Resolution 942). He hankered after direct dealings with the Americans.

As the Bihac crisis subsided, the UN had been seeking an indefinite ceasefire from the parties. The Serbs saw some attraction in this. The Bosnian Government was predictably more cautious. Nonetheless, it was the end of the campaigning season and the UN were making progress. Jimmy Carter then arrived on the scene shortly before Christmas and met a beaming Karadzic in Pale in full view of the world's media. The Bosnian Government was none too happy. But a Cessation of Hostilities Agreement for an initial period of 4 months was signed on 23 December and came into effect on 1 January.

The agreement contained within it measures to achieve a lasting ceasefire through separation of forces, exchange of liaison officers and so on. The Bosnian Government in fact blocked implementation of any measures which could entrench the halt in the war. The greater prize of bringing the Serbs on board for a political settlement eluded President Carter. I thought that if Karadzic was prepared to find a way out he could do so with least loss of face through Carter. But all the Carter mission achieved on that front, I fear, was to give Karadzic confidence that the international community would eventually agree to negotiate changes in the Contact Group Plan and would give up its insistence that the plan had to be accepted unless both sides agreed changes to it. With both sides seeming still to think they could win the war, I was not hopeful that the time gained would enable the negotiation of a peace agreement.

President Carter remained in the wings but did not return to Bosnia. No doubt he would have done so if Karadzic had shown a real willingness to deal.

Macedonia

In 1994 our Ministers lost some of their focus on Macedonia. After the efforts of 1993 the state was more secure. The economic situation was still precarious and reform (notably privatisation) slow. But enough international support was forthcoming and enough trade coming through (including illicit movements over the FRY border) to keep the country going.

The Foreign Secretary would have liked a solution to the dispute between Macedonia and Greece over the name of the state and the flag (the Greeks considered the Vergina star as a Greek emblem as it had been inscribed on Alexander The Great's tomb). Douglas Hurd talked to President Gligorov about this and found him inflexible. The Macedonians felt they could afford to wait for a better chance of a reasonable deal once the whipped-up nationalist fervour in Greece had time to subside and the interest of businessmen in northern Greece in resuming business dealings with Macedonia began to make an impression.

Meanwhile, Cyrus Vance continued patiently trying to

broker a package settling all the arguments. The Macedonian waiting game worked. A deal was done in 1995 by which the Macedonians gave up the Vergina star and the Greeks lifted their blockade at the border. The Greek said they would accept some compound name not excluding the word "Macedonia". But the Macedonians were not going to compromise much if at all on that. I do not blame them.

A British Embassy in Sarajevo

With a Cessation of Hostilities in place and the Bosnian case against the UK before the ECJ dropped I thought it right to open a British Embassy in Sarajevo. I had the impression that my energetic Deputy in EAU Robert Barnett used a visit to Sarajevo accompanying Lady Lynda Chalker (Minister for Overseas Development) to shape the job. I did not regard him as available after only just over a year in his present job: I needed him in EAU.

Nonetheless, once it was clear that he was regarded as available I backed his candidacy. There was no-one else running who was remotely as well qualified. The thought crossed my mind that I might apply. On reflection it made no sense from an office point of view and I doubted that my family would like the idea!

Robert set up the post in very difficult circumstances and on his own. He built bridges with the Bosnians. He worked through some dangerous times, particularly during the November Bihac crisis when Sarajevo too was heavily shelled. I spoke to him on the phone against a background of war noise. Some on our own side, notably the military, were not so enamoured with him. In the end all involved came to the view that a year was enough for him in Sarajevo. He deservedly moved on to promotion to Counsellor but did not stay long in the Diplomatic Service after that.

British Embassy Sarajevo

The establishment of the Embassy in Sarajevo completed the network of UK posts in former Yugoslavia. But one remained without its own building – Tirana. We had a broom cupboard, as we called it, in the French Embassy from which to operate there. Throughout my time working on former Yugoslavia I was frustrated by our failure to close a deal with the Albanian Government on a property for the Embassy. Our pre-war legation was now the site of a large government guest-house. The Albanians said they could not afford to give it up. They offered a series of other buildings, each of which fell through owing to claims made by former owners. The Albanians either could not or would not make it happen.

Our patience ran thin, and Ministers decided that we should if necessary withhold the return of pre-war gold belonging to the Albanians on which we had come to an understanding before my time when agreeing to resume diplomatic relations. The consolation was that the issue looked close to being wrapped up, through an exchange of our claim to the guest-house site for another villa, as I finished my tour at FCO in April 1996.

1995

The Contact Group tries again

The Contact Group, and within that the four close Allies, were under pressure to find a political way forward as the winter ceasefire wore on. Richard Holbrooke (US Assistant Secretary) was now taking a closer interest. The US Administration was running out of tactics to delay action being pressed for by Congress to lift the arms embargo.

The next Presidential campaign was coming on to the horizon. Senator Dole, leading proponent of lifting the arms embargo, was President Clinton's likely rival. The Administration wanted to defuse the problem of Bosnia. That suited Holbrooke. He wanted to move things. I imagine that he was frustrated by the weakness of the cards in the American hand. He said on several occasions that the US should have been there on the ground, while in the same breath castigating the Europeans for their lack of robustness. The Administration's need coincided with his interest.

Holbrooke's personality led to fractious meetings. He was the most senior in the group in that he had been an Assistant Secretary years previously and now appeared to float free of the State Department hierarchy. He had links with President Clinton. He was a clever speaker. His voice was always hushed. He often began with compliments, particularly to the Germans (he had been Ambassador in

Bonn and maintained that Germany was the major European partner of the US of the future). He then often said quite outrageous things. Pauline Neville-Jones was not of a temperament simply to be rolled over by this. Holbrooke did not take kindly to anyone standing up to him. One of his US colleagues told me that after his arrival in a country some those who worked to him commented "The Ego has landed".

The Contact Group representatives (William Ehrman for the UK) were despatched to Sarajevo and Pale in January 1995 to see if they could bring Karadzic to the negotiating table on the back of the talks he had held with President Carter before Christmas. They tried out some ideas. The Contact Group Plan remained on the table and had to be the way forward. Karadzic was offered a face-saver. The Contact Group Plan was described as a "starting point" for negotiations.

The Bosnian government was suspicious. It was explained to them that this formula reflected the reality that there could be a period for discussion between the parties in which mutual agreement could be reached on changes. This had always been the position. Now it was being made explicit. Karadzic would not buy it because of the implication that failure of the parties to reach agreement would mean that the CG Plan had to be accepted.

On 25 January, the day after Karadzic had baulked at these ideas, we had a meeting of the four Political Directors in London. Holbrooke pressed an unhappy Wolfgang Ischinger to agree that the Contact Group should try alternative wording on Karadzic. So we told our representatives to stay in Sarajevo. At this point the new Russian, Zotov, and Michael Steiner were already determined to leave and did so as soon as the snow allowed.

William Ehrman soldiered on. There was no consensus

on another CG trip to Pale, which would certainly have been seen as an act of weakness by the Bosnian Government. William acted as spokesman in a bizarre conversation by radio telephone during which Karadzic apparently stood outside in the snow. William asked him if he accepted the various points in the CG proposal. Karadzic said he did not, but they were "very nice gentlemen" and he looked forward to further discussions with them. The Bosnian Serbs shelled Sarajevo on the following evening despite the ceasefire. These were the last political negotiations with Karadzic.

At an office meeting on the following Monday the Foreign Secretary doubted that we could pursue both a negotiation with the Bosnian Serbs (Plan A) and the mutual recognition route (Plan B) with Milosevic. We did not draw a line under the direct route with Karadzic but there were no more proposals the Contact Group could make. The ball was in his court. He never played it back.

We were back on Plan B. On 9 February 1995, I went with Pauline Neville-Jones and William Ehrman to Paris for discussions with the French Foreign Ministry. The French planned a series of steps on Plan B leading to a meeting of Presidents Milosevic, Izetbegovic and Tudjman in Paris in the middle of March. How the Presidents were to be brought to agreement on the substance so that this meeting could take place had not been worked out. The French were more willing than the Anglo-Saxons to launch initiatives while unclear how or even whether they will work.

Our contribution was to be Pauline Neville-Jones adding her formidable powers as a negotiator to the effort in Belgrade to persuade Milosevic to move. We knew the odds were against success, but there was no better avenue to pursue. The Contact Group now became in reality the Political Directors. They had a stormy meeting on 14 February, but the big news was that the US agreed to full sanctions for the FRY if their more demanding version of Plan B was accepted. This showed what Holbrooke and his Deputy Assistant Secretary Bob Frasure could achieve. They both wanted a result.

The Russians were not helpful on this. The problem appeared to be Foreign Minister Kozyrev himself, although the political realities behind him in Moscow evidently reduced his freedom of manoeuvre. The Russians insisted on a lifting of sanctions against the FRY. They would not accept any linkage between sanctions and the situation in Croatia. All this undermined the Contact Group negotiating position, led at this time by the UK and France.

Milosevic did not close the door. He strung the process out with counter-proposals. He seemed to accept that time was not plentiful and that a resumption of the fighting with possibly devastating consequences would be inevitable if there were no political breakthrough. But he did not seem to believe that we would be prepared to pull out our troops, an option which the Foreign Secretary was in fact increasingly bringing up the agenda for discussion with the Defence Secretary and a reluctant Prime Minister.

The Americans were keener than ever to keep UNPROFOR. Holbrooke became a major player on former Yugoslavia by agreeing a deal with Tudjman, bruited before the world's media, which would allow the UN forces to stay in Croatia after expiry of their mandate at the end of March.

Meanwhile, the Foreign Secretary hankered increasingly after a Plan C as he did not believe Milosevic was negotiating seriously on mutual recognition. On 10 March I submitted a first paper on the Foreign Secretary's interest in a new single negotiator. I was sceptical that the US would accept. The response from Private Office on 13 February was that the Foreign Secretary thought "we had to move the furniture". He had in mind the former Swedish Prime Minister Carl Bildt to replace Lord Owen and to be accepted by all as the single negotiator.

All Pauline's efforts to persuade Milosevic to budge on Plan B were failing to bring him to accept, although she did manage to reach agreement that he would be expected to recognise not the current Republic of Bosnia and Herzegovina but just "Bosnia and Herzegovina". This would help Milosevic to argue that he was not recognising the present government in Sarajevo but something new. It was a fix which was helpful at Dayton.

The Bosnian Government were at this stage keen to secure recognition from the FRY. I saw Prime Minister Silajdzic one-to-one during a stopover at Gatwick airport on 15 March. He was interested while not hopeful that Milosevic was ready to move. Pauline was just about able to persuade the Foreign Secretary, for example at an office meeting on 17 March, that Plan B still had some life in it. A Contact Group meeting on 27 March agreed to have another go at Milosevic; Pauline dutifully reflected the Foreign Secretary's scepticism.

In the following period, the calm before the inevitable storm, I enjoyed another trip to Washington on 4-5 April, calling on Bob Frasure – now getting into negotiations himself with Milosevic – and Sandy Vershbow (National Security Council) among others. We managed an EAU Heads of Mission meeting in Zagreb on 24-25 April over which the Permanent Under-Secretary presided.

As April proceeded matters drifted towards the rocks. The US played tough on renewal of the Stage I sanctions suspension for Milosevic. They eventually insisted on cutting the renewal period from 100 to 75 days. Then two French soldiers were killed in Sarajevo on 14 April, in the midst of the French Presidential campaign: the French insisted on a Security Council Resolution which in truth was only declaratory and did not change anything on the ground but at least served as an expression of their anger. Ivor Roberts, our ebullient Chargé d'Affaires in Belgrade, managed on 26 April to inch Milosevic forward on a mutual recognition package by bringing him to agree that the statement of recognition had to be in the present and not the future tense. But, despite UN efforts to secure a prolongation, the Cessation of Hostilities Agreement in Bosnia expired on 30 April.

There were two shocks on 1 May. First, the Croatian army moved into western Slavonia. The pretext was that the highway through the Sector, opened as part of Lord Owen's successful mediation on a package of economic and confidence-building measures, had been blocked. In fact the problem had appeared to be on its way to resolution (it had arisen from a couple of incidents for which both sides shared the blame). In the following days the Croatians left no doubt about their intention to gain control of this the most vulnerable of the four sectors in Croatia held by the Serbs. In the process, there were some unsavoury roundings-up of Serb civilians and the lives of UN peacekeepers were put in danger. Some defended Croatia's action as simply taking what was theirs. For example, the Commission representative put on a pro-Croatian performance at the Ad Hoc Group on 12 May. But this was the beginning of Croatia's slide from grace in the eyes of some of its erstwhile supporters.

The second shock was a visit from William Ehrman to tell me that he was to be the next Private Secretary and so would shortly be vacating his position as Contact Group representative. I had by this point begun to wish to see light at the end of the EAU tunnel. The job was the most intense I had ever had, seven days a week. I had told Personnel that I would like to move in the autumn or in the following spring at the latest. The chance of a change had now arisen earlier than expected.

The job of Contact Group representative was not what it had been. The work was now really done at Political Director level. The prospects were uncertain: I could find myself without a post after a few months. The ideal would have been to have my next one lined up. Unfortunately, Washington – my first choice – had been bagged (and he deserved it) by the outgoing Private Secretary John Sawers. The other possibilities, New York and Bonn, could not be taken any further as things stood because of doubt about the timing of the respective incumbents' next moves. I had to take something of a shot in the dark. I opted to move from EAU. There was really no other sensible choice once my plea to be allowed to combine the two jobs had been turned down. I had loved EAU, with its bright and hard-working staff – none more so than PAs Alyson Garden and Kim Bowers who drove me mad with their chatter but were just first-class in delivering the goods.

In April, the Foreign Secretary gave the UN Secretary General formal notice that we would "redeploy" our contingent from Gorazde at the next roulement (within 6 months). On 16 May there was heavy shelling of Sarajevo. The Foreign Secretary informed the UN that the UK did not oppose a tough response.

General Smith's Ultimatum and the Consequences

General Rupert Smith had been thinking about the coming crisis ever since assuming the command of UNPROFOR in Bosnia and probably well before during his previous job in the MOD (in which he had been the best UK military interlocutor we ever had). He saw that UNPROFOR would be in an impossible position unless there were political progress or the force was given the authority and military capacity to move across the line from peacekeeping to peace enforcement.

On 24 May General Smith issued an ultimatum to the Serbs that shelling of safe areas had to end by noon the following day and heavy weapons returned to depots around Sarajevo. There was a second ultimatum calling on both sides to move other heavy weapons outside the Sarajevo exclusion zone. The Serbs did not comply. An air strike was carried out against an ammunition dump near Pale. The Serbs raised the stakes with further shelling. 71 people were killed in Tuzla town centre. There was a second air strike against the same target – this time apparently successful. The Serbs took international hostages, aid personnel and soldiers, around Sarajevo.

I came into work on Saturday 27 May to collaborate on a paper to be drafted by the Cabinet Office for the following evening. We met in COBR (Cabinet Office Briefing Rooms). The Chief of Defence Staff drove this preliminary meeting, blaming the military crisis on the lack of political progress and insisting that we should negotiate with Pale.

The following morning the Prime Minister wanted a briefing in COBR before going to Lord's for an England v. West Indies one-day cricket international. After the briefing he spoke from COBR to the newly-inaugurated President Chirac. John Major, as so often, demonstrated that he had a strong grip on Bosnia policy. One comment to us was memorable: "Smart arses on both sides of the Atlantic who said all was needed were a few good whacks had better start rewriting their memoirs". He was right. It was never as simple as that, although I believe that we would have brought the Serbs to a deal more quickly had we used air power more decisively against them and sooner.

Later on 28 May 30 British soldiers of the Royal Welch

Fusiliers were taken hostage in Gorazde. As we met with the Foreign Secretary in the early evening shortly before the OPD I had no inkling of the likely impact on this on our policy. Overseas Policy (OPD) meetings had not previously produced surprises. In fact the Serb hostage-taking of our soldiers turned out to be a big mistake with serious consequences for the Serbs and their timing, just before the OPD meeting, could not have been worse. The PM was not in a mood to let this go by. He had the support of the Committee in deciding to send reinforcements to Bosnia to ensure the safety of the UK troops. It was also decided to issue a private warning to Karadzic and Mladic that they would be held personally responsible if any UK hostages were harmed.

It was a bold move. We had no clear idea about what the extra troops were supposed to do. I went to No. 10 on 30 May to help brief the PM in advance of a press conference. He said he was comfortable with the decision, but later became impatient when Defence Secretary Malcolm Rifkind could not say what the role of the reinforcements would be. At another meeting around the Cabinet table on 31 May the PM became angry that the message to Karadzic and Mladic, which was to be in his name, had not yet been passed. He called the message which I had drafted "wishy-washy". I trooped out to a neighbouring room to order a changed version. Such an episode might have terrified me a couple of years previously. But this did not cause any lost sleep. In fact it was helpful as I had been having problems clearing the message with the Foreign Secretary's party at a NATO Ministerial at Noordwijk. The message was delivered.

I spent 1 June as part of a largely MOD team talking to the French in Paris. They did not like our view that the reinforcements, which they as well as we had now decided to send, should be under UN command. The French were suspicious of our reinforcements seeing them as an attempt to take centre stage. In fact the creation of the Rapid Reaction Force from the reinforcements and some of the existing UK forces in Central Bosnia may well be seen by historians as a French project. We should not mind too much. We did come round to the French point of view that the Rapid Reaction Force should wear camouflage rather than UN blue berets to underline that this force was different from UNPROFOR. President Chirac was driving hard. French pressure had brought us to the disastrous safe areas policy. This time their pressure getting us to move further had positive results.

On 13 June the last of the UK hostages were released. Eventually all the hostages came out unharmed. Karadzic admitted publicly that taking them had been a mistake. Previously, the Serbs had limited hostage-taking at moments of crisis to small-scale operations. This time they engaged the vital interest of a power which could bite back. The episode had been the first stage of a rewriting of the rules on the ground in Bosnia. We were now assembling a force capable of looking after itself and inflicting pain if the Serbs misbehaved.

The Frasure and Bildt Efforts on Plan B

The prospects on the political side were far from good. Bob Frasure had had long talks one-to-one with Milosevic in Belgrade and on 18 May we heard that he had a deal having made some concessions to Milosevic to which the UK and France would certainly not object. Frasure spoke later of paying what was necessary for the services of the rat-catcher (he will rightly be remembered for many things and among those should be his brilliant one-liners). The Germans did not like the deal, but that was not the crucial point. Bob was required by Washington to go back to Milosevic to insist on an American right to re-impose sanctions if the FRY misbehaved.

Milosevic would not accept this. Nor in fact would we since this was a decision for the UN Security Council which the US could not arrogate to itself.

Part of the reason why Frasure was not given full backing from Washington for the deal with Milosevic must have been the growing coolness of the Bosnian Government to the recognition package. When I saw Prime Minister Silajdzic again on 7 June, this time accompanying Douglas Hogg at a meeting at Heathrow airport, he was pretty dismissive about the package. The use of air strikes and the Bosnian Army's (over-optimistic) hopes of breaking the Serb grip around Sarajevo had emboldened the Bosnian Government.

Silajdzic reserved his strongest criticism for our insistence that the Rapid Reaction Force should not be misinterpreted as a military intervention to impose a solution. In fact the Bosnian Government, and even more the Croats, were reluctant to let the RRF cross their lines presumably for fear that it might interfere with their own military operations. The US, too, were unhelpful. The Administration required a statement of the RRF's intentions, apparently to secure Congressional agreement to fund the Force through the UN. In the end only partial funding was agreed as UN Security Resolution 998 authorised the higher troop ceiling for UNPROFOR. This left a sour taste: the US had long been urging a more robust policy on the ground, did nothing itself and would now not properly back Allies prepared to do something.

Carl Bildt was now on the scene, having first been sounded out by the Foreign Secretary who then secured EU support for him. David Owen showed remarkable grace in bowing out. Right up to the end he was working hard to make his contribution. He had strongly supported the effort to secure a recognition package with Milosevic. He had discussed this at his office in Queen Anne's Gate with William and me on 2

June as I took over as the Contact Group representative and he prepared for a farewell dinner with Milosevic in Belgrade.

I went with Carl Bildt to see the Prime Minister at No 10 on 12 June. John Major gave him a lot of his time. But there was not much to say at that stage. The PM volunteered that three-quarters of the Conservative Party would cheer if he announced the withdrawal of UK troops from Bosnia. Given the US attitude it was tempting then to ask whether the effort was worthwhile.

Bildt arrived with plenty of advantages. He did not have the history of conflict with the US which dragged down David Owen. He had superb contacts in all the major capitals. But he was new to the subject and there was a lot to learn. He did not come from a country which could give him decisive backing when needed. For that he would have to depend on us.

23 June was my last day in charge of EAU. The previous day John Major announced that he would stand in a leadership election. He beat John Redwood easily enough. The greater significance for the FCO was that Douglas Hurd chose this opportunity to stand down as Foreign Secretary after 6 years. His last day was 5 July. At a party for him given by the PUS I was honoured that he remembered me among those he mentioned in his reply to John Coles's speech. I had had countless Office meetings with him, often at short notice. He rightly saw Bosnia as a key test for UK diplomacy and spent a great deal of his time on it. His final success was the appointment of his preferred successor, Malcolm Rifkind. The most fascinating switch in the government was Michael Portillo as Defence Secretary.

We did not have long to wait for our first office meeting with our new chief. This was held on 7 July. Both he and new junior Minister Sir Nicholas Bonsor (Douglas Hogg had at last gained his deserved promotion to the Cabinet as Agriculture

Secretary, which gave me more pleasure than anything in a long time) were anxious that the first use of the RRF should be successful. Meetings with the new Foreign Secretary were much less frequent than with Douglas Hurd, who had not only set down the political guidelines for policy but had helped steer it as if also a senior official.

The Srebrenica crisis and the second London Conference
On 9 July I had a call from Stephen Gomersall, the Deputy Permanent Representative in New York, about reports of the Serbs advancing within one and a half miles of the centre of Srebrenica. This was the beginning of terrible tragedy with huge loss of civilian life, which proved to be a further turning point in our policy towards the Serbs.

The Contact Group met on the evening of 12 July in the Old Admiralty Building. Holbrooke was ill with 'flu and not in good temper. He made it clear he thought we were wimps for not defending Srebrenica as he said President Chirac had advocated. Of course this was a way of deflecting blame. Pauline reacted badly to this. The upshot was a highly dramatic occasion which dragged on beyond midnight. Holbrooke repeatedly disrupted the meeting to take and make telephone calls.

With President Chirac talking in public of Daladier and Chamberlain, the PM decided on 14 July to grasp the initiative by calling an international meeting of Foreign and Defence Ministers in London on the following Friday. Like the decision to reinforce our troops this had been prompted by anger over Serb behaviour. By overrunning Srebrenica the Serbs had broken the tacit understanding which underlay Resolution 836. At that time we did not know the extent of Serb atrocities against the men of Srebrenica.

With my successor Kim Darroch about to have a much

needed holiday abroad I slid back into the Head of EAU slot to oversee the preparation for the Conference. It was one of the hardest weeks I can remember. The practical arrangements at Lancaster House were inevitably imperfect although not seriously so. There was nothing we could do about the excessive heat on the day. The policy preparation was even more difficult. The focus quickly trained on Gorazde as the test of the international community's resolve since of the other two eastern enclaves Srebrenica had been taken by the Serbs and Zepa was already going the same way. The Americans were reported in the press as being ready to offer Apache helicopters to help in an operation to reinforce and save Gorazde.

We had by now already withdrawn our battalion from Gorazde and had no intention of putting our troops in a position in which they could be overrun or taken hostage. OPD on the evening of Sunday 16 July decided that there should be "timely and militarily effective" use of air power to deter attack against Gorazde and that we should be prepared to switch a battalion in theatre to Sarajevo to support the French there. The Monday, Tuesday and Wednesday were tough. The only respite was a meeting at 1 Carlton Gardens on 19 July with Douglas Hurd to brief him in advance of his interview with the team researching for the TV programme "Death of Yugoslavia" and on the Bosnia debate in Parliament that day.

On Thursday 20 July the officials began to gather in London. The Four had a pol/mil meeting in the afternoon. The French pressed for French/UK reinforcement of Gorazde. Our position was firm, with the OPD decision behind us. The US did not really want to be dragged into sharing the military risks. I think they were relieved by our dismissal of the idea that Apache helicopters would make the crucial difference in a reinforcement operation. Our line was that getting the troops into the enclave was only the first problem. Keeping a sizeable force in Gorazde supplied would be impossible without entering into war. It would be much better to withdraw UN forces to comparative safety and to deter the Serbs with a threat of disproportionate air strikes which we were fully prepared to carry out.

21 July 1995 was an amazing day. Having arrived at home at 0020 I was up again at 0500 and in London for a cup of coffee with Carl Bildt and the Foreign Secretary at 0730 followed by a breakfast of the four Foreign Ministers at 0800. Having opened the meeting in a sweltering Lancaster House the Prime Minister handed over the chairmanship to the Foreign Secretary who is brilliant on these occasions. The Prime Minister stayed on in the UK Ministerial room banging heads together throughout the morning. He was particularly concerned that this risky forward move in military policy should be accompanied by a decisive effort to move the political process. He explained all this forcefully in particular to Warren Christopher. He pressed both him and the nearly new French Foreign Minister Charette hard on supporting Bildt's effort to close a recognition deal with Milosevic.

Our other main problem, on the other side of the spectrum, was the Russian position. They did not want to be associated with a policy supporting NATO air strikes. We saw no chance of reaching agreement with them on a conference paper. Instead we used the draft discussed among the Four as a Chairman's statement to the press in the early evening after the end of the Conference. Kozyrev disliked the bounce intensely. We had no choice.

At 1930 we had a meeting of Contact Group Ministers again in Lancaster House. It amounted to little. The Ministers were too tired after a long hot day after a long hot political season. Bildt pressed for support for his efforts to agree a revamped recognition package with Milosevic. But Warren

Christopher was not prepared to give more on sanctions relief and the US position on a sanctions re-imposition mechanism remained an obstacle.

Clearing the path for a political settlement

The creation of the Rapid Reaction Force and the London Conference of 21 July were two essential precursors to a real change in the situation in Bosnia. They were necessary preconditions but very far off from being sufficient.

The first further step, a small one, was for NATO to decide soon after the London Conference that the threat of a disproportionate use of force in the event of an attack on Gorazde should be extended to cover Sarajevo. We had resisted extension at the London Conference, and remained wary about treating the other two remaining safe areas in the same way as Gorazde: the military circumstances were quite different. But with the immediate threat to Gorazde fading there was sense in including Sarajevo. It would in any event destroy the credibility of the new international policy if there were no reaction to a Serb atrocity against Sarajevo.

The second major development was the Croatian intervention in the Krajina. This looked imminent on 2 August. The Croatians had gathered a force estimated at 100,000. Thorvald Stoltenberg tried to mediate and it seemed that he might be getting towards a meeting in Geneva. But having had a successful warm-up in western Slavonia in May the Croatians were confident of success. They attacked on 4 August and had clearly won within 48 hours. The Croatian Serb army, strong on paper, had been overwhelmed by the fast, US-style thrusts of the new Croatian forces. Our military analysts had called it wrong. They had expected much sterner Serb resistance.

Milosevic and the Yugoslav army did not react. They did

not have time to do so, and the Yugoslav army had problems enough caused by evasion of National Service and scarcity of resources. But there was in any event no indication that Belgrade would intervene in this fight any more than over western Slavonia. The Croatians judged this correctly and I was not surprised. I had been struck during visits to Belgrade how little people there cared about the Krajina – an area a long way from them and certainly not a priority.

A much more intriguing and important question was whether Milosevic would try to defend the last Serb-held area – eastern Slavonia. Some in Croatia wanted to complete the process of "liberation" straightaway and did not believe that Milosevic would or could stop them. Tudjman opted for caution. It is possible that his forces could have overrun eastern Slavonia. We knew that the Croatian Army had been improving fast and the action in Krajina proved that. But the risk of war with the FRY was too great. Tudjman always envisaged that he and Milosevic would decide the future of the area together. A war did not fit into this picture.

The third, and the most important, development was the US initiative for a political settlement. The PM had pressed hard at the London Conference for action. The only avenue open at that point was the recognition package with Milosevic, although this was facing an uphill struggle in view of the lack of Bosnian and US enthusiasm and Milosevic's stalling. It would be much better to return to Plan A if possible. The US proposed precisely that. The initial US presentation in European capitals came from Tony Lake, the National Security Advisor, in mid-August. He was stealing a march on the holidaying Holbrooke. The UK responded positively.

The media were reporting in these early days that the Croatian success in Krajina had simplified the situation and opened the way for a political initiative. I have no doubt that the policy gurus in Washington were saying this. But I suspect that the initiative would have been taken at some point anyway.

Death of Bob Frasure

On 19 August I heard on the radio that Bob Frasure and his colleagues Nelson Drew and Jo Kruzel had been killed when their armoured car fell into a ravine after trying to make way for a French vehicle on the dangerous road over Mount Igman to Sarajevo. Bob was one of the best. In the tough Bosnia business he was always absolutely honest and straightforward. I had last seen him in July in my room in the FCO. He had just spent a weekend visiting old haunts in London. I went with Pauline to Washington for a memorial service for the three on 23 August at Fort Myer, Virginia. President Clinton spoke with warmth and simplicity a ceremony conducted with a sincerity that other nations would find hard to match.

This appalling accident did, I am certain, serve to reinforce US determination to secure a peace settlement. Whatever one might think of Richard Holbrooke he was not a cold man. He had been close by on the Igman road in another vehicle. He was visibly affected by what happened. With the loss of Bob Frasure he took full charge of the negotiating effort himself, leaving John Kornblum temporarily in charge of the European Bureau at the State Department. This meant more ruthless direction. It also meant much less cooperation with the Europeans. The US are never enthusiastic team players. Bob Frasure was the best we could have in that regard, and Holbrooke probably the worst. The Dayton talks could not have succeeded without Holbrooke. Yet if Bob Frasure had been there it would have been a more harmonious and cooperative effort – and I think there would still have been a successful outcome.

Meeting with the Bosnian Serbs at Chevening

It was not clear where our new single negotiator Carl Bildt would fit into the new political process. At his request the UK fixed an unpublicised meeting for him with a Bosnian Serb team at the Foreign Secretary's house Chevening. Malcolm Rifkind wanted reassurance that this was politically safe. I went to see him at the flat at 1 Carlton Gardens on the evening of 24 August. The house was being decorated and the Foreign Secretary was unfamiliar with the flat. I showed him the way to the sitting room! The box of children's bricks there during Douglas Hurd's time had gone.

I was an observer at the Chevening weekend (26-27 August). Carl Bildt was accompanied by his team – General de Lapresle, David Austin and General Chris Elliott. The Serbs were led by Assembly speaker Krajisnik, who had with him General Tolimir, "Foreign Minister " Buha, Lukic and Zametica. The Serbs claimed without any conviction that they had come to hear proposals for a settlement. Bildt made it very clear that was not the game right now. He sought some flexibility on a solution for Sarajevo. Krajisnik brought out all the old maps, offering nothing like enough. Tolimir was particularly hardline.

The Bosnian Serbs could make nothing of this opportunity to get out ahead of the game. That was no surprise. All sides had shown a preference in the end for a solution which they could say was forced upon them. No-one wanted to take responsibility for concessions. The important point about this meeting was to show the Bosnian Serbs that they were being listened to. Once there was a settlement we should want them to sell it to their people.

Air Campaign against the Serbs

The following day was the beginning of the fourth element which set the stage for Dayton. A shell killed 30 people near the market-place in Sarajevo. The response was considered at a meeting of the four Political Directors in Paris the following day, followed by an enlarged Contact Group (the Americans had invited the Italians and Canadians to a meeting in Washington in the margin of the previous week's memorial service and created a precedent).

Neither President Chirac nor the US negotiating team were at this point advocating a massive NATO air campaign. Rod Lyne later told me that No 10 had telephone calls from the Americans and that Holbrooke was at first against air strikes. It took a while before the Americans were singing with one voice. As we saw it the policy was already in place, decided at the London Conference. It was now for NATO and the UN commanders to carry it out.

As I arrived in Geneva on 30 August for a Contact Group meeting with the Islamic Contact Group I heard that the NATO air campaign had begun. The question we asked ourselves at a Cabinet Office meeting on 31 August was how the dogs of war would be called off. There were enough targets only for a couple of weeks. Mladic fed worries about sustaining the policy by saying that the North Vietnamese had withstood years of bombing. Neither this nor any other useful business was dealt with at a meeting of the enlarged Contact Group at Petersberg on Saturday 2 September. This was a media show for Klaus Kinkel in the company of the ever more popular Holbrooke.

The Croatian and Bosnian Armies take the initiative
It took until 14 September for a deal to be worked out in Belgrade to allow the suspension of the air campaign. Meanwhile the damage to Serb communications was severe. The Croatians and Bosnians took advantage on the battlefield. Both armies, particularly the powerful Croatians, moved

forward in western Bosnia. It was for a time unclear whether the Croatians would also take the largest Serb town Banja Luka and/or cut the northern corridor to eastern Bosnia. Either action would have created hundreds of thousands of Serb refugees in addition to those who had recently fled from Krajina.

The Croats appeared in two minds. They held off and the Serb defences rallied. They Croatians may have been persuaded by a combination of the difficulty of the task and the danger of engaging Milosevic's vital interest. The upshot was that by the time of the ceasefire of 5 October the two sides were holding percentages of territory much closer to the 51/49 division. This was a helpful outcome for the US negotiating team, although for a while as the Croatians were sweeping forward and the NATO air strikes continuing some must have been wondering whether the approach should switch to an effort to defeat the Serbs on the battlefield.

The Geneva and New York Agreed Principles

The first text building towards a peace settlement was the Agreed Principles adopted in Geneva on 8 September. In advance of this Milosevic had extracted an agreement from the Bosnian Serbs to accept that he would lead a combined Serb delegation at the peace negotiations. At last he had decided to take charge. The Geneva meeting brought the three Presidents together for the first time since the days of Lord Owen's Bosnia negotiations. The big gain on the Bosnian Government side was that the territorial integrity of Bosnia was accepted. For the Serbs the even bigger gain was acceptance of two entities, one of which would be the Republika Srpska.

The US technique in dealing with the parties was sound. They insisted on having the text tied up before the meeting to avoid complications. On the Serb side they dealt entirely with Belgrade. Milosevic shared little if anything with the Bosnian Serbs.

The meeting also demonstrated how the US were to treat the European members of the Contact Group. We were not shown a text of the principles until the morning of 8 September. We were witnesses to the occasion rather than participants. The outcome was what counted above all for all of us. It could only be achieved through deploying the power of US diplomacy. But it should have been possible for the Americans to bring us into the inside track. We would not have obstructed progress!

The air strikes were suspended on 17 September as I accompanied the Foreign Secretary on a visit to Belgrade. We spent the following morning and afternoon in Sarajevo, including a helicopter trip up to Mount Igman. We were in Zagreb for the evening. One of my tasks was to set up a meeting for the Foreign Secretary with Holbrooke. He tried through his staff to fix it so that Malcolm Rifkind would call on him at his hotel. Typical Holbrooke. He then agreed to come to our Ambassador's residence after the Foreign Secretary's return from a dinner with his Croatian opposite number. He addressed himself to "Malcolm" throughout with barely an exchange with his UK counterpart Pauline Neville-Jones.

The second preparatory meeting with the three parties, this time the Foreign Ministers, was held in New York on 26 September. The plenary lasted for only 30 minutes. The day was largely devoted to US efforts to bring the Bosnian Government to accept the further principles they had worked out. The occasion was an eye-opener for the Americans. They were used to tough bargaining. None are tougher in negotiation than they. But the Bosnian deviousness, even with a superpower, was more than they had reckoned with. They were angry that Foreign Minister Sacirbey had sought to claw back an agreement secured by Warren Christopher at a very early hour of the morning on the telephone with Izetbegovic in Sarajevo.

Once the text had been agreed, Holbrooke spoke on the telephone to the President in Washington who immediately appeared live on television to announce the result. This was the first occasion on which the President had done this. If there were any doubters about US resolve I thought that this day should have convinced them.

European Preparations

On 2 October I went with the Foreign Secretary to Luxembourg for the monthly Foreign Ministers' meeting. It was a depressing affair. A succession of inexpert interventions. No wonder the Americans refused to deal directly with the EU on these matters. Some would argue that the Ministers could not contribute sensibly since they were kept out of the process. But the real problem was a lack of international political vision. After visits to Paris and Vienna I finished the week in Rome for an enlarged Contact Group meeting designed to keep the Italians happy. The Italians hosted it well. It was a largely substance-free occasion. Holbrooke enjoyed poking the Europeans in the eye by referring to the house in Sarajevo where Archduke Ferdinand had been laid out in 1914 – a house "redolent of failure".

In the middle of October we became involved in a scramble for our piece of the Bosnia action. The US had announced that proximity talks would begin at Dayton, Ohio, on 31 October (eventually 1 November) and continue for as long as necessary. We then heard that the US had agreed that the Peace Agreement should then be signed in Paris. No 10 bade Pauline quickly to come up with a UK response. She hit upon the idea of a Peace Implementation Conference (around the end of November and preferably before the French occasion). There was a shower of further meetings to prepare for Dayton. The most substantive and business-like, surprisingly, was in Moscow on 17 October. The Americans were working hard bilaterally to reach agreement on Russian participation in the implementation force IFOR. The Russians insisted on a special arrangement as they would not serve in a NATO-led operation. The circle was squared by a loose subordination of the Russian forces to an American commander outside the NATO framework. I had to draft a telegram after arriving late that evening in Brussels (Ad Hoc Group the following day). The chance to spend another night at the wonderful Ambassador's residence looking over the Moskva to the Kremlin was adequate advance compensation!

The last European coordination meeting was held in Paris on 26 October. We had General Jeremy Mackenzie (Deputy SACEUR) to brief us on IFOR. It was a depressing occasion. There was no coherent lead either from Carl Bildt or any of the three European states. I was not encouraged by this to add to my weariness by making another return trip across the Atlantic for the preparation with the US (on which we had been insisting). Pauline went accompanied by MOD representation.

The EU Foreign Ministers agreed a policy paper on 30 October which the European Three represented at Dayton could take as their broad guideline. My excellent Spanish colleague, Santiago Cabanas, had led the drafting of this (Spain had the Presidency). He consulted me at the very beginning sending an early version to my home personal computer by fax. I cannot convey how revolutionary this use of technology seemed to me in 1993! I could not sufficiently master my new computer to return my comments by the same means. But Santiago took and used the thoughts I passed to him by telephone. The EU can work reasonably on foreign policy issues such as Bosnia when sensible and competent people like Santiago are running things and are making sure that the states most involved in the matters concerned are on board.

The Dayton Peace Conference

I intended to keep a full diary of my time at Wright-Patterson Air Force Base at Dayton, Ohio. This unfortunately lapsed after the first few days. But my recollections remained sharp when I wrote about it five months later. This is not the place for a day-by-day account of the talks. That is better done by the 85 telegrams and other faxes and internal paperwork produced by the UK Delegation. What follows are broad lines and impressions.

The base and our set-up

The delegations representing the non-US Contact Group governments were led by Political Directors. Each was limited by the US to Principal plus seven. This was determined by the bedrooms available. Each of these delegations was allocated one side of a corridor in one of the two-storey blocks usually occupied by visiting officers. The UK was on the first floor with the Germans opposite. Downstairs were the French and Russians. Each delegation had one spare room for use as an office. The Principal had a sitting room adjoining the bedroom. All others had a simple but entirely adequate bedroom only.

I was the number two in our team. The others we nominated at the beginning were Michael Wood (Legal Adviser); Colonel David Leakey (MOD); Matthew Rycroft (from EAU); George Busby (from our Embassy in Belgrade, a Serbian speaker); and two Personal Assistants (Yvonne

Ratcliffe, Pauline's PA who handed over to mine Avril McCallister after ten days, and the Head of EAU's PA Alyson Garden). We had also to accommodate Susan Scholefield (MOD) on our corridor in the first week or so. The MOD, understandably in view of the large force we were preparing to commit, wanted more representation at the discussions on the military implementation annex. The upshot was that the two PAs had to share a room until Susan went home for a few days. When she returned she found accommodation elsewhere on the base and then returned to the corridor a few days before the end when George Busby left.

The Dayton base proved to be a good location. It would not have been the first choice of many. The Americans looked at other more glamorous possibilities on Long Island and in Florida, but the set-up at Dayton was deemed superior. The organisation was first-rate. The accommodation blocks were very close together, making it simple to set up impromptu meetings. There were larger rooms at the Hope Conference

Wright-Patterson Air Force Base

251

Centre which was just five minutes' walk away. It was remote, unglamorous, a place you wouldn't want to spend too long in especially during the drab late autumn of Ohio.

The Hope also supplied food: three large meals a day at the functional cafeteria "Packy's", which was well used by all and provided opportunities to buttonhole people who were otherwise hard to get hold of. Each delegation could whistle up a couple of "vans" to take people off the base. There was tough security on the perimeter, including sniffer dogs. This was sometimes too inflexible. Jacques Blot, head of the French delegation, refused to be searched and was held up for an hour one lunch-time with a European coordination meeting awaiting him inside.

The Americans were rightly concerned that the parties, notably the Bosnian Government, would use the media as a weapon during the talks. One of the ground rules was that the only briefing of the media should be by the State Department spokesman Nick Burns in Washington. This generally held well until the later stages of the talks when breaches mattered less because the process was so far down the road. The media were allowed into the base shortly before the talks began and again at the opening and other ceremonies. There was little incentive to hang around the perimeter of this huge base. The weather was cold and sometimes bitterly cold.

We arrived at Wright-Patterson at 2045 on 31 October and sent the first two telegrams from UKDEL Dayton before the working day ended at 0230. The working hours were longer than they needed to have been. Pauline was brilliant, but effective use of her team's time was not always one of her strengths. The effect of a long succession of days ending always well beyond midnight and sometimes after 0400 followed by a new day at 0730 was to stultify creative thought. Apart from our first weekend at Dayton when there were a few hours at

Packy's

slow pace the activity was non-stop and by no means all of it was necessary. The Germans were not idle, and yet always managed to close their office before we did. Michael Steiner, known as a workaholic, described the UK delegation as "bessessen" (possessed).

Opening Ceremony

The opening ceremony on 1 November was a piece of US stage management. In front of the world's media the Principals walked into the arena one by one introduced by a master of ceremonies like latter-day gladiators. Each had his/her place at a round table in the centre of the room with delegations radiating from the table in pie slices. Izetbegovic tried to put Milosevic at a disadvantage by focussing on "terrorism" in Banja Luka (the US press majored on this and related human rights and War Crimes themes throughout the talks). Milosevic was nettled: he invited anyone who so wished to visit Banja Luka. He maintained that the territorial arrangements were what needed to be settled as the constitutional lines were already set by the Geneva and New York principles. Tudjman highlighted the problem of eastern Slavonia.

The Americans decided to go for the maximum in terms of coverage and specificity in the peace agreement. This was a New-World can-do approach and entirely fitted to the circumstances. What could not be agreed among the parties at Dayton was most unlikely to be agreed elsewhere. The framework of a General Agreement and 11 annexes survived throughout the talks although the content naturally changed in the course of negotiation.

There were two negotiations – among the Contact Group on implementation and with the parties on substance.

Negotiations on Implementation

The intra Contact Group discussion began by focussing on military implementation. This was mostly an issue for the US, UK and France with the Germans present as a lesser but still active player. The Russians had to be brought in later. There were long and difficult discussions picking up from sessions in Washington immediately before Dayton. Lurking in the background was the figure of General Joulwan acting as the top US military figure rather than NATO's SACEUR. Nothing could be agreed without his chop. The imperatives behind his position seemed to be that military implementation should be restricted to straightforwardly military tasks, while insisting at the same time that no activities on the civilian side should be allowed to impinge on the freedom of action of the military commanders.

The French had one card to play on this – namely that their

historic agreement to become fully integrated into this NATO operation could be withdrawn if the US did not allow a proper mandate for the High Representative who, the EU believed, should be the central figure in civilian implementation. Jacques Blot made this point in explosive style. The US may have thought this a bluff but I suspect that they could not afford to ignore it in view of the high stakes involved. The issue was not resolved in the military annex (Annex 1A) but left for the discussion of civilian implementation (Annex 10).

Annex 10 was a protracted negotiation. The US had produced a first draft before Dayton. This envisaged a Senior Implementation Co-ordinator (SICOR) who would pull together the work of the various players on the civilian side. The individual involved would have a lowly status compared with the mighty Commander of IFOR. This did not fit in with the European concept, originating with the French, of an authoritative High Representative who should be a European in view of the overwhelmingly European input and the US command of the military operation (although the Europeans were making the majority contribution to this too).

On the way out to Dayton I had a go at drafting a new Annex 10. The Europeans insisted that this, rather than the US draft, should be the basis for discussion (not unreasonable as we were working on US drafts in most other areas). Our draft sought to give the High Representative a role in monitoring the overall implementation of the peace settlement and the authority to call meetings with the IFOR Commander to resolve questions where their competencies overlapped.

We were not helped in this negotiation by a US turf battle which gave the lead on civilian implementation to Bob Gallucci while on other matters the political lead lay with the European Bureau at State. Gallucci was new to Yugoslavia (having come from earning considerable credit dealing with North Korea) and unaware of the history of the linked negotiation on military implementation. He shuttled between Dayton and Washington, causing the negotiation to be even further stretched out.

We were also not helped by the backseat driving of General Joulwan. He baulked at giving the civilian coordinator a role in "overall monitoring" even though it had been precisely this language which had been agreed at NATO. After days of argument (including Pauline on the phone to Joulwan) we settled on "monitoring"! The arrangements for coordination between the military commander and the civilian coordinator were even more difficult, with Joulwan refusing to accept anything which might hint that the Military were not all powerful. A compromise had eventually to be reached. But a lot of bad blood was unnecessarily created along the way. Jacques Blot was fierce and brought Paris into action with demarches in Washington. Wolfgang Ischinger, of wonderfully calm temperament, made it clear that the Europeans would not give way.

Potentially most serious of all, Carl Bildt was so outraged by the US performance that he looked to be walking away from the post of High Representative for which he was the only candidate. Without him the European concept of civilian implementation would be in deep trouble. Increasingly we were seeking as best we could to tailor the mandate to fit him. He was particularly offended by the behaviour of Joulwan. He once said during a negotiating session, in his typically understated way (although he was clearly very angry), that as a former Prime Minister he could not understand that a military officer was being allowed to dictate a political agreement: in Sweden such a general would have been banished to look after one of the outer islands. It took all Pauline's persuasive power with support from London to prevent him from making a firm decision that he would not take the job.

I had some doubts whether such a senior politician however talented was right for the job as it came to be specified. Carl Bildt said at that time that he envisaged spending a good proportion of his time travelling internationally and made it clear that he would need an office in Brussels as well as in Sarajevo. This gave rise to the question whether he would also be able to tackle the everyday issues on the ground.

The Americans saw an opening here to keep their SICOR (who would of course be an American) as the man in charge in theatre while the High Representative carried out international duties. This would have been hopeless since the High Representative would only have authority if he were the man responsible on the ground. The Germans were angling for the post of Senior Deputy to be written into the Agreement (this was Steiner's undeclared bid – he eventually secured just this title but only once out in the field in the New Year). The eventual text left the issue of staff structure to the High Representative, which was as it should be.

Another tricky aspect of this issue was the appointment of the High Representative. The Americans would not allow him to be established by the UN, as the French would have preferred and we would have been happy with. In the end the parties called in the text for the appointment of the High Representative. It was understood that the appointment would be made by the London Peace Implementation Conference.

Of the rest of the negotiations on the civilian side, the most important and difficult were on the Constitution (in which Michael Wood became deeply involved, impressing all in this and other matters by his competence and imagination) and the elections. The conundrum in the Constitution was how to give substance to the blocking mechanism promised to each party in the Agreed Principles while at the same time encouraging the system to work. The best which could be done was to bring the Constitutional Court into the picture to determine whether a vital interest was at stake which could justify use of the blocking mechanism.

On the elections, the US wanted the OSCE Mission with an American in charge to run the elections, to ensure these took place properly and did not hinder the withdrawal of US troops at the end of the year as the President had promised Congress. The Europeans insisted that the parties should take more responsibility than this for their elections. The upshot was agreement that there should be a Provisional Election Commission, including the parties, to supervise the elections. The Americans tried nonetheless to bounce us with a new draft of the elections annex right at the end of the talks. Wolfgang Ischinger made it clear (and it came best from the "favourite" European) that Germany would not put up with this. The Americans backed off.

We were all uncomfortable with the police annex (Annex 11). With the military restricting their role there would clearly be a gap when it came to civil order, freedom of movement. The US focussed on this only in the run-up to Dayton. For a while they talked of the possibility of an intrusive Haiti-style police operation. But they were not themselves prepared to head up and man such an operation. I think they appreciated our view that their concept would not work in Bosnia. The only source of large numbers of police would be UNCIVPOL and then significant numbers would only be volunteered if the mandate was seen as practicable by the sending states. So the police role was limited to an Assistance mission, training and monitoring the police forces in the new Bosnia. The Americans did not like this, and we agreed that there would be problems. But it would have been wrong to expect of international police a security role, which really only the military were equipped for.

Negotiations with the parties

The Americans kept the Contact Group at arm's length from the core of the negotiation with the parties, involving us closely only when they needed help or our agreement. This was evidently the way Holbrooke wanted to play it. His staff was, presumably on instructions, uncommunicative. This had the effect of cementing solidarity and cooperation between the Europeans and to a surprising degree with the Russians too.

The Americans began with the parties focussing on the constitutional aspects and leaving the map on one side. It was soon apparent that there were two obstacles to be overcome before the Bosnia negotiation could be brought to closure.

The first was the future of the Bosniac/Croat Federation. This was to be one of the two entities of the new Bosnia. But the two parties were at loggerheads about the relationship it should have with the central government and how power should be shared. Without a functioning Federation the Dayton blueprint could not work. The Bosnian Government insisted on progress before allowing the overall negotiation to proceed further.

Holbrooke delegated the Federation negotiation to Michael Steiner. He sensibly concentrated on the fundamentals gaining agreement to a definition of the respective responsibilities of the Federation and central governments, and a timetable for implementation. An initialling ceremony was held on 9 November with the press invited in for the event. I doubt anyone believed that this agreement would be properly carried out any more than its many predecessors. But it was enough to be going on with. For the Croats it was important to show that the Dayton talks were not just a matter of sorting out the differences between the Muslims and Serbs. The Croats later achieved their most important aim of being recognised as a constituent people.

The second obstacle was Eastern Slavonia. The risk of war there upsetting any deal on Bosnia was clear for all to see. Tudjman insisted on the resolution of the problem. Milosevic's drive for a Bosnia settlement forced him to drop his customary hands-off attitude towards Croatia issues. Yet the deal had also to have the agreement of the local Serb leadership. The US Ambassador in Croatia, Galbraith, and Thorvald Stoltenberg talked in theatre. Stoltenberg had with him in the later stages at his request an FCO officer, Julian Braithwaite, who acted as an adviser and a two-way channel of communication. Julian contacted me regularly in Dayton. On 5 November he rang me on my mobile phone as we were at dinner at a Dayton Chinese restaurant "Shades of Jade" and he had just arrived in Belgrade in the small hours. His enthusiasm for the task still came through.

The text which Galbraith and Stoltenberg were pushing became too difficult to nail down. The exigencies of Dayton nonetheless demanded some agreement. The answer was to strip the text, putting the weight on a transitional period of UN administration. The Agreement was signed on 12 November. I do not know on what understandings between Milosevic and Tudjman, if any, this agreement was built. The FRY claimed that the next stage, an agreement on normalisation of relations, was also settled and that this included an understanding that Croatia would give the FRY the strategically important Prevlaka peninsula in return for land above Dubrovnik. If that is so Milosevic made an error in not closing the deal there and then. Tudjman discovered on his return home after Dayton that surrendering Prevlaka was difficult to sell domestically and backed off.

There were a lot of questions left unanswered by the Basic Agreement on Eastern Slavonia which caused plenty of trouble in the weeks ahead. But it was enough to clear the way for the Bosnia negotiation. Coincidentally on Sunday 12 November the widows of Frasure, Kruzel and Drew visited Dayton. I had the opportunity for a good talk with Bob Frasure's widow. Amazingly she recalled my name. Her dignity and belief in the Bosnia peace effort were inspiring. She had a particularly long meeting with President Milosevic. I like to think that this hard and ruthless man had been genuinely attracted by Bob's personality and had been touched by his death.

The Dayton end game

The stage was set for the denouement. Warren Christopher came to Dayton for a big push on 14 November. It did not work. The Bosnian Government said they were not convinced the Americans would deploy their troops. An outsider hearing some of the rhetoric from Congress might have believed this. But the US had committed itself to a troop presence in Bosnia to implement an agreement and could not back out. In reality I suspect that the Bosnian Government considered there were more concessions to be had. They were right.

The US delegation then sought to gear up the process for a deal at the weekend. Christopher returned on Friday 18 November. This was billed as the final effort. We all doubted that the talks could be extended beyond Thanksgiving the following Thursday at the very latest.

The key as in all Bosnia negotiations was the map. Serious talking on this did not start until the second half of the Dayton negotiations. The Americans were unwilling to put down a concept of their own. When the negotiation on the documents officially ended at midnight on Saturday 18 November, the map was still far from agreed. The greatest difficulty was of course Sarajevo. The Americans had run through a number of variations, even exploring the idea of a Brussels-style solution whereby an undivided Sarajevo would be in effect a third entity.

The news on the morning of Monday 20 November was gloomy. Milosevic and Silajdzic had agreed on a map during the night, but Granic had objected when he saw it and Izetbegovic had pulled the plug. Pauline and I bumped into Izetbegovic and Silajdzic on a walk nearby (all the Yugoslavs – most notably the FRY – conducted their sensitive internal discussions in the open air, assuming I suppose that their accommodation was bugged). She then had a phone call on her mobile from the Foreign Secretary seeking news as we walked around the golf course on a bright chilly morning. The tension was palpable. All the Allied big guns, including President Clinton, had already been deployed to speak on the telephone especially to Izetbegovic. Surely this stubborn man would not hold out when so much, in particular a US troop presence, was on offer?

In the afternoon I met Simonovic, the Croatian Vice Foreign Minister outside the Croatian block. He told me that the Croatians were offering a deal whereby they would give up more land to the Serbs around Glamoc and the Posavina and the Muslims would cede some in the Ozren. But as we went to bed there was still no deal.

The final breakthrough on the morning of 21 November was achieved by Milosevic who evidently decided that he would do whatever was necessary to secure an agreement. I saw him early in the morning with one aide standing in a snow flurry waiting outside the US block adjacent to ours. He was ushered in by Holbrooke's wife. He gave away more in Sarajevo than was ever thought likely, so that the city would be united within the Federation. He reportedly told Silajdzic that the Muslims deserved to have Sarajevo after suffering the siege. In return he insisted that the Serbs had to be found enough land to give them 49%. He also conceded on a number of minor points in other documents so that the deal could go through.

The initialling ceremony was held in the afternoon of 21 November. The Bosnian Serbs were absent. Pressure had been applied on Krajisnik, leader of the Bosnian Serb team, to initial it. But the map must have been a nightmare for him. He is said to have had some kind of seizure when he saw it! The final European battle was to secure a place for our principals and not just Carl Bildt at the table on the dais. It reflects on the US dismissal of our role that there should have been any question about this. The mood at the ceremony was a suitable mixture of satisfaction and sobriety in the face of the daunting challenge of implementation.

We took a flight home that evening from Cincinnati. My last contact with the parties was at the airport. Mo Sacirbey, who had at one point been ostracised for allegedly smuggling a girlfriend in as a member of the German delegation, came up to me and asked whether I had heard that Milosevic had

Before the initialling ceremony

Map of the division of Bosnia

withdrawn his agreement. For a split second I was beginning to take this in before realising that I was being taken in.

It was wonderful after three weeks to be leaving and to have the prospect of seeing Judy and the children again. On arriving home at 1030 the next day I found a letter from the Foreign Office Honours Section saying that I had been put forward for inclusion in the New Year's Honours list – a CMG. I told Judy but no-one else.

Peace Implementation Conference, Lancaster House London, 8-9 December

This was Pauline Neville-Jones's creation. The idea was to create structures to govern the political arrangements for

Bosnia and to consider how work would be taken forward on the remaining issues from the break-up of Yugoslavia. The British team worked on the idea at Dayton where she insisted we should do a lot of the spade work. She spent most of an afternoon and evening drafting a paper sitting at the word processor with my PA Alyson Garden. We had to think through how to make the PIC membership comprehensive including a wide range of states and organisations but also to invent a Steering Board to ensure the key players could get things done. The PIC was a superb achievement for which Pauline has not been given all the credit she deserves.

During Dayton, the FCO was faced with decisions on how much it should risk spending to ensure that the Conference could be staged properly soon after a peace agreement, while aware that there was no guarantee this timing would work. Our advice from Dayton was eagerly sought every morning in the final stages of the negotiations. In the end the FCO had to commit to some hundreds of thousands of pounds of expenditure to keep open our options. The gamble paid off.

The focus of our preparation in the run-up was the Conference Document which, unlike the July Conference, we wanted to have adopted by the participants. The crunch day was Wednesday 5 December. We sat down in Pauline's room at 1030 to start the redrafting process. We first had a general look at the structure. Then experts on the various aspects were invited in. It took until 0100 to produce a version which Pauline was prepared to issue to the rest of the G8. At the time I thought that this painful procedure had been unnecessary. But looking back it was a crucial effort which ensured that we had a good enough document to make agreement possible, and to earn considerable foreign admiration, at the Conference itself. I learned a lot.

Following this work in London, there was a G8 preparatory

meeting in Brussels. There was not all that much of a response to our hard work. The occasion was more memorable for the return journey. I spurned the offer of a lift on the Foreign Secretary's plane to Northolt for a commercial flight to Gatwick (just 10 minutes from home). The 1840 British Airways flight was loaded and ready to leave when it was announced that the first officer had slipped on the ice outside, injured herself and been declared unfit to fly. We were rebooked on a Sabena departure to Heathrow which arrived there at 2100. It then took 4 hours by taxi to come through the traffic on the M25 and M23 which was obstructed by broken-down vehicles whose drivers a sudden cold snap had taken by surprise. And I am usually a lucky traveller!

On the day preceding the Conference the Americans came in with a list of amendments, some of them described as deal-breakers. They were not heard with great sympathy. The treatment meted out to the Europeans at Dayton was fresh in our memory. The US team of officials was led by Bob Gallucci. Holbrooke did not show.

Surprisingly, the Conference began on schedule at 1600 on Friday 8 December. This depended on the prompt arrival of a flight which we laid on from the OSCE Foreign Ministerial meeting in Budapest. Prime Minister John Major made an impressive and forceful introduction. The Foreign Secretary chaired. He gave the large cast little opportunity to hinder the acclamation of Carl Bildt as High Representative. The objective of the day was achieved. Carl Bildt said to me in passing that "it was all our fault", meaning the shape of the role he was take on and how it would be governed. The task was full of difficulties. But I don't know how better we could have swung the international community behind the High Representative.

We worked on the Conference Document into the night.

I arrived home at 0400. I was up again at 0630. I helped out at a meeting in the margin on Eastern Slavonia from 0900 to 1100; Sir Nicholas Bonsor chaired. There was little we could do except to highlight the issues and exhort action. Having pressed for the Basic Agreement the US was doing nothing at that stage to implement it.

The rest of the day was a whirl as we accommodated changes to the document where we could and fought off others. It came together for a finish at 1730. The Foreign Secretary gave a kind-sounding reception to a series of speakers in a final session who wanted further changes. He allowed none and brought down the gavel sharply to end the Conference.

At the end I wondered how much the Conference would be remembered. It was essential to give the many organisations involved in civilian implementation an understanding of how the whole affair could work. It was essential to appoint the High Representative and create the new PIC Steering Board to support and guide him. It was necessary to wind up the old ICFY and make provision for a continuation of some of its tasks, notably Kosovo and succession issues, under the PIC. But it was probably not such a seminal event as the July Conference which decisively changed the international military policy towards the Serbs.

The next stop was Paris on 13 December for the lead-in to the signature of the Bosnia Peace Agreement on the following day. In fact it was the fine setting of Royaumont near Chantilly: the conference was transferred from Paris because of the transport strike there. The Contact Group Ministers touched hands with the OIC Contact Group Ministers and then the French held a first meeting on a new Balkan Stability Pact process. The Dayton texts were signed in Paris on 14

December in the company of Heads of State and Foreign Ministers.

The Germans had their turn in the post-Dayton action on 18 December at Petersberg. There was a meeting of the Four Political Directors in the afternoon after the main business – setting the tramlines for the arms control process agreed at Dayton. The evening was the occasion of the first get-together of the PIC Steering Board. After an early morning visit to the Embassy in Bonn to dictate telegrams, I went back to London with Pauline. She was emotional having heard glowing farewell tributes from so many people and in particular from Foreign Minister Kinkel. I could understand her refusal to become Ambassador at Bonn when she had set her heart on Paris and achieved so much on Bosnia.

Last things on Former Yugoslavia

Starting 1996 I had to find enough useful work to occupy me for some weeks while my next post was being decided. There were a number of highlights. First, I signed off at the EU Ad Hoc Group at the January and February meetings. The Group had been my introduction to the new Common Foreign and Security Policy and helped me to understand the possibilities and limits of European cooperation at this time of the EU's development.

Second, I had the opportunity to make a final visit to Sarajevo on 18 January, accompanying new Political Director Jeremy Greenstock on a Contact Group visit. It was a first effort to remind the parties, in this case the Muslims, of their obligations to carry out the Dayton provisions to the letter.

The occasion had added spice as it was Holbrooke's farewell visit there. To some extent the rest of the Contact Group served as extras in the backdrop to his visit: hence the refusal of the French Political Director to participate. We travelled on a US C17 from Frankfurt airbase. Holbrooke invited the other principals one by one for individual audiences. The most memorable of the meetings in Sarajevo was a briefing from "Stuffy" Leighton Smith, Commander IFOR, and Holbrooke's attempt to get him to toe his line! We were ferried to Rome in the evening where the Europeans were joining a meeting of EU Foreign Ministers. I dictated my telegram at Hotel "Lord Byron" and left early the following morning.

Third, I went with Judy, James and Katy to Buckingham Palace on 23 February for my investiture in the Order of St Michael and St George (CMG). Afterwards, we had some champagne with EAU so I could thank them for their help. Jeremy Greenstock held a farewell reception for me on 29 February.

Don't read the next two paragraphs if family history bores you!

A few years later, looking into family history, I discovered a diplomat, a half first cousin three times removed – Hammond Smith Shipley – who was awarded the CMG in 1896, exactly a hundred years before me, for his work as British Delegate on the Sassoun Commission which looked into the alleged Turkish massacres of Armenians of August-September 1894, one of the vexed foreign-policy question of the day just as Bosnia was in the first half of the 1990s.

He wrote:

"The Armenians were massacred without distinction of age or sex...it is not too much to say they were absolutely hunted down like wild beasts, being killed wherever they met;" (British Blue Book, Turkey, No. I, Part I, p. 206).

After receiving the CMG,
Buckingham Palace, 1996

To me he does not seem a distant kinsman. A central figure in my family history is my great-great-great-grandmother Mary (née) Dexter. I am descended from the union with her first husband, Samuel Squire (Squire was my mother's maiden name). Samuel Squire died at 25 in a workplace accident. Mary married again, to John Shipley, an enterprising man active in Nottingham's vibrant textile industry. A daughter, Mary Squire Shipley, ended up maid to an Austrian countess, married an Irish vet in Vienna and died an old lady in Russia as the Foreign Office were trying to extricate her from Jaroslavl north of Moscow in the chaos following the Revolution. A son, Hammond (a Shipley family Christian name) Shipley, somehow married a lady of a well-to-do family with the result that their two sons, far from going into service like their aunt, studied at Oxford University in the 1880s. The younger, Arthur Granville Shipley, became an Anglican clergyman; the elder, Hammond Smith (his mother's maiden name) Shipley became a career diplomat. He served in remote places, mostly in the old Ottoman

Empire and including what became Yugoslavia, as well as Persia. He retired in 1918 on a Foreign Office pension and died in 1930 in Pontefract where his brother was vicar. He did not marry and has no descendants. His brother's only child was killed at 21 in World War I. Mary Squire Shipley and other siblings similarly have no living descendants. But I have been forunate to be given a photo by another distant cousin.

Retrospective on Former Yugoslavia

I was in the right place at the right time. I wanted to head a department to work on a front-rank policy issue. I was given my chance. I became immersed in former Yugoslavia policy but still able to maintain some emotional detachment. The

Hammond Smith Shipley

271

pace and excitement bowled me along. Once I felt sufficiently confident after the first few months I started to travel abroad to promote the international diplomacy aspect of the role. I felt I could never tire of European and transatlantic trips. Just as well given what was to come in my final jobs in the Service.

What about the fate of the region? Richard Holbrooke said at the end of the Dayton Conference that he feared the huge effort made to achieve an agreement by the US superpower (and allies) might have only delivered the most expensive ceasefire in history. Despite all the problems since, it has been a lot more than that. There are tensions and not enough reconciliation and co-operation between the two entities in Bosnia. But there is no war. You can travel freely around the country. The economy is weak but people are living much better than 20 years ago.

I was asked why the Dayton Conference did not also try to settle the disputes over Kosovo and other issues arising from the break-up of former Yugoslavia. With the world, led by the US superpower, focussed on the region at Dayton should not advantage have been taken to force solutions on all outstanding matters? It's a tempting argument and had some traction at the time. On the other hand, where people had been dying in large numbers was Bosnia. It was going to be difficult enough to force a settlement to that. Getting Milosevic also to concede on Kosovo, part of the territory of the Serbian state, would be hugely difficult if not impossible. The effort of trying to achieve this would make it more difficult to achieve a solution for Bosnia.

As for Kosovo, war came in 1999 and led to the toppling of Milosevic. It proved to be the last large-scale western military intervention in the region.

The end state in the region needs to include all these

states – Bosnia, Serbia, Montenegro, Kosovo, Macedonia and Albania – in the European Union in some form. That needs more time and western care and attention. It will not be easy as the tide within the EU in favour of enlargement is past the flood and is ebbing.

PART III

DIRECTOR PERSONNEL

Foreign Secretary Jack Straw asked me over from my office in the Old Admiralty Building across Horse Guards' Parade into his grand office in the main building in King Charles Street to talk about the budget for Personnel. One of his staff put his head round the door and said "Alan, Craig Murray is looking for you." "Ok, say I'll be back in my office shortly.""No. He says he's been there. He's now outside here wanting to see you." "He'll have to wait a bit". When I eventually came out he was gone. It certainly wasn't usual for staff to lie in wait uninvited outside the Foreign Secretary's office. Craig Murray moved on to a higher level. He ran as a candidate for Jack Straw's Blackburn constituency at the following general election.

Another dilemma. What do we do if our man on Tristan da Cunha won't leave the island when his successor arrives? There's only a ship there every 6 weeks.

People behaved differently towards me when I became the Director of Personnel in the FCO in early 2002, eventually with a seat on the FCO Management Board too. Some grand folk in the Service who had hitherto not taken much care in their relationship with me became solicitous. Others railed against me about the unfairness of it all, not granting them the posting of their dreams. I held on to the thought that it wasn't me they were reacting to or against: it was my function.

I dislike the term Human Resources. People are human

beings, and not to be classified with inanimate inputs – office equipment or buildings or cash. In teacher training I learned not to talk of pupils as A-level or whatever "material". I wasn't going to have the true treasure of the Foreign Office – its staff – relegated to being bits of material.

I changed my mind about a lot of things! First was the decision to take the job of Director Personnel in the first place. I was approached in late August 2001, after the incumbent Denise Holt had been selected as Ambassador at Mexico City and wanted a successor by Christmas. Christopher Hum, the Chief Clerk (Deputy Under Secretary for the Administration) spoke to me first. Fair enough. I told him when I started as Director South East Europe after returning to London from Berlin in late 2000 that I had an interest in FCO corporate issues. Then Denise spoke to me about the job, most eloquently but also in a measured way. Finally John Kerr, the Permanent Under Secretary, invited me in. I thought about it, and then declined.

I wasn't sure it was right for me to move away from foreign policy jobs, and I wanted to build on my restart on the Balkans to produce a blinding second year of achievement before abolishing the position altogether. 2001 had been fascinating, especially work to forestall a conflict in Macedonia.

John Kerr pointed out that there were no other suitable Director-level jobs on the horizon. I replied that things had a habit of turning up and I was sure something would over the next year – a point he acknowledged.

A few days later I made an about-turn. It was after all an opportunity, which would not recur, to branch out into a different area. The job had a well-defined area of responsibility. I would have a lot of scope. I would not suffer the frustration of more senior people crowding my space as did the Political Director on Regional Directors whenever there were big-ticket regional issues. I felt I'd regret not striking down this path. I was selected, with the blessing of the PUS-designate, Michael Jay, then still Ambassador in Paris – my favourite PUS (alongside David Gillmore, who allowed the BBC Panorama team freedom to film what they wanted to make the excellent programme True Brits showing diplomats at work home and abroad).

From Personnel to Human Resources

So how did I end up changing the name to Human Resources? The great thing about working in the Administration is the opportunity to change things. I inherited from my predecessor papers documenting ideas about how Personnel could change for the better. In other organisations, in the public and private sectors, Personnel was becoming leaner and using technology better, freeing up resources for the front line. Gut feel: standing still was not an option!

This both enthused and worried me. Enthused, because there might be a project here where I could really make things better. Worried, because I didn't understand where it might lead and wanted above all things to avoid a lot of effort which only succeeded in moving the deckchairs on board the ship. Change projects don't have a good track record in the FCO. I left the papers in the too-difficult tray and gave myself time to find out what Personnel really did.

I have a need to reduce complex issues to a coherent picture I can see before my eyes and which I can communicate to others in simple terms. In time it came to me that the key was to think of Personnel in terms of service delivery. I had entered for the first time a field in which I wasn't developing/delivering FCO objectives but supporting the FCO in doing this. It followed that we should deliver a service to give that support. Otherwise how could we justify our existence? Sounds obvious, but Personnel can end up doing things for all sorts of other reasons, not least the management fashion of the day. I needed this simple idea as an anchor and yardstick to deal with the array of ideas people would have on what we should do – ideas which would inevitably point in several different directions.

The starting point was to conduct a Review of Service Delivery in Personnel Directorate. I needed the right person to lead it. Until then I was not sure it was worth going ahead.

I had a stroke of luck. One day in early summer 2002 Andy Heyn, Head of Personnel Management Unit 1 (which dealt with the European side of the Office), presented himself. He was interested in the idea, interested in project work, wanted a new challenge and saw this as a development opportunity towards gaining promotion to the Senior Management Structure.

The start was slow. I wondered whether, as in other areas of work in Personnel, this would be a case of plenty of effort without an end product. It didn't turn out that way. Andy brought in Susan Frew, also from Personnel Management. He also found the right consultancy: people from Cap Gemini Ernst and Young who understood they were dancing to a tune whose big themes were already composed and who were there to help the development of these rather than to strike out in any new direction. You can tell I am sceptical about the use of management consultants.

I set Andy three objectives in the Review: to devise a better service for the FCO; to devise a better service for individual officers; and to make the best use of new technology coming on stream (particularly the new Management Information system Prism which was being developed at that time, and the new Intranet we were promised). It soon became clear, as the FCO's finances worsened, that there was an underlying fourth objective – to do all this and make savings in Personnel.

At a formative time in this process, 5 February 2002, I joined a group visit of HR Directors organised by the Whitehall & Industry Group to the IBM European centre for HR located near Portsmouth. IBM had revolutionised their HR operation, on the back of criticism that it was not relevant to business needs. The most immediately striking aspect was their "Ask HR" service for staff. This was a single phone number for everyone in their European theatre to ring with any enquiry about HR. Front-line operators would either answer direct or would pass to experts while keeping track of the enquiry and ensuring it was answered within a specified time. There were surveys to measure customer satisfaction. A second point was the development of a brilliant intranet on which staff could themselves find many of the answers they were seeking. The front-line operators would often refer enquirers to the intranet, with the idea that eventually more staff would get used to the idea of helping themselves. All sounds obvious in 2015. It wasn't to me in 2002.

Andy and Susan never deviated from pursuing the objectives I set. They conducted a review by visiting other organisations and asking people in the FCO what they thought, including servicing a Steering Group of people from the FCO outside Personnel who had ideas of their own and hankered after a wider review, which risked in my view losing the tight focus of improving service delivery.

After the Review came the proposals. The big-ticket items were: to create HR Managers located within the front-line Directorates to give direct advice and support to managers; and to create HR Direct (the FCO version of IBM's Ask HR) to deal with all enquiries from individuals. The FCO Board agreed to this in March 2003.

Implementing this meant dismantling structures and

working practices to which staff in Personnel and the wider FCO had become accustomed. We set about abolishing the Personnel Management Units, which had comprised 60 to 70 people dealing with both managerial and individual issues. Most controversially it meant taking away from staff an individual personnel officer responsible for giving them career advice and shepherding them through the boarding process as they changed jobs in the Service. This, we found during the benchmarking process with other organisations, was a system unique to the FCO. Views on its merits were divided. The Personnel Management Officers themselves, as Andy and Sue knew from direct experience, were maids of all work answering enquiries on every conceivable issue and risked being mistresses of none.

The toughest part was taking away jobs, particularly in the PMUs, and getting the right people into the new ones. In June/July 2003 I chaired internal selection boards for the new jobs. There was a fair bit of grumbling about undue speed. But most of this subsided pretty quickly and the plus point for staff was that they could quickly see where they were going.

The next step was to train people for their new roles. In some cases this involved also a thinking-through of what would and would not be offered (for example, the new careers team of 7 people for the whole Service would focus on giving careers advice to new entrants). It was not always an easy process getting the staff to work out the detail of how things would be done in the new structure rather than looking to me and the Review Team to give them the answers. But it did happen. There were some tremendous awaydays. It was a joy to see some individuals taking advantage of this opportunity to create new ways of doing things.

The Review was implemented on time and on budget. It went fully into operation on 21 January 2004 with the opening of HR Direct and the full functioning of the HR Managers. Both these innovations got off to a flying start, thanks to the enthusiasm of the staff.

We weren't helped by the technology. Prism failed to deliver on time. Although no-one would admit it openly and we all tried to sing a happy tune, the project was in difficulties at an early stage owing to unanticipated pressure for over-complicated processes for security reasons. We were also completely reliant on outside consultants not only to develop the system but to remain for years to come in the background ensuring it remained operational. Unhealthy. By then it was too late to go back to the drawing board.

The concept of Prism was wonderful – bringing personnel, payroll, finance and procurement together in an integrated system. In practice the extra complications forced on us meant compromises in what it would deliver for us, a loss in workforce savings, delay and the risk that we'd have terrible problems getting it to work efficiently. The Project Team worked its socks off nonetheless to deliver a system and we all talked up Prism while being increasingly aware of its defects. It was a classic "I wouldn't start from here" situation, but we felt we had no choice but to keep on buggering on and to make the best of it. Later, when I was No 2 in Washington, I was probed by the visiting Foreign Affairs Committee about Prism. By that time I was able to say that we had got it to work.

The new Intranet also failed to deliver on time.

The upshot of being let down by these two projects was that the new HR Directorate structure had to operate with workarounds.

Yes, HR Directorate. I did change the name.

In the end I concluded – to the amusement of colleagues and the Permanent Under Secretary who knew my view about the term HR – that my personal objection was getting in the way. Nearly all Whitehall Departments and most of the wider public as well as the private sector used the term (some had moved on to "Human Capital Development" – but that was no better!). The Personnel Directors' Group led from the Cabinet Office by Alice Perkins had been renamed the HR Directors' Group. It was important for the FCO to counteract our image of being stuck-in-the mud: I wanted to make a contribution to this in my area. In short, adopting the term HR helped to convey the modern approach I felt the outcome of the Review was giving us. What's in a name!

I was sometimes asked about the change of name in the briefings I gave on the changes in London and at posts abroad. I told it like it was.

Visits abroad

His Excellency The Governor (of an Overseas Territory)
I was determined not to become desk-bound by the huge amount of process in HR, particularly meetings. I needed to see colleagues in their working environment in UK and abroad so that I had the context in which to do my bit. I thought it important they had the chance also to see me (and complain). So I made time for travel. Not that it was a hard decision. Days of wall-to-wall meetings in London were not an unalloyed joyful prospect.

The first outing was for a Heads of Andean Missions' Conference in Caracas in late April 2002. The highlight was a visit on the way out there to Grand Cayman. I wanted to find out about the work in the Overseas Territories: Cayman offered itself as relatively accessible. What did a Governor do?

Peter Smith, the Governor, was happy for me to come even though he was in the last ten days of his posting and about to retire from the Service. What I saw was a job which ranged from being the local celebrity and attending events at parish-pump level to dealing with policy on international finance working with Whitehall. The Governor had a very small personal staff and yet big responsibilities working through or with (which is it?) the local government. This brought home to me the dilemma that the UK wants these remnants of Empire as far as possible to run themselves (the age of colonialism is long dead and these places too would be independent if they were viable as states and wanted to go that way). But the UK is responsible for the territories and has to carry the can if things go wrong, for example in financial transactions. So we do need a measure of control – rights to go with the responsibilities.

The risk is that the Governor will find himself in an impossible position – blamed for everything by the locals but without the powers and the support from London to do the job properly. Having said all that, what great jobs! How few people know about them, including in the FCO.

I asked Peter Smith what had been his greatest challenge. He said it had been when the prison had burned down and the inmates had escaped. He had had to beg the Metropolitan Police to come out and help!

What a place! The Governor's House was on the beach, just a few steps from the most wonderful warm turquoise sea (I went for a swim at first light – around 0630). A huge cruise ship was at anchor outside the harbour (too big to land). I was told that such vessels catered for the newly-wed, the over-fed and the nearly-dead. Wonderful seafood. The people so relaxed to someone coming from the hurly-burly of London. That, too, is life in the FCO.

There are big challenges in all these territories. I'll say more about the Falkland Islands, Bermuda, and Turks and Caicos later on. How about Gibraltar? Selecting the Governor there is a key task. The position has often been held by a former military person or someone with military experience. What about Montserrat, where much of the island was devastated by the volcano?

I went to Brussels, Berlin and Washington. Staff at big posts in the developed world often have special issues. They are not always seen as friendly places to work. But most of my time was spent in more difficult environments. I concentrated on places where there were big challenges and where there were selection decisions coming up on new Heads of Mission.

On the Front Line

First to Saudi Arabia, arriving in Riyadh on 3 October 2002. Riyadh is a unique place to serve. The city is as modern in many ways as you can get. Good shopping and healthcare. A lot of it looked American. Life in the diplomatic quarter was comfortable. The housing was good; childcare was inexpensive and readily available; the club offered a swimming pool and sports facilities. Getting out to the desert was a joy. But it was alien, even for those used to other parts of the Arab world. For women there were the issues of having to cover up when in town and not being allowed to drive.

Staff are made aware of what it is like before they are posted to such places. As I discovered, some take to it and see the good parts as a bonus; others are negative. The contrast was between those who wanted to leave as soon as possible and were counting the days and one couple who had been in Jedda and Riyadh and wanted to complete the set by serving in Al-Khobar, our third post in the country (I visited all three on this trip).

I offered to make a small contribution from the HR budget towards a scheme to make a driver available to women who didn't have their own, so that all women had flexibility to go out of the diplomatic quarter under their own steam and did not have to rely on their spouses. It was no more than a gesture, and only for one year. But it was appreciated. It is important to show that the Centre listens.

Not far in the background were concerns about security. The Embassy building and the living accommodation relied a great deal on restrictions to access to the whole diplomatic quarter, which looked to me by no means watertight. Only a few months after I visited there was a bomb attack on another compound which also damaged the wonderful British school I saw. It felt like a place where something awful could happen, and all the more dangerous because daily life seemed so comfortable.

There came a moment in late 2002 and early 2003 when it unclear whether we had strong candidates to replace our Ambassador Derek Plumbly, our leading Arabist at the time, at the end of his tour of duty. We needed someone who could motivate staff in these difficult circumstances as well as fulfil the highly important role of the Ambassador on the political and commercial fronts. The Riyadh job was counted among the weightiest Ambassadorships (rating higher than, for example, Rome). I thought briefly about throwing my own hat into the ring. Most likely I wouldn't have got it. I had only been Director Personnel for a year. Yet, as I learned as Director Personnel dealing with my colleagues, opportunities come up unexpectedly and these can be big moments in a career. Anyhow I didn't try it and there was no serious suggestion from anyone else that I should.

On 15 January 2003 I went to Nigeria. Twenty-five years after being Assistant Desk Officer in FCO for Nigeria in Near East and North Africa Department I was able to make my familiarisation visit! I was met at Lagos airport by a fixer who got me through and safely into the armoured car for the journey to the High Commission. This was a reflection of the potential to run into nasty situations in and around the airport. An official vehicle had stopped some bullets a year earlier, caught in crossfire.

Lagos is a city for which the word teeming should have been invented. Fifteen going on twenty-five million people then sprawled around the original town. There was no option of going downtown for a drink here!

Yet I liked what I saw. The weather was warm and welcoming: I was treated to a dinner under the stars hosted by the Deputy High Commissioner David Wyatt. The staff accommodation was good. The UK counted for something. With the US not so very strongly engaged in Africa our High Commissioner had the opportunity to be regarded as a particularly important interlocutor, and Philip Thomas had succeeded in getting alongside people from the President down.

The visa section in Lagos was our biggest in the world, and had its problems in coping with the volume of applications. As always on these trips I had a good look at this part of the mission's work. I was struck by the extent of the effort into checking for possible fraud. Some applicants showed an amazing professionalism in this area. If only the talent spent on this were used instead in creating wealth for the Nigerian people!

I had had some idea of what Lagos would be like. By contrast Abuja was a blank sheet of paper. A new city created in the savannah in the centre of the country but far away from any other major population centre. When I was in West Africa Department in 1978-1979 Abuja had been a project to help knit the country together after the Civil War. Now, it had actually happened and was gathering pace because the Federal Government was based there. Already the shanty towns around the planned part of the capital were mushrooming.

The population was estimated at 3-4 million and growing fast. The High Commission in Abuja had organised itself well and with foresight: we had a good well-used staff compound, criticised years previously as a white elephant.

As in all these trips, I spent a lot of time with the Head of Mission, in this case the High Commissioner Philip Thomas. It's easily overlooked how isolated Heads of Mission can feel. So often they told me that they had no-one to talk to, being themselves the boss and having no FCO interlocutor at the same level (unlike during a London posting). Of course, with the Personnel Director they wanted to discuss their staff and their own future. So it was on this trip. Philip Thomas wanted to become Consul General New York, a highly sought-after post. He got it, and so our paths were to cross again when I was posted to Washington.

On 4 March I went by Aeroflot to Moscow. The following day was one of those bright sunny and very cold ones such as I enjoyed in the cold winter of 86-87 in Berlin. From the excellent new Embassy building there was a superb view over the frozen Moskva river. The mission was humming led by Roderic Lyne, an impressive bilateral Ambassador and unsurpassable as our representative in Russia.

From Moscow to St Petersburg. It was a treat to see this city coming out into the world after the end of the Cold War. The local staff exemplified this: all relatively new and young, eager to learn and improve, and looking to the future. The Consulate was well set up in a new office with the bubbly and highly able Consul General, Barbara Hay, living over the shop. The view across the frozen river was stunning, as was my first visit to the Hermitage. A city bound to become a major destination for weekend trips from the UK.

The visit to Africa from 1-6 June was together with Dave Fish, the HR Director at DFID. At that time, Clare Short had been Secretary of State for DFID for 6 years. She had been a powerful Minister, giving her Department focus on one objective – reducing poverty – and securing a level of resources for her programmes of which other departments could only dream. On the downside, DFID was not co-operating well on foreign policy issues of concern to other departments. There was still aversion among some in DFID to the idea of close co-operation with the FCO from which DFID had secured a "divorce" in 1997.

Dave Fish operated within this framework, working loyally to his Secretary of State. At the same time, as someone who had worked overseas with our High Commission in Kenya, he knew the realities of life abroad and the value of co-operation. We demonstrably travelled together and saw the High Commissioners and Heads of DFID offices together. We produced a joint minute at the end with recommendations on FCO-DFID co-operation.

We visited Uganda, Tanzania and Zimbabwe. Three different FCO-DFID relationships.

In Kampala, the High Commissioner was Adam Wood, whose home department was DFID. There didn't seem any particular problem in FCO-DFID co-operation. But it was evident that the separation of the two offices across the capital city which has serious traffic congestion was a factor hampering development of greater synergies at all levels in the missions.

In Dar-Es-Salaam we saw the new building of 5 floors – one each for FCO, DFID, the Germans, the Dutch and the Commission. The High Commissioner, Richard Clarke, had the best access of any foreigner to the President. His position was based to an important extent on the DFID programme of budget support for the Tanzanian government: he operated as the person responsible to both departments for securing their objectives in the country.

In Zimbabwe there was little DFID could do other than offer emergency humanitarian aid while the government of President Mugabe continued its chronic mismanagement and blamed Britain for the impoverishment of this country. The Zimbabwean government would not see the High Commissioner, Brian Donnelly, on official business. Surely the day would come when more was possible, and Zimbabwe would attract a serious DFID reconstruction programme. When that day came we would want to ensure FCO and DFID were pulling together in-country. Writing in 2015, Comrade Bob is still in charge!

The visit was also a chance for me to understand what qualities we should be looking for as we considered the succession to these High Commissioners. In the case of Tanzania, the issue presented itself much sooner than I had expected as the incumbent wanted to leave the Service. We do ask a lot of our leaders overseas. They mostly carry on in a seemingly effortless way. Yet behind the façade there are many stresses which the Office should be listening to with greater sympathy than I was sometimes able to muster.

In Dar-Es-Salaam I had also to look at the relations between staff. I had been told by the High Commissioner, the Africa Directorate and my own staff that things had been difficult and affecting the operation of the Post. There had been a hope that things would improve once staff moved out of unsatisfactory temporary office accommodation and into the new building. But what I found was lingering ill-feeling on a scale I hadn't experienced at any other post. On return to London I sent a couple of colleagues to investigate further and recommend what to do.

We took the hard decision to short-tour one member of staff in the interest of the functioning of the mission as a whole. We did this elsewhere on occasion for various reasons.

Iraq after the 2003 invasion

I went to Iraq as HR Director to look at the situation of FCO staff working there. There had been a number of attacks in late October on the Green Zone in Baghdad where our staff were working with the Coalition Provisional Authority (CPA). On 27 October the Al-Rashid Hotel, used by CPA staff, was hit by a rocket attack. The UK lead in Baghdad, Sir Jeremy Greenstock, was worried that it would lead staff to walk. On 28 October, I participated in a meeting of COBR, the government's crisis machinery in the Cabinet Office. Jeremy spoke to us via a live secure video-link from Baghdad. We were told that the risks to staff were increasing and there was a need to make their situation more secure. Staff in Baghdad were inevitably unsettled. He asked for a Personnel visit. I went with a Welfare Officer, Diane Wilton, and with Dave Fish, as many of the staff were DFID contractors. We had collected some messages from other HR Directors in Whitehall who had staff from their Departments out there

The FCO had prepared in advance of the conclusion of the fighting for the establishment of a new Embassy in Baghdad. We had flat-pack buildings ready to move on a low-loader from Kuwait to be set up on the compound of our old Embassy in Baghdad once security allowed. But we didn't really know how the allied governmental operation would function after the end of the fighting. As it turned out the old Embassy compound was insufficiently secure and civilian authority for the transitional period to a new Iraqi government was vested in the Coalition Provisional Authority.

The CPA was 90-95% American. But in view of the UK commitment to the allied effort there had also to be a sizeable British effort. Jeremy Greenstock was prevailed upon by the Prime Minister to go out there for 6 months after his term at the UN finished in July. It fell to me to talk through his package with him – a reversal of roles from the days when he had been my first Personnel Officer.

I flew to Kuwait overnight on 9 November. We arrived early morning, had a chance to recover a little at the Ambassador's residence, and then went to the military airport for our flight to Baghdad. Nothing was ever easy about Baghdad. The irritable commuter to London would forget complaints about leaves on the line if faced by the risk of missiles and terrorism! We had trouble landing in Baghdad because of a sandstorm. I suppose that brought with it the blessing that we might be less easy to target by ground-to-air missiles.

We were taken by Control Risks, private contractors, to the Green Zone in Baghdad, formerly Saddam's government zone. All the foreign operations had been concentrated there because of the growing security threat. We had a meeting and dinner with Jeremy Greenstock and staff. The security briefing was grim. I was used from my time on the Assessments Staff to pessimism among analysts – their instinct was in that direction. No-one ever shot a pessimistic analyst. I did not want to believe that we were losing the peace after the war. But the prognosis we were given was all too believable. After the euphoria of the initial period after the end of the fighting and the toppling of Saddam there were a lot of disaffected Iraqis, particularly among the Sunnis, who did not feel they had a stake in the provisional government arrangements overseen by the Coalition. Our staff needed to be better protected.

The Green Zone was a large swathe of Central Baghdad, shielded on two sides by the river and defended by several rings of coalition security on the other two. It was an area about the size of Kensington and Chelsea, I was told. It was certainly big. Inside, our people worked in the CPA building alongside the Americans and in the British Embassy operation from an excellent villa, formerly occupied I believe by a member of

Saddam's family. They ate free of charge at a canteen, with food provided in a massive operation by Kellogg, Brown and Root who were paid costs plus three per cent for their trouble. They slept in containers, though many in fact slept in their offices around this time as the containers were not hardened against incoming missiles.

In this atmosphere the focus was on getting the job done. While that job seemed to staff worthwhile they were prepared to put up with the inconveniences and risks. My task was to underline the message from London that their work was considered high-priority (they knew that but needed to hear it) and that their safety was even more important to us. That meant taking every reasonable security precaution, even though these could make their work more difficult to carry through and made everyday life even more difficult.

We managed one meal at a restaurant outside the Green Zone. Coming back we heard there had been a mortar attack and were careful to keep out of the way of the US Rapid Response Team. Next morning we inspected the craters in the car park in front of the CPA building. No-one had been hurt.

The next day, 11 November, we saw the Canal Hotel building used by the UN as the HQ for their Assistance Mission until destroyed by a suicide car bomb on 19 August 2003. Over 20 people had been killed, mostly by flying glass (I decided never again to complain about ugly bomb curtains in London) and including the UN Special Representative, the much-loved Brazilian Sergio Vieira de Mello. This was a salutary reminder of the need to improve security for our own staff if we were to continue to have civilians in Iraq. We talked to UK staff who were in surprisingly good heart despite the dangers – one had very nearly been seriously injured or worse when a mortar had hit a nearby hotel, since evacuated by our staff. The plan was to relocate the sleeping containers into the basement of the Convention Centre, which would provide shelter from shelling.

I had a chance to see how staff lived. Life was work, eat and sleep with diminishing opportunities to get out of the Green Zone except with armed guard. There was a risk of over-eating and over-drinking, which required self-discipline and time in the gym to counteract. Some contractors went out to work in Iraqi Ministries to help to them on to their feet, but even that was beginning to look a system living on borrowed time as security worsened. After a second bomb attack in September, all UN staff had left Iraq.

Four youngsters on our staff did decide to go home. But that wasn't so very damaging to the operation in view of the continuous coming and going of personnel in Iraq in any event. We expected staff to serve 6 weeks and then take a week away from Iraq. We looked for commitments of 6 months at a time.

Some stayed longer. Visiting the CPA in Baghdad you could understand why. Looking through the television tube in UK you saw violent chaos. Sitting in the Green Zone you saw a job to be done and a chance to take a level of responsibility not available in many places in our network. With the right security, people were able to visit ministries to help these get going in the new world after Saddam. Others worked out in the governorates, though this was increasingly difficult as the security situation worsened towards the end of 2003 and even more so in Spring 2004. Most worked at CPA itself.

On 12 November, Control Risks took us to the airport for a flight to Basra. I met up with Hilary Synnott, Henry Hogger and Robert Wilson, leading the British civilian team there in the Coalition Provisional Authority South. We had a chance to see something of the area in a drive outside the compound. The compound, adjoined to the British military zone on the

Shatt-el-Arab, had only recently been taken over and the space was rapidly filling with containers as more advisers from a surprisingly wide range of countries were coming in. It felt safer than Baghdad, lacking the feverish atmosphere of the Baghdad Green Zone. The British military were using the tactics of Northern Ireland to try to get along with the Iraqis in the south: it seemed the right way at the time but the outcome was not so positive. It was possible to get out of the compound if escorted.

Then, in the afternoon, there was news of an attack on Italian carabinieri at Nasiriyah with large numbers killed. We were locked down following intelligence that the compound could come under attack. We put on heavy flak jackets and helmets and wondered how long we would be staying there.

We did get away in the afternoon of the following day. We went in military convoy to the airport and met up with an Italian who had escaped the attack at Nasiriyah. Together we joined a convoy organised by Andy Bearpark. I had known him since the early 1990s. He was then in charge of the emergency assistance programme of ODA (in 1997 to become DFID) and had been unfailingly effective in getting things done in Bosnia. I remember once asking him after a Ministerial request to beef up our effort in a particular area of Bosnia what could we do quickly. He asked how much; I said half a million pounds; he said "done" and did it. Andy was at that time described in the press as the only civil service mandarin with a diamond earring. He left ODA, went on to work in other crisis areas – I saw him in Kosovo – and was now a contractor in Iraq.

The convoy was protected by a group of tough gun-toting South Africans who communicated in Afrikaans. If they had seen danger, I am sure they would have fired first and asked questions later. They got us to Kuwait. We dropped off the Italian at his Embassy and went to the Marriott Hotel. Early the next morning, Saturday 15 November, I caught a flight to Heathrow. Back at home that evening Iraq seemed an unreal experience.

It is surprising and fortunate we did not suffer FCO casualties in Iraq. The risks were mitigated but could not be removed. There were people in Iraq who did not want the international community there and would take any opportunity to kill. In 1984-85 when on the Lebanon desk in London, our Ministers had been anxious about the risk of harm coming to our Embassy staff in Beirut. We had several evacuations, often resulting from a Ministerial concern on a Friday as the weekend loomed. But since that time, Ministerial readiness to embrace risk to staff had increased – in Bosnia, in Kosovo, in Afghanistan – and a readiness to spend what it took to protect. Sometimes deaths were caused by accidents, in turn made more likely by the security provisions needed against the high level of threat – in Bosnia we lost people using helicopters.

Death in Istanbul

It was back into the office on the Monday 17 November 2003. US President George Bush came to London and stopped the traffic as I tried to get to work on Wednesday. On Thursday 20 November I was in the office of the Permanent Under Secretary Michael Jay when his outer-office staff came in to tell us of a bomb attack against the British Consulate General in Istanbul and the HSBC HQ. This followed attacks on 15 November on two synagogues in the city.

We soon learned that our Consul General Roger Short had been killed along with around 10 locally-employed staff, Turkish and British. FCO emergency plans were already good by this time. The immediate reaction was to send a Rapid Deployment Team with varied skills to Istanbul. The big question in the first hour was whether the Foreign Secretary should fly out there straightaway.

My own first take on this was that the Foreign Secretary's presence in the immediate aftermath was more likely to get in the way than help. This was the decision of George Bush on the day after Hurricane Katrina struck in 2005 – and his reputation has ever since been damaged by the impression he did not care as he looked over New Orleans from his aircraft rather than seeing it on the ground. Foreign Secretary Jack Straw was only a few months into the job but was an experienced Minister and politician. He understood the likely domestic reaction to a visit or no visit. He decided to go and joined the Rapid Deployment Team at Gatwick for the flight that afternoon. He was right to go. Staff there appreciated it and the media reaction was positive.

Afghanistan

On Saturday 22 November I left on Emirates for Dubai, overnighted in the Meridien and took a UN flight early the following morning getting up at 0130 UK time. The weather was clear and the view over the mountains breathtaking. In Kabul I saw the site of the new British Embassy and visited the DFID office.

The following morning I went to Mazar-es-Sharif. Here was a name I had seen so often in intelligence reports when in the Assessments Staff. Now it had a British-led Provincial Reconstruction Team and a member of the FCO in charge, Jackie Wilson-Smith – one of our rare Dari speakers. She had a photo with her surrounded by warlords who had also figured in these intelligence reports. Mazar surprised me by its broad central street and tourist shops. But it did still feel like frontier country. A visit to a fort just outside the town reinforced that impression. I saw the forest where the Taleban had been defeated and heard how an SAS soldier had miraculously escaped a B52 bombing when a tank turret had been blown off its mounting and covered him.

Security was already tight at Kabul. Our people couldn't leave the compound unless under armed guard. At times of particularly high alert the army deployed armoured vehicles to beef up the protection of the entrance against storming or a suicide bomb attempt.

This was a recognisable Embassy operation, albeit in extreme security conditions – quite unlike the massive US-led operation in Baghdad. Team spirit was everything in getting the job done. These were people with great inner resources. They worked and lived together, with only small impersonal containers (called pods) to which to retire for a bit of privacy. The new Embassy, on the site of the old Bulgarian Embassy, was going to be bigger with more hardened accommodation but not so very different in terms of lifestyle.

What a spectacular country. I've seen a fair bit around the world, and you do lose your sense of wonder as time goes by. But I shall remember the flight to Mazar. The RAF Hercules soared up the mountains giving us a close view on this clear day. And they swooped down valleys. I'm sure you could see some isolated spots where man may never have set foot. And I had such a great view from the cockpit.

Pakistan

The next stop was Islamabad, courtesy of a UN flight over the Khyber Pass and with the Siachen Glacier in the distance. Security was the biggest issue again. The compound was spacious and impressive with swimming pool, football pitches, tennis and squash courts as well as catering facilities. The advantages of a long-established mission were in stark contrast to Kabul, where we had abandoned our Embassy years previously and so had to start from scratch in a difficult environment.

These advantages in Islamabad did not make it an easy posting. At times of tension it was an unaccompanied post, that is no partners or dependents. I understood the wish of staff to relax this whenever possible, which we did. But there were also evacuations, such as when there was a risk of war, even nuclear war, between Pakistan and India in 2002 over Kashmir and only a core of staff were left and they were packed up and ready to move at short notice.

A joy of earlier days in Islamabad had been to go into the Murree Hills, summer retreat for the British during the days of empire and now for Pakistanis, and enjoy the spectacular scenery. Now staff were largely confined to the compound and careful travel for others between home and work. Even visits to the town had to be thought through.

The High Commissioner Mark Lyall Grant was understandably focussed on how to attract good staff from UK to work in Islamabad. The need was great as this was one of the largest posts we had, because of the size of the visa section, and not everything could be done by local staff. Mark was strikingly good at the outward-facing element of his role mixing empathy with straight-talking as he did later as our Permanent Representative at the UN. He showed me a local newspaper reporting his visit to Lyallpur, present-day Faisalabad. The name was a tribute to Mark's ancestor Sir James Lyall, Lt Governor of Punjab. Mark pointed out that news of the Pakistani PM had been relegated to the inside pages by news of his visit.

I flew on a thousand miles to Karachi, a post always in the spotlight in discussion about how much risk we should take. I was greeted by an armed guard and taken to the lovely peaceful green compound, a haven of calm within the menacing hustle of the city. I sat up till late with David Pearey, the Deputy High Commissioner in charge of the post. Next day I had a drive round the city to get an understanding of the challenge for staff and returned to the quiet of the compound and played croquet, which seemed entirely fitting.

From Karachi I went via Dubai to a Regional Heads of Mission Conference in Sri Lanka, a chance to talk with staff collectively about HR policies and individually about themselves. The journey back to London included a stop at Male. I was impressed by the altitude reading as we waited at the airport – 12 feet.

In London

I spent most of my time in London. The Review of Personnel Directorate was the theme I chose to drive myself. Most other work came to me.

Handling emergency operations in FCO was essential to our reputation. We came to manage this better. We had plenty of practice owing to the Iraq war, the renewed threat of war between India and Pakistan in Spring 2003 and the Istanbul bombing. In each case the emergency rooms in the Foreign Office Main Building basement were opened, and there was for some of the time also a 24-hour consular emergency operation from the Old Admiralty Building across Horse Guards Parade from the Main building in King Charles Street. We did our bit preparing in advance lists of people for shifts. I had seen in the first Iraq war in the Cabinet Office that it's essential to operate on the basis that the emergency will continue for a long time and staffing will need to be sustainable. We benefited from the willingness of staff to rally round in an emergency. That's always been a strength in the FCO.

I came to the job believing we had to do something to force the pace on increasing ethnic minority representation in the FCO. Working with Anwar Choudhury on his bid to become High Commissioner in Bangladesh and seeing it succeed did give me some pleasure. Unfortunately, he was attacked and wounded there and had an unsatisfactory role when back in London but I had the pleasure of seeing him in action as Ambassador in Peru in 2014 when I visited Lima after my retirement from the Diplomatic Service. I had ideas to bring in more people but time ran out on me. Other organisations, for example the BBC, have done better. The Service has not yet the critical mass of people from ethnic minorities in senior positions to ensure we shall reach the kind of levels we need to be able to say we are representative of British society. This is even more important now that there is something of a backlash against multiculturalism, complicated by terrorism carried out in the name of Islam.

There were not enough senior women either. I persuaded a couple from outside to join us mid-career. If I'd been in the job longer I think I could have raided other organisations for a few more. It's important to avoid any sense that women are being promoted or appointed to senior positions just to improve the stats on female representation. Women who are in these positions by right are the first to say that. It might help to be a woman when candidates for a particular job look otherwise about level-pegging. I don't have a problem with that. We do have a problem that not enough of our home-grown women who have come through the ranks are coming through to senior positions. Too many leave mid-career. This may have to do with the peripatetic lifestyle which is less appealing to those who put family first – and still more women than men do that – or is the culture still too macho?

I have made a note to check in 2025 whether we still have

under-representation of women and ethnic minorities. I really don't know if we'll have cracked it by then.

The FCO Selection System

The HR Director used to be seen primarily as the person who operates the appointment system. This is much less the case in 2015 than it was 2001-4, as selection at least up to the most senior levels is now led by the Line Manager under rules drawn up by HR.

The FCO operates a system of fixed-term appointments: up to four years overseas; up to three years at home. This helps promote flexibility and reduces the risks of coasting in jobs, which is why fixed-term appointments were also introduced in 2004 for the Senior Civil Service in Home Departments. Early in my career, I recall reading an Annual Review by a senior Ambassador in which he wrote : "As I said in my fifth Annual Review and will say in my seventh… " Not healthy. On the other hand, it can lead to a culture in which people are focussing on impressing in order to capture their next job rather than on developing in their current one. The system has generally served well and I hope will continue, adapted to promote greater professionalism and curb the persistent tendency to value the gifted amateur.

All jobs are advertised, and staff in the right grade or with an appropriate promotion ticket can bid. Some jobs are also open to other parts of the Civil Service and on occasions are advertised publicly. It can mean that staff bid for several jobs without success. That can be because they have been unlucky. Or it can be that they are bidding too narrowly and perhaps unrealistically.

The HR Director was particularly involved in appointments in the Senior Management Structure (the FCO equivalent of the Senior Civil Service), chairing the No 2 Board (consisting of Directors) – which decided on junior and middle-ranking Ambassadorial posts and Heads of FCO Departments – and acting as Secretary to the No 1 Board (consisting of Directors-General) which takes senior appointments. The Boards took their roles seriously and, for the most part, came to sound conclusions based on hard-headed but fair discussion.

I felt this particularly of the No 2 Board. Most members prepared themselves thoroughly for the discussions and acted collegiately to arrive at the best result for the Office. Where I had a strong view that they were in danger of not coming to a good conclusion it was possible to have a frank debate and ensure that the decisions were well informed. The run-up to the Board was crucial in preparing the ground: I had Nigel Haywood – later to star on TV as Governor to the Falklands – and then Howard Drake successively as my deputies in charge of preparing the No 2 Board and both did this with great commitment and authority.

The decisions taken by the board can have big consequences. Before my time, Craig Murray had been entrusted with the role of Ambassador in Uzbekistan. This did not work out well. Craig will have his version of the story. Heads of Mission do sometimes attract criticism for their behaviour. The FCO has to take a view on the fairness of any criticism and the impact on the UK position. There are many cases, and that is the norm, where the FCO has supported Heads of Mission who have attracted criticism or made an error of judgement in a particular moment which has caused embarrassment. But there is a line beyond which the FCO may draw the conclusion that a Head of Mission ceases to be effective.

This difficult case had its odd moments as in the beginning of this section on Personnel. Craig Murray eventually left the Service, on generous terms which would not be available I suspect nowadays. He did not win in the general election against Jack Straw in Blackburn.

The members of the Board were experienced and talented senior people, who knew well the requirements of many of the jobs and the people under consideration. Permanent Under Secretary Michael Jay was conscious of his responsibility in the chair.

There was a risk of discussions developing a momentum in a certain direction, and then other members going with the flow, and not coming to the best solution. The question for the HR Director in these circumstances was to what extent to intervene. I was conscious that as HR Director I was Secretary and not a Board Member. I had to examine my own motivation too: I might prefer a certain solution, for example because it fitted in a chain of other appointments and would make good use of all the staff coming available although not necessarily ensure the best qualified bidder was appointed to a particular job.

I was mostly seeking to ensure the Board had full information before it and to mitigate what are called the "halos and horns" effects – candidates being branded with a good or bad reputation on the basis of thin evidence which then becomes magnified in its impact on the decision-making process. As I came to know the landscape and candidates – usually even better than the Board members – it was reasonable that I should steer them. For the last few No 1 Boards in my time, I wrote a Steering Brief with recommendations (some firmer than others). The core of my role was ensuring every candidate had a fair hearing and the Board understood what the position in question required and what each candidate would bring to it.

Every decision mattered greatly to the individuals considered for selection and to the success of the FCO.

The Resident at Tristan da Cunha was a post which posed unusual issues. Not someone Ministers were likely to hear much from or about, unless of course the appointee himself was a problem. There was no rush of volunteers, just as there was not for St Helena. We were a bit concerned that the present incumbent might be reluctant to leave and wondered what would happen if he would not get on to the ship which passed by once every 6 weeks. We found a successor and the predecessor did leave.

In the case of Riyadh, we found ourselves at that moment – surprisingly – without a strong field for a key job. In an earlier meeting with him I had mentioned Riyadh as a possible future target to Sherard Cowper-Coles, an Arabist then serving as Ambassador in Israel. Without checking further with him, I included him among the candidates for the No 1 Board and they chose him. Sherard was aghast when I told him of the selection, saying that he had not applied for it, and has since reminded me of this! He did a great job there.

The No 1 Board was conscious of a special responsibility both to select the best candidates for the top posts overseas – Ambassadors to the EU in Brussels, Washington, to the UN in New York, Beijing, Tokyo, New Delhi, Riyadh, Paris, Berlin, Abuja etc – and while the UK had forces there in Baghdad and Kabul too. At the same time it wanted to make the best use of the skills and experience of the talent available at that moment.

The Ambassador in Washington has to be one of very best diplomats, on top of the issues, able to lead policy and people, and with the confidence of No 10. As David Manning fitted that bill so much better than anyone else at the time, it seemed disingenuous to invite bids from others. We sent a message to staff saying that the appointment would be handled in this way without going through a Board discussion about other candidates and why we were doing this. It's right to be open about these things. David Manning was outstanding in the job. It hadn't entered my head that I would end up being his Deputy in Washington.

There were occasions, very few, when No 1 Board decisions had to be reviewed – sometimes because the appointee withdrew. On other occasions, the Board decided not to appoint a candidate not because he would not do well in that role but because they thought he would be even better elsewhere. The result was that other candidates, who were perhaps not the very best in the field before the Board but still perfectly well suited to the role, were selected.

I cannot think of an appointment we made to a top job overseas which did not work out well. Yet, I am conscious that some other candidates might have done equally well, and some dreams for which individuals had striven in exemplary fashion for decades were not realised for reasons no fault of their own but just because of the circumstances when the decision came to be made. Had the decision needed to be made a year earlier or later they might have been selected for the job of their dreams.

From the position of HR Director I could see why life is a bitch sometimes. I could only sympathise with those who missed out and celebrate with those who are successful.

Ministers

Boards make recommendations. These have to be ratified. For the senior appointments (No 1 and No 2 Boards), the recommendations went to Ministers. Why? Because that was the system. It didn't correspond to the situation in the Home Civil Service, where Ministers' right to be involved was more circumscribed. None of this is set in stone. The move towards Political Advisers and larger ministerial staffs, and the focus on the appointment of Permanent Secretaries and other top officials, is leading to a call for greater Ministerial involvement in appointments.

It would be retrograde to retreat from the long-established

principle of appointment on merit. The UK learned this in the nineteenth century from experience in India where political appointments were not getting the job done and so competitive exams and training, including in languages, were introduced. These principles took longer to be established in the Home Civil Service and Diplomatic Service. They have proved their worth.

I didn't have problems with Ministers during my time as HR Director. I don't recall any occasion on which a junior Minister attempted to overturn a recommendation from the No1 Board. They had an opportunity to express a view on the candidates before the Board was held. In the case of Baroness Amos, a highly able Minister who knew her patch (particularly Africa), this was rightly an important factor. From other junior Ministers, except in cases where the jobs were very close to them (Private Secretaries, press officers), we tended to receive inputs based on a cursory knowledge of one candidate's achievements, the others being unknown to them. I suspect that Ministers felt they ought to comment and so came up sometimes with unhelpful comments. Perhaps we shouldn't have been asking them at all.

This is not to say that officials know it all and Ministers should stay out of it. We were required to consult the Foreign Secretary on senior appointments abroad and at home and No 10 on the most senior. Michael Jay would check well ahead of decision time, so that we wouldn't end up with a disagreement between the Board and the Foreign Secretary.

I am uneasy about political appointments. The government needs to be comfortable with Ambassadors in key places like Washington and EU Brussels. Should there be strongly qualified people from beyond the Diplomatic or wider Civil Service, then also fine in my opinion to consider them as long they are subject to the same rules as others both as candidates in a selection process and the discipline applied once in post.

Political appointments are commonplace in other Diplomatic Services. The US Service has a large number of friends of the President as its Ambassadors: some effective, many not. The Germans have a few such appointments at any one time, usually to reward a politician. We have had very few. Jim Callaghan appointed his son-in-law Peter Jay to Washington; Margaret Thatcher twice appointed retired Ambassadors whom she trusted to Washington. More recently, the post of High Commissioner at Canberra became for a while regarded as a chasse gardée for a political appointment.

Parliament has understandably taken an interest in such appointments. In many countries, including the US and Brazil (my last two posts) there is a process of interviewing and confirming all Ambassadorial appointments by Parliament (the Senate in these two cases). There are risks in this that an appointment for the public good of a civil servant could be blocked for some unrelated reason. But it might give greater transparency to political appointments.

There was a wish among some Ministers for more. Not so bad if they were looking at people who would have a lot to bring. But I felt that these jobs were at risk of being seen as an extension of political patronage and with the risk of the appointment of people who were not the best option for the country but needed to be found a berth.

Political patronage is not helpful as we see in the creation of peerages and award of other honours to people who have donated money or helped political parties or provided political services to a government. This seems corrupt like the political sinecures of the 18th century. It seems to get worse the longer governments are in power. It would be good to have more information in the public domain about these awards in the public interest.

Looking Back at HR

The drawback of this job was that it took me out of foreign affairs. Wouldn't it have been better to be Ambassador somewhere and use what I had learned in home policy jobs and as an overseas operator in Berlin, harnessing public diplomacy to the cause? A number of Ambassadorships went by for which I could have bid but I felt unable to leave HR so soon. As 2004 wore on I started to think that I might have missed the boat. There were no suitable ones coming up in 2005.

But HR was a unique experience, thanks in particular to Michael Jay. In my policy jobs I had worked to Ministers. In this one, the Permanent Under Secretary was the key senior reference point. Not a day would go by when we were both in London that I wouldn't have a meeting or telephone call or several of one, the other or both, with him. He would listen as well as talk. He was the first Head of our Service with the view that management and policy work cannot and should not be separated. As HR Director I understood how important it was to our staff to feel understood and valued. I felt understood and valued by Michael Jay.

I learned about the Office, posts and people and systems. I had more influence on the Office in this job than in any other.

I enjoyed reforming HR in the FCO. I went to my next jobs overseas better equipped for the administrative dimensions of the role. Yet, when I look back, I see the foreign-policy aspects of my career as those which remain most vivid and meaningful. There are always fights over the allocation and organisation of the decreasing resources at the FCO's disposition. In the end these are not the things which matter most.

Most of all I enjoyed the sense of making a difference to departments at home and Embassies overseas – and to individual people. HR handled the hopes and fears of people who were our colleagues as well as delivering services – payroll, health and safety etc. So many people came into my room. The best general advice I could give was to stay flexible about the course of a career – for reasons beyond an individual's control, a particular much-wanted position might not be attainable at a particular moment. Also, unexpected opportunities could arise.

There were some amazing people in the Service. David Manning, Jeremy Greenstock and Michael Jay were the best of their generation and genuinely warm people too. For bravery, Nick Browne was the top candidate. For expertise, there were many candidates – expert Japanologists in Tokyo, Sinologists in Beijing, Arabists, Africanists, EU experts, experts on political/military affairs etc etc. We maintained our excellence in languages. More was – rightly – expected of Ambassadors overseas and senior staff at home in managing their people, money, programmes and estates.

My expectation was to go abroad next as an Ambassador. I knew from my experience running Personnel that that was both realistic and right in career terms. I failed in a bid for Germany. I was asked by Michael Jay and David Manning to be Deputy Head of Mission (Deputy Ambassador) at Washington. I was reluctant to be a Deputy at a large Post for the second time. But Washington was special. The family liked the idea. I liked the idea of working with David Manning. So, after saying "no" twice, I became a candidate. I stepped out of the No 1 Selection Board when it came to discussion of this job. Michael Jay invited me back and the Board were generous in their congratulations.

4.

THE UNITED STATES

I LOST THE QUEEN'S CONSORT

On 4 May 2007 I was accompanying the Duke of Edinburgh at the Jamestown settlement in Virginia as Deputy Head of Mission, with the Ambassador accompanying the Queen. This was the culmination of a huge amount of planning for this central leg of a State Visit to the United States. The Duke of Edinburgh was free to roam around the site as The Queen processed.

Suddenly, I found I had lost him. I scurried about only to find he had made his way to his car and left! That in turn meant I had missed the convoy and consequently the transfer by helicopter to Norfolk where he was to visit a warship on which he had served in WW2. I had been there on a preparatory visit to see what he would do, been assured by his staff that he would leap up the steep gangway from the quay up to the ship, and was familiar with what would happen on board. But I wasn't there on the day to see him do this, What an idiot I felt!

So I tagged on to the party with the Queen. The Duke did not miss me in the slightest. In the rush of events I managed to play it down. But it was not a career highlight to lose the consort of your monarch.

A farcical start

There was a mess-up on the US side on arrival in the US of the Queen's party. Timing as so often on these occasions was tight so we were a little nervous as we waited on a blustery afternoon at Richmond airport for the plane to land. The flight was actually a little early but for some reason was made to hold until the scheduled time to land – 1500. The plane drew up, a red carpet was with difficulty laid out in the stiff breeze. The steps were wheeled up to the waiting plane. But they were not high enough to allow egress. There ensued a search, lasting 15 minutes, for suitable steps. Meanwhile, we could see through the aircraft's windows a visibly irritated Queen's party wanting to get out!

★★★

Just a short time into my posting in Washington in 2004, I had been visited at the Embassy by a delegation from the Commonwealth of Virginia. They told me that they represented the Jamestown Commission and were mandated by the Commonwealth Assembly to organise for June 2007 the commemoration of the 400th anniversary of the founding of Jamestown, the oldest continuously-inhabited European settlement in what is now the United States.

I had only been dimly aware of Jamestown. Like many people, I had heard a great deal about the Pilgrim Fathers and their settlement in Massachusetts in the 1620s, often thought of as the first European settlers. I learned about the Jamestown settlement, founded by a London joint-stock company hoping to profit from the riches of the Americas, especially gold.

The Jamestown settlement went through times of great want but survived, just, to become the first capital of Virginia.

The site of the original settlement had been lost and had long been thought to have been covered up by the adjacent James River. There was now no town at all there. Recent and ongoing archaeological work had revealed that the site was in fact on the bank of the river. It was being thoroughly investigated. Some of the finds were already available to view though the work was far from complete.

I was fascinated too by the impact of the settlement back home in the Britain of the early 1600s. Shakespeare wrote "The Tempest" based on the story of shipwreck in Bermuda of a ship bound for Jamestown. Pocahontas, whatever she did or did not do to help John Smith in 1607, became a celebrity in London when she came to live in Gravesend as Rebecca married to John Rolfe. The Jamestown story deserved to be better known.

The delegation, through their spokesman Chip Mann of the Jamestown Commission, explained their plans to me. A new Visitors' Centre would be built at Jamestown. The finds of the current investigation would be displayed. There would be seminars in Virginia on the legacy of the settlement, notably on the Rule of Law, involving international experts. The President of the United States would be invited to visit.

Their big ask of the UK was for a visit to Jamestown by the Queen. She had visited in 1957 for the 350th anniversary. It would be the highlight of the 400th anniversary if she could come again.

Requests for visits by the Queen are heard by British diplomats around the world with great frequency. She cannot go everywhere and there are good reasons not to go to some places. But I thought this idea had some chance. More important, so did David Manning. We passed it back to London. The fact that the initial response was not negative gave reason to hope. Having David Manning on the case was another! The Virginia team did their bit with the White House getting them to issue an invitation for a State Visit.

I saw Chip Mann and others involved a number of times. I went down to Jamestown to see for myself and to visit nearby Williamsburg, which had become the second capital of Virginia after Jamestown and had, since the 1920s, been preserved as Colonial Williamsburg of the pre-revolutionary period – a tourist attraction and a focus of study of that era. Their enthusiasm was infectious.

Chip and colleagues rang me from time to time to ask whether the Queen would be coming. All I could tell him was that we had done what we could from the US end so that a decision could be made in London. I did not want to tempt fate or raise their hopes, even though I felt positive about the prospects. Even in January 2006 the line from London was still that no decision had been made. We finally had the green light in the summer of 2006 for a visit in May 2007, not in early June 2007 at the time of the anniversary celebrations. No matter – there would be events throughout the year. Maybe it was even better to come at a different time. On 24 August 2006, I went to the West Wing to see Mary Haines about precise dates matching the availability of the Queen and the President.

The visit was fixed for either side of a weekend which, happily, coincided with the Kentucky Derby and allowed the Queen to spend the weekend at the ranch not far way of former US Ambassador to London 2001-2004 Will Farish. He had been notable during his tenure for his long absences leaving his Deputy to run things. But he had shared with the Queen a great love of horses and that would be the focus of the weekend allowing for a breather from two sets of two days of full-on events.

The first two days were Virginia. We rushed from the airport into Richmond. There was a fabulously enthusiastic reception, especially during the walkabout escorted by young Governor Tim Kaine – the big chance in a provincial town to

State Visit to the United States
by The Queen and The Duke of Edinburgh
3-8 May, 2007

The Royal Visit
May 3-4, 2

Alan Charlton

OFFICIAL
Issued by the British Embassy, Washington DC

The Queen in a carriage in Williamsburg and my credentials

see the Queen. This included a meeting with leaders of the Virginia Indians, who – I was told – had found the Crown during the pre-revolution period more reliable in living up to agreements with the Indians than the Republic which succeeded it. The Queen spoke to a joint session of the Virginia Assembly.

It was down to Williamsburg for a horse-drawn procession from the Capitol building to the Williamsburg Inn, where she had stayed in 2007 too. Friday 4 May was the centrepiece visit to Jamestown to see the finds of the archaeologists. In the afternoon, having missed the helicopter with the Duke of Edinburgh to Norfolk, I tagged along at a lovely occasion at William and Mary College following lunch at neighbouring Williamsburg. The students were wonderfully enthusiastic.

The Queen made a number of speeches. She alluded gently to the contrast of the progressive Virginia of 2007 with the segregated South of 1957 at the time of her previous visit. It is a great asset to have a Head of State who can bear witness

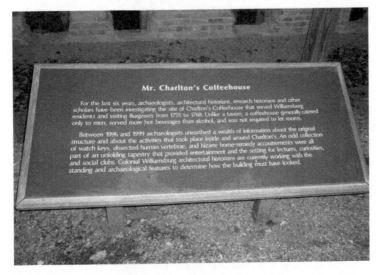

Charlton plaque at Colonial Williamsburg

to such huge change over half a century.

Judy and I visited colonial Williamsburg a number of times privately. I found there a Charlton of 18th century North America. He had a coffee house and made wigs. No relation as far as I know.

David and Catherine Manning made the trip to Kentucky for the Derby and Will Farish weekend. I stayed in Washington. I went out to Dulles on Saturday afternoon to meet Foreign Secretary Margaret Beckett. As usual, she wanted everyone around her at the hotel – this time, the Hay Adams.

The Monday was great. The sun shone. Judy and I went to Blair House opposite the White House, allocated to the Queen for the visit – a bit of old America. We had toe marks for our places in the fourth row during the Arrivals Ceremony on the White House lawn. There was a handshake with the President in the receiving line before lunch in the White House. In the afternoon we had a garden party at the Ambassador's Residence. The Embassy had made a big effort to make the guest list varied

The President and Mrs Bush
request the pleasure of the company of
Mr and Mrs Charlton
at a performance in honor of
Her Majesty Queen Elizabeth II
and
His Royal Highness The Prince Philip
Duke of Edinburgh
to be held at
The White House
on Monday, May 7, 2007
at eight-thirty o'clock

White Tie   East Entrance

and interesting. The stand-out for me was meeting Mickey Rooney, someone of the generation of the Queen and Duke who had been famous almost as long as they had. I went around with the Duke of Edinburgh who tried not to shake hands too much – entirely understandable given the impact handshaking must have over the years (I have a hand problem and so sympathise!) but not easy to avoid with enthusiastic crowds of Americans.

The evening was devoted to the State dinner at the White House. Judy and I were hosted by Joe Hagan. Laura Bush had said earlier on TV that she had insisted, despite the President's dislike of dressing up, that the event was special and should be white-tie. The menu was news in the media. So was the invitation to the dinner to the winning jockey of the Kentucky Derby, Calvin Borel. He was filmed picking up his evening dress at a shop and then arriving at the White House.

Tuesday 8 May was a nice moment for me. I had led on the longest single event of the visit – to the NASA Goddard Space Flight Center, 30 minutes drive into Maryland. I went in the car with the Duke of Edinburgh on the way there – he talked about the importance of Science. Goddard is a centre of Science. We had chosen it as the future-oriented counterpoint to the focus on the past at Jamestown.

I then went with Margaret Beckett on some calls on Capitol Hill in the afternoon. First she had a one-on-one lunch with Condi Rice. Then we saw Speaker of the House of Representatives Nancy Pelosi, followed by Tom Lantos, Chair of the House Foreign Affairs Committee and then the Congressional UK caucus.

The evening was the return dinner at the Residence. A diplomat's dream to have the President of the United States and First Lady at the Residence. The Queen made a laconic reference to Dubya's lapse on dates in his public remarks at the arrivals ceremony on the White House lawn the day before. He commented that the old-fashioned look she had given him on that occasion reminded him of his mother.

I saw Hillary Clinton out of the Residence – she lived nearby. Then I went upstairs to meet the Queen and the Duke

Hillary Clinton

who were ready to leave for the airport. They awarded me the CVO, Commander of the Victorian Order, for my part in the visit. We got to talk about the Olympics in London in 2012. The Queen said they wouldn't be around for that. Far from it – she arrived at the Olympic Stadium leaping out of a helicopter!

Other Royals came to the US too around this time. The Prince of Wales with the Duchess of Cornwall had visited in November 2005 and were given a dinner at the White House, memorable for a performance by cellist Yo Yo Ma. The US had not been one of those countries on which the Prince had previously focussed, but his work with young people and business meant he had something to say in the US. The Duke of York together with Sarah Ferguson represented the UK with great dignity at a commemoration of 9/11 in New York; he also came to Washington to support the whisky industry, announcing that he didn't drink the stuff himself. The Earl of Wessex charmed with his modesty and workmanlike approach; I enjoyed the conversation in the car when I went to meet him at Dulles airport. We in Washington fortunately did not find ourselves having to meet minor royals who were just using the airport not on official business as did our colleagues at the Consulate in New York.

PART II

SPECIAL RELATIONSHIP?

As a British diplomat in the US you are frequently asked, mostly by other Brits, whether there is – or still is – a special relationship between the UK and the US.

Living and working there you can see that most countries, perhaps all countries, have a special relationship with the US. Canada and Mexico clearly do as the two land neighbours, both of whom the US tried in part to incorporate into their country in earlier imperial days and both of whose economies are now so interlinked with the US. Many other countries have big communities of immigrants – the Italians, Jews, Greeks, and now especially the countries of Central America. Others have had their recent political direction defined by their interaction with the US – Japan, Germany, Philippines for example. Others have important links of history, such as France. Russia wants to be seen as on a par with the US as was the Soviet Union in the time of the Cold War. China and India are increasingly key relationships for both sides as they grow as powers. For Brazil and many others, the story of US development is one to admire and emulate even if they have reservations about US policies both foreign and domestic.

The UK is in a special position. There are ties of family and history about which quite a lot of Americans care, as we see by their interest in genealogy and in visiting the UK. Americans are also to the forefront of fans of modern Britain as we see by the numbers of them living especially in London and enjoying theatres, museums and stately homes. Speaking the same language is important. The triumph of English as the sole language in the US in the nineteenth century, despite large immigration from elsewhere, was a big factor underlying the potential for growth in the bilateral relationship in the twentieth century.

Yet having the same language has not been a sufficient condition for the closeness of the relationship in the last hundred years. It has taken a congruence of interests and dedicated leadership to bring that about. A central figure in this – recognised by his statue in front of the British Embassy in Massachusetts Avenue – was Winston Churchill, who is revered as much in the US as in the UK.

The US has always been moving between isolationism and involvement in the world. As a huge, largely self-sufficient country with unthreatening neighbours, focussing on its internal development is a natural inclination. The UK has not had that possibility as a small country dependent on its connections around the world for its prosperity. We have generally sought to avoid becoming more entangled in the complex affairs of continental Europe than our economic interests demand. At times we have intervened to defend those interests. We celebrate the leadership of Marlborough of a European coalition to prevent the hegemony of Louis XIV (not easy as France's population was four times Britain's in 1700). We celebrate Nelson and Wellington as central figures in the struggle to prevent the domination of Europe, for good or ill, by a new French overlord – Napoleon – a hundred years later. We celebrate Churchill as the leader who embodied resistance to German domination in World War II.

The difference in the twentieth century was that the US and Germany had become the two greatest economies in the world. In World War I it was the late intervention of the US which tipped the balance, forced Germany into a desperate and almost successful offensive in 1918 and then made the Allied offensive thereafter decisive. Yet the US experience of losing so many men on the fields of Europe in World War I led to a determination among many Americans not to repeat the experience when the war clouds gathered again in the 1930s and war restarted in Europe in 1939.

Enter Churchill. Having weathered the Battle of Britain in 1940 he saw the crucial importance of moving from saving the country to winning the war as depending on the involvement of the United States. He used his personal connection with the country, being one-quarter American and one-eighth Iroquois. He used the sympathy of Roosevelt to move in the direction of a strategic alliance. The cornerstone of this was the Atlantic Charter of 1941.

The alliance in World War II led to defence and intelligence relationships, which remain central to the UK's security to this day. I had the chance to see this up close while working in Washington. Added to it was the new field of what the US have called Homeland Security. Not having experienced the threat of invasion in the last 200 years the terrible shock of the attacks of 9 November 2001 was even greater on US government and people than they might have been in other countries.

The Churchill label was powerful in the US. His famous sayings were as much currency in Washington as in London. It was a pleasure to host a reception at our house for his granddaughter Celia Sandys about her leadership programme.

Homeland Security was big during my years in Washington. A Joint Contact Group developed between the relevant parts of the two governments and agencies to foster co-operation. There was a high-level meeting every six months. I would host the dinner at our house at Edgevale Terrace when the meeting was held in the US and came to know the people involved. I am sure Churchill would have approved of this entirely logical extension of the relationship!

The links between the two countries work well even though there are always areas of difficulty. One of those in my time was the concern in the US about a threat from radical Islam in Europe, including and even especially the UK. Briton Richard Reid was arrested with a bomb in his shoe at a US airport. The attacks in London of 7 and 21 July 2005 underlined the potential. There were calls in the US for the introduction of visas for Brits to enter the US.

On 22 September 2004, Yousuf Islam, formerly Cat Stevens, was arrested on arrival for the UK in the US: this was cack-handed. There reports of nuns being harassed at the airport. The queues at immigration became excessively long and the attitude of immigration officials hostile. This got better over time. The US seems to have refined its procedures over the years.

Another problem area, with the rest of the world rather than specifically with the UK, was the detention camp at Guantanamo Bay. In the aftermath of 9/11 there was huge sympathy for the US in the western world and beyond and an understanding of the importance of pursuing the perpetrators. The US term "War on Terror" was not to everyone's taste. But there was a general view that it was necessary to get tough with those who would attack us at home or abroad. Criticism of transporting detainees from far away to a US camp outside US jurisdiction was muted at that time.

This could not last and the US was slow to see how its image in the world was being damaged and with it the degree of international co-operation it would receive. The transfer of detainees was of questionable legality at best. The treatment of some detainees, as this came to light, was seen as crossing the boundary into torture. Water-boarding in particular, immersing detainees close to the point of drowning, was seen as adopting the kind of behaviour the western world had left behind. Then there was the issue of legal process: when and how would the detainees face a proper trial? For the UK, and for other countries, there was also the bilateral question of giving the detainees of their nationality or who had been resident in their country. proper consular and political support.

These questions became ever more difficult. US officials in the National Security Council and the State Department sought a way forward of course within the limits of the policy set by the government. Our consular officials were allowed to visit Guantanamo to meet detainees with British nationality and later British residents. There were moves to set up military courts but the progress towards these was slow, no doubt owing to the expected difficulty of securing convictions in some cases.

On 29 June 2006, Phil Zelikow and John Bellinger of the State Department came to the Embassy to give a briefing on how the administration proposed to deal with the problem issues in a definitive way. No-one doubted the wish to do this. We welcomed their initiative to come to us to talk about it, recognising that the US had to take action. This proved too difficult. Some detainees were released and some were tried. But we have seen in the following Obama Presidency how difficult it has proved to close the camp down while fears remained that releasing some detainees would increase the threat against the US. Indeed, some of those released are reported to have taken up the fight against the US again.

Tony Blair

After Churchill, the British leader who commanded the most widespread respect with the US had been Mrs Thatcher. She was seen to have stood beside President Reagan at a tricky time in the Cold War. He was willing to conclude arms reduction treaties while at the same time ready to stiffen the defences of Europe, most controversially at the time by stationing a new generation of medium-range missiles in Germany and elsewhere. Her iron determination was seen as being in the mould of Churchill. Lady Thatcher continued to visit Washington at least once a year, staying with a team at a hotel, even though her health had deteriorated considerably. Her appearance at the funeral of President Reagan in June 2004 was especially poignant.

Other British Prime Ministers since the War were received in Washington and had close relations with the US President. It was Tony Blair who took this to a new height in peacetime.

Some in the UK continue to seek ever more detail about his relationship with President Bush, especially over the UK decision to join the US in the invasion of Iraq in 2003. Perhaps it is my wont to see things as simpler than they are. But, as it looked to me, Tony Blair believed in the centrality of our alliance with the US, thought that meant being alongside the US wherever possible and he may well have wanted to take the opportunity of US activism after 9/11 to remove Saddam Hussein. The UK government came to the view, not without internal dissent, that there was a legal base for action in the long Iraqi defiance of UN Security Council Resolutions and what we believed, wrongly as it turned out, was a continuing Iraqi programme of development of chemical, biological and nuclear weapons.

The UK government did itself no favours by the so-called

"dodgy dossier" attempting to make more of the case against Saddam than the available information would allow – although not going as far as to claim a link with the 9/11 plot, as I have mentioned above Paul Wolfowitz propounded.

It may be that the Blair government was guilty of hubris in following the US lead without being clearer on the plans for "the day after". The big difference compared with 1991 was that the Allies would have to take on responsibility for administering Iraq after the fighting was over. There were people on the US side who had an almost mystic belief in the power of democracy to lead Iraqis to a better future. Yes – there were such Iraqis who believed in democracy, in Iraq and returning from exile. But there were also a lot of others, notably Sunnis, who felt they would be disadvantaged in the new set-up and others, the Shia, who felt they should be dominating power. The Kurds, of course, wanted out of Iraq or – as has happened – enough autonomy to separate themselves in terms of their security and prosperity.

Perhaps the Blair government just gambled that things would turn out well enough. The Kosovo intervention had been a bit of a leap in the dark. It turned out well enough even if there were serious issues to be resolved about the situation of the minority Serb population and areas and the political status (still yet to be accepted as a state at the UN by a significant minority of members). Sierra Leone had been another risky intervention but successful. Afghanistan, in 2003, was not going so badly at that point. The West, having been so reluctant to intervene during the Bosnia War 1991-1995, had also failed to intervene to prevent a massacre in Rwanda in 1994. But there was a record of more successful military action from 1995 to 2003. Western governments were now readier to contemplate intervention and they were sick of Saddam's ducking and diving over compliance with Security Council Resolutions.

The domestic reaction in the UK to the outcome in Iraq has dented Tony Blair's reputation (though a lot of Brits would still prefer him over his successors as Labour leader because of his pragmatic domestic policies). The dissatisfaction over Iraq has coloured the view of the UK body politic in relation to military interventions.

In 2011, David Cameron's government led with France on the intervention in Libya, but again there was insufficient thought about what would happen the day after and Libya is a mess. Gaddafi had after all done what he promised to the US and UK: he stopped his WMD programme. Was it right to intervene to remove him? Also later, the UK was at the forefront of diplomacy in the fight against the Asad regime in Syria, until the government lost a vote in Parliament in September 2013 – a shock from which Foreign Secretary William Hague never seemed to recover and he left office the following summer, a year before the end of the coalition government's term.

The strength of the personal relationship between Tony Blair and the President set the tone for the relationship of the Embassy with the Administration. The co-operation on homeland security was outstanding at a policy and practical level. We worked towards the long-cherished UK goal of an Arms Trade Treaty including on collaboration on access to information which the CIA were reluctant to allow. On the back of Tony Blair's achievement of a parliamentary vote in support of the next-generation nuclear deterrent ongoing co-operation in that field was secured.

Northern Ireland

There are some areas where the US has been part of the problem as well as part of the solution. Northern Ireland was such a case. In the past, the IRA had raised money in the pubs of Boston and some members of Congress had openly supported their cause if not their methods. Over time, accelerating during the premiership of John Major and again during Tony Blair's time, the UK government understood the need to engage the US administration and Congress positively and put aside irritation that the US and other foreigners were in effect messing with our internal affairs. An important step was engaging Senator Mitchell and others in the peace process and giving them real influence.

This made a difference. I went with successive Northern Ireland Secretaries to visit key players in Washington. One call together with John Reid on Senator Edward Kennedy had a touch of comedy, an episode to brighten a diplomat's day (not that such a fabulous posting as Washington needs much joy added to it!). It was hot summer. Senator Kennedy had been outside talking to some union protesters and entered in his shirt and red braces bathed in sweat. With him came one of his dogs who made a beeline for the sitting John Reid, jumped on him and started licking his face. Not every minute of the official engagements of one of Her Majesty's Secretaries of State is replete with dignity!

I recall Hillary Clinton, then a Senator, being ready to help by using what contacts and influence she had, for example with the Protestant community. The same was true of senior officials at State, such as John Bellinger, and at the White House.

We started to take a broader view of the annual celebration of St Patrick's Day in Washington, which included a reception by the President. Once, our main preoccupation had been to persuade the White House not to invite Sinn Fein. We now sought to combine the occasion with an event of our own at the Embassy supporting the peace process. The way forward had to be together with the Irish government and the political parties in the North, even including those who had strong links with the IRA such as Gerry Adams and Martin McGuinness.

I was amazed to find myself hosting breakfast for Ian Paisley and Martin McGuinness on 7 December 2007 at the Willard hotel in Washington, one of the first occasions they travelled abroad together. Their joshing of each other, after the hatred of so many years, underlined the maturity which had arrived in the peace process, however intractable some issues remained.

When Tony Blair made his final visit to Washington as Prime Minister on 16-17 May 2007 it was a moment to reflect on what had been achieved on Northern Ireland. At short notice, the Ambassador invited a large number of people who had played a role on Northern Ireland. Senator Edward Kennedy came. So did Congressman Pete King, once one of the strongest critics of UK policy. Tony Blair, with his customary grace, had his photo taken with everyone who wanted that memento and stayed at the event until the end.

On the second afternoon of that last visit by Tony Blair as Prime Minister I found myself called upon to help with a phone call to him from President Sarkozy. Tony Blair understood French well but his staff, taking the note, were not so confident – so I gave the gist to them. It was the extrovert Sarkozy telling him that he had to stand for the new post of President of Europe. But it was soon clear that European partners were not going to accept such as powerful figure in this position, especially a Brit. A pity. In fact, the EU went in the other direction towards personalities who were not well-known and not likely to wield real power and influence. Having Tony Blair as EU President would have had a huge impact on the European relationship with the US and perhaps the UK too. The right person from the right country could make a difference. That was also true of former Irish Prime

Minister John Bruton's appointment as EU Ambassador in Washington instead of an unknown Eurocrat as was the usual practice.

The strong relationship between Prime Minister and President helped us too in a range of policy areas. One of the most difficult has always been the Middle East Peace Process, notably Israel/Palestine. Here again Tony Blair was greatly involved, and continued to be so after stepping down as Prime Minister. There are plenty of knowledgeable experts in the US who would support a solution on similar lines to those supported by the UK and EU – a territorial settlement based on the pre-1967 borders with some adjustments, some arrangement to share Jerusalem, recognition of Israel and security measures backed by the international community. The Americans have unique leverage with the parties, especially Israel. But there are also those in the US who support Israel continuing to create facts on the ground. A big difference has always been that the UK sees the Israeli settlements as contrary to international law. There is no consensus in the US to join in with this view – which gives Israelis the perspective that they can continue on their current path and still ultimately have US protection.

I saw a fair bit of the thinkers and players on the US side. Dennis Ross had unparalleled expertise of negotiation. Dan Fried, Phil Zelikow and others were pragmatists looking for a way forward.

The scope for moving forward was narrow. There was a view in Washington, particularly after 9/11, that the issues for the US in the Middle East had moved on and the Israel/Palestine dispute was no longer the central question. The Administration started to talk about the Broader Middle East, encompassing Iran and Afghanistan as well as the Arabian Peninsula and Egypt. I sat in on several conversations with leading players from the FCO and No 10 in Washington. I saw these people myself and especially enjoyed breakfasts with Dennis Ross at my house as he was on his way into the State Department.

The Americans had no time for Yasser Arafat. They had, with distaste, tried to bring him into negotiations but found him unwilling to commit. When he died, in mysterious circumstances, on 27 October 2004, the Americans felt an obstacle to peace had disappeared. The opposite was the case. If they could have brought Arafat to negotiate and agree a deal – and I admit I do not know whether this was possible though I wanted to believe it was – there would have been a real chance of wide acceptance around the world because Arafat was such a key personality in world politics. We have seen since his death the split between Hamas and the more traditional Palestinian organisations as well as the growth of radical Islam in the whole region and beyond. The goalposts for a negotiation have shifted considerably.

A joy of working in the Washington Embassy was that there was an important angle for us to pursue in just about every foreign-policy issue in the world – whether regional or global. So I got to talk about issues in Africa, Asia, South America and also the issues of global warming, poverty reduction, global trade.

This included a role on Bermuda. The island had decided in a referendum to remain an overseas territory under UK sovereignty probably so as to keep the useful UK passport and also, crucially, to bolster its image as a centre for financial services which could be trusted. The US Congress was suspicious of these islands in the Caribbean. So about every 6 months the Bermudan Prime Minister would come with a team to Washington to talk to Congress and would come to the Embassy to see either the Ambassador or, if he was

British Governor's Residence in Bermuda

unavailable, me. We also visited Bermuda in April 2006 to talk to the government, including a call on the Premier, and understand better how the island functioned. We stayed the weekend at the Princess hotel in Hamilton. I enjoyed drinking a Dark and Stormy at the Pickled Onion. The Governor John Vereker and his wife Judy kindly hosted us at the Residence for a couple of nights thereafter.

Members of the Falklands Islands Legislative Council also came by once a year linked with their visit to the UN in New York for the annual decolonisation session. Here were two residents saying the people wanted to remain under British Falklands rule and did not want to be considered as oppressed under colonial rule. That did not suit the agenda of Argentina and allies. We met them in Washington as part of their work to ensure the Administration understood their situation.

The traditional position of the US was not to take a view on sovereignty of the islands. The US aversion to colonies and empire, understandably except their own, continued in attenuated form even into the 21st century. But the Argentina of the Kirchners had done itself no favours by its graceless treatment of George Bush when he visited Argentina in 2005 for the Summit of the Americas. The anti-US rhetoric of the Argentine government was also not helpful to their cause. I know the Administration enjoyed tearing a strip off the Argentine Ambassador when some further egregious insult from Buenos Aires gave them the opportunity. Dubya was a President who took more of an interest in Latin America than any other, at least since Teddy Roosevelt, and Argentina took no advantage of it. That helped the Falklands cause.

A major aspect of life in the Embassy was handling visitors from the UK. We had sometimes to be strict and say we could not look after some would-be visitors at particular times (when we had the Prime Minister, senior Cabinet or just a lot of visitors). This often did not go down well as people in London have tight schedules. We had to be straight sometimes with Junior Ministers about the level of access they would achieve in Washington unless they had some special angle (some just wanted to come to Washington). Americans did not understand Junior Ministers as they do not have an equivalent.

Domesticity

When the Ambassador was out of town or had to deal with another visitor it fell to me to host them. Our house at Edgevale Terrace, less than 10 minutes' walk from the Embassy off Massachusetts Avenue, was set up to handle this. We had a team of three Filipinas, all related, as the permanent staff – the senior one was the cook and housekeeper – and they had contacts with many more who could work as additional staff for events. The house was lovely. Large enough for receptions and meals and to offer accommodation, but still cosy enough to feel like a home (unlike the residence where the Ambassador and wife had a flat above the grand shop). Unlike European destinations, Washington is too far in distance and time for a one-day visit so the possibility of accommodation at Edgevale Terrace – if the prestigious Ambassadorial Luytens residence was not available – was eagerly accepted.

Although close to Massachusetts Avenue our setting had a touch of countryside as we were facing the long strip of land through Washington which is Rock Creek Park. Very early in the morning there were sometimes deer in the road. They ate anything which grew above ground level in the unfenced front garden. I once saw a coyote early in the morning. We had chipmunks in the back garden and once I saw a family of raccoons there. The birds were beautiful, especially the red cardinals. We had fireflies in May-June.

Soon after we arrived we experienced a plague of cicadas, which hits Washington in full force every 17 years. There were thousands of them outside the front door. The screech they made reminded me of Psycho. They were big, ugly and harmless. Within a few weeks all that was left were the husks.

We had a large number of Ministers, parliamentarians, officials and others from UK to stay and for events. I liked breakfasts and lunches as working occasions with structured discussion. Dinners tended to start and finish early unless they involved people we knew pretty well. I had one invitation to dinner at the Senate for 1730! The Bush administration started early in the morning and Congress seemed to be going in the same direction. Quite a change compared with the legendary late-night parties of previous generations in Washington.

These visits were helpful to the Embassy in getting us in to see senior people. They were also interesting opportunities to hear a bit about politics at home. I particularly enjoyed those who were discursive, like Charles Clarke and Peter Hain. Others provided memorable moments. When David Miliband came on 5-6 June 2007 as Secretary of State for Environment, Food and Rural Affairs one journalist floated with him the possibility that he might become Foreign Secretary. This was an entirely new idea to me. He responded quietly: "That would be nice". He was appointed Foreign Secretary on 28 June. He must have had more than an inkling when he came to Washington of what was to come.

John Reid came to Washington in several of his different Ministerial positions. When he came as Northern Ireland Secretary he and his party arrived at the house late at night on 17 June 2007 and he had his staff hopping about even later. I admired him and liked his politics but working with him would not have been easy. We went down to the National Security Council the next day and had to walk briefly in the sunshine. This made me realise how used I had become to the fierce Washington summers. He asked if it was always as hot as this. Hotter than Glasgow, for sure. Perhaps Teddy Kennedy's dog (in the episode I've already described) was licking the sweat from his face.

Parliamentary committees from both Houses and on all issues loved to visit. The Americans could relate to these as their congressional committees went overseas too. That didn't make it easier to gain high-level meetings unless there were some compelling reasons or personal contacts. In the US and elsewhere there was a risk that committees would fall into their London mode and start hectoring people they visited as if they were taking evidence. As a senior diplomat you had to watch your step with them. They could be friendly one minute and in investigatory mode the next.

We also saw individual MPs who wanted to see us. Not all did. George Galloway was not in touch with us when he came to Washington to give evidence to the Senate on the UN food-for-oil programme for Iraq on 17 May 2005. I am not a fan of Mr Galloway, not least because of his relationship with President Milosevic, the main cause of the terrible Bosnia War, but he is a skilled political operator and he gave the Senate more than they bargained for – not that that made any impact on policy.

My role included supervising the British Consulates around the US and acting as line manager to the Consuls, except the Consul-General in New York who reported to the Ambassador. We had Miami, Orlando, Atlanta, New York, Boston, Chicago, Denver, San Francisco, Los Angeles and Houston. It was important to hear views "outside the beltway" as Americans talked about travelling outside Washington (the beltway being the motorway around the District of Columbia). The Consulates ranged in size and function – trade promotion and consular work being the staples of their purpose. They were all special in their way.

Chicago had the most stunning residence, an apartment on the 63rd floor with a panoramic view of the lake and downtown. You went up in the lift and entered the apartment to be greeted by the most amazing view through the glass on the two floors (the door gave on to the upper floor). Chicago had great music – we saw a concert conducted by Haitink there – and was a special place for a St Patrick's Day celebration with the river turned green and people of all races enjoying the party.

Boston was the most atmospheric. The Consul-General's residence then was an old town house in Chestnut Street, a perfect counterpoint to the modern office building used by the Consulate-General just over the bridge in Cambridge. On 25 October 2008, I met Tim Berners Lee, inventor of the internet, there playing with the Consul-General's young child in the margin of an event for the visiting President of the Royal Society Lord Rees.

Los Angeles had a residence well suited to the annual party of people invited to the Oscars. They had a team which worked on film because of its substantial contribution to prosperity back home. They also covered Orange county and San Diego, in themselves huge economies of importance to the UK.

San Francisco had given up a large residence and acquired a house in a nice area where US senator Diane Feinstein lived. The House of Commons Foreign Affairs Committee asked several years in a row why the FCO had made this change losing such a grand residence, which some of them had visited. One complained that it was like moving from Westminster to Ealing. I wondered what was wrong with that. We did not need a house of that size.

The Consulate-General also covered Silicon Valley, which I visited a couple of times and learned the importance for the future of international collaboration on innovation and the opportunity for such hotspots as Cambridge in the UK. We closed our Consulate in Seattle so San Francisco had also to cover Washington State: I tried to introduce the idea that the Deputy Consul General should have a special responsibility for the state and visit regularly but I don't think it took root.

Atlanta was our Consulate-General for the South East minus Florida. It was the Cinderella of the Consulates as UKTI did not see it as so important commercially as other areas, despite the economic rise of the Carolinas. For that reason the possibility of closure arose whenever there was a review of the US network of Posts. I always hoped we can could adopt the opposite path and make more of our investment in Atlanta. You can make a case for anything and the FCO has to cut its cloth according to the money available. Yet we could not steel ourselves to covering all this territory either from Miami or Washington.

Miami was at risk of closure during my time. At a meeting with Jack Straw in Washington we basically agreed a deal dropping the idea of closing Miami but also dropping for now the idea of a major build at our Washington Embassy site (and instead just doing what was necessary to give it a longer lease of life: the basic support systems – water and electrical – were on their last legs). Miami grew in importance and became a Consulate-General in line with the others mentioned above.

We also had a Consulate in Orlando entirely of locally-engaged staff and entirely focussed on the consular issues arising from the attraction of Disney and the related holiday areas. Vast numbers of Brits came through Sanford Airport alone, some with little money. A few ended up in prison. I was struck that the fragmentation of the US judicial system between city and counties at that time meant that some of these prisoners were notified to the consulate and some not. Some prisoners could be found online.

Denver was a one-person operation opened to take advantage of a strong welcome in Colorado and kept even though UKTI moved out. This post was an interesting case for the debate between those on the one hand who believed we should spread our resources in more posts and trust our staff to deliver through the deeper local knowledge and stronger local contacts and those on the other hand who believed we were better off concentrating staff and money in fewer posts – UKTI at this time sought to have staff only in four posts (New York, LA, Chicago, Houston) meaning that the viability of others – even San Francisco – was in question. Perhaps unsurprisingly we carved something of a middle path between these two ideas – but Denver was bound to be vulnerable despite its small cost and strong local standing.

That leaves the Consulate-General at Houston. This city is the world's capital of oil and gas, a key industry for the UK (as well as being the largest city of the South). I loved Texas – Austin, San Antonio, Galveston – but Houston was not my favourite. The city centre is made for the car and the subterranean shopper.

Hurricane Katrina was the biggest test for the staff there in my time. On 3 June 2005 I was at FCO in London for crisis management training. The FCO was acutely aware that one of its main vulnerabilities was response to consular emergencies. Of course we had always known that. Yet, for some of us, this was not top of our thoughts. We saw foreign-policy issues and emergencies as the core of our mission; the consular dimensions were important but for others to deal with. The point this training was getting across was that senior staff needed to see consular emergencies as top of their agenda and be prepared to react fast. Ministers already understood this, as Jack Straw had shown in his decision to travel immediately to Istanbul when the Consulate-General there was bombed and the Consul General and others killed.

The training at FCO was designed to shock the senses. Just as we were easing into an introductory session alarm bells rang. We learned of a consular emergency and before we had drawn breath we were being asked to make decisions and respond to media interest. The training made an impression on me. I understood the need to have a clear idea of how to organise staff and the importance of command, control and leading from the front.

On 31 August 2005, the levees broke and New Orleans was flooded after Hurricane Katrina had hit. It wasn't the first hurricane or the last in what was a particularly severe hurricane season. What was different was the impact. It soon became clear that lives would be lost.

I had a lunch in Washington with two former members of the administration, Frank Miller and Marc Grossman. I was in charge of the Embassy in the Ambassador's absence. By the end of the lunch I had decided I needed to go down to Houston myself to supervise the consular response. I had already sent our Head of Consular, Graeme Wise, down there earlier in the day. The FCO training persuaded me I needed to be there too, especially as our Consul General was away on a duty visit to Aberdeen, the UK centre for oil and gas. There were reports of a party of young Brits being marooned in a hotel in New Orleans. There would certainly be other Brits affected. I formed an Emergency Response operation at the Embassy, named myself Crisis Manager and others as my Deputies and to lead on the various aspects of the effort. I got on a plane to Houston that afternoon. I arrived at 2120 together with a press officer from the Embassy.

The authorities in Texas had decided to evacuate people from New Orleans, sent in buses and set up an emergency reception area with beds and medical attention organised by the Red Cross at the Houston Astrodome. I and a few others from the Consulate were there all night as people arrived on the buses. In the confusion the buses had simply allowed anyone to board and brought them to Houston. In a situation of uncertain safety the buses did not reach, for example, the hotel in New Orleans where the party of British youngsters was stuck. Just one Brit arrived that night in Houston on the buses. Our team helped point people in the right direction. We were the only foreign country represented at that time.

On 2 September Consul General Judith Slater returned to Houston, and a Rapid Response team from UK was in the field following up leads about Brits who might have been caught up in the storm in the states of Louisiana and Mississippi. I went back to Washington. The operation continued. We sought permission from the Louisiana state and city authorities to go into New Orleans itself, especially to the hotel where the young Brits were staying. There was no electricity, so the batteries of mobile phones could not be recharged and we heard nothing more from the party of youngsters. There were rumours of looting and violence. The authorities did not want us to enter the city.

This did not go down well in London as there was pressure from the media about what we were doing to help the youngsters and any other Brits in New Orleans. Some media reporters were getting into the city. I was clear that we could not go in while the US authorities were saying we should not do so, both because we were stationed in the US accredited to them and should obey their rules and because the risks to our own staff of entering the city at that stage had to be borne in mind.

By 5 September there was a very strong media focus in the US and UK on the situation, especially in New Orleans. I received a message from the Prime Minister's party, then in Beijing, that I should get on to the media. I did a live interview in Washington with Sky News on a roof with the iconic dome of the Capitol Building as the backdrop. I gave the three messages: our sympathy for those caught up in the disaster; the dedication of the whole Embassy and network to helping Brits affected; and our admiration for the work of the US authorities with whom we were co-operating closely. The interview was in several pieces as Sky monitored the helicopter of President Bush coming in to land at the White House.

We organised staff throughout the network to staff teams in the field. We had no shortage of volunteers. They needed to be self-sufficient and resilient, with satellite phones and water. Some hardly slept. A stringer for one UK paper wrote that our Consul whom she saw at a hotel in Louisiana was a coward because he had not gone into New Orleans. She wrote that she was only a girl in a skirt but could do better. His young son read this. The man concerned was one of the most dedicated consular officers I have met and went days with very little sleep and not always finding a hotel bed.

Ministers were on edge too. I was concerned that they were implying we were not doing enough. This got through to Lord Triesman, then a Minister at the FCO. He rang me from UK having pulled off a motorway. He said I need not be concerned. He came to Washington the following week.

The youngsters in New Orleans got away after a few days, fortunately unscathed by the violence. We did eventually find that a couple of longstanding residents of UK extraction had died in the flooding.

There were other alarms. Hurricane Rita later in September was the fourth-most intense tropical cyclone ever observed in the Gulf of Mexico, stronger than Katrina. It killed around 100 people in the Caribbean and Florida and caused more flooding in New Orleans and Louisiana but not the devastation there of Katrina. People were advised to evacuate Houston and the chaotic traffic out of the city created its own problems and caused some fatalities. I spoke to our Consul General Judith Slater who decided to stay home that morning having told staff not to report for duty at the office downtown. It turned out that she took the right decision. But this showed the difficulty of getting the response right. Hurricane Wilma later in October was the most intense cyclone ever recorded in the Atlantic basin. Fortunately, it did its worst out at sea.

Travelling around the US

One of the wonders of life as a diplomat is the chance to travel in the host country. With no small children at home the US posting was a special opportunity.

In Washington DC itself, walking was a pleasure – in

the crisp cold winter making snowmen, the glory of spring including cherry blossom at Kenwood, the hot summer introduced by fireflies, the balmy autumn with warm weather lasting sometimes into November.

Washington was said to have northern charm and southern efficiency. It's true that it was unloved by visitors in its earlier history. The story goes that it was chosen as the capital of the Union not only as a compromise between the North and South and because George Washington had an interest in the area, but also because its unhealthy climate encouraged legislators not to tarry – the quicker they worked the quicker they could leave the place and go home. The advent of air conditioning after WW II helped.

Now people are desperate for property in formerly insalubrious areas. The gentrification is moving steadily across the District. The newer Virginia and Maryland suburbs are expensive. All this has its downside as poorer people are edged out. But Washington has become a desirable place to live. We loved the walks through historic streets, the developing riverside areas, the parks.

A Civil War story. On our visit to Washington before starting work there I sat next to an American lady at a dinner party in what was to become our house. She had lived in Washington for some time but had been born of a southern family. The conversation came to the Civil War because I mentioned that I had been watching the wonderful Ken Burns TV series on the Civil War, which is so immediate because it is told in photographs and diary extracts. She said she had heard from her grandmother how Union General Sherman in his sweep through the South to the sea at the end of the War had not only destroyed the crops and economy to bring the south to its knees but had waged terror through rape of women. She related this to me with a shiver of barely repressed rage as if she had heard just yesterday of these events which happened 150 years previously. The other side of the coin is the horror of slavery for which the South has greater responsibility than the North. The North and South are reconciled now. But that does not mean all is forgotten or even forgiven.

Nearby Washington there are reminders of US history. Mount Vernon of course – early on in my time I was on the former Presidential yacht Sequoia, now for private hire, with new Home Office Minister Hazel Blears and others attending an international event sailing down the Potomac to George Washington's former home, now a museum. There are falls upstream in the Potomac which we always favoured when we had family and friends visiting. There are Civil War battlefields – in Virginia and of course Gettysburg in Pennsylvania – all with Rangers to help you understand. There is Harper's Ferry of John Brown fame in glorious country. All doable in day trips.

A special place for me was Charlottesville. Monticello and the University of Virginia are reminders of the great legacy of Thomas Jefferson. My reason for visiting several times was different. On 18 December 2004 the King's College Cambridge choir came to our house after the final performance at Washington National Cathedral of their US pre-Christmas tour. We had invited all alumni of King's living in the proximity to the party. It was memorable. We had a log fire crackling. The older boys sang some wonderful Barber Shop quartets. The young boys raced around the house.

One invitee, Adam Watson, wrote to me to say he would have loved to come, but now being somewhat frail at 90 years of age he felt unable to make the trip from his home in Charlottesville. He invited us to come and visit him. We did so on 10 April 2005, meeting Adam and his wife Andie, a southern lady a little younger than he and not reconciled to modernity such as seat belts as we discovered when she drove us around at one point.

Adam escorted us on a tour of the Lawn, the centrepiece of the University of Virginia where he was still a Professor of Political Theory.

His life story was fascinating. He had studied in Germany in the 1930s and seen the rise of Hitler. He had joined the Foreign Office – or was it SIS? – before the War and served in Moscow where he had seen Churchill during the latter's visit to talk to Stalin in 1942. He heard him talk about the War late into the night in the Embassy. Then, he was Head of Chancery at the Embassy in Washington in the late 1940s. I so wish I had recorded what he said about that time. He had been a roving government envoy to Africa during the period of independence in the 1950s. In the early 1960s he had been the first British Ambassador to Cuba in the Castro era. He had found a connection with Castro discussing agriculture – Adam's father had run a farm and his brother still did, in Sussex, which Adam visited every summer. Adam had then left diplomacy and joined the British car industry, then still one of the strongest in the world but the wrong choices were made about foreign investments. Later still, he started a new life in the US.

He spoke German, Spanish and French beautifully as so few Brits nowadays can who are not professional linguists. He continued to write about political theory. He continued to teach. Sadly, his health deteriorated after this visit when he still able to walk with us around the Lawn. I learned this by email from Andie. I visited again on 20 May 2007. We had lunch, as previously, at Farmington House with its wonderful calm atmosphere and views across the countryside. Adam was clearly in decline. He died on 1 November 2007. I went to a memorial service for him in Charlottesville.

By halfway in my time in Washington, I realised that I could tick off all 50 states of the Union, adding visits before our posting to ones during it. My fiftieth state was North

Dakota when I visited Bismarck on 6 October 2008. People often ask about favourites. The easy but true answer is that all the states had something wonderful: in Californiathe drive along the coast from Los Angeles to San Francisco; the national parks; the mountains; San Diego. Alaska was unforgettable. We flew from Anchorage to Dead Horse (I have the T-shirt) airport in the far north by the oil refinery and came back down in a bus through the tundra and saw the wonders of Denali National Park and a clear view of the summit of Mt McKinley. Key West in Florida felt special too, the southernmost point of the US and looking towards the Caribbean and especially Cuba, which one day will be connected with Florida again. Visiting Dodge City in Kansas was special, and talking in his office in Washington about the ageless series Gunsmoke set in Dodge with Senator Pat Roberts of Kansas (who had kindly hosted our son Tim as an intern in his Washington DC office). Las Vegas in Nevada – a place to relax and enjoy. Coffee and beignets in New Orleans. Beale Street and the Rock and Soul Museum in Memphis. The charm of Charleston and especially Savannah in the south. Hawaii coffee fields. New Hampshire in the autumn. New York of course. This is not a travel book, so I'll leave it there!

The so-called fly-over states had their own charm. After visiting Oklahoma City and Tulsa I gave a lecture at the Oral Roberts University. I was introduced by a delightful young man from Africa called Blessed Moreover.

The mass of farmland is a wonder to behold in some of these states. On 18 August 2007 I drove from Des Moines, Iowa, some 250 miles round trip to the small town of Waverly. I saw little else but maize and other cereals en route.

PART III

MEETING
INTERESTING PEOPLE

The purpose of the drive through Iowa was to see Senator Barack Obama on the Presidential campaign trail – the Iowa caucus being the first of the state primaries scheduled for the 2008 Presidential election. He spoke on energy security at a meeting in a large factory hangar. The response was interesting. Helpers had to keep putting out chairs for Iowans and people who had come by bus from elsewhere. There were several hundred people there, not counting the media. All white. A man in a stetson next to me said he reckoned this guy better than others he had seen. Obama looked a million dollars in black shirt with sleeves half-rolled up and black trousers. He was slim, energetic and confident. He spoke in a way everyone could understand without being patronising. He answered questions without evasion. I could already see him as President.

I had met him a couple of times in the Senate. Once had been a chance encounter in the corridors when accompanying John Reid on 19 June 2007. The other was a call by David Lammy MP. Obama asked if we could help with the dying wish of a child to appear as an extra on a Harry Potter film: Obama's staff had got stuck with Equity rules. I later heard that Mr Lammy's staff did manage to arrange this.

John McCain, to become the Republican candidate for the Presidency, was friendly towards our Embassy. He was a thoroughly decent man with some conservative views but able to appeal across the party divide in a way that few younger Republicans can. I was involved in several meetings with him at the Senate. One stands especially in memory. On 2 March 2006 the Foreign Affairs Committee had a call on him. He perched on his desk as the Committee members found seats around. They were thrilled. It's the kind of moment which made these trips for parliamentarians, who were not going to be received at a very high level in the Administration.

Surprise Party for Condoleeza Rice

The Washington Residence is a place of renown in the Service. Official visitors are anxious to stay there. Ambassadors are anxious to limit the strain on the staff. It is furiously busy and the Ambassador in exhausting perpetual motion. I have some understanding for previous Ambassador Chris Meyer who wrote that he found himself once in another house in Washington saying automatically to someone "Welcome to the British Embassy".

An especially memorable night was the surprise 50th birthday party for Condoleeza Rice. This had been arranged in secrecy between the residence and Condi's White House – she was then still National Security Advisor and about to be appointed Secretary of State.

It was 13 November 2004, just ten days after George Bush was re-elected. Condi was driven with her aunt towards – she thought – Georgetown for a birthday dinner at a restaurant when the car went into the Embassy. She told me she had not immediately thought too much of that as she visited the Embassy to practise with her chamber music group. I knew that as I had seen her playing the piano there and once amazing a couple of former US Senators with whom David and I were having dinner when she popped her head around the door.

As she entered the Residence this time she saw all the guests snaking up the staircase in black-tie – including the President and First Lady, many others from government past and present (Vice-President Cheney had been scheduled to attend but was taken to hospital that day with a heart issue), her family, friends from Berkeley where she had been Provost, pianist Van Cliburn. David and Catherine Manning had kindly also invited Judy and me. Condi was whisked upstairs, dressed in a scarlet gown by her favourite New York designer Oscar de la Renta and had a ball. I have a recollection of dancing the conga holding on to the First Lady.

The internet was already busy in 2006. But social media were still young. Somehow no news of the event seeped out at first. There was nothing in the newspapers – and how the social columns would have loved it! I was asked weeks later by diplomats from other Embassies about it and said

Condoleeza Rice at her surprise 50th birthday party at the British Residence
Washington

nothing. I wonder if it would be possible to keep such an event quiet nowadays? News did leak out eventually, and in the following year was the subject of some carping about the cost in the UK and a written Parliamentary Question after the New Statesman called it a "ludicrously lavish extravaganza". Hosting a party with such a guest list for $9,500 seems to me a not unreasonable use of public money. The FCO spent that kind of money and more, in short order, chasing Freedom of Information requests for MPs who wanted to see every public document with their names on it and for the media on fishing expeditions.

I admired Condi Rice. She had a rigid work ethic. She was up very early in the morning and on her treadmill to keep in shape before travelling to the State Department ahead of most of her staff. She was entirely unpretentious and unstuffy. She prepared in a typically disciplined way for the role of Secretary of State, reading every treaty to which the US was party. Very rarely did she show any emotion.

One occasion she did show just the slightest touch was at her inauguration as Secretary with a small number of people at the State Department for the swearing-in, of which I was lucky enough to be one. In her remarks, she asked rhetorically what the first holder of the office (Thomas Jefferson, one of the largest slaveholders of the time, who never acknowledged his children by a black slave) would have thought of her as a successor as Secretary of State. She noted that he supported the idea that a black should be counted as two-thirds of a person in the population count of the States of the Union. She did not develop this train of thought further. She did not need to.

This had additional spice for me as I love US history and prefer the more prosaic John Adams over the more colourful Thomas Jefferson, who was unrepentant about the lack of liberty for such a large proportion of the population while proclaiming the new republic as the land of the free. Of course there were real economic and political issues about how to develop the United States without slavery and to keep together the north and the south of the new Republic. George Washington freed his slaves when he died. Jefferson did not do that. I suppose my view is also coloured by the fact that Jefferson leant more to the France of Emperor Napoleon Bonaparte than to the UK of an increasingly liberal foreign policy towards independence movements in the Americas led by George Canning.

There was chatter about Condi running for President. She was always clear that she had no such intention. She said publicly that her greatest aspiration was to be President of her favourite football (American) team. I suspect she wasn't the sort of person who would have relished the business of running for office.

There were some great characters in Washington. One such was Arnaud de Borchgrave, of noble Belgian extraction, father-in-law of Robin Niblett then deputy at CSIS and later Director of Chatham House in London, and always to be seen at major think-tank events. Arnaud was in his eighties but still very much on the ball, on his treadmill every morning and looking pretty fit. On 26 September 2006, coming down the lift after a book launch by Madeleine Albright at CFR (Committee for Foreign Relations) he told me that he had just visited a stonemason to order his headstone. I took the bait, saying that he had many years ahead of him. He asked me if I could guess the inscription. I did what seemed required, asking him to tell me. The answer was: "I saw this coming".

The diplomat overseas has to form working relationships with people relevant to the areas he covers. In the Blair years it was even easier in Washington than normal. I could see key people at State and NSC and elsewhere. Marc Grossman as the Under-Secretary Political was especially good with his very limited time and I kept seeing him after his (temporary) retirement to private sector consulting. John Bolton was regarded by some in the UK and US as an extreme right-winger. I found him extremely knowledgeable, helpful and courteous when he was Under-Secretary for Defence at State Department; the same went for his successor Bob Joseph. Dan Fried, a political appointment in the second Bush term, wanted to get things done and was imaginative in exploring new avenues. Fran Townsend, Homeland Security at NSC, was a delight to work with.

Then there were the Burnses at State Department, neither of them related as far as I know with Ken Burns the maker of great documentaries such as that on the Civil War. Nick Burns became Under-Secretary Political. He wasn't quite as accessible as Marc Grossman and he saw more of the Ambassador but I could get to see him if needed. Bill Burns was in Washington occasionally but mostly away in Moscow as Ambassador. I had known him in Jordan over 20 years previously. Paula Dobriansky worked incredibly hard as Under Secretary for Global Affairs and regularly accrued more responsibilities. Kristin Silverberg was the talented young lead on UN affairs. On the Middle East, Eliot Cohen came with a reputation for leaning towards Israel but that is generally true in Washington and I had no doubt he wanted an Israel/Palestine settlement if one was negotiable.

Henrietta Fore was Under-Secretary for Management, M, who was naturally keen to meet James Bond's "M", Judi Dench. I exchanged notes with Henrietta from my time on the FCO Board about management reform and she kindly invited me to meetings of the Advisory Board set up by Condi Rice about the "Embassy of the Future". I went to the launch of the Report at CSIS, another of the great think tanks in Washington, on 15 October 2008. The high-calibre committee of businessmen, academics etc recommended an increase in the State Department's staffing of 1,000 people. A minority report recommended at least 2,000 additional staff. This is a striking contrast with the FCO's struggle for much of my time in service even to maintain its budget in real terms despite the understanding that the UK's security and prosperity depends so much on our connections around the world. The excellent new Permanent Under Secretary, Simon McDonald, will have all to do to ensure the Service manages to remain among the best while having to make more savings in the coming years

Beyond the circle of acquaintances connected through work we enjoyed the company of former members of the Administration such as Dan Poneman, who was part of a rock band including the Hungarian Ambassador and a former member of Steely Dan called "Coalition of the Willing." The Folger Library run by Gail Paster with its wonderful Shakespeare collection and scholarship was a joy. Our interest in the theatre there led to us hosting a reception for our hero Derek Jacobi.

Colleagues from other Embassies are always an important part of diplomatic life overseas. Sometimes it's possible to join forces to add weight on certain issues – the EU as a club does this in particular. Individuals make a difference. John Bruton, former Irish Prime Minister, became EU Ambassador in Washington. He worked hard using his CV, nationality and personal charm to reach all parts of Congress and beyond. He lived quite close to us off Massachusetts Avenue. The EU machine does not much like such appointments and I am no unqualified fan of political as opposed to career Ambassadors. He was remarkably effective without in any way being too grand to rub shoulders with other diplomats. Wolfgang

Ischinger, whom I had known in Bosnia days, became German Ambassador. The French Embassy I admired: having been in the doghouse of US opinion for speaking out against US policy on Iraq they worked their way back to co-operation on many foreign-policy issues, which is as it should be.

A Deputy Head of Mission has to be able to deputise for the Ambassador and do the foreign policy, the speeches and the calls that the Ambassador would do. I liked to think of that as my primary role. Of course, even then, you are not the Ambassador and only in charge in an acting capacity. The bread and butter of the Deputy has to include overseeing the work of the Embassy, including the administrative side, and perhaps leading on particular projects.

Writing annual reports on all the Heads of Section in Washington and the Heads of our Consulates-General was a major and laborious exercise. What I thought more important was trying to help them including with a view to their further careers, using the knowledge I had gained as HR Director in London.

Everyone has his or her path. Not all are ambitious. But, unsurprisingly, many who came to the US were strong performers with potential to do even bigger jobs. Sebastian Wood went on to be Ambassador to China and next Germany; Frank Baker Ambassador to Kuwait; Susan Le Jeune became HR Director and then Ambassador to Austria; Julian Braithwaite became Consular Director and then moved to NATO; Matthew Gould became Ambassador to Israel; Andrew Seaton was Consul-General in Hong Kong; Martin Uden Ambassador to Korea; John Rankin High Commissioner to Sri Lanka; Judith Slater Deputy High Commissioner to South Africa and Singapore and soon Consul-General in Istanbul. The First and Second Secretaries have moved onwards and many upwards too.

Washington was another opportunity to work with the military and MOD as in pre-unification Berlin and in London over Bosnia. We also had a Treasury representation, an Agriculture attaché, a Scottish Affairs Team and others. Whitehall on the Potomac was the strapline. I enjoyed working with the Science and Innovation team; Jack Straw gave the first ever speech by a UK Foreign Secretary devoted to Science in Washington at Howard University on 13 May 2005. I learned to see the power of diplomacy in promoting UK science and – linked with that – promoting UK Higher Education in general. More of that when we come to Brazil.

I would not have gone to Washington to work for any other Ambassador than David Manning. When he left in September 2008 at the end of his term I was ready to go too.

We enjoyed a great send-off dinner hosted by the new Ambassador Nigel Sheinwald and his wife Julia. Being invited to the British Ambassador's residence in Washington is a hot ticket and well over a hundred came. I've found the text of my speech for the evening. I mentioned that I had hosted then Environment Secretary Margaret Beckett there on my first day in Washington. This farewell dinner was the other bookend.

A British diplomat's speech on such occasions invariably includes an amusing story. I used the grandeur of the setting to contrast with the austerity of a dinner at the British Embassy in Moscow hosted for Foreign Secretary Ernest Bevin just after the end of World War II at the house of Ambassador Sir Morris Peterson, Lady Peterson and their elderly Scotch terrier Brindel. Ernest Bevin recounted later that they had given him with the cheese what appeared to be dog biscuits. By way of a joke he said at the end of the meal: "Lady Peterson – these look like dog biscuits". "As a matter of fact they are" she replied "but we like them." After a pause Mr Bevin said: "I hope I'm not depriving Brindel of his dinner". "That's quite all right, Secretary of State" she said "Brindel won't eat them".

We left the snows of Washington in late January 2008 for a holiday in the summer of New Zealand and Australia.

5.

BRAZIL

THE LUCKY COUNTRY

A Brazilian ascended to Heaven. At the pearly gates he thanked his maker for the wonderful country in which he'd lived his life. "It has beautiful forests, mighty rivers, a lovely climate, mineral and oil riches, no enemies. Thank you, Lord". The Almighty stroked his long beard and replied. "You are right. Of all the places in my creation it is among the very best. But I did play one trick, my son. I put the Brazilians in it." It was a Brazilian who told me the story and I have heard several other versions of it.

The Brazilians are proud of their country. They are patriotic. Just listen to how they belt out the national anthem at big sporting events. It is a long anthem and is foreshortened at international competitions such as the World Cup so that no anthem is played longer than others. But a home crowd will carry on singing after the music stops. The Brazilians are of many different races, religions and social classes. They are unified by the flag, the anthem and the football team.

Like other nations, they do not take kindly to people from outside running them down. Yet they are acutely self-critical. They will speak frankly about what is wrong in their country and the difficulty in putting it right. It's an attractive quality.

I was British Ambassador in Brazil for 4 years and 7 months from December 2008. I had a month in the country before that improving my Portuguese, living in Campinas with Language School owner Pierre Coudry (a Brazilian with a French father, whom I later appointed British Honorary Consu). I had worked hard at King's College London with

*President Lula receiving my credentials from The Queen as her Ambassador
to Brazil, Planalto Palace, Brasilia, 2009*

Elizabeth the Second,

by the Grace of God of the United Kingdom
of Great Britain and Northern Ireland and
of Her other Realms and Territories Queen,
Head of the Commonwealth,
Defender of the Faith.

To His Excellency Luiz Inácio Lula da Silva,
President of the Federative Republic of Brazil.
Sendeth Greeting!
Our Good Friend!
Being desirous to maintain, without interruption, the
relations of friendship and good understanding which happily subsist
between Our Realm and the Federative Republic of Brazil, We have
made choice of Our Trusty and Well-beloved Alan Charlton,
Companion of Our Most Distinguished Order of Saint Michael and
Saint George and Commander of Our Royal Victorian Order, to reside
with You in the character of Our Ambassador Extraordinary and
Plenipotentiary.

The

an excellent Brazilian teacher Mariangela Spinillo to reach the Diplomatic Service Higher Standard by then – I was later thrilled to meet Brazilian TV News presenter William Bonner and wife Fátima Bernardes whose programmes I had watched on video as part of my instruction. Pierre, his wife Marina, daughters and friends also helped me see something of Brazilian schools, business, the media and academia. It did not seem an alien place when I arrived: a European language, a history of European immigration and traditions, a European culture; African, native American, Japanese, Middle Eastern influences; North America as the model for many aspiring families. All these aspects I could understand and relate to.

So, on my first day, I was confident I would get to know the country. With each day that passed I learned more and yet became more puzzled about how it really worked. The country has many recognisable parts. But there is more to Brazil than that. Brazil is one of a kind in the way it does things and does not apologise for this uniqueness. When I left, I felt I was still a way from really understanding the country. I'm still working on that.

PART I

ROYAL MAGIC

A Night at the Opera

It was the nearest thing to the Oscars I shall experience. It was a dark hot evening in Manaus, the heart of the Amazon. The square was brilliantly floodlit so that nothing could be seen of the hundreds, perhaps thousands, of people watching. A voice boomed through the PA system announcing our arrival in excited Portuguese, spreading some of the magic dust of royalty on to the crowd.

We got out of the cars. "Here he is" said The Voice. "Prince Charles" – pronounced Shar...lez. "He doesn't look bad for a chap of sixty". There was no translation into English and I didn't offer one.

I clambered out after the Prince of Wales. We walked through the square to the Opera House with The Voice continuing a running commentary every step of the way.

The opening scene of the film "Fitzcarraldo" has Claudia Cardinale and Klaus Kinski arriving by boat at the Opera House over a hundred years ago to hear Caruso sing. In those days, Manaus was still living the boom of its world rubber monopoly. It was one of the richest cities in the world. They sent their laundry down the Amazon to Paris, so I was told.

The building of an Italianate Opera House (Teatro Amazonas) in the jungle, 900 miles from the Atlantic, the city's conduit of supply, reflected the wealth and ambition of the time. Performances by the greats of the day such as Caruso (though I'm not sure he actually performed there) underlined the importance of the city.

The British played their part in the development of Manaus. The floating dock, the electrification, the trams (called "bondes" around Brazil to this day after the financial instruments used to finance them in London). I was asked by a Brazilian company to help inaugurate a new housing development in Manaus with the name London attached to it: the style was apparently reminiscent of architecture of 100 years previously in the city. I wasn't able to make the trip.

It was not only what the Brits did for Manaus which is remembered, but perhaps even more what they did to it. The bounder who ran off with Lydia Bennett in the Jane Austen's wonderful "Pride and Prejudice" was one Mr Wickham. A good name for a villain! There was a bad Mr Wickham in Brazil too.

Some outstanding Brits visited the Amazon in the nineteenth century, were welcomed and advanced scientific knowledge of flora and fauna and the people of the region. Wallace, Bates and Spruce were three of these, their extraordinary efforts and achievements set out in John Hemming's rich "Naturalists in Paradise".

Henry Wickham was not seen in the same light. The story goes that he took as a way of making his fortune from the Brazilian Amazon some 70,000 rubber seeds to the Royal Botanical Gardens at Kew in London in 1876. These seeds were the stock which launched the rubber plantations of Malaya and elsewhere in Asia. Rubber from the new Asian plantations undercut Amazonian production. When Wallace, Bates and Spruce were active in the 1840s-1860s the rubber industry in Amazonia was growing. Entrepreneurs thereafter, some from overseas, became wealthy. But when the Manaus Opera House was in full swing in the early 1900s the seeds of the decline of Manaus were already germinating on the other side of the world. By 1920 the Brazilian rubber industry was reduced to 2% of world production.

Henry Wickham reportedly was paid £700 by Kew for his seeds and talked the talk of the man who gave rubber to the British Empire. In later life he was rewarded by the British (he became Sir Henry) and Americans and able to live a comfortable old age.

Manaus declined from riches to poverty in the first half of the 20th century. The opera house declined with it. Then, after World War 2 when the Brazilian government wanted to boost the economic development of the region. Manaus was made a free-trade area; is now a thriving functional city home to two million people and producing among other things millions of motorcycles a year, including British Triumphs; the Opera House is restored to its former glory and has a season around May every year.

Back to 2009. Prince Charles was escorted to the top floor of the Opera House for a reception. It is a beautifully ornate room. The cost of shipping the precious materials and workmen from Europe must have been huge. When tourists visit they have to slide along the parquet floor in oversize slippers so as not to damage it. Then we went downstairs to the concert hall. You felt as if you were in Milan. The Amazonas Philharmonic Orchestra performed a programme of pieces by British and Brazilian composers to an invited audience.

On another visit to the Opera House, looking around the museum celebrating its history, I saw a pair of Dame Margot Fonteyn's ballet shoes on display. She was a frequent visitor, and had Latin American and Brazilian family links. It would have been wonderful to see her perform.

Meet our Leopard

I made other visits to Manaus. One included a visit with my Defence Attaché to the Army Jungle Warfare School on the edge of the city. The precise programme I was given included the British Ambassador being photographed with the School mascot.

I was grouped together with officers and soldiers for the photo first thing the following morning. They brought on the mascot. It was a lean and hungry-looking leopard controlled by two soldiers through stiff steel chains linked to a steel collar. I wondered if he/she had already enjoyed a satisfactory breakfast. The two guardians held the leopard in position for the photo, not too far away from me. I am sure he/she was very nice as leopards go but I was not inclined to attempt closer acquaintance.

Selva! is the cry of greeting with which I was received by the men when I visited the Jungle Training School – the reply is, you guessed it, Selva! It means Forest or Wood. The men looked very fit and had loud voices. They were taught to survive in the jungle, learning what can be eaten and what cannot, and which plants and fruits can be helpful when dealing with injuries and illness days away from a hospital.

As I was being briefed by the General in charge of the Amazon region, I was struck, not for the first time, by the underlying concern of the Brazilians that foreigners could invade the region. This has historical roots. The confederates of the US South, had they not been defeated in the Civil War, might have tried to expand not only to Mexico and Cuba but further south. After the Congress of Berlin the European Powers made a grab for Empire in Africa and Asia – might they try to colonise parts of South America? The pretext could have been that the territory was scarcely used and populated – this was a driver to the Brazilian government to seek development in the region. Some Brazilians claim to be concerned nowadays by the US Atlantic Fleet.

So, I was told, the main task of the Brazilian Armed Forces remained to defend the country, notably the Amazon, against invaders. The logistics are such that few places can be reached by road and many not even by air. The rivers are the main conduit. Looking at a map of the deployment of his forces I pointed to one near the border with Peru and asked how far away it was – over 2,000 miles!

In fact, the most serious threat to Brazil is the use of the territory, especially the rivers, to transport cocaine and derivatives from Peru, Bolivia and Colombia. The General told me that combating this was a civil police responsibility with the army playing only a supporting role. I think this situation has moved on somewhat in the last few years. The threat of drugs – transit and consumption – is so dangerous to Brazilian society that they need every tool in the box to bear down on it.

A visit to Manaus is not complete without experiencing the meeting of the waters as the rivers Negro and Solimões merge by the city, the first a black stream and the second muddy. The two streams carry along beside each other for a short distance before merging. I have seen the phenomenon from a ship and from a helicopter. A wonder of nature in Amazonia. My only regret is that I have not been more ambitious and explored more of the region, following at least some of the travels of those irrepressible naturalists Wallace, Bates and Spruce in the mid-nineteenth century.

Dancing in the jungle…with serious purpose

The Prince of Wales is a celebrity in Brazil. He has visited several times. Whenever he visits a moment is replayed on

Brazilian TV from his youth in 1978 when a mulatta woman Pina danced with him in the street. The lady became famous and was featured on the front cover of Brazil's premier weekly magazine Veja.

So when the Prince visited Brazil in March 2009 the media were on the look-out for more dancing scenes. In Rio, he walked through a sea of intent dark faces in the Complexo do Maré favella as he went to visit the inspiring Luta Pela Paz, founded by Luke Dowdney to help children of this violent district gain discipline in their lives through boxing, capoeira (artistic shadow boxing to African drums) and other sport and to learn skills such as IT outside school. On the way there were a few female attempts to engage him in a dance. But this was not a place to linger. When I had visited previously there had been an exchange of gunfire in the next street.

The media were better satisfied by his visit to the Maguire people on the bank of the Tapajós River in the Amazon. He

Tapajós River

danced with the lovely 20-year-old Anaya, moving well in a jive for chap of sixty. The Governor of the State (Pará), Ana Julia Carepa, had her moment to be twirled around. She then went on his arm in a walk in the jungle. I was not impressed by her gate-crashing the event; but it was her state after all! I came to appreciate her better on another visit to Pará in a delegation of EU Ambassadors in a discussion about the environment. Controlling deforestation in Pará is a very difficult challenge; the state is by no means all powerful; and it seemed to me she was trying hard to do the right things.

The purpose of Prince Charles' visit to the Maguari was to show how such village communities were trying to make a living sustainably. They made articles from local rubber for tourists. They fished. They grew traditional manioc and made their flour from it. No doubt the Prince likes dancing. But it was the villagers and the message about the environment which were centre-stage.

Saving the Planet

The Prince had made a keynote speech two days previously in Rio, in the classical Itamaraty Palace formerly the home of the Foreign Ministry when Rio was the capital. The Prince was introduced by Luciano Coutinho, President of the Brazilian Development Bank, in charge of the Amazon Fund to promote sustainability in the rainforest. The Prince spoke about the urgency of action by the international community to prevent dangerous global warming before it was too late. The message which got through to the media was that we only had a short time to prevent catastrophic global warming.

The day before, the Prince had delivered his message to President Lula in Brasilia. We had had some difficulty in arranging a slot for this meeting as the President had an engagement in the evening. I confess to being rather nervous when the Prince's plane arrived late at Brasilia airport that afternoon and I knew the first engagement, at the Congress building, would be difficult to control.

The Prince was greeted on a slope leading up to the Congress entrance by a photogenic honour guard of soldiers dressed in historical uniforms forming a line on both sides. He then had to make his way through a heaving scrum of people on the way to the room designated for the meeting with congressional leaders. My heart sank. This was not going to be an intimate conversation with a few senior members. It appeared any member had the right to gate-crash. At least we enjoyed a flash of typically Brazilian humour as we went into the meeting room when a man in the crowd hoisted a placard asking the Prince if he would like to buy a castle – a nice echo of a corruption story then running in the Brazilian media about a Brazilian Congressman who had his castle's security and other services paid out of his expense account.

The meeting room was even more packed than I had feared, including with people we had not expected. Former President Collor presented himself with grace and charm, saying he had received the Prince in his former function (from which he was later impeached) on an earlier visit. The meeting ran over time, making us even further behind schedule.

Time for Tea

The next engagement was my reception in the Embassy garden, lush from the seasonal tropical rain – it had poured down the previous afternoon. The large crowd of guests had waited patiently in the hot sun for their moment, excited about the opportunity to witness British royalty at an afternoon tea engagement, something exotic for Brazilians. The guests had been piped in on the bagpipes of a chap from São Paulo who was a regular at the annual Queen's Birthday Party at the Residence.

The Prince of Wales and Duchess of Cornwall arrived to the playing of a Brazilian military band, walking down the steps with me as commentator with the mike this time as they made their progress towards me. We stood to attention for the National Anthems, the Brazilians singing along lustily to their own.

Time was tight. We had the guests arranged in groups and the Prince and Duchess on separate progresses to meet as many as possible. But the time had almost run out as they started to talk to people. Yet we could not risk being late for the President, especially as it had been a struggle to nail down the appointment.

Then came one of those moments of serendipity. We received a message that the President was not yet ready to receive the Prince and asking us to hold our departure for the Palace until we heard from them again. It later became known that this was because there had been a power failure at the President's palace, the Planalto (since thoroughly renovated as its vital functions were beginning to fail by 2009 – after nearly 50 years since it was built). There was embarrassment on the Brazilian side and hence no reason given for the delay. Fine, to my mind. It meant we could do the reception justice. The guests loved it.

The eventual meeting with the President was remarkable. Here, meeting the heir to the British throne, was the first President of Brazil from humble origins, having as a child scraped a subsistence living with his family in the interior of the poor northeast of the country, moved to the metropolis of São Paulo selling nuts and shining shoes to support his mother until he became an apprentice in the car industry, trade union leader, three times loser in Presidential elections and now President and highly regarded at home and abroad.

Lula had paid a State Visit to UK in 2006. There were stories about how amazed he was to be accommodated in Buckingham Palace and how he called out to his wife Marisa that he was taking a shower there etc. He had spent time with the Queen.

I had mentioned the Prince's impending visit when we were invited with other British Ambassadors and their spouses to see the Queen at Buckingham Palace exactly a year previously. When I told her that the Prince would be visiting Brazil and addressing the issue of climate change she confirmed that her son was always talking about that. She recalled in vivid detail, as if it were yesterday, her own visit to Brazil talking about the cities and other places she had seen and giving a view on each.

I knew she had visited Brazil but, to my shame, had not checked when. Once back home I discovered this had been in 1968! It was a visit, I was to discover during my time as Ambassador, etched in the memory of many Brazilians. She and the Duke of Edinburgh had flown out to Brazil and then used the Royal Yacht for events and a Rolls Royce transported to Brazil on the Britannia. We created an exhibition of photos and news stories of the 1968 visit to celebrate the Diamond Jubilee in 2012 and exhibited it in several cities. So the glow of a visit by the Queen can last more than forty years.

I was not sure how the meeting between Royal Prince and People's President would go. The Prince described with passion and gesticulation his concern about climate change and the importance of Brazil's role. I was a little nervous about how this would go down, as the Brazilians are sensitive to suggestions that global warming is their fault. They like to point out, fairly enough, that it was the historical pollution of western countries which had created the dangerous levels of greenhouse gases in the atmosphere: they did not take kindly to those responsible for these emissions telling them how Brazil should look after its rainforest, part of Brazilian sovereign territory.

As it happened, I could see that Lula was impressed by the passion and eloquence of the Prince's remarks. He does not speak foreign languages. His interpreters are simply outstanding, conveying not only the literal translation but also the sense of the interlocutor's remarks. But Lula appears to glean a great deal also from the way people speak and their body language, which need no interpretation. This was not a meeting characterised by a gap between two people separated by their totally different backgrounds. It was a discussion of ideas and policy. The meeting lasted much longer than scheduled. Lula has that skill of top-rank politicians and statesmen of being able to listen to what others are saying as well as being a formidable speaker and advocate himself. I felt the discussion had made an impression on him.

2009 was a key year for the international debate about climate change, leading up to the Copenhagen Summit in December which was billed as the moment for a new international agreement to tackle global warming. It was a major part of the Embassy's work to press the case for ambition with government, business, academics and the media. We had a balancing act: we were determined to make an impact on the domestic debate but without being seen to interfere in the country's internal affairs and risk being castigated as an historic polluter calling the kettle black. We tried not to leave fingerprints on the debates we launched. For example, we contributed towards a scientific documentary for TV but had only the name of one of our local staff on the credits, not the Embassy.

President Lula, encouraged and pressed through the year by many in his own country including the media as well as the Prince, went to Copenhagen having just announced new commitments to reduce deforestation in the Amazon and limit Brazilian greenhouse gas emissions. There was also an electoral dimension as Lula had decided to promote his Chief of Staff Dilma Rousseff as the candidate to succeed him in the 2010 Presidential election: she needed to show her green credentials to meet the challenge of iconic environmentalist Marina Silva, then emerging as a Presidential candidate. Marina Silva had called on me in June that year to say she wanted to make a difference in Brazilian life.

Lula went to Copenhagen serious about negotiating a deal, despite the traditional caution of his Foreign Ministry which wanted a more negative line blaming the West. This was very encouraging – he was widely respected and Brazil was a key country. Unfortunately, not all other key countries were so convinced of the urgency. What did emerge was the centrality of Brazil, India and China together with the US in the debate.

The Prince also chaired a meeting of Governors of the Brazilian states of the Amazon region while in Manaus. This was the second of the two asks I made of Governor Eduardo Braga of Amazonas when I spoke to him in advance about what he could do to help with the visit of the Prince – the first was the event at the Opera House. The two biggest hitters present were Eduardo Braga and Blairo Maggi of the soya-growing state of Mato Grosso – a man who had been awarded by Greenpeace its annual award of shame The Golden Chainsaw for his farming exploits at the expense of the forest but was now talking about a better compromise between environment and development. It's hard to tell how much impact such a meeting makes. I suspect the impact is slow-burning. These are not the occasions for decisions, but can be important in shaping opinion.

On our way to meet the Maguari we had sailed along the Tapajós in a ship in which the Prince chaired a seminar on the science of global warming with a fascinating selection of Brazilian experts. It was a way of using the time well while seeing the country from the river.

This journey reminded me of a reconnaissance visit I had made the previous November with excellent visit organiser Kate Reynolds from our Embassy to a number of villages on either side of the Tapajós as we looked for the right place to focus a number of activities for the Prince's visit. As happened not infrequently in Brazil, we became later and later as the day wore on so that we left the last village shortly before dusk. Within a few minutes of leaving the shore we were enveloped in total darkness: there was no moon and no lights from the shores. I reflected that the river was 8-10 miles wide at this point. It felt like sailing on the open sea. I fervently hoped that the pilot of the small boat knew where he was going!

We also enjoyed looking at boats during the recce trip. We saw one which Norwegian Prime Minister Stoltenberg had used previously for a fact-finding visit to the region – the Norwegians are important supporters of the Amazon Fund. It looked like something which had sailed along the Mississippi in yesteryear and was in fact named Carolina do Norte. I could just imagine following the local practice of retiring to a hammock on deck and letting the world drift by as you glided slowly down the river.

This recce visit left me, right at the beginning of my time working in Brazil, impressed by the diversity of Brazil's population, one of the country's great strengths. In looking at possible scientific work the Prince could see in action in the rainforest we met a young academic from a local university, an expert in soil science. He had a square white face and hair with a reddish tinge. He spoke only Portuguese. I asked him if he had Russian parentage. He said he was of Russian and Ukrainian extraction but his father was black and so were his siblings. He described himself as white on the outside and black on the inside.

While in Manaus the Prince also promoted the cause of sustainable agriculture in a visit to a model farm. He was in his element looking at pigs and discussing the merits of anaerobic digesters. He also went with his wife, who had a separate programme in Manaus, to a wonderful charity teaching children to make musical instruments from non-noble wood from the rainforest (avoiding the need to cull the rare mahogany trees often used for the neck of the instrument) and finding markets in São Paulo and abroad.

I saw the Prince in action again on global warming the following month in London. In the margin of the G20 summit he chaired a meeting on 1 April 2010 at Clarence House including President Sarkozy, Chancellor Merkel, President Yudhoyono, Prime Minister Berlusconi, Prime Minister Aso, Secretary of State Hillary Clinton and Foreign Minister Celso Amorim of Brazil. He knew the limitations of his position. He does not speak for governments and has no executive power. But a Prince of Wales has convening power. He uses it to encourage movement in the right direction.

His visit was followed up by people involved in his Rainforest Trust coming to Brasilia over the years I was Ambassador. They would stay with me at the Ambassadorial residence in Brasilia as a base for their meetings.

The conversation the Prince's staff held with the Brazilians morphed into a discussion on global food security, where Brazil – as a top producer with scope for more – is a key player (though the Prince's opposition to GM is a complication). DID played a role in encouraging Brazil to share its agricultural experience and expertise with African countries.

While Caroline Spelman was Secretary of State for Environment, Food and Rural Affairs I had hopes that agriculture would become an important element of bilateral relations with Brazil. She came out to Brazil, struck up a close relationship with the Brazilian Environment Minister – woman to woman – and impressed in talking to the Agriculture Ministry with her understanding "as a farmer's daughter" of the needs of the food producers. She left Brazilian officials breathless by the pace of her walking at Chapada dos Veadeiros, a National Park a couple of hours from Brasilia: one chap was taken to hospital – fortunately he recovered. Unfortunately, the dialogue between governments on Agriculture was not sustained. One problem with Brazil is that the other party often has to make a lot of the running. The US has the stamina to do that on a range of policy areas; the UK often does not.

My residence in Brasilia became home to the royal couple for two of their four nights in Brazil. I had rather expected that they would choose the Brasilia 5-star hotel but his recce team were convinced he wouldn't want to go there – I imagine for reasons of lack of privacy and because of its glitzy and expensive modern architecture. I could see the attraction of my residence for peace and quiet. But I rather doubt the architecture, in tune with Oscar Niemeyer's style for Brasilia, and marble floors would cause it to be ranked among his favourite buildings. I offered to move out and leave the residence entirely to them. They didn't want that. I am glad they stayed there. Residences are kept to be used.

This was the last of four staffed residences I lived in – Bonn, Berlin, Washington, Brasilia. You have furniture,

Terrace of the British Ambassador's residence in Brasilia, the best spot for that quiet diplomatic chat over a drink or to host Ministers from the UK for breakfast outside

crockery, cutlery, pictures etc provided with the house – and staff to cook and clean so that you can use the house to the maximum for events. You live in a goldfish bowl on public view, which can be wearing. It gives the misleading impression to visitors that you are rich, rather than the reality of living on a civil-service wage. Some residences have better private areas than others. You never feel the house is more than the temporary home it is. It's a place of work where you happen to live. That's fine for a few years. But there is, in the end, no place like your real home in UK.

Harry Mania

I loved the Sixties. I was more observer than participant. But I was thrilled by the sense that there was something new and ever better in popular culture. Teenagers no longer thought they should act and dress like small version of the older generations. In 1963-7 there was new music and fashion every week. The Rolling Stones assumed they would soon be history. Amazing that they remain one of the biggest rock-and-roll attractions over 50 years later. They played to over a million people on Copacabana Beach in 2006.

Beatlemania was a phenomenon of the early to mid-sixties. Youngsters would scream and shout just catching sight of their popular heroes, not just the Beatles but the other groups of the day. It was an expression of the excitement of the times. I was never myself in a hotel besieged by a highly excited crowd of fans until Prince Harry came on his first visit to Brazil in March 2012. He arrived in Rio early in the morning and went to his hotel in Copacabana. The crowds soon started to form, mostly girls and women. When we came out of the hotel to attend events they pressed forward, noisily. Some managed to get past security into the hotel lobby.

As long as security was maintained the hullaballoo was fine by me, the British Ambassador. The purpose of this visit was to promote the British brand and British business in particular. As an Ambassador you need to use whatever your country has to make it distinctive and special. The Royal Family can be a very strong card for the UK. The Queen is the most famous woman in the world. Prince Harry has a strong personal appeal. I am sure William and Kate will be huge when they visit Brazil as no doubt they will. The Princess Royal is very well respected. We hoped to have a visit by the Earl of Wessex to promote the Duke of Edinburgh's award scheme – that did not materialise in my time. The Duke of York is not such a strong card nowadays in Brazil as he is in some other countries, after allegations about some of his contacts around the world: his staff were disappointed when I told them I was not sure if he visited that he would be received by the President and what stories the media would run. Other countries have other assets; our Royals are matchless.

We played on that. My staff came up with the idea of running a competition inviting young women to tell us online why they would like to meet Prince Harry. Whoever was deemed to give the best answer (and I did not get involved in the judging process) was to meet Prince Harry at our Gala Event on Sugarloaf Mountain and also appear on the hugely popular Sunday TV programme Fantástico.

The Sugarloaf event was very ambitious. We hired the

Prince Harry and Eduardo Paes, Mayor of Rio de Janeiro, at GREAT event on Sugar Loaf Mountain Rio, 2012

site for the night with money largely raised from commercial sponsorship and branded it GREAT (the GREAT campaign to promote Britain). At the foot we had British cars and motorbikes and samba dancers to greet the Prince as we arrived. The cable cars going up were decorated as London underground carriages with "Mind the Gap" greeting passengers.

At the top, we had a stationary cable car with James Bond memorabilia to mark the scene in Moonraker when 007 struggles with Jaws on a cable car suspended in mid-air on the way up to Sugar Loaf. There were booths set up by company sponsors, notably BP and BG. There was a Groucho's Bar offering a GREAT cocktail, a well-known DJ, the FA Cup on display, lots of examples of British innovation and style. We made a DVD to the sounds of Adele's Rolling in The Deep.

Prince Harry toured all this. He was then introduced in the auditorium by a video from David Beckham to give his speech, the first he had made in support of British business. He thanked Mr Beckham as someone who used to play football and then spoke really well about his first impressions of Brazil and what the UK had to offer.

He met the winner of the Meet Prince Harry competition and many others besides, including some of the models there to showcase British fashion on the catwalk.

He was interviewed by the Luciana Gimenez, mother of Mick Jagger's son Lucas. I had met her before at a TV station in São Paulo. She had become a celebrity in Brazilian soap operas. Luciana interviewed me too, a great honour and also a strain on my neck muscles as she is tall and was wearing high heels too.

Rio Mayor Eduardo Paes came to the event with his wife and young children. He stayed on till very late through that beautiful balmy night on his own talking to the Prince about his life growing up in Rio.

The next day, Saturday, brought more crowds, this time early in the morning on Flamengo beach. Prince Harry ran the charity mile along the road bordering the beach, with a mask depicting his brother Prince William covering his face. He then played on the sand with great energy and in seriously hot weather rugby, beach volleyball and more with enthusiastic youngsters. I tried to do some commentating in Portuguese on the public address. The media loved the whole occasion. Photos made the front of the Sunday papers in the UK.

Harry in the Favelas

The most daring event that day was a visit to Complexo do Alemão, a collection of favelas (shanty towns) in Rio on and between hills recently connected by a cable car as a way of helping the residents. Introducing the Prince to Brazil would not have been complete without showing him the less advantaged and their culture and aspirations.

Complexo do Alemão had already been included in the programme of pacification of the favelas. This sinister-sounding term was an attempt by the city and state authorities to turn the favelas into part of the city and their residents into fellow citizens rather than outlaws living illegally. The favelas had grown fast in the middle decades of the twentieth century as Brazilians moved in millions from the interior to the cities in search of a better life. They constructed their homes wherever they could, in the case of Rio largely on the hills overlooking the middle-class areas along the beaches.

Overwhelmed by this flood of people, Governors and

Mayors of Rio had tried to remove some of these houses in the 1970s causing disastrous social conflict. A succession of Governors and Mayors, some corrupt, had then ignored the issue or found ways to buy the votes of these people. Governors and Mayors had also often been at odds with each other and with federal government, weakening the impact of their actions. Only in recent years have more enlightened, ambitious and honest leaders sought to make these favelas part of the City and State working together and leveraging federal support too.

Led by the heroic modest state security chief José Mariano Beltrame, a man whose life has been threatened so many times, the plan has been to send in shock police and military forces to cleanse certain favelas of the gang bosses and then follow up with public services – education, social, youth and connecting utilities officially (this has the disadvantage for residents of ending free and illegal access to phone lines and electricity). The jury is out on whether the authorities will have the willpower to carry this programme through beyond the 2016 Olympics and how successful pacification will turn out to be in the long term. But it is the right idea.

I once asked the Mariano Beltrame what his worst fear was. He said it was that after his term in office things would go back to how they had been before. That shocked me. Surely that could not happen. Rio's old ways of governance had led to its decline and to alienation – Rio voters famously voted for a rhino and a monkey in local elections before a law was passed stipulating that candidates, even those written on to ballot papers by the voters, had to be human beings. I think it's positive, that Rio voted for Deputy Governor Pezão to succeed his former boss Sergio Cabral as Governor from 2014 and provide some continuity. There is an important decision to be made by the people of Rio on who should succeed Eduardo Paes as Mayor in 2016. Leadership is crucial in Rio and elsewhere. It has to come from the state and city authorities with support from federal government.

Complexo do Alemão in 2012 was still edgy. Security was tight for the Prince's travel on the cable car, walk through the narrow streets and arrival at a community centre which the Embassy was supporting. He was wonderful with the young kids. His appearance on a stage in front of a crowd of enthusiastic youngsters and saying a few words of Portuguese was the first item on the Rio 6pm TV news.

This was all good for me as Ambassador. Yet I nearly did not make it. As happened 5 years previously in Jamestown Virginia – when I lost touch with his visiting grandfather the Duke of Edinburgh and missed the convoy leaving for the next event to Norfolk Virginia – so in Rio I missed the convoy and saw it racing away without me from the hotel on Copacabana and the adoring crowd around it as it headed to Complexo do Alemão. I found a driver to take me at frightening speed to the cable car terminus, caught a following cable car and managed to catch up. Ambassadors are meant to keep out of photo shot but in the end we bear the responsibility and need to be around. Losing two princes in a career is not Great.

The Prince handled the adulation with aplomb and was not averse to meeting beautiful women. What he especially seemed to enjoy was meeting young children – a pointer for future visits.

He went out to lunch with the staff on the first day to a typical churrascaria – a buffet with everything and meat carved from skewers by waiters touring the room. He loved the food and joined in the occasion as one of the team. He was clearly excited to be in Brazil for the first time.

He went on to visit the Pantanal and play polo in São Paulo state to raise money for his Sentebale charity. He went back to Brazil in 2014, after my time, and gave a heartfelt media interview about helping children. He could become a key link between Brazil and the UK.

PART II

WHAT DID THE BRITISH EVER DO FOR BRAZIL?

Independence, Olympics, Gorillas

I've mentioned the Brit Henry Wickham who Brazilians believe robbed them of their rubber industry.

The Brazilians also blamed us for pressing them to abolish slavery in the nineteenth century because – they claim – we wanted a level playing field with production of sugar and other crops in the West Indies where slavery had been abolished. Brazil had made enslavement of native Brazilian Indians illegal a long time previously but saw no alternative for their economy than continuing to import black slaves from Africa. In the UK, pressure from civil society and religious conviction meant that no government could fail to take a tough line against the trade in slaves to both Brazil and the United States and to argue for the abolition of slavery in these countries.

The Brazilians felt they had no choice but to agree to clauses committing themselves to abolish slavery in bilateral agreements with the UK on trade and finance between the countries. This led to the phrase, now in everyday use in Brazil, "para ingles ver" "for the English to see" – in other words, for appearances' sake. Brazilian governments signed up to abolition simply because the UK so insisted. But they could not see how the Brazilian economy could operate without slave labour.

Slavery was eventually abolished in 1888 when the Princess Regent Isabel signed the Lei Aurea (Golden Law). The following year, the Emperor (a decent liberal and popular Victorian figure) was invited by the political and military elite to go into exile and a Republic was proclaimed.

Brazilians have a pretty positive view of the contribution made by their Emperors. In 1991 there was a referendum on the form of government Brazil should have – presidential, parliamentary or monarchist. It is hard to believe the return of the monarchy was a serious proposition but the fact that the option was offered, over a hundred years after its abolition, tells us theirs wasn't seen as so bad a period.

The time of the Brazilian Emperors – 1822 to 1889 – coincided with a period of British pre-eminence in Brazil. The UK was the most important trading partner, the most important investor, ran much of the shipping, built railways and founded utility companies. Loans to the Brazilian government were arranged through the City of London through Rothschilds. There were British communities in the major cities, notably Rio and São Paulo.

Even in the first part of the twentieth century, the UK was a major player although being eclipsed by the United States. Brazil was still much in the thoughts of British business. I was struck that Billy Bunter, the schoolboy created by Frank Richards, spent one holiday in Brazil at the farm belonging to a relative of a school friend in the book "Billy Bunter in Brazil". In those days of the British Empire, Brazil was apparently also seen as familiar territory.

In 1931, the then Prince of Wales – later Edward VIII and Duke of Windsor – visited Brazil with his brother Prince

George (later Duke of Kent) to help shore up the fading trade and investment connection. The Prince was known as the "Empire salesman" and had just been to Australia and New Zealand. Including Brazil (and Argentina) on this trip underlines the perceived value of the link to the UK.

As in so many other parts of the world, the exhausting UK effort in the First World War led to retreat in the UK position in Brazil. In the Second World War the UK had to call in all the assets it could to pay for LendLease and the war in general. The UK position in Brazil was seriously degraded. Yet the large number of names on memorials to the dead in both World Wars in Anglican churches in Rio and São Paulo show that there were strong communities up to this time; I was moved by the Remembrance Day services I attended in both citites.

The US started to become the key relationship for Brazil after World War I. This was consolidated by World War II. But I don't see that it was inevitable that the UK position would slide even further after World War II. The Germans, Italians, French and others took a long view and invested much more in Brazil than the UK. The other European countries had their own economic problems at this time: the UK was not alone in struggling post-war. The UK car industry was powerful in the 1950s. Could it not have invested in Brazil as others did? No point crying over spilt milk perhaps. It's good to see Jaguar Landrover investing in Brazil – yes, a difficult market but a huge consumer base and a good bet for the long term, as it was in the 1950s.

Let's also go back to Brazil's formation as an independent country. A big moment in the Napoleonic Wars was the French decision to invade the Iberian Peninsula in 1808. The British decided to take on the French with local allies. The rise of Wellington began.

It was a big moment for Brazil too.

The oldest continuing alliance in the world was forged in the late fourteenth century between the Kings of Portugal and England. Over the centuries since, this had continued to make sense against the two superpowers France and Spain. As French forces sped towards Lisbon in 1808, the Portuguese departed – Royal Family, advisers, treasury and archives – to Brazil escorted by the Royal Navy. There was a joint interest in keeping the Portuguese government operating. This was no sudden whim. The plan had existed for years.

From 1808-1821 Brazil was the seat of government of the Portuguese empire including Portugal. The reward was Portuguese agreement to open Brazil to international trade with a special tariff for the UK.

When the Portuguese King João returned to Lisbon in 1821 he left his son Pedro in charge of Brazil. Pedro declared Brazil's independence from Portugal in 1822. Declarations are one thing; control of the country another. How was the new Brazilian Emperor Pedro to remove the Portuguese from his territory? Portugal was itself in domestic political turmoil. But Brazil was the jewel in the Portuguese crown, from which a lot of Portuguese wealth derived. The declaration may have been a put-up job between father King João and son Pedro I of Brazil. But that does not mean it would have been acceptable to those wielding political power in Portugal.

In Spanish South America liberation movements were led by soldiers, notably the Liberator Simon Bolívar. Bolívar had help from tough British Napoleonic war veterans, officially barred by the British government from taking part but in practice allowed to leave the country for this purpose without hindrance. The British government did not want to upset Spain and other powers in Europe by taking Bolívar's side: the co-operation of the European Powers was key to keeping the peace in Europe. But George Canning, Britain's

Brasilia residence dining room with portrait of George Canning

greatest Foreign Minister, believed the liberation movements were the future and gave them important political and moral support.

The portrait of George Canning looked down on the dining table of my residence in Brasilia. He served as Foreign Minister at a time when the Prime Minister was Lord Liverpool, a man who held the government together rather than led it. Canning led on foreign affairs. He had a clear vision of the world after over 20 years of war against France. This included a new order in Latin America. He was in touch with James Monroe about the Monroe Doctrine, both interested in preventing the Iberian powers regaining control over Latin America. The US example of development was attractive in Latin America, though US interference (notably after World War II) was not.

Brazil did not need to recruit British veterans for a land struggle against the Portuguese on the Bolívar model against Spain. Brazil is a vast country. There were then few roads.

What was needed was not a land army but a strong navy to expel the Portuguese from the key ports.

Admiral Thomas Cochrane was the decisive figure. His is the other large portrait in the British residence in Brasilia, by the main entrance.

Cochrane was glamorous and controversial. He had been a daring and successful sea captain in the Napoleonic Wars. He had entered Parliament as Member for Westminster. Then he was accused of what we might now call insider dealing. It was alleged he was among a group of men behind rumours in 1814 that Napoleon had died. This caused the stock market to rise. He was among those who sold large amounts of government stock at an inflated price which of course fell once it was clear the rumours were untrue.

Cochrane was sentenced to a year of imprisonment. His knighthood was ignominiously revoked. He was not popular with the Prince Regent owing to his radical politics supporting electoral reform. Like John Wilkes a generation before, Cochrane was re-elected by his constituents despite his official disgrace. The evidence against Cochrane was not negligible. But it was circumstantial. Sixty years later his descendants were awarded a sum of compensation as damages for wrongful conviction.

Cochrane left the UK. He became a gun for hire in the cause of liberation. At the behest of Chilean leader Bernardo O'Higgins he became a Chilean citizen and Vice-Admiral and took control of the Chilean navy against Spain, including in the struggle for Peru.

The call then came from Brazil for Cochrane to take charge of the Brazilian navy. He recruited new sailors, largely from the UK and US, and set about pushing the Portuguese out of the north-eastern and northern ports. In recognition of his achievements, he was created by the

Brazilian Emperor Marquess of Maranhão and ceded land in the area.

As happened in Chile, he became embroiled in controversy about pay. He took his own reward from ports he attacked in Maranhão and made off in a Brazilian ship to UK in 1825. There followed a long dispute about who owed what to whom. When on a state visit to the UK in the 1980s, President Sarney of Brazil, himself from Maranhão, is said to have kicked Cochrane's tomb in Westminster Abbey calling him a corsair.

Cochrane went on to fight in the Greek war of independence in 1823. His knighthood was reinstated and he was re-enlisted as an Admiral of the Royal Navy in 1831 after the death of George IV. He became venerated by the Brazilians as a liberator. Several other senior British naval officers served in the Brazilian navy with him and after him.

In September 2010, to mark the 150th anniversary of Cochrane's death, I hosted a dinner in Rio on board HMS Ocean – the largest ship in the Royal Navy. Sitting next to me was Admiral Bittencourt, in charge of the Brazilian Navy museum. Cochrane may have been a bit of a rogue. But he played a big part at a crucial moment in ensuring the new Brazilian Emperor had control over the far reaches of his territory. Spanish America divided into different states. Brazil might have been divided too had Cochrane not been successful.

Declaring independence was the first step for the new Brazilian Emperor. Securing control of the territory the second. The third step had to be gaining recognition as an independent state from the Powers of Europe.

British diplomacy played a central part. The Powers victorious over Napoleon were governed by conservative leaders reacting against revolutionary movements. They were not likely instinctively to be happy about liberation movements in South America. George Canning's leadership was crucial. He persuaded the Concert of Europe not to kick up a fuss. His diplomats worked with the Portuguese on a face-saving deal whereby Portugal would accept Brazilian independence.

My favourite work of art in the Brazilian Foreign Ministry in Brasilia shows British diplomat Charles Stuart handing over the terms of independence agreed by Portugal to the Brazilian Emperor Pedro I in 1825. This was the moment for Britain to recognise Brazilian independence without upsetting its allies in Europe. I admire the bright red suit worn by Charles Stuart for the occasion. I would have liked one of those as my uniform as British Ambassador...

Nowadays, Brazil has a lot of important partners in the region and around the world. The UK is one of many. Others are considerably more important in terms of trade and investment, political co-operation and other fields. That does not mean the UK is unimportant.

Looking at the whole world, South America is perhaps the least important of the continents for the UK. We live and trade in Europe. North America is our strategic ally. Asia is an economic powerhouse. Africa feels close to us and is an affair of the heart. Still, South America and Brazil in particular have done well over the last 20 years. The UK needs to have a global reach. We can do better with Brazil and other countries in South America. The French, Germans, Italians and others try harder than we.

The World Seen From Brazil

Brazilian foreign policy is often a source of puzzlement and frustration to governments in the West. The House of Commons Foreign Affairs Committee on a visit to Brasilia were told by ex-President Collor, then Chair of the Brazilian Congressional equivalent, that when he had visited the White House to see President Bush Senior he had said he was against Brazil intervening externally in any place, at any time and for any reason. Not all Brazilians would be so categorical. But this is the basic view of the foreign-policy elite.

After the troubles of interventions in Iraq and Afghanistan, the appetite in UK for interventions overseas is much reduced – and President Obama has focussed on ending the US commitments in these places and not beginning new ones. Even so, we are strongly influenced by the lesson of passivity in face of the Nazi threat before World War II and the sense that we should be ready to help others, for example in Africa.

Brazil's view comes from its history. Apart from the wasteful Paraguay Wars in the nineteenth century, Brazil did not get involved in military conflict in its own region. It settled border disputes, generally successfully, by negotiation and shows of strength. It kept out of the affairs of its neighbours.

In fact, for most of the nineteenth century Brazil had little contact with others in the Americas. It was a monarchy unlike the Spanish-speaking states. It was politically relatively stable compared to the Spanish-speaking republics. It was an Atlantic Power looking towards Europe where it had its main trading partners and intellectual influences. After the abolition of slavery in 1888 most of its immigration came from Europe too.

As US power rose in the last 30 years before World War I, Brazilian foreign policy took its US links ever more seriously. The Spanish-speaking countries were often at odds during this time with the US, for example over their intervention in Cuba. Brazil was not.

This has changed in the last 20 years. Brazil wants greater co-operation between countries in South America, excluding the United States whose support for the dictatorships in the region was seen as self-serving.

The links with Europe in the nineteenth century, the US in the twentieth and now in South America have not changed Brazil's basic world view. It sees all countries as having a right to a share of international governance though with some big countries, such as Brazil and the US, being included in governing councils. This was the Brazilian argument in the pre-WWI conference at The Hague, at the League of Nations in the 1920s and regarding the United Nations and its Security Council in the last 60 years.

Brasil believes firmly in the principle of non-interference in the internal affairs of other countries. Like China, it perhaps does so because of a historic fear of foreign interference in its own domestic affairs. Brazilian involvement in world governance, yes. Intervention, no.

There is a tension between claiming a position in the UN Security Council and being ready to carry out responsibilities such as peacekeeping. Under President Lula Brazil took command of the UN peacekeeping effort in Haiti. It has become involved in UNIFIL (Lebanon) to a much smaller extent. But this may prove a surge of activity at a time when Brazil was pressing for a UN Security Council Permanent seat.

Brazil is a big country, with a different history and language from its neighbours, focussed on its own development. It will not be persuaded to join what it sees as foreign adventures.

And The Winner is...

My time as Ambassador gained a new dimension on 2 October 2009. I was at the Copacabana Palace hotel in Rio with Dilma Rousseff, then Chief of Staff to President Lula, Pezão (big foot) the amiable Deputy Governor (now Governor) of Rio, the Deputy Mayor and many of those involved in Brazil's bid for the 2016 Olympic Games. Their leaders – Lula, Governor Sergio Cabral, Mayor Paes, Carlos Nuzman heading the Brazilian Olympic Committee – were in Copenhagen for the last push in Rio's campaign and to await the decision.

Outside the hotel, on Copacabana beach, there was a large crowd enjoying the sunshine and waiting expectantly for news on the large video screens of the final stages of the decision-making process on the host city.

There was a gasp in the room when Chicago was eliminated in the first round of voting. The home city of President Barack Obama had been seen as a dark horse in the race which might just come through on the rails. Confidence grew about Rio's chances. In the next round Tokyo was eliminated. Then the final round: an envelope was opened and a slip of paper revealed bearing the words Rio de Janeiro.

I congratulated Dilma, Pezão and many more as the representative of the country holding the 2012 Games. I underlined how closely those responsible for the London Games wanted to work with Rio. They kindly invited me to sit at the table of an impromptu press conference.

This was a big moment for Brazil. It was the third time Rio had been a candidate to host the Games (previously 1936, 2008) and the first time it had been among the final few in the competition. With Brazil having hosted the 2007 pan-American Games, set to host the Earth Summit plus 20 in Rio in 2012, awarded the World Cup for 2014, it seemed it had transcended its reputation as a Country of the Future and was now in the front rank in the family of nations.

Amazingly, this was the first time the Olympic Games were to be held in South America. Brazil has not traditionally been strongly connected with its regional neighbours, although this has started to change a bit. But there was a sense among Brazilians that they would be holding the torch for their sub-continent.

London, 2012: Good Evening, Mr Bond

I went back to London for the opening of the 2012 Olympic/Paralympic Games because Dilma Rousseff, now President of Brazil, was invited to talks with David Cameron while she was in town for the ceremony. It was a friendly meeting at No 10. Dilma spoke in Portuguese but clearly understood most of what David Cameron was saying. She loved the artwork.

The morning following the opening of the Olympics I went to the Foreign Secretary's house in Carlton Gardens for the meeting of the two Foreign Ministers, accompanied by the two Ambassadors. The Brazilians said they had enjoyed the ceremony (though I wondered how much they had understood of the references to periods in British history) and commented, tongue in cheek, that Dilma was wondering if she like the Queen at London 2012 would be required to arrive at the 2016 Opening Ceremony in Rio by parachute.

Dilma was re-elected in 2014 for a second four-year term which stretches beyond Rio 2016. If she stays to the end I wonder what she has in mind for the big opening night?

I watched the London 2012 opening ceremony on TV. I

did go to the closing ceremony, together with the Brazilian delegation, which had a special role as the next hosts. Earlier that Sunday I went with Brazilian Minister of Sport Aldo Rebelo to the BT Tower where we were by met by BT Chairman Sir Martin Rake. The purpose was to explain the challenges of providing telecommunications in London and round the world for such a huge event of global interest. It was a huge task of planning for London 2102 just to accommodate the expected sevenfold increase compared with Beijing 2008 in the need for bandwidth to accommodate everything from media companies to individual smart phones transmitting live the 100 metres final back home to Shanghai or Mumbai. You could have brilliant Games but if the world could not see them live on their screens around the world they would be a flop.

The Brazilian Sports Ministry had for some years been a fiefdom of one of the Communist Parties in Brazil and part of the governing coalition. Unlike his predecessor, a charming man who enjoyed the luxuries of life and did not seem well suited to his party, this particular Minister was a true believer in his politics. He saw sport as a means to help liberate the lower classes. He was fascinated by what he was shown in the BT Tower. I liked him. He later became Minister for Science and Technology and then Defence Minister in Dilma's second term.

Yet, for Aldo Rebelo, one of the key moments, I suspect, was at the top of the tower when he asked me (I was acting as interpreter as he spoke no English) in which direction lay Highgate cemetery. He said Britain was a great country because it had given shelter to Karl Marx at a time when he could not have continued in his native Germany. Aldo Rebelo had visited London for the first time years previously to visit Karl Marx's grave at Highgate Cemetery.

Olympic Legacy

Beijing 2008 gave a big boost to understanding of China's emergence as the world's second economic power after the US. The Chinese did not seem so concerned about value for money for their spending. The striking Bird's Nest stadium has not since been used except as a tourist attraction.

For Brazil, as for the UK, that was not going to be enough. London 2012 was a big success as an event. The transport links, seen as a potential problem, worked well – not least because a lot of Brits stayed out of the city, went on holiday elsewhere or worked at home. They were also friendly Games. Londoners, and the UK more widely, got into the spirit of the event. The crowds were huge, including for the Paralympic events. After leaving the BT Tower that Sunday morning, I watched the marathon pass by Trafalgar Square. There was a wonderful relaxed atmosphere.

But the excitement of the summer would inevitably fade. There needed to be an answer to questions which would be asked in the years to come whether it had all been worthwhile. The biggest single legacy promises to be the revitalisation of Stratford in London. It was a polluted decaying former industrial area. The ground was cleared of its poisons, the canal restored as a working waterway, power lines sunk underground, the rubble of old buildings used as foundations for the new stadia. Above all there was a plan for it to become a new residential and business area after the Olympics/ Paralympics in addition to usage of the stadia. This is part of the wave of new development in the East of London.

Brazilians feared that Brazil might not cover itself in glory in hosting the Games. But they feared even more that there would be no lasting legacy. The reputation of the 2007 Pan-American Games was soiled by stories of corruption, fat cats making big bucks at public expense through inflated contracts. The World Cup in 2014 has not helped as, despite what politicians said in advance, some of the stadia are white elephants.

On 25 March 2010, I sat with the visiting Olympics Minister Tessa Jowell, Governor Sergio Cabral and Mayor Eduardo Paes in Rio. The Mayor asked how the International Olympic Committee would react if he modified Brazil's plans away from those submitted to win the bid. He wanted the revitalisation of Rio downtown area to be a legacy of the Games and to help with this he wanted to move some functions there. Tessa said the IOC would not like it but the Mayor should do what he thought was right. It was his city and his opportunity to make a difference to it.

In January 2015, we walked through the downtown area in Rio from the cruise-ship terminal at Mauá (I had been lecturing on board during the journey from Southampton). The new Museum of Tomorrow (in partnership with the London Science Museum) was taking shape nearby. The ugly overhead road past the docks I had used so many times had been dismantled. Old buildings were being revitalised. There was vigorous work in train moving forward with a new tram line, pedestrianisation, opening up ways to walk to historic buildings and locations which had been hidden away for years.

Perhaps not everything will be finished by the time of the Olympics. But there is a real promise of something very special having changed by then. It will be great to see crowds of tourists discovering the glories of old Rio, including places lined to the UK such as the fascinating British Cemetery (Cemetério dos Ingleses).

Sorry to lurch into a story about the dead. But I like these cemeteries. When the British were granted special tariffs for trade after escorting the Portuguese court including the Queen and Prince Regent and his government from Lisbon in front of the invading French in 1808, a stream of British merchants and adventurers came to Brazil. Many died young, struck down by yellow fever and other tropical diseases. There was nowhere to bury them as the Catholic Church at that time would not accept non-Catholics into their graveyards.

The Portuguese Prince Regent gave the British the right to have their own cemeteries. These were created in Rio, Salvador, Recife and probably other cities. They were the first non-Catholic cemeteries in Brazil. They were used not only by the British but by other non-Catholics – Americans, Germans, Jews, Muslims. The cemetery in Salvador in a lovely spot above the sea has been recently restored. The Recife cemetery has a famous Brazilian, General Abreu e Lima, who as a young man fought with the liberator Simon Bolívar in Venezuela. When he died in 1869 in his native Recife the Catholic Church refused to have him buried in their cemeteries because he was a freemason. And so he went to the British cemetery. It is a strong reason why the local authorities have designated the cemetery as a site of national historical importance. There is now a district of Recife named after Abreu e Lima and even a oil refinery along the coast intended as a joint project between Venezuela and Brazil.

The cemetery in Rio remains looked after by the British community in liaison with the city authorities. Originally it was in a lovely spot with a view to the sea, captured in a painting by the traveller and confidante of the Brazilian Empress Maria Graham. It has been for decades hemmed in by favelas and not easy to access. I visited a couple of times. The Rio downtown revitalisation will open up the cemetery once again to more visitors.

The Only Gorilla in South America

I especially enjoyed visiting the state of Minas Gerais when I was Ambassador. I'll say more about it when I get on to football. But let's concentrate now on the story of Idi Amin, who was the only gorilla in South America (or so I was told).

I went to see the Mayor of Belo Horizonte, capital of Minas Gerais for the first time on 29 April 2009. At the end of the meeting, Marcio Lacerda said there was something else he would like to discuss although he was somewhat hesitant to mention it as it was perhaps not the kind of business a diplomat would usually be involved in.

It concerned the gorilla at the zoological gardens on the outskirts of Belo Horizonte. He was a silverback male weighing 100 kilos who had an area specially created for him.

Idi, the only gorilla in South America, at Belo Horizonte zoo. He was a famous personality, visited by school groups learning the imporance of saving endangered species. I was involved in some gorilla diplomacy with the Mayor of Belo Horizonte

He had lived there for over 30 years. His politically-incorrect name belonged to the times of his arrival. He had become a well-known personality visited by generations of Mineiros and especially by schoolchildren learning about the importance of protecting endangered species.

The mayor continued that Idi was now in his late thirties, currently healthy but not likely to live for many more years. The zoo, with the support of the city, had been trying for some time to bring some females so that he could mate. As he had been born in the wild, unlike most gorillas in captivity around the world, he could help strengthen the blood lines of the gorillas remaining on this earth.

The organisation which arranged transfer of gorillas between zoos was the Aspinall Foundation in Kent. A discussion was in train with them. Understandably they imposed strict conditions for example concerning the habitat in which the gorillas would live. The conversation was moving slowly. The mayor said that I, as the British Ambassador, could be their ace card.

Being new to gorilla diplomacy, I was cautious about what I could do to help. I said the Foundation would no doubt make a decision according to their criteria and not because of any advocacy on my part. But I said I would speak to them.

Once I was back in Brasilia I rang the Aspinall Foundation on a couple of occasions. They were well aware of what Belo Horizonte had to offer and optimistic that it would work out though it could take time as there would have to be careful planning. Meanwhile, I went to visit Idi in the zoo. He was magnificent and rightly the centre of attention of the zoo visitors. He did indeed have an impressive habitat – trees, water and a cave in which to retreat.

Some months later, two young females born in UK were flown to Rio and then taken to Belo Horizonte accompanied by a team from the Aspinall Foundation. It was not only a matter of getting them there safely but also helping with the socialisation process. Idi had not had any female company for at least 25 years after a previous female companion had died. He was now to share his world with two, both around half his size. I went to see then together with Judy and brother-in-law David in November 2010. We were allowed to go down to the cave to look through the window at them.

Sadly, Idi died a few months later leaving the compound to his two British companions. I keep a photo of him.

PART III

FOOTBALL AND
FORMULA 1

It is well known in Brazil that football was introduced by Charles Miller, the son of British expatriates born in São Paulo. He went to Southampton for his schooling, played games there – football, rugby, cricket – and returned to Brazil in 1896 determined to spread the gospel. It was the good news of football which fell on fertile ground. A league was created in São Paulo based on teams representing British companies – Charles Miller played for the São Paulo Railway Company which operated the route through the jungle down from the city to the port of Santos. Other clubs joined in – in the case of Rio one of the early clubs was Rio Cricket, whose members were British expatriates from Niteroi just over the Guanabara Bay from the City. The pavilion and ground are still there and I was enthusiastically received when I visited as Ambassador but the members of what is now a social club (though still with ground where cricket could be played) are nowadays all Brazilian and cricket is foreign to them.

Charles Miller was a figure in São Paulo football for decades until his death in 1953. The Museum of Football in São Paulo is situated on Charles Miller Square. It contains plenty about Charles Miller himself. I accompanied Prime Minister Gordon Brown on a visit there in March 2009. He had a conversation with Brazilian football great Socrates about the Brazil-Scotland match in the 1978 World Cup.

I was frequently asked by Brazilian kids which Brazilian team I supported. This allegiance is important in Brazil (as it is in Britain) so much so that in Portuguese a Brazilian says not just that he supports a certain club but that he is that club.

I am Fluminense, one of the big Rio football clubs. Having denied any allegiance for four and a half years while Ambassador, thinking that it would be risky to declare support for any Brazilian club, I decided at an event at the wonderful Fluminense centre to take the plunge. It was on impulse. But it was near the end of my time; the club had been founded by Oscar Cox, of British-Brazilian extraction, and I loved their Exeter City connection.

The Fluminense museum tells of the trophies the club has won and the great players who have worn the club's colours. It also has a room about Exeter City. This was the first foreign professional team Fluminense played against. It happened on 22 July 1914 in Rio. The room has photos and press reporting of the event reporting the brutal tactics of the Exeter players. It even has what is alleged to be the original ball. Fluminense won. The Exeter team left soon after and were back home in time for World War 1.

The occasion for my visit was a reception to celebrate the Brazil-England friendly on 30 May 2013, the first competitive match at the reopened and refurbished Maracanã stadium; the result was a diplomatic 2-2 draw. I was presented of course with a Fluminense shirt with its vertical maroon and green stripes and also with a shirt to advertise the coming centenary of the Fluminense-Exeter city match. Exeter were invited to play again at Fluminense in July 2014 and did so. I kept the Fluminense shirt and gave the Exeter City one to my wife's nephew and his wife, both of whom studied at Exeter University and are Exeter City fans.

Fluminense was the last in the stable of clubs around the world I had come to support. My home team is Nottingham Forest; I had a season ticket for the Trent End as a teenager in the 1960s. Crawley Town is the club I go to watch regularly nowadays. I became an avid Schalke fan when we were living in Gelsenkirchen while I was teaching – heady days of Klaus Fischer. We watched Blau-Weiss and Hertha BSC in Berlin. I took a bit of interest in DC United when in Washington. I look out for the results of all of these. Another enrichment from a career working overseas.

Bobby Charlton (no relation, unfortunately)

The Brazil-England match at the Maracanã in May 2013 was the second of a double-header of friendlies. The first was at Wembley on 6 February 2013 celebrating the centenary of the Football Association. It was a cold un-Brazilian night and yet a great occasion with Brazilians living in UK turning out in big numbers, as they did when I went to watch Brazil play a friendly against Ukraine at Pride Park in Derby in October 2010. The Wembley match was unusually high in quality for a friendly. In fact it was the best of the best performances I have seen from an England team – they won 2-1.

For me the match was memorable for my one and only meeting with Bobby Charlton. I admired him hugely as a player. I watched him play several times when Manchester United visited my team Nottingham Forest in that amazing sixties line-up including George Best and Denis Law. One such occasion was as part of the record crowd ever at City Ground Nottingham in 1968, just short of 50,000, well above official capacity. I followed Bobby Charlton's recovery after the Munich air crash in 1958. I watched on TV his key role in England winning the World Cup in 1966 and Manchester United the European Cup in 1968. Who knows if England might have won the World Cup again if he had not been substituted when England led West Germany in the World Cup quarter-final in 1970?

Timidly, I went up to his table at a dinner before the England-Brazil match and introduced myself to him and his charming wife Norma. They said they had heard that a Charlton was British Ambassador in Brazil and were proud of that. I said I hoped I was related to them: there was a story that my Charlton family came from the northeast of England, the strongest concentration of people with the Charlton surname, in the 18th century, but I had no proof one way or the other. They were enchanting. Sometimes the good guys do come out on top.

Pele

I suppose the nearest Brazilian equivalent to Bobby Charlton is Pele, probably the most famous footballer of all time. Meeting him took my breath away. This happened by chance during the London 2012 Olympics as I was awaiting the Brazilian Vice-President in the Foreign Office courtyard before a conference on combating hunger. Pele came walking through, a wonderfully fit 70-year-old. We had a few minutes' conversation in Portuguese and then English, which he speaks very well. I had in my mind the iconic swapping of shirts between Pele and Bobby Moore after the 1970 World Cup game.

Too much cake?

England first played in the World Cup finals in Brazil in 1950. They based themselves in Nova Lima, a town near Belo

Horizonte in Minas Gerais where there had been a British community for a hundred years owing to the British gold mine at nearby Morro Velho. The mine had been one of the most technologically advanced in the world, thanks to the oversight of the Chalmers family for many years. The company also introduced the idea of healthcare for its workers in a hospital. There is now a fascinating museum showing all this.

When I visited the Nova Lima country club where the squad had trained and been entertained I was shown the gifts the FA had given to the club and hundreds of photos, including of Tom Finney and Stanley Matthews. The club still had some of the trappings of its time as a centre of the British community. There was a snooker table, preserved but not used. I imagined there was cricket equipment stowed away somewhere gathering dust.

Belo Horizonte was the scene of one of the biggest upsets in World Cup history. The star-studded England team, admittedly without Stanley Matthews for this match, lost 1-0 to a scratch team from the USA. A Brit once told me that he strained through bad reception to hear the result on his radio in England and thought it must have been 10-0 to England, more what he expected.

The England squad were treated to wonderful hospitality. The British community was then declining but still strong. There were also photos of them celebrating the coronation of 1952. The community has now faded away or been submerged in Brazilian culture – though British surnames remain common enough (we had a Samuel Lloyd from Nova Lima representing VisitBritain in Brazil, and there is still an Episcopalian, formerly Anglican, church proud of its British heritage.)

I found some customs remained, including eating queca – British-style cake – which I haven't come across elsewhere in

Brazil. Perhaps the England boys had a slice too many before playing the USA?

I had a chance to see some of England's preparation for the 2014 World Cup in Brazil when I watched the squad train at the Urca military facility under Sugar Loaf mountain before the friendly with Brazil in May 2013. I enjoyed a conversation with Roy Hodgson who wanted of course for England to do well in the tournament but also to do it right – preparing well and with community engagement. He was worried about the heat of Rio and feared having to play in Manaus (which came about). I don't think it was the heat which defeated England in 2014. The squad was not as strong as in 1950 and for some reason didn't find the extra gear needed to succeed in such a tournament.

The Love of the Game

My knowledge of football was handy during my Ambassadorship in Brazil. During the 2010 World Cup in South Africa, I was on a morning radio show in Rio chatting to the host between other stories and music when the station's reporter in South Africa came on the line and asked me about the relative merits of the 1966 and 1970 England World Cup squads. Who'd have thought that would have been useful for a British Ambassador?

I found in Brazil a compendious knowledge of British football and adherents of just about every club there. After briefing a meeting of editors at the Rio newspaper O Globo on UK-Brazil relations, I was taken by the Sports Editor to his desk where he showed me photos of himself and his son at the City Ground Nottingham – he professed eternal support for Nottingham Forest.

I have from my time in Brazil also one those "Where were you when..." sporting memories. The other English club I support, with my sons, is Crawley Town, as we have had a house there since 1979. While we were spending a weekend at a holiday resort in Florianopolis in the south of Brazil in February 2011, I watched on TV their unforgettable 5ᵗʰ round FA cup tie away to Manchester United in which they played so well and unluckily lost 1-0, though still a non-league club at that time. I loved hearing the well-briefed Brazilian commentators try to pronounce the names of the players and praise Crawley's performance. I was glad that our son James was at Old Trafford in person to see the match.

Don't watch football and drive!

Brazil has a shockingly bad reputation for road safety. More than 40,000 people are killed every year. There are several factors. Too many people drink and drive – the Rio campaign of zero tolerance and blanket checks of an evening has had a major positive effect: people know they'll be caught and so don't risk it. Lorry drivers carry on for very long hours travelling across this huge country. The bus drivers seem especially dangerous. Many roads are poorly made and have dangerous potholes. The safety standards of cars manufactured in Brazil are often lower than equivalents in Europe.

In the margin of the São Paulo Grand Prix of 2012 I co-hosted a seminar on road safety together with former World Champion Emerson Fittipaldi, one of the few survivors among top drivers of his era when the casualty rate in Formula 1 was especially high. Safety has been improved greatly in that sport. The purpose of the event, linked to a campaign by the UN Secretary General to reduce deaths world-wide and personal involvement of President Dilma Rousseff, was to look at what could be done to halve the death rate in Brazil by 2020.

Brazil has shown it can mount successful public education campaigns. It did this to raise consciousness about AIDS. It did it about smoking. Education will be a key element in road safety.

I avoided Brazil's roads when I could. I travelled a lot between cities but almost always by air. On the roads, overtaking was a particular danger. I was told that some companies in the oil centre Macaé forbade employees to use the main road from there to São Paulo until the road had been widened. I recall some heart-stopping moments on that road and others.

My most vivid memory in a car had nothing to do with the state of the roads. One sunny afternoon not far from the beach in Rio I hailed a taxi to take me to Galeão airport. A young man in his twenties picked me up. He had a video screen on his dashboard with a live broadcast running of a Botafogo-Fluminense local derby. He rushed me to the airport. Taxi drivers often do that. They know the roads well and drive all the time and are highly skilled. In this case only a percentage of his attention was devoted to the job, probably more than enough in his view but less than I would have liked. He watched the screen, listened to the commentary on the car radio and, at one stage, phoned a friend about it. He thumped the steering wheel in frustration when the wrong team scored – I think he was Botafogo. We arrived without mishap but with the driver in a bad mood as his team was losing and the passenger's nerves somewhat frazzled.

The São Paulo Grand Prix

After football the second big sport in Brazil is Formula 1. The Brazilian Grand Prix, in recent years at Interlagos in São Paulo, is a key event in the Brazilian sporting calendar. I went to three of them.

Formula 1 is a important industry for the UK. A large number of F1 teams are based in the Home Counties. The UK is a leader in the engineering and design of the cars. We exploited this every year with an event at the Brazilian-British Centre in São Paulo organised by our Consulate-General. It was a chance to showcase UK excellence and invite Brazilian personalities to rub shoulders with the famous Brits leading this world-wide sport.

UK plc is fortunate to have the Brazilian-British Centre. It is the home to a number of UK organisations – the Consulate-General, British Chamber of Commerce, British Council, BBC and Cultura Inglesa (the landlord of the building – a not-for-profit company which provides English language teaching embedded in British culture around São Paulo). There is also a library, cafeteria, a pub and impressive spaces for exhibitions and receptions. Every British Embassy around the world would be happy to have such a facility.

The Brazilians have a special affection for Ferrari. Thousands turn up at the Grand Prix with the Ferrari colours. Many Brazilians do have an Italian heritage. But there is more to it than that, I suspect. The history and image of Ferrari have claimed a special place in Brazilian fans' consciousness.

Of course, the Brazilians want to cheer on Brazilian drivers. Ayrton Senna was and is no less than a national hero. He was a brilliant and daring driver, a world champion, admired around the world. At the time he was a top driver, he also gave Brazilians a feeling that their country was achieving something. This was a depressing time in Brazil itself with uncertainty about democracy and a sliding economy, and hyperinflation wrecking lives. Senna's races were watched on TV by huge numbers of Brazilians. They loved him. It is rare around the world to see the name of a sports figure on so many roads, bridges and airports.

I saw the crowning of two British world champions – Jensen Button and Lewis Hamilton – and had the chance to see the pit lane and talk to some of the drivers and team chiefs. We also had visitors from UK. In 2008, just before the ambassadorial term began Cabinet Minister Tessa Jowell, whose Department included responsibility for sport, was our guest of honour, meeting up with the Brazilian Sports Minister.

It's great being at the event and meeting people. But, in truth, it's easier to follow the race on TV screens than on what you can see of the track at various vantage points. The Lewis Hamilton world championship depended on him making at least fifth place in the São Paulo race. People watching on TV in UK would have known he had managed that – just – before I did at the track.

The sporting event I most enjoyed was the Brazilian School Games in Cuiabá in 2013. This brought together leading youngsters from each state of Brazil for finals in swimming, volleyball and several other disciplines including chess. I was there because England sent a team, the only foreign competitors, following up the participation of a Brazilian team in the English school games in the UK Olympic year, 2012. The heat of Cuiabá was a challenge for the English competitors. They did their very best in volleyball where the Brazilians are nationally very strong. In swimming there were some high achievers among the English, including a few who had participated in the Olympics. What an experience for the English and young Brazilians to meet in remote Cuiabá!

Cricket ought to be a top sport in Brazil. At least that's my view even if I doubt I'd have many Brazilians agreeing with me. They have the weather for it. There is a traditional game called Bate played on the beach which looks like cricket. Football caught on; cricket sadly didn't. There is an annual match between the British Ambassador's XI and the Australian Ambassador's XI in Brasilia, followed by a gala ball at the British residence to raise money for cricket in Brazil: I held this event 5 times and had 139 people there at the last one. I went to watch the match earlier in the day but did not play – I should have done so. The Aussies won more often than the Brits in my time. The good news is that there is a bit of a spread of cricket around the main Brazilian cities. It'll never become huge. But, who knows, perhaps there might be a Brazilian team challenging to get into the Cricket World Cup one day. Call me a dreamer. Who would have expected to see Afghanistan in the World Cup?

PART IV

LIVING IN BRAZIL

I'm asked by Brits about to visit Brazil whether it is safe. The statistics for homicide, road accidents and crime are not encouraging. Most of those affected are from the poorest parts of Brazilian society. But there have been some nasty incidents involving foreigners. At carnival time in 2009 a group of young Brits were among those who experienced the trauma of being woken at night in a hostel in Rio and robbed at gunpoint. The Rio authorities were horrified about this. They were horrified too in August 2013 when an American tourist was raped taking one of the minibuses from Copacabana which used to tour unlicensed – they introduced restrictions on these.

I never felt personally threatened even when walking the streets of Brazil's cities.

I warned visitors from London who intended to spend free time on their own in the cities not to become a consular problem. When it came to Ministers it was not always popular that we wanted to monitor what they were doing in Rio at a weekend. A female civil servant visiting on duty from London did not come back after an evening out in Rio. We spoke to her colleagues, called the police and hospitals. Fortunately, she turned up in the morning not really clear what she had been up to all night but, after checks, apparently with no lasting repercussions. What to do at night in London would be her own choice and not the business of her Department. In Brazil, it was the business of the Ambassador.

Diplomats are used to the possibility of being targets themselves for crime or terrorism and take precautions according to the perceived level of threat. In the days of the military dictatorship in Brazil, a US Ambassador was kidnapped. Embassies are guarded in Brasilia without being turned into the fortresses as in more dangerous parts of the world. A driver was held up in broad daylight at gunpoint just outside an Embassy near our own. There were desperate people around.

Freak accidents can hit anyone and perhaps in Brazil as often as anywhere. My colleague the Portuguese Ambassador was badly injured by a shot from a ceremonial cannon! Fortunately he made a very good if slow recovery.

Brazil was not seen as a high-risk country for British diplomats while I was there. Even so, the British Embassy was better guarded than most in Brasilia. We had checks, double gates and ramps at the main entrance. We had our own guard force, on duty around the clock. It was disturbing when we discovered from close-circuit TV film several days after the event that a young man with a machete had climbed over our external fence in the middle of the night and had been on the residence roof. It seems he was only looking for fruit from our trees. We did at least make sure there were no overhanging branches to facilitate scaling the fence.

The most dramatic albeit also comic security event of my time concerned a package which the security guards stopped at the gatehouse of the Embassy. It was addressed to me but there was apparently no information as to who had sent it nor about its contents. In line with standard policy, it was taken outside the Embassy. As there was no safe way of determining whether or not it was benign, the guards blew it up on some waste ground nearby.

It turned out to be a gift of pottery from the state of Piauí sent to me by a Federal Senator from that state, Heráclito Fortes, a larger-than-life figure then on the political scene. I told Heráclito what had happened and he graciously sent another, which I displayed in the residence for him to see when he visited the Embassy a couple of weeks later.

There are exotic diseases in Brazil such as Chagas. You need to take seriously the standard vaccinations for yellow fever, tetanus etc. The greatest risk in Brasilia was dengue. This is spread by a bite from a certain type of mosquito, most likely bred in stagnant water in cities. Having at one time almost eliminated the disease in Brazil it has made a comeback in recent years. Brazilians are rather ashamed of that, since it is the result of failure to eradicate stagnant water in cities. The wife of one of our diplomats in Brasilia was very ill for a quite a time with it.

Brasilia had even better weather than Amman. We had no heating in the house because we did not need it – you just put on a sweater if the temperature fell a bit in the winter. In the dry season many days were brilliantly sunny. Yet it was never oppressively hot – 33 degrees was about as high as it went. Situated on the high plain, it was also rarely oppressively humid.

Some people suffered from the opposite problem. There was sometimes very low humidity in the dry season between May and September, even in single figures as in the Sahara desert. Those with respiratory difficulties in particular found this hard. It got worse if there were forest fires fanning smoke into the city.

Personally I loved the low humidity. I have with me the memory of walking the 10km around the Central Park (Parque da Cidade) early on many a weekend morning under a perfect blue sky in shorts and sandals, 30 degrees and very dry. Beats a damp Saturday in UK.

While it was often inconvenient for pedestrians, Brasilia had the merit of being easy to get around by car, unlike the other major Brazilian cities where it was sensible to build in large slabs of time between appointments for long traffic delays. The Brasilienses, natives of Brasilia, are always quick to praise the advantages of living there.

The British Ambassador lives on a plot of land in a row of Embassies (including France and the US) where we built both the Embassy and his residence, all within a tropical garden with water features.

I ate bananas, papaya and mangoes from the garden. It was ablaze with colour around the year. We decorated the house with flowers from it. Orchids flourished. Exotic birds came to visit. I occasionally saw a toucan. Common were hawks and egrets. Outside the compound on nearby waste ground there were burrowing owls. Visiting Ministerial trade envoy Ken Clarke enjoyed using some down time to sit on the residence veranda and note the birds he saw in his journal.

Around Brasilia there were monkeys aplenty. Once when I was driving out of the zoological gardens in Brasilia I was struck by a group of monkeys swinging through the trees outside the perimeter. Perhaps they were watching us rather than vice-versa.

Yet Brasilia is not seen as a paradise by everyone. It was built out of nothing. As promised, President Kubitschek inaugurated the new capital on 21 April 1960 within his 5-year term having sounded the starting pistol in 1955. Countries were offered plots of land on which to build new embassies. The UK was one of those which took up the offer. But that did not mean quick transfer of Ambassadors to Brasilia as their base. Into the late 1960s British Ambassador Russell was still hosting his famous parties for Rio society at his residence there with his daughter Georgiana as hostess. That kind of event was not happening in Brasilia. Eventually the Brazilian government had to force Ambassadors and Embassies to move to Brasilia by threatening to cut off their privileges should they not do so.

Some Brazilian civil servants were also reluctant. I was told by an eminent Brazilian Rubens Ricupero that in 1963 there were only a handful of Brazilian diplomats stationed in Brasilia, using some offices in the Ministry of Health pending construction of their new Foreign Ministry in Brasilia. One night the Duty Officer received a call that Bobby Kennedy would be landing at Brasilia airport on a sudden visit to see the Brazilian President. The young Duty officer went to the airport and escorted Bobby Kennedy to the Presidential Palace – there was no senior Brazilian Foreign Ministry official in Brasilia to do this.

Some Brazilians work in Brasilia in the week and go home elsewhere at weekends. This is less of a trend nowadays. But the capital still feels a lot emptier at weekends. I can only recall meeting one person who regularly did the opposite – leave São Paulo at the weekend for Brasilia because he liked the peace and quiet of his house by the lake built as a key feature of Brasilia's original design. Most Brazilians would say – even though there are now good restaurants and the city is on the circuit for touring music acts – that Brasilia still lacks the soul of a major city.

São Paulo is and never has been the capital of Brazil. It is the centre of industry, finance and culture (except for TV and film where Rio probably leads). Brasilia will never challenge this. It means the Ambassador, forced to reside in Brasilia, will find himself on an aeroplane to São Paulo and elsewhere on a regular basis.

Even Boring can be Exciting

Brazil is such a bright and colourful place. The greatest example of this is Carnival. We twice went to the Sambódromo in Rio for one of the two nights before Shrove Tuesday when the top 12 samba schools parade competing for the championship of the year.

Gaudy costumes, sumptuous human flesh, breathtaking acrobatics, mind-numbing anthems, thunderous drumming, and an atmosphere of joy and excitement all through the night. It's hot and steamy. At the same time you are aware of the amazing achievement by each school in putting together a procession of 2000-3000 people, floats, bands, dancers, acrobats and showing their best in no more and not much less than 75 minutes half a mile from one end of the sambadrome to the other in front of 72,000 spectators.

When it all comes to an end about 0630, the sun is rising again and you can then repair to the beach for breakfast. For the judging of the performances you have to wait until the Wednesday. That determines which school is the winner and which school is relegated from the top twelve. Marks are given by judges in several categories – the acrobats, floats, drummers, dancing queen, costumes, choreography etc. All are tabulated on a big screen at an outdoor stadium for the live and television audiences to see. The winning school parades again on the following Saturday. The one relegated is replaced by another in the top 12 for the following year.

Compare and contrast 5 pm on a Friday afternoon in December 2009 in a large hall in Brasilia, a city people work in but many leave as the weekend approaches. I was asked by my staff to give a presentation on public finance as part of a seminar part-sponsored by the Embassy seeking to help with a drive for better governance. I expressed doubt about whether this might be the best use of the Ambassador's time, particularly with the weekend beckoning. Would anyone be interested? Would anyone even turn up? They told me how much the organisers were looking forward to it. I had heard that before, I thought, but gave it a go.

I walked into the hall and saw 500 people there, not in a state of slumber or packing for the weekend but in full debate about public finance. I cannot recall what it was I said except that getting public finance right – efficient, transparent, free of corruption – was a good idea, and the UK wanted to offer its own experience and expertise such as it was. A sea of faces watched and listened with attention. There were some intelligent questions. I walked out, bewildered, and went for a pre-weekend swim to reflect.

The stereotype of a Brazilian in the mind of a European is of someone exotic and extrovert, used to improvisation and perhaps not so good at timekeeping. All this is to be found. But they are also ambitious, focussed and prepared to work hard. A taxi driver in São Paulo may well work extra shifts so as to afford private school for his kids. A woman may travel long distances by bus early in the morning to work as a maid in a middle-class apartment, have a shop job in the afternoon and come home to do the housework and cook for the family in the early evening.

There is no culture of siesta. People in the big cities may take a little longer for lunch than in Europe but they may well also work later in the evening.

Exotic Places

In February 2015, nineteen months after leaving Brazil as Ambassador, I did an event with Michael Palin on travel in

Brazil. It was at the Senate House, home of the Institute of Latin American Studies (ILAS) of the University of London where I am a Fellow (nice title though I don't really know what it means). The idea of the event was to honour the memory of travel writer John Brooks who had left a legacy to ILAS, which has been used for events/grants over many years.

Michael Palin and I sat in easy chairs in front of an audience of 200 in the splendid William Beveridge Hall. My job was to engage him in stories about the travel in Brazil which underpinned his TV series and book. I added the odd detail from my experience.

We talked about Rio – the beautiful city. We talked about São Paulo – a great city, and one where, Michael Palin shrewdly observed, you can be what you want to be.

It made me think of some other places I had visited.

Panel with Michael Palin on travelling in Brazil, Senate House London, organised by Prof Linda Newson of the Institute of Latin American Studies

Michael mentioned that in Recife the attractive long walkway along the seafront has at regular intervals shark warnings, which I have never seen elsewhere in Brazil. This reminded me that in Palmas, a new city which is capital of the state of Tocantins founded only in 1988, a Rio-style beach has been created along the Tocantins River. Palmas is hundreds of miles from the coast and the hottest place I have visited in Brazil. I can see that putting down some sand and some beach bars could be an attractive proposition for the population who might enjoy there some hours of weekend relaxation with the family. But I thought the effect more than slightly dulled by the notices warning against entering the river because of the piranhas, necessary though those undoubtedly were.

Michael Palin's book highlights some amazing characters he met while in Brazil, especially women. One story remains in his mind. He started his journeys in Brazil in the far north visiting the Yanomami tribe in the state of Roraima. At night he slept in the communal living space, a large hall with thatched roof. Needing to make a call of nature he went outside in pitch darkness, he found his way far enough from the sleeping quarters to perform the function. Then came the problem of finding his way back. He was in the jungle, a foreign and hostile environment. There was no light. But a woman in the hut had thought of this. She was holding open a flap and the light from within was the guide he needed.

He met powerful businesswomen, artists, religious leaders, models, and many others. Yet the single simple act of kindness of an Indian woman in Roraima remained especially important.

It seems odd to speak of Brazil still being male-dominated when there is a female President. In fact, women are not well represented in Congress. This is even more the case in business. So I was especially happy to be invited to a small group of influential female businesswomen for a breakfast meeting in São Paulo. I came away thinking Brazil will have many more senior women in this sector in the coming years.

Brilliant Britto

Talking of Recife brings to mind the celebrated pop-artist Romero Britto, a native of that city. He is so well known that he and his work were used as the theme by a samba school for their parade in the Sambadrome. He paraded aboard one of the floats himself.

Romero created a portrait of the Queen for her Diamond Jubilee in 2012, which went to Buckingham Palace. He kindly accepted an invitation to come to my Party at the Ambassador's residence in Brasilia in May 2012 to help us celebrate the Jubilee. There are copies of this portrait now in the Residence,

The Queen by Romero Britto

425

the Embassy itself and in our Consulates in São Paulo and Rio.

I saw Romero again in 2014 in Miami, where he is now based. He graciously showed me his gallery and studio. Miami has become Portuguese as well as Spanish-speaking as so many Brazilians visit to shop and relax, bank their money there and invest in real estate. Romero is part of the scenery of Miami. He even has a shop on board a cruise liner operating from there.

Dazzling diversity

Brazil is a very big country. It is a unique mix of races – Native American, Portuguese, Africans from various parts, Italian, German, Arab, Jewish and Japanese are the main groups I came across.

Just think about the ladies for a moment. You see tall blonde and blue-eyed air hostesses and models from the south of Brazil. You see dark black beauties, for example in Salvador. You see reddish-brown Indian women of differing statures. You see full-blooded Japanese women.

Most people are a blend. Early Portuguese settlers often had Indian (native American) wives; there are different words for native American Indians (Indios) and Asian Indians (Indianos) – there are perhaps surprisingly few of the latter in the Brazilian mix. Around 50% of people claimed to be black in the last census. I recall one of the rising diplomats in the Brazilian Foreign Ministry was part Japanese and part black and maybe other things too; I was proud that she said she had felt at home in multicultural London. They are all proud to be Brazilian and all speak Portuguese, except for some of the older generation of Indians.

May I Take an Indian Spear on Board the Plane?

The Indians are fascinating. Unlike in Argentina, the remote locations of some of them and then enlightened Brazilian policies in the twentieth century enabled many tribes to survive. Most of them live on land specifically allocated to them by the Brazilian government, some 11% of Brazilian territory. There are still some who have never had contact with the outside world, notably groups in Amazonia near the border with Peru. Brazilian government policy is to monitor these people from the air but not to force contact on them. Contact is invariably dangerous unless carefully handled as these people have little resistance to diseases common to others.

I visited Palmeira dos Indios in the northeastern state of Alagoas. The purpose was to visit a school there partnered on a British Council scheme with a school in Tuxford, in my native Nottinghamshire, which I also visited later on. The schools were in contact through a British Council programme, which was also helping with leadership training for the youngsters. While at the school I was treated to a display of the crafts of the local Indians and also of their dancing.

Now it is common when making visits for the Ambassador to be given gifts as he/she arrives and leaves. Often these are heavy coffee-table books, some of which somehow are left at the airport before going home, or pictures, or examples of local pottery. As I left the school at Palmeira dos Indios they thrust a spear into my hand. It was an ornamental spear but a spear nonetheless.

I immediately decided I wanted to keep and display it in the Residence. Flashing through my mind, though, was an occasion in the US having visited the Baseball Museum and Slugger Factory in Louisville Kentucky being told when I got to security at the airport that I could not take the miniature baseball bat given out as a souvenir of the visit on to my flight back to Washington DC. I had to leave it behind in the airport. I could see that other travellers had encountered the same problem as there were quite a number of bats in a basket provided for the purpose. I wondered if the bats were recycled to the museum?

Fortunately, in Palmeira dos Indios, there was a solution. I asked the accompanying British Council representative if she would take it home and then send it to me by post. She did. It was displayed in the Residence. I now have it at home.

Respect the Earth, White Man

Ed Miliband visited Brazil from 1-5 August 2009 as Secretary of State for Environment, Food and Rural Affairs. I admired his energy. We covered a huge amount of ground.

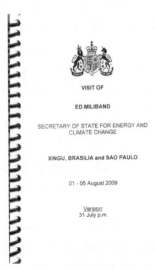

Ed Miliband programme

It included a visit to the Xingú National Park. We had in advance to produce medical certificates to show that we had had no communicable diseases recently. It being winter in Brazil, flu was a particular concern.

We arrived courtesy of a Greenpeace Cessna aircraft from Cuiabá. The set piece was an event in a traditional open hall with thatched roof. Representatives of 16 tribes had found their way to the spot, some paddling considerable distances along the Xingú River to meet the White Chief. Each declaimed in his own language, translated into Portuguese often by his son. There was one speech at the end by a woman. Ed Miliband was then presented with a petition. The bottom line was that, like the North American Indians in the nineteenth century, the Indians in Brazil were facing serious encroachment from the Whites (by which they meant non-Indians). The Whites did not respect the land and the rivers.

In response to questions, they said the climate was becoming hotter, the rivers polluted, their way of life thereby endangered. They spoke against the controversial plan to build a hydro-electric plant upstream at Belo Monte. This issue has become internationalised with Indians visiting European national parliaments in their war paint to leverage pressure on the Brazilian government, who say the Indians' concerns are unfounded and hydro-electric power is the greenest there is.

Where there are Indians there should be Cowboys.

And there were. The cowboys are very much still in business in Brazil and retain their traditions. We went from seeing the Indians on the Xingú River to visiting a ranch at Bangue-Bangue (yes, it means bang-bang-cowboys shooting at each other – and is also a shorthand for Western films).

A group of cowboys met us off the plane, in their full gear including rifles and pennants. They looked rather more menacing than the Indians. I imagine they saw us as the enemy ready to criticise them for their use of the land. They escorted us to the farm.

The farmers explained that they did retain and where necessary re-grow trees and shrubs next to rivers in accordance with the spirit of the law if not always the letter.

They were certainly not like the rogues who had devastated the environment in other parts of the Amazon (Prince Charles saw some of this in the state of Pará). They found the environmental regulations too onerous but understood the need for compromise.

One of my Brazilian favourites, Federal Environment Minister Izabella Teixeira, later brokered a sensible compromise on these laws in the so-called Forest Code, after decades of trench warfare between the long-feuding environmental and farming lobbies in Brazil. Neither side liked it. Nor are they ever going to like each other. But the principle that both views have to be accommodated is getting through. The compromise seems fair to me. Brazil retains stronger laws than anything in UK but gives the farmers more flexibility.

Is Ethanol Evil?

Ed Miliband also experienced the Brazilian side of the debate on whether ethanol should be encouraged as a fuel to replace petrol/gas. We took him straight from arrival from the airport on arrival from UK to an ethanol plant in the interior of São Paulo state to see the efficiency of the process. Sugar cane can be turned in modern plants into either sugar or ethanol and the waste products used to generate electricity for the plant, nearby towns and to fertilise the fields. Experts told us of their expectations that the process would be improved in the future to be carbon-positive, that is a net benefit in terms of the emission of greenhouse gases which cause global warming. The Sugar Cane Industry of course had an interest in saying this to us. Ed Miliband then went to Brasilia to hear the views of the NGOs. In a Saturday afternoon meeting at the Residence he heard concerns from them about some of the old-fashioned processes still used and the exploitation of labour. But and they were clear that the ethanol produced from maize in the US made much less environmental sense.

But they saw that the future in Brazil was with processes of which environmental groups should approve. They were unhappy that European NGOs continued to campaign against ethanol irrespective of how it was produced. This had a caused a rift in some cases between the Brazilian and European wings of global NGOs.

He later heard more of the same from some of Brazil's grandees such as former President Fernando Henrique Cardoso, Foreign Minister Celso Amorim, Energy Minister Lobão, Governor of São Paulo Jose Serra and former Environment and Finance Minister Rubens Ricupero. He finished off his visit by meeting the oil and gas industry, in which there is plenty of UK involvement.

Giant Anteaters

The Amazon with its forests and rivers is magnificent. There are dolphins and other amazing fish, you can see some birds, you can hear the monkeys. Yet it is not the best place to see wildlife. That is the Pantanal, the wetlands in the west of Brazil about the size of Wales with ranches and farms of various sizes but no towns.

We spent a few days there in late June 2009, flying into the heart of the area by small private plane from a private airfield on its edge at Aquidauana in the state of Mato Grosso do Sul. We stayed at a lovely lodge and were escorted on safaris by jeep, kayak and on foot during the day and at night.

Formidable footprints and the red-light district

We saw anteaters and giant anteaters in the meadows, identified over 100 species of birds including several varieties of toucans as well as storks and vultures, weird-looking tapirs, caimans by the hundred in the water with otters large and small, snakes of huge dimensions.

The king of that jungle is the jaguar. They do not show themselves readily. But we did see their footprints by the water...

At night we saw nightjars and other birds. We came to a clearing in the forest at one point with a view over the river. There were hundreds of red lights. Yet there was no town anywhere near. These were the eyes of the caimans, we were told.

In the forest we both heard and saw howler and other monkeys. Wild pigs rushed by us. We were fully covered up having been warned of the risk of being attacked by ticks.

By our comfortable chalets, raccoons came by at night and foxes in the morning. The noises of the forest were many and varied. Some pheasant-like birds roosted in the low trees right by us at night and woke us with a dawn chorus which sounded like Zebedee's spring - Boing! - in the Magic Roundabout.

It was such a full experience that I don't think, years later, I have fully assimilated it.

Rubber supports Carnival

A work trip to the state of Acre, in the far west of Brazil, also took me to the forest. That well-run state has leading ideas on how to avoid encouraging deforestation and to provide alternative livelihoods.

I saw traditional rubber-tapping in the forest and had a go myself. It seems a slow business. You make a cut in the tree bark, let the latex tickle into a container and then move to the next tree. At the end of the day you collect it all up.

But to what purpose? Brazilian rubber is not a competitive export. What is produced in Acre should ideally find a use in Acre so that the rubber tapper can earn a decent income. Enter Carnival. It is a time of year in the big Brazilian cities when there is considerable conviviality of a carnal nature. The Brazilian government, which has with some success for years been promoting safe sex, provides condoms in large numbers free of charge.

I visited the state-of-the-art factory by the forest. It was a spotless and fully automated process employing a couple of hundred people, mostly women. They were delighted to have good jobs in a modern facility helping the forest workers and people wanting a good time in cities like São Paulo, three hours' flight away.

I flew north, courtesy of WWF, over where a new road was being built to connect the rest of Brazil with neighbouring Peru and the Pacific. New roads in the rain forest tend to attract people who want to develop the land, pushing out the residents and encroaching on the forest. You can see the process particularly in Pará. The idea here is to support the residents, helping them get their goods to market so that they do not feel forced to sell up, as well as to try to stop newcomers destroying the forest. Sky TV are doing great work raising money for this purpose.

You just feel in Acre that the money will not be subverted or frittered away and so it is worthwhile helping. The modest Governor of the State came to my hotel to walk me to his office in the capital Rio Branco. He comes from a long line of leaders who have the welfare of the forest and its people at heart.

The former Federal Environment Minister and Senator Marina Silva is from Acre. She lived in the forest until as a teenager she had to go into the town and take work as a maid so that she could be treated for arsenic poisoning. She came to see me at my residence in Brasilia in June 2009 to say she was determined to lead a campaign for a different kind of national leadership of Brazil. Her campaigns in the 2010 and 2014. Presidential elections have made an amazing impact in view of the lack of any serious party machine behind her. She speaks no English, she is frail, and yet she has such charisma. She worked in her youth with the legendary Chico Mendes. He was murdered in 1988 by people who saw his environmental idea as bad for their business. I went to see his simple house, now a museum and shrine.

Little London

Brazilians mostly live in cities. In fact, Brazil has a higher percentage of the population in urban areas than does the UK. When I speak to people in São Paulo and Rio about the rain forest for many of them it is little closer than it is to the good folk of Nottingham where I come from. Why would you want to go there, I was asked?

Cities are created out of the countryside. One remarkable example is Londrina, Little London. I was invited by the young black mayor of Londrina Homero Barbosa Neto to attend an event to mark the 75th anniversary of the city in 2009. It was held on Black Consciousness Day which helped to attract some high-profile guests from around the country.

The city is in the southern state of Paraná which has been developed considerably by European immigration over the last hundred years. There are Italians, Germans as elsewhere and also a large number of eastern Europeans from various parts. This is reflected in the churches.

Londrina was founded by Londoners. A company gained authorisation to build a railway and lay out the town. As part of a wider visit to South America aimed at boosting the UK's flagging trade, Edward Prince of Wales visited the area in 1931 together with his brother Prince George, Duke of Kent, a visit much commented upon by the German media, presumably wondering if this was an effort to add Brazil to the British sphere of influence. The splendid city museum tells the story how it has grown into a city of 250,000 now. I did meet one grandson of an original London founder. There is also a splendid British school there, which I visited. But, otherwise, the city has little British about it except its history.

Brazilian nicknames

A Brazilian once told me she was ashamed that Brazilians are so often known by nicknames rather than their real names, suggesting that little is taken seriously in Brazil. I suppose those of us who follow football are used to Pele, Hulk etc. It is more unusual for a Head of State to be known universally by his nickname. Luis Inácio da Silva was always known as Lula (Squid). Eventually he changed his name legallyto Luis Inácio Lula da Silva, so it wasn't really a nickname any more by the time he became President of Brazil!

Another nickname you come across a lot in Brazil is Tiradentes (teeth-puller). This was the nickname given to one of the young men who rose up against the then Portuguese state in the so-called Inconfidência Mineira in 1789. It was a warning note that the rule of those designated by the distant Portuguese Crown was not popular in an age when North America and Europe was vibrating with talk of revolutionary political change. Brazil was rich in gold but the Brazilians were not benefiting much. Poor Tiradentes, real name Joaqim José da Silva Xavier, was executed in grisly fashion in Rio de Janeiro in what is now Tiradentes Square: the clemency granted by the Portuguese Crown to other conspirators was not extended to him. At least there is a public holiday nowadays bearing his name.

There is also a lovely small town in Minas Gerais called Tiradentes, one of a number of towns (Ouro Preto, formerly capital of the state, is the most substantial) which became rich in the colonial era because they were on the Royal Road along

Ouro Preto

which gold passed from the mines to the sea. We stayed at a relaxing guest house serving afternoon tea British-style which fitted the relaxed pace of the town.

There are two outlets of the Royal Road to the sea. One is Rio. The other is Paraty. When I was learning Portuguese before starting as Ambassador I caught a glimpse of this graceful town with its cobbled streets and elegant low-rise houses and restaurants. I was treated to a catamaran voyage over the weekend stopping at islands for oysters and fried fish served on a banana leaf. Idyllic.

Everyone to his god

Visiting São Luis on the north coast underlined the diversity of religious belief in Brazil but also how these beliefs are nowadays tolerated and can intertwine. We experienced the festival of São João (St. John) in mid-June. The traditional story Bumba Meu Boi is enacted in the street. Basically, it is about a bull is killed and comes back to life, a pregnant girl, a cowboy and a priest. The dancing and drumming are African, the costumes a mixture of African and European.

The European masters tried to suppress the gods of their African slaves. What happened was that the African deities started to have their equivalents in Christian saints. The depiction of Christian figures looks decidedly African some times, for example in Salvador, the most African of Brazilian cities. Nowadays, religions such as candomblé are treated with respect in Brazil. The superstition in them has long taken hold in figures of speech and customs such as wearing white at New Year in Rio and jumping seven times over the waves in homage to Iemanjá.

Tolerance is a great virtue and one which seems to come

naturally to Brazilians. They are a spiritual people, though the number of atheists while still small does rise with each successive census. The fastest-growing group is the Evangelical Christians especially among the poorer people. They are to be found everywhere from shacks in villages to huge US-style halls holding thousands of worshippers in the big cities. Their ministers are close to their flock and deal with their problems. They form a caucus in Congress on matters of conscience.

The flip-side of tolerance is that Brazilians may sometimes be too willing to let things pass which should be stopped. The corruption between big politics and big business in Brazil is a case in point. There are individuals well known to be corrupt

Planting a tree at Itaipú. Tree-planting is an Ambassadorial fucntion, along with shaking thousands of hands, having your picture taken every day and giving a speech every other day

and even with convictions who continue to be voted back into Congress or other offices. Justice takes far too long to be administered and the rich seem to avoid it forever. More impatience with these people could force on to the agenda stronger disincentives to curb bad behaviour.

The Big Falls and the Big Dam

There is a lot of water in Brazil. The Amazon quickly convinces you of that. Down in the southwest, water produces a big part of Brazil's (and Paraguay's) power at the Itaipú dam. I visited in 2011courtesy of the Federal Ministry of Mines and Energy, including down where the turbines operate. It is a joint project with Paraguay. The border between the two countries is marked halfway along the top of the dam. The Boardroom and Control Room are similarly half in each country.

Itaipú dams the River Paraná. It produces about as much energy as the huge Three Gorges dam in China. It took a long time to build and to bring into service. Nothing comes easy in this part of the world, especially collaborative projects. Paraguay receives an annual payment from Brazil for use of more than its share of the power generated.

Tony Blair visited together with President Fernando Henrique Cardoso in 2001 and planted a tree. I planted another tree next to it. Talking of Tony Blair, he came to Brazil to give some lectures during my time as Ambassador. One was in São Paulo at breakfast time. I was stunned by the achievement of the organisers to have hundreds of Brazilians in their seats, including some very senior ones, so early in the morning so that the event could start on time; contrast this with party-political events in Brazil where I learned to turn up at least an hour late in order not to waste too much time hanging about.

When I met Tony Blair the previous evening I was struck by his understanding of Brazil.

The big attraction of the area is the nearby Iguaçu Falls. The Cataratas hotel on the Brazilian side is one of my favourite places in Brazil. There are views over the Falls. The hotel is inside a National Park. On the Argentine side there are walkways over the Falls. The Falls are spectacular, on a much bigger scale than Niagara. The area has its own micro-climate encouraging yellow butterflies and cuatis. Beautiful.

PART V

THE DARKER SIDE

Brazilian is a country of light and colour. It is a lucky country, blessed with so many natural advantages.

The most appalling disaster in my time as Ambassador was the fire at the Kiss night club in Santa Maria in the southern state of Rio Grande do Sul. Hundreds of youngsters, many of them students at the Federal University of Santa Maria celebrating a freshers' ball, were enjoying a Saturday night out with live acts on 27 January 2013. The night club was far too full.

I watched news coming in on live TV in the early hours of Sunday morning. Large numbers were taken to hospital. It became clear that a band playing in the night club had let off a flare while performing on stage. This had caused a fire in flammable acoustic foam in the ceiling which had released poisonous smoke. People rushed to the exits but a large number simply could not get out in time. There were insufficient exits; night-club staff did not recognise the severity of the incident quickly enough. 242 people died and hundreds more injured. 90% of the dead died from suffocation. Many bodies were retrieved from the bathrooms. It was the second highest death toll from a fire in Brazilian history.

The scenes outside the night club early that morning were heartrending. People who had escaped were looking for friends. Relatives were seeking news of loved ones. The emergency services were operating in full swing yet there were few lives to save.

There was an anguished reaction from Brazilians. Why should such terrible and preventable accidents keep occurring in what was by this time the world's seventh economy? How could the club be allowed to operate far above its crowd capacity, without emergency exits, poor signage and staff who did not seem sufficiently aware of their role (they had locked the crowd in)?

I telephoned Embassy staff to ask them to check whether there were any Brits caught up in the disaster who would need our help. The Consular team swung into action. It was not easy to get information from the emergency services and hospitals but our staff managed to ascertain with a fair degree of certainty that there appeared to be no British nationals involved.

There was an outpouring of sympathy around the world. I arranged for the Queen to send a message to the Brazilian President. One positive development from the event was a connection made by De Montfort University Leicester with Santa Maria University which has a led to an exchange of student visits and exploration of longer-term co-operation.

Yet those of us living in Brazil were left to reflect on places we had visited in the country which were equally unsafe and where such a disaster was still waiting to happen. The owners of Kiss had lied to the safety authorities about the emergency exits in order to speed up the licensing process. They were subjected to investigation and criminal proceeding. But the state authorities, too, were criticised for failing to check safety with sufficient care. Brazilians do not have confidence that such terrible tragedies could not happen again.

It's the same with landslips. Every winter when it rains heavily there is loss of life not so much from flooding but rather because of mudslides engulfing housing which should not have been built where it was. In January 2013, some 250 people died in the hills above Rio and many more were made homeless. We heard plenty about all this from Brits who had homes in what is usually a delightful area and had done their best to help.

Very often casualties in Brazil following torrential rain are caused by mudslides which sweep away houses built in their path – and where they should not be. Rio state has introduced an early-warning system and they do now have an emergency centre to co-ordinate responses. But how about other states?

Air France disaster

The Foreign Office rightly tells Ambassadors that we are in the public eye at no time more than when there are natural disasters. I experienced this when Hurricane Katrina hit New Orleans in 2005. I found myself ordered to get on to live TV when stories gathered pace about a group of British youngsters being stranded in the city.

In that respect the terrible Air France disaster of 2009 was rather different. I geared up the Embassy to give it top priority. Yet it was slow burner. This was not one of those cases where there were people to rescue. It soon became clear there were not this time – all 228 passengers and crew were killed. Wreckage and bodies were slow to be found. Some never were.

AF447 disappeared on 1 June en route from Rio de Janeiro to Paris. It was last heard of in mid-Atlantic well out to sea from Brazil. I called a teleconference of our posts including London at 0900 our time to start up an emergency operation. We knew soon that there were 5 people with British nationality on the passenger manifest.

On 6 June two bodies were found and some wreckage including a bag with a boarding card 2k for one of the missing

Brits. By 24 June 80 bodies, and some parts, had been found. These were taken by Brazilian frigates to the nearest Brazilian territory, the island of Fernando de Noronha but soon transferred to the mainland in Recife.

Our task became largely one of helping with the identification of the British bodies. We had the help of a team of Disaster Victim Identification experts from the West Midlands police. They liaised with the authorities in Recife and with the Brazilian government and Interpol working with our Embassy team. They also liaised with representatives of other countries who had victims on board, most of all of course the French who lost 61 citizens and the Germans who had 26 on board; there had been 59 Brazilians including Prince Pedro Luis of Orleans-Braganza, descendant of Emperor Pedro II.

The expertise of the DVI team was of great help to all of these countries. Their calmness in the face of bureaucratic delays was admirable. Armed with dental records and DNA taken from the homes of the British victims, a couple of matches were found.

The aircraft's flight recorders were not recovered until May 2011.

The French enquiry into the disaster reported on 5 July 2012. The aircraft crashed after temporary inconsistencies between airspeed measurements caused the autopilot to disconnect after which the crew reacted wrongly and there followed an aerodynamic stall from the plane did not recover. It was the worst disaster in the history of French civil aviation.

The disappearance of Malaysian Airlines flight 370 in 2014 evoked memories of the Air France crash – remote, difficult to find the plane, no survivors, questions about what happened. The difference is that as of November 2015 the plane has still not been found; we do now have an explanation from the

French authorities about the cause of the Air France crash. I wonder why after AF447 it did not become mandatory for civil aircraft to carry tracking devices?

Fiona Conroy

Fiona was the lead of our Science and Innovation network in Brazil, a vibrant and talented late-thirties civil servant aware of her African racial origins and also a Londoner through and through. She and her husband had a young daughter.

We had waited some time for her appointment and arrival in Brasilia. I was an enthusiast for our Science and Innovation work, an area where organisations and people in both countries saw big value in working together. She was the first Head of the S & I network we had from UK, based in Brasilia to work with the Brazilian government while also overseeing a small team in the Consulate-General in São Paulo. She was knowledgeable, energetic, charismatic and fun. After her first few months in the job she was starting to make a difference.

The Foreign Office has operated an open-door approach among staff ever since I joined in 1978 and, I imagine, a long time before that. This means that even the most senior people have the door of their office open for people to walk in unless they are in a meeting or conducting a sensitive phone call.

Fiona used to come in and see me from time to time as she knew I was hungry to hear how she intended to take her work forward and how I as the Ambassador could help. She lit up any room she walked into – with her smile, bouncy body language and positive narrative.

Out of nowhere, I took a call late one evening from my Deputy Colin Reynolds (he and his predecessor Martyn Roper were both excellent) to tell me that Fiona had been taken to hospital and was in a very serious condition. She died not long afterwards. None of us had had any idea that she was so unwell. She had been complaining for a while of not being quite right. But her collapse was sudden and unexpected.

A week later the staff gathered in the Embassy grounds between our offices and the Embassy club in the sunshine to remember her, plant a tree in her memory and inaugurate a plaque with her smiling face and a bench where people could sit and think of her. I am not good at getting through my words on sad occasions. I just about managed it. Others spoke eloquently, including her husband. Some film was shown of her giving a presentation at an awayday. She was taken back to London for a family funeral.

PART VI

TWO PRIME MINISTERS IN BRAZIL AND A DEPUTY PRIME MINISTER TWICE

"Gordon, we must show our people we have a plan…"
President Lula

British Ambassadors in Brazil have always had to struggle to attract visits by the British Prime Minister. These are phenomenally busy people leading the government, having to report to Parliament, heading their party and looking after a constituency. The political leaders of most countries often do some of this work but very few all of it. They can find more time to travel. British Prime Ministers have to travel to Brussels and the key European countries. They love travelling to the US. China and India are top for trade visits. Latin America is a lower priority.

Tony Blair had visited in 2001 towards the end of the Presidency of Fernando Henrique Cardoso, who was a social democrat with whom the UK could relate with not too much difficulty. When I arrived in Brazil in 2008 the reputation of President Lula was becoming a strong attraction. Prime Minister Gordon Brown had been in touch with him for many years and met him outside Brazil. The PM was keen to visit but finding the opportunity during his frenetically busy premiership was a challenge.

The financial and economic crisis of 2008 shocked the world and reverberates to this day. Brazil had been badly affected by previous crises and many in Brazil feared the worst this time too. While I was on language training in Campinas in November 2008 some companies were talking about the risk of failures and not being paid.

The previously little-known G20 including the world's largest economies shot to prominence as the G7 and G8 were clearly not sufficiently global to be the right fora to find global responses to a global crisis. This was in line with the Brazilian determination to see the membership of key global bodies reflecting the growing power of countries outside Europe and North America.

The UK was in the chair of the G20. Gordon Brown called a summit meeting in London for 2 April 2009. His consultations in advance of the Summit included travel to several of the member states. He came to Brazil on 26 March for a two-day visit (following on to a Progressive Governance meeting of social democratic leaders in Santiago after that). As well as the Chancellor Alastair Darling, Cabinet Ministers Peter Mandelson and Douglas Alexander and Sarah Brown were among the party. After arriving at Brasilia airport at 0650 they milled about at the Residence until Lula was ready for us. He is not generally an early riser.

The centrepiece of his visit to Brazil was a meeting with President Lula at his official residence in Brasilia, the Alvorada Palace. This is one of the original buildings designed by Oscar Niemeyer for the new capital in Brasilia and ready for the inauguration in 1960. It is very much in the Niemeyer style of concrete curves. It looks remarkably small for a palace compared to those left behind in Rio de Janeiro. The line-up in the small library used for the meeting was Gordon Brown and the Chancellor of the Exchequer Alastair Darling opposite Lula and his Finance Minister Guido Mantega with the Brazilian Ambassador and I also in the front row (in accordance with Brazilian protocol rather than our importance at the event) and other Ministers and senior people behind us.

Gordon Brown began with a fast detailed summary of the issues for the G20 summit and ideas on how to tackle them. Lula paused. Hoarse from smoking his favourite cigarillos, which I think he has now given up after his throat cancer scare, he thanked Gordon Brown for all the help and advice he had received from him, especially in the early days of his presidency. He then said that he was not an expert on the detailed economic points and would leave Guido Mantega to comment on those. What he did know was that the summit the following week was a big moment. The people in our countries were worried about what would happen. It was essential that the leaders could return from London telling them that there was a plan to tackle the crisis.

Typical Lula. He so understood the politics of the moment. Straight to the heart of the matter.

In the press conference outside the Palace Lula spoke for a very long time and threw in a remark that the world crisis was the fault of those who were white and had blue eyes. They did not understand economics. Challenged by the media, he said he could not think of a single black banker. I can't imagine he made this up on the spot. Whether he had planned to say it – it seemed a bit rude to his friend Gordon Brown – I do not know.

I thought of the visit of Ed Miliband to see the Indian tribes in the Xingu. They saw Lula as the White Man causing them problems!

Lula later told his people that the shock of the world crisis was causing no more than a "marolinha" (wavelet) in Brazil. That was true. Buoyed by the commodity boom, with China in particular buying its food and iron ore, Brazil's economy had just a short period of negative growth before bouncing back with 7.2 % growth in 2010, the highest for years, while the western world was struggling.

The Prime Ministerial party spent the rest of the day in São Paulo. Gordon Brown gave a speech at FAAP (Fundação Armandao Alvares Penteado) University. The highlight was a tour of the Football Museum and a chat with Socrates. They left the following morning after a long day.

I went back to London a few days later to accompany President Lula's party. The G20 was deemed a success in showing at least a degree of co-operation between the major economies in tackling the crisis. My sharpest memory is of Lula arriving to inaugurate the new London office of the Brazilian Development Bank BNDES right by the Mansion house. It wasn't so much what he said, impressive though that was. It was his entrance, readiness to hug everyone (including me) and have photographs taken. All with a smile and the best of humour.

He was out of politics for a while curing his cancer. He then focussed on the re-election as President in 2014 of his protégée Dilma Rousseff as well as on his visits overseas, notably to Africa. If the circumstances are right, he could be a candidate for President again in 2018 although he will then be in his seventies.

David Cameron and a Teddy Bear

David Cameron has been vigorous in visits overseas to promote British business. He is very good at it, remembering the requirements of individual companies on the delegation and making himself available to them. Brazil had to be on the list of visits, though in the end it was rather low on it.

As often happens, his people decided he should come to Brazil following a visit to the United States. I can understand that it may make sense for the Prime Minister's diary to group long-distance visits overseas. But planners are sometimes challenged as regards world geography. You don't just drop down to Brazil from the US. The length of the journey from New York/Washington DC to São Paulo is not much different than from London and the time difference is greater for half the year.

David Cameron arrived on a Virgin Atlantic plane in São Paulo early in the morning of 27 September 2012 with a delegation of business people, university representatives and some gold-medal winners from the London Olympics. Trade Minister Lord Green and Universities/Science Minister David Willetts had already had a good day's programme in São Paulo.

It was a drizzly, chilly, murky morning. My fingers were crossed that the weather would not prevent the two waiting helicopters from taking the Prime Minister and some of his party up to Sorocaba for a formal inauguration of the new JCB plant there manufacturing diggers, in particular for a huge order from the Brazilian government. JCB had already expanded into China, India and Russia. There were a lot of holes to dig in Brazil.

The manager of the Sorocaba factory was a Mexican whose wife had worked at our Consulate and had sadly died. I once asked him why JCB had decided on Brazil rather than Mexico as their Latin America centre. He said because of corruption in Mexico. Brazil is not free of that at high levels; but evidently, for a Mexican, it was a better bet than Mexico. I was able to help JCB move along the Brazilian bureaucracy by mentioning to the Governor of São Paulo an issue over a large tax repayment owed to them.

The PM was in his element at a business event at FIESP, the powerful São Paulo Trade and Industry Federation – with the requirements of businesses large and small in his delegation at the front of his mind. We flew over to Rio for several events in the Palacio da Cidade, the Mayor's official residence (Eduardo Paes has not lived there) and formerly Residence of the British Ambassador when the capital was Rio. On another occasion when on a podium there with the Mayor I said that I would support any move to return the Brazilian capital to Rio if in return I could have my house back.

It is a splendid building with imposing steps leading up to the main door and then an imposing staircase up to two grand reception rooms, with smaller ones behind. The British government, in a period of austerity and global retreat after the Second World War, decided South America merited more attention and invested in the construction of this building (as well as in an existing large house in the Recoleta district of Buenos Aires for our Ambassador to Argentina).

In the modern way for high-level visits we grouped several events in the single building so that the PM could drop into each one.

The following morning, after the PM had visited Luta pela Paz and Luke Dowdney, we took a Webjet (since gone bust) charter to Brasilia – the Virgin plane having relocated to Brasilia. I imagine the Brazilians were pretty amazed by out taking a budget flight even if a charter. I can't imagine the French President doing this.

Half the conversation with President Dilma was on bilateral matters, mostly trade and economic. David Cameron was reassuring about the tough UK rhetoric against immigration, pledging that Brazilian students on the President's Science without Borders scheme would be welcome and that they could study additional English if they needed it to reach the language standard for their course. She had raised the point at their meeting in London in July on the eve of the London Olympics.

This programme was a sudden idea she had had when told by President Obama how the Chinese were sending their students in huge numbers to the USA (and of course

To Alan,

with thanks, best wishes —

David Ca—.

THE RT HON DAVID CAMERON MP
THE PRIME MINISTER

David Cameron

to UK and other countries). She told her Education Minister Aloizio Mercadante to arrange for 100,000 Brazilian students to go overseas in her 4-year term. These students, mostly undergraduates spending a year of their course abroad, were supported by government and business scholarships. The UK had a quota of 10,000, which we just about met.

It was struggle to persuade the Brazilian government that these students were welcome, so the PM's words were important. I was asked out of the blue by the Brazilian government in May 2013 whether we could take over 2000 additional students, whom the President wanted to relocate from Portugal. We had the advantage of high reputation in our university sector. But we failed. The Home Office insisted that any students improving their English in UK before their course started would have to return to Brazil to apply for their visa for their course. This was hopeless. The students' grants included only money for one return flight and many students had no funds to pay for another one. The students went elsewhere. The UK lost £36 million in income to our economy. Our reputation took a knock and I fear this has affected how we are viewed as a partner in the second stage of Science without Borders from 2015.

If I have a regret about my time in Brazil it is that I didn't make bigger waves about this offer. I had only a few months to go before leaving the Diplomatic Service. I felt very strongly that the government was not acting in the country's best interest. But I was still immersed in the culture that you could put your case, as I did, but then you had to get on with carrying out government policy. Correct. But there was later criticism in parliament of the missed opportunity. I could have had one last go in a telegram to be widely circulated in Whitehall setting out the case.

Universities and Science Minister David Willetts tried to

help. Advisers at No 10 didn't want to see a problem. The FCO didn't want to push it. The moment was politically difficult as UKIP had done well and the Conservatives badly at the local elections a few days previously. Yet, I suspect UKIP would not have been against the idea!

Yes, there were some bogus overseas students coming to the UK, mostly from other parts of the world, using their applications to enter the country and then disappearing as illegal immigrants. But these students are financially supported by the Brazilian government, have a return ticket, and cannot complete their qualification until they return to Brazil. The big problem was the government promise to reduce immigration below 100,000 a year – without introducing identity cards, with no comprehensive system to count people as they leave the country (and so no way of knowing if people overstay), and no way of limiting immigration from the EU.

The other half of David Cameron's meeting with Dilma was tough going on foreign affairs as the President criticised western intervention, led by the UK and France, in Libya and intervention in general in other countries.

There is a debate always to be had about the legality and efficacy of intervention. But the Brazilian approach comes close to opposing intervention in principle in all circumstances – indeed this is what former President Collor said had been his policy when I took a visiting UK parliamentary committee to meet him in his position as Chair of the Congressional Foreign Relations Committee. When I once asked a Brazilian whether he thought it had been wrong for Brazil to join the fight against the Axis in World War 2, I was told that Brazil had only declared war after its ships had been attacked by the Germans – in other words, not because Germany had been wrong to invade Poland, France etc.

So often I found myself easily on the same wavelength on

big international issues when I was overseas. But there were always some issues where there was a big divide. In Germany, it was over the trend towards ever closer union of the EU which the Germans felt had to be on the right side of history and the UK did not. In the US, it was over healthcare. Americans saw our NHS as a socialist system which could stop people having the treatment of their choice. In Brazil the big divide was over foreign policy.

David Cameron did the right thing, put over his case and did not rise to some tough wording of the Brazilian position.

The meeting ended in smiles. It had been agreed that gifts between the two Presidents would be handed to aides so that time was not spent on giving and receiving. Nonetheless, I had suggested that it would be nice touch if the PM gave Dilma something for her young grandson, whom she adored. He gave her a teddy bear. She hugged it and smiled.

Coming out of the meeting, we had our gold-medal winners stationed on her path inside the Presidential palace (the Planalto, which Prince Charles had visited). She stopped to talk to Anthony Joshua and Nicola Adams, two charming British boxing champions – the first about twice the size of the second.

Off to the airport. David Cameron seemed happy with the visit and ready to mix with the delegation and the media on the return flight from Brasilia to London on the Virgin Atlantic charter. A few days later I bumped into the Prime Minister while meeting officials at No 10 and he said he thought it had been right to visit the three cities as I had wanted rather than two as his staff had suggested. It is always a dilemma for top-level visitors to Brazil. Rio gives such wonderful photo opportunities and has the 2016 Olympics; São Paulo is the business, finance and cultural centre; you may well have to go to Brasilia if you want to meet the President.

Nick Clegg – UK Rep for Latin America?

Ambassadors are always fighting for senior Ministerial attention. It's different if you are in Washington, Brussels or Paris – and nowadays in China and India. You are then flooded with visitors, some coming without strong purpose. But, elsewhere, it is struggle for Ambassadors to attract attention. High-level visits force Whitehall to pay attention to your bailiwick for while at least so that the visitor can have a productive programme.

The coalition government formed in 2010 gave Ambassadors opportunities. It was a fixed-term, so we knew we would have 5 years to work in. In the wake of the financial crisis it was clear that our economy and living standards would be depressed because the government would have to tighten spending because of the huge budget deficit and mountain of debt inherited and people would be constrained in their outgoings so domestic demand was not going to rise quickly any time soon. Increasing exports and revenue from investments outward and inward was a way of growing the economy. That was an area where senior government Ministers could help overseas in support of business.

For the first time we had a Deputy Prime Minister who was the leader of another political party and an interest in creating his own profile. This was not the Deputy of the style of Willie Whitelaw, a sage troubleshooter within government keeping the show on the road. Nor a John Prescott, appealing to parts of the Labour movement Tony Blair could not reach. Nick Clegg was keen to act as an alternative to the PM as far as possible.

He also speaks foreign languages, sadly unusual among UK Ministers nowadays, unlike many foreign counterparts. He speaks Dutch, because of his mother. He also speaks

Spanish with his Spanish wife and his bilingual children. The latter was an unusual asset which marked him out for a role with Latin America, receiving visitors in London and making visits overseas to Spanish-speaking countries.

Brazil is 36 times the size of the UK, half the landmass of South America, half the population, a lot more than half of the economy and higher-ranked in 2013 among world economies than the UK on Purchasing Power Parity, the ever more popular comparative measure taking into account what people can buy with the volume of wealth generated.

But they speak Portuguese. Brazilians don't hear much European Portuguese. Portuguese visitors to Brazil outside the big cities may be asked where they learned their language as it can sound non-native to a Brazilian. Portugal is exposed to Brazilian TV and music in Brazilian Portuguese all the time.

As for Spanish, only half the people in South America speak it. It is meant to be compulsory to learn it at school in Brazil. That doesn't translate into familiarity. Brazilians may be able to puzzle out what a Spanish speaker is saying in simple everyday situations. The Spanish speakers understand little of what the Brazilians say in return.

Nick Clegg's staff were keen to advertise his Spanish to me. I said it didn't help much in Brazil – not the reply they wanted. The Deputy Prime Minister caught on to this after his first visit. I had to relay from the embarrassed staff of his opposite number the Brazilian Vice-President that they wished Nick Clegg would speak to him in English as he could understand that a little and it made it easier for the excellent interpreters who worked for the Brazilian Presidency.

Nick Clegg's visit to Brazil was scheduled for February 2011. With him would be a delegation of business people and university leaders. We had had good visits already from Cabinet Ministers in the new government – Caroline Spelman on Environment/Agriculture and Vince Cable on Business. This was a chance to operate at a higher level in the Brazilian government.

I was nervous because we had not secured a meeting with the new President Dilma Rousseff. I knew the Brazilian Foreign Ministry was pushing on our behalf. It was unfortunately not unusual in Brazil, though desperately bad for Ambassadorial nerves, for such meetings to slot into – or out of – place right at the last minute. I had been clear that the Brazilians were capable of insisting on the protocol of the Deputy Prime Minister being received by his opposite number, the Brazilian Vice-President, and no higher.

The additional problem was that no-one – Brazilian or British – seemed to have a way into Dilma's office. I tried my message on Brazilian Ministers – Aloizio Mercadante, Fernando Pimentel – she had known for very many years. Whether the message got through I do not know. It was already clear the new President would be more restrictive on receiving visitors than her predecessor President Lula. She would see whom she had to see – Presidents and Prime Ministers. She made a few exceptions – the US Vice-President and some high-ranking female visitors. I kept on asking and – as happens all the time in Brazil – getting no answer.

A week before the visit we were warned by London that votes in Parliament on electoral boundary reform and a referendum on introducing an alternative-vote system were threatening to derail the visit. It was finally called off with 48 hours' notice, much to the disgruntlement of the delegation which had planned to accompany him. The referendum on the Alternative Vote happened; I voted for it; but it came nowhere near the threshold need to pass. The electoral boundaries were not reformed – a much worse dent in our parliamentary democracy as this threatened to skew the result of the next general election.

It's not great revving up an Embassy machine and the host country for a senior visit and then calling it off for reasons they will find difficult to understand. But it happens. The Brazilians do this themselves. I could not tell whether the UK reputation was seriously damaged by the postponement – probably not, I thought and hoped.

Nick Clegg ended up making two visits to Brazil, both around my birthday – 21 June – in 2011 and 2012. We crammed a lot in.

We had a stroke of luck with the timing of the first visit. President Dilma had just come up with the Science Without Borders Scheme. The idea was to accelerate innovation in Brazil by exposing large numbers of students in STEM subjects (Science, Technology, engineering and Maths) to courses at the world's best universities. The good news for the UK was not only that the President took notice of the global university league tables, where our universities were second only to the US, but also her Ministers were under huge pressure to deliver the 100,000 students overseas from a standing start in less than 4 years.

So, for once, the Brazilians were at least as keen as the UK to engage. The universities delegation, under Minister of Science and Universities David Willetts, had serious meetings. Universities UK became the negotiating partner with the Brazilians. Nick Clegg established what we needed to do. UUK, with Joanna Newman as the negotiator, got on with forging a deal after this promising start. The Brazilians needed it to be easy to deliver. So UUK offered a single price for a year at any UK university. This helped get over Brazilian resentment at paying what they considered "taxes", that is student fees at overseas rates.

What a boon for UK universities! Most UK universities participated in the scheme, received Brazilian students and found them a delight. It was especially interesting for places like the University of Derby, a young university closely linked to local business and so able to find placements to enhance the study period, and for up-and-comers like De Montfort University Leicester which had the largest cohort of Brazilians in 2014.

The downside for the Brazilians was that the elite UK universities – Oxford, Cambridge, King's College, UCL etc – did not find it worth their while to accept Brazilian undergraduates. When President Dilma was re-elected and continued the scheme it was clear that they would need a different formula for the following years which would include these elite universities too.

I tried to help along a deal on the lines for Further Education. The Association of Colleges (AoC) played a similar role to UUK for tertiary education in offering the Brazilians a framework for training their youngsters in UK. I know some Further Ed Colleges in the UK are keen to have more foreign students. Various Brazilian agencies, AoC and the Embassy sat around my dining table on 21 March 2013 seeking to seal an outline deal. The additional dimension is the need for more pastoral care in view of the youth of the students. We got rather stuck on periods of study. I left the table feeling that there were blockages on the Brazilian side but not seeing how they would be removed. Sadly, the deal didn't go forward.

Nick Clegg's second visit was to lead the UK delegation to the Rio + 20 Earth Summit. It was meant to be at summit level, and the UK government certainly took global warming and sustainability seriously. Prime Minister John Major had led for the UK at the original Earth Summit in Rio in 1992. But the fact was that there was going to be no breakthrough agreement at Rio + 20 and I could not recommend that this was an occasion to which the Prime Minister had to come.

On both visits Nick Clegg was a first-rate operator, handling meetings with skill and our promotional events with panache including at our UK pavilion near the Rio + 20 conference site. He wanted to use his rowing prowess in 2012 and we arranged for him to have an early-morning outing on the Rio Lagoon with Brazilian rowers. But it had to be called off as we had thunder and lightning.

PART VII

FOREIGN AFFAIRS

The FCO had good reasons to be grateful to William Hague as Foreign Secretary for 4 years of the coalition government. He protected the small FCO budget from cuts in the first years of the coalition – we basically had to manage with so-called flat cash (no uplift for inflation).

He talked up the importance of the FCO within government. This was one period where the FCO was not pushed around by an all-powerful Treasury and/or ignored by No 10 Downing Street as had happened in some previous governments. The FCO budget is small change in the greater scheme of things. The Treasury have always had bigger fish to fry. But the FCO has also suffered from being an easy target. We are not well organised with backers from industry, academia, the armed forces ready to speak on our behalf as you might see in the United States where the State Department has a serious high-level Advisory Committee. So the FCO budget has often been squeezed. With William Hague at the helm, a former Party leader and genuinely big hitter yet no longer with an aspiration to be Prime Minister, a man who helped the Chancellor George Osborne in his career, the FCO for once was not going to be under exceptional pressure.

That does not mean we didn't have to be efficient. William Hague with his background at McKinseys knew how to push for improvement. At the same time he was no lover of management speak, which is all-pervasive weed in Whitehall. I only wish he had spoken out even more on that.

He encouraged ambition.

He cared about the institution. Famously, he said publicly when he visited the FCO library, recently emptied of original treaties and books given to King's College and other universities, that all he had found was Albert the Anaconda, a stuffed snake which had presided over the library for the top of a bookcase for time immemorial. The Library was re-opened, to some extent restocked but with a different and more modern purpose.

The FCO Language School, closed for good reasons a few years ago, was re-opened in new premises in the basement of the FCO main building, on a more sustainable model – providing excellent facilities in the prestigious building at King Charles Street for contract teachers to use with groups of diplomats and sometimes individuals (such as Ambassadors for whom an ability to speak well in the language of their country is so important) rather than employing teachers directly and struggling to match the ever-changing demand with the staffing.

When William Hague left the Foreign Office in 2014 he had set in train the formation of a Diplomatic Academy, an institution many Diplomatic Services have around the world for training staff (including in Brazil – the Rio Branco Institute). Again, this was conceived in an imaginative and flexible way to suit our needs and resources available rather than slavishly follow a model from another country. If done well, it will give coherence to our training and development effort, which has been piecemeal hitherto.

He wanted the FCO not only to be the leader on political and security issues overseas and become ever better at consular protection but also saw the FCO as an Economic Department especially able to make a difference for UK business. He did not like the trend of recent years of reducing the UK diplomatic footprint overseas. He wanted more staffing for Embassies in the so-called emerging powers such as China and India (and Brazil was on this list too, though lower down) and wanted diplomatic missions re-opened in some places where we had closed and opened in new places.

Wet blankets in FCO asked what we should stop doing in order to take on his new priorities. He said we should do it all! Right! It was for the FCO to find ways of reallocating resources in accordance with his vision.

I drew on his expansionist vision to suggest opening a new British Consulate in the northeastern city of Recife. The rationale was that the North East was a coming region of Brazil with opportunities for UK business; it had a Governor in Eduardo Campos who was dynamic, internationally oriented and could one day be Brazilian President (sadly he was killed in a plane crash in August 2014 while campaigning for the Presidency); it would be good for the UK to develop contacts outside the traditional spheres in Brasilia and São Paulo where there was more hunger for contact and sense of adventure.

I said we could open the Consulate on a shoestring in the first instance by having our Consul General in São Paulo John Doddrell oversee it by being designated also as Consul General Recife – this fitted him well as his wife was from Recife and he knew the city well and liked working there – and appointing a locally-engaged Consul (I already had in mind Gareth Moore, then working for us on consular matters and living in Natal). It worked. London supported. The Foreign Secretary enjoyed announcing the opening of this new mission and the re-opening of our Embassy in Paraguay, for the years since its closure a major bone of contention with that country.

He promised to visit Brazil. He saw the role of the Foreign

Secretary as being broader than the traditional focus on the EU, Middle East and the crises of the day – although his time too became increasingly taken up with these matters. But I could not claim Brazil should be among his top priorities to visit. What I wanted was for him to commit to a yearly meeting with the Brazilian Foreign Minister, alternating location between Brazil and UK. It would then be for me and FCO to ensure these meetings were valuable. I knew the Brazilian side would take them seriously and were much more likely to engage on joint working with the prospect of some new step forward being prepared for the annual meeting. It all sounds like process – but that was the way to make things happen with Brazil.

Again, we had a false start. He was going to visit Brazil in early April 2011 and then the crisis in Libya caused him to postpone. He eventually visited in January 2012 – January is usually a quieter time for Foreign Secretaries when they make trips far afield. It wasn't ideal for us as January is the summer holiday in Brazil. But it worked well enough.

Day 1 was Brasilia – talks at the Foreign Ministry.

Day 2 was in Rio. We had a seminar on the Arab Spring, an effort to launch more debate on hot foreign affairs issues in Brazil – civil society is growing in influence but discussion of international issues is still largely left to the Brazilian Foreign Ministry (known as Itamaraty after the Palace they occupied in Rio). We had organised a conference involving Chatham House in Rio on "Brazil and The World" for the abortive April 2011 visit: it had gone ahead but without the Foreign Ministers.

I organised a dinner for him to shoot the breeze with interesting Brazilians outside government. He liked that. It included one of my favourite Brazilians, Ellen Gracie Northfleet. She was the first woman to be Brazilian Chief

Justice. When Gordon Brown visited Brasilia, Lula said how highly he esteemed her and sought our support for her election to an international legal position. She stepped down from the Supreme Court in 2011 and went to live and practise in Rio.

Her name suggests a link with the Anglo-Saxon world. She explained to me that her family had lived in London up to the time of the Great Fire – hence the surname, north of the Fleet River – and then emigrated to the colony of Virginia. After the Civil War, her family was one of a number from the former confederate states to emigrate to Brazil, settling in the deep South – Rio Grande do Sul. Another aspect of the diversity which is Brazil.

The Falkland Islands – a stone in my shoe?

I was asked in a public session of the conference involving Chatham House and the Brazilian think tank CEBRI in 2011 whether the Falkland Islands were a stone in my shoe as British Ambassador to Brazil. It was a good question. I said it was true the British and Brazilian governments had different views on the sovereignty of the islands but we were able to talk about these and they did not get in the way of working together in many political and economic areas.

The Falklands did become a more difficult issue for me as Lula handed over the Presidency to Dilma at the end 2010. On 29 December 2010, I received a phone call from the Brazilian Foreign Ministry to say that our applications for the two Royal Navy ships HMS Clyde and HMS Gloucester to visit Brazilian ports had been turned down. I wasn't given a reason.

It had been a regular practice for Royal Navy ships to make reprovisioning visits to Brazil when going out to, or returning from, duties in the South Atlantic including visiting the Falklands. HMS Gloucester had, for instance, stopped in Fortaleza in December 2009 and I had hosted a lunch and evening reception on board. Similarly, I had given a lunch on board HMS Portland in Rio in May 2010 and we had used the ship to host an exhibition for the UK Defence Industry.

The rhetoric at regional political meetings was ever more reflecting the Argentine wish to create a hostile environment for the UK over the Islands. At these meetings other countries would have a range of concerns and goals. Argentina would just press for action and stronger words on the Falklands. President Cristina Kirchner gave the impression that it just required a big push to force the UK to negotiate. The UK government was always ready to talk about co-operation in the region. We would not talk about handing over sovereignty unless the Falkland Islanders wanted that.

The intensifying pressure from Argentina on its neighbours and the sharpening of rhetoric bothered me and fellow British Ambassadors in the region. But, on the other hand, the media in Brazil barely bothered to report such developments and the rhetoric had had no practical effect.

Quite why this changed just as Dilma was becoming President only the Brazilians will know. Perhaps to get her relationship with Argentina off to a good start.

It is a difficult relationship for Brazil to manage. Argentina is the most important neighbour and central to Brazil's interest to see closer political and economic co-operation in South America. If Argentina is not pulling in the same direction, Brazil will find it hard to achieve agreement in the region.

There is a historical-psychological dimension. Argentina was after World War 1 among the most successful economies in the world. Similarly, it was well placed after World War 2 as an advanced country offering primary products. It had always been a more sophisticated society. There is no city of European format like Buenos Aires in Brazil. Argentinians were, until recently, better educated and more advanced in the sciences.

Nowadays, Argentina has dubious credentials to be within the G20 group of countries as its economy is well below that threshold and sinking further. After long looking down on Brazil, the Argentine economy is now considerably smaller than São Paulo. At the same time, Argentina has been making life difficult for Brazilian business there. It's a great achievement of the last 25 years that the rivalry between the two countries has been replaced by structures of co-operation, for example in nuclear collaboration and the Common Market of the South (MERCOSUR) agreement. But the bilateral relationship looks to not a few Brazilians as largely take from Argentina and no give.

I had several sessions with the Foreign Ministry, Defence Ministry and the Brazilian Navy to investigate what was happening. As so often in Brazil, the situation was murky. They said there had been a decision to change their policy and they would not revert. Still, they also stressed that permission to visit would be decided on a case-by-case basis, so we could not call this a ban. They were clear it was linked to the role of the ships in the Falklands but unclear how they would treat applications for ships' visits which were not sailing there or back. They wanted to keep the temperature down and did not publicise what they were doing. I left them in no doubt that there was no chance at all of a change in the British view about the sovereignty of the islands because the status quo was what the Islanders wanted and they had a right to determine their own future.

I had to interpret what I thought was going on and advise London accordingly. I was certain that Argentine pressure lay behind the change. It might have been seen as a good way for Dilma to start her relationship with President Cristina

Fernandez de Kirchner. There might also have been a link with the visit of HMS Ocean in September 2010 and joint Brazilian-British marine manoeuvres at that time. We knew the Argentinians had complained to Brazil about this.

Brazil had always supported the Argentine claim to the islands. They also disliked having a foreign presence on South American territory, though they did not speak out strongly against this nor against French sovereignty over their neighbour French Guiana. There were some claims that the UK was militarising the region through its garrison on the islands, stationing of Typhoon aircraft and operation of warships; there were also complaints about stationing nuclear weapons. None of this stood up. Very few Brazilians knew anything about these issues, about the islands or cared about their sovereignty. For the Brazilian government, their policy was mostly a matter of handling their bilateral relations with Argentina (essential) and the UK (important). As so often in diplomacy, the trick for them was to how to derive benefit from both.

I suspected there were differing views in the Brazilian camp. Nothing would change for the better during the current Brazilian and Argentine Presidencies. But beyond that, it was not impossible to imagine a quiet relaxation of the situation. I thought we should apply for ships which were not warships and for warships which were not going to or from the Falklands. I advised we would do best to stay calm. We had to make clear that we did not like this and wanted it to stop. But making a public fuss would almost certainly help hardliners in Brazil and lead to a harder edge to their policy. This is not easy advice to give on an issue as sensitive as the Falklands where Ministers understandably and rightly want to shout their indignation from the rooftops.

We received permission for HMS Protector to visit Rio

in December 2011. Protector was a scientific ship on its way south to replace the damaged Antarctic survey ship. On 21 December I was on board Protector on a balmy Rio night surrounded by senior members of the Brazilian Navy and other guests and looking at vessels of the Brazilian fleet including several – like the former Sir Galahad and Belvedere – which had seen service in the Falklands War of 1982 for the Royal Navy before being sold to Brazil.

I took a call on my mobile phone from the Brazilian Deputy Foreign Minister. I had been pressing for a high-level Foreign Ministry comment on a statement made at a regional meeting the previous week which included wording about barring Falklands-flagged ships from regional ports. The reaction to my phone calls had been that I should not worry about this – there would be no difficulty in practice. I asked for a reply to a simple question: has anything changed regarding access for ships from the Falklands to Brazilian ports? The Deputy Foreign Minister told me that nothing had changed and I should follow up at working level.

I did this immediately after Christmas and was reassured that banning any ships not caught by prohibitions in the international Law of the Sea would require changes in Brazilian legislation. There had been no changes in Brazilian legislation. Brazilian negotiators had insisted that the text about Falklands-flagged ships should contain the phrase that any action against them should be "subject to national and international law".

This is what diplomats do. The Brazilians had gone along with Argentine rhetoric but ensured it would have no effect on Brazilian actions. The Argentine Foreign Minister declared publicly that he had checked with Brazil and been told Brazil would stick to the statement about Falklands-flagged ships. What he did not say is that this would not change anything in practice. When we heard some time later that a ship had encountered difficulties with the authorities at a southern port, the Foreign Ministry ensured the problem was resolved.

Meanwhile, I had been doing my bit to help BAE Systems in a negotiation to sell three Offshore Patrol Vessels to Brazil. The Brazilian Defence Minister told me there had to be a political dimension to the deal in the sense that the British government needed to show its support for the sale – we arranged through a letter from our Ministry of Defence. We also supported a visit by the Head of the Brazilian Navy and the Brazilian Ambassador to see the ships being built in Portsmouth. It was great to hear the Brazilians talk in Portuguese about "their ships" although the negotiations had yet to be concluded. The ships have since made visits to ports in Africa on their way back to Brazil.

This was a good deal all round. These were the kind of state-of-the art modern ships Brazil really needed in my view for the Navy's task of defending its offshore oil fields; the prestige projects of a nuclear submarine and a new aircraft carrier seemed more about image projection. The Brazilian Defence Minister had secured agreement for the President to procure them as a target of opportunity. BAE Systems had been building them for Trinidad and Tobago only to be told after an election there that the ships were not wanted after all – so the company wanted to sell them quickly. The Brazilians have the option to build more of the same type in Brazil under licence from the company.

We didn't have the same opportunity on fighter aircraft as the Brazilian short list omitted the Typhoon (probably rightly as Brazil doesn't need a plane of this sophistication). The US F18 looked to me the best fit for Brazil, except that the Brazilians did not believe Congress would allow sufficient transfer of technology – the US option stayed in the game owing to brilliant work by US Ambassador Tom

Shannon ensuring it was made as attractive as possible to the Brazilians.

I and many others heard President Lula say in his speech at the Independence Day Parade on 7 September 2009 in Brasilia that Brazil intended to buy the French Rafale (from his friend Nicolas Sarkozy, there at his side). The Brazilian Air Force was not convinced and forced a re-evaluation of the options. The best option for UK interests was the Swedish Gripen as it would have over 20% value of UK components. For a long time, the Swedes seemed outmatched by the diplomatic power of the US and an ever more annoyed France. But, in 2014, the Brazilians decided to buy Gripen – which the Brazilian company EMBRAER could build with SAAB.

I visited the Falklands in January 2012. It was fascinating week, travelling around the islands and speaking to hundreds of islanders. I was left in no doubt that the Falklanders had become even stronger in their views about Argentina as the Argentine President shouted ever louder about ignoring the Islanders' wishes and negotiating with the UK about handing over sovereignty (not going to happen). Younger Islanders were forthright in their views about the current Argentine government. I detected that some of the senior political figures actually found the situation easier than when former Argentine Foreign Minister Di Tella had sought to charm them during the Menem Presidency. At the same time, everyone wanted closer links with South America, and Brazil in particular. We tried to help in the Embassy and Consulates with practical contacts on trade, sport, culture.

There were many reminders of the war on the islands. Thirty years on there was still debris of various kinds, including Israeli-built war planes acquired by Argentina and brought down. The British war memorial and Argentine cemetery are places of pilgrimage. People who were children during the war and held for weeks by the Argentine military still suffer post-traumatic stress.

The Falklanders' referendum on sovereignty in March 2013 produced a 99.8% vote in favour of retaining the Islands' current political status as an Overseas Territory of the UK. That was no surprise for me having seen many of them just a year before.

It was good publicity in Brazil too. The most common line on TV and in the press was that Argentina was making such a fuss over the Falklands in order to deflect attention from the increasingly difficult domestic situation – just as the Argentine junta had done in 1982 – but this time Argentina would not try a military invasion.

The Ronnie Biggs hangover

One of the longstanding sores in the bilateral relationship had been Brazilian refusal to extradite the convicted Great Train robber Ronnie Biggs back to UK. Brazilian law does not make extradition easy. It did not consider the possibility in this case because Mr Biggs had a Brazilian child. He became something of a celebrity in Rio.

During my time the Italians were very upset over the Brazilian decision not to extradite Cesare Battisti, convicted of four murders in the 1970s. There were those in the ruling Workers' Party who saw Battisti as a political activist not unlike themselves during the Brazilian military dictatorship. The Italian body politic and the media made clear their disgust and a lot of Brazilians too. The issue is not over. Battisti may yet be deported to another country.

I found myself having to handle the case of Michael

Misick, former Premier of the Turks and Caicos Islands. He was wanted back in the Turks and Caicos to answer charges of corruption. By this time we had a mutual legal assistance agreement with Brazil and established that this applied also to overseas territories such as the Turks and Caicos. Mr Misick was arrested by the Brazilian police.

There followed a long political struggle within Brazil on whether to send him back to the Turks and Caicos or allow him to stay accepting his contention that he was being persecuted. I knew this was finely balanced. The Federal Justice Minister and Supreme Court kept up a dialogue with me, understanding there was a lot at stake regarding Brazil's reputation in UK and beyond. There were tricky moments such as when he was released on bail. But eventually, in January 2014, six months after my departure as Ambassador, he was extradited to the Turks and Caicos. It was a good decision for Brazil showing it meant what it said about legal co-operation with other countries. It must have been tough for the Justice Interior Minister against the backdrop of some domestic internal pressure.

These two areas – the Falklands and Michael Misick – were difficult issues. Yet as an Ambassador you rather welcome having some grit in the oyster. When things are going swimmingly you might wonder whether the contacts and reputation you have tried to build up in the country really make much difference. It is when the going gets rougher that these are of value. These issues were also ones for the Ambassador to address personally and give you a good reason to deal with your host country at a high level of seniority.

Don't get the impression my time in Brazil was all about stones in the shoe and grit in the oyster. Most of what I did was looking to help the UK increase trade and investment and looking to increase foreign-policy co-operation. We had a strong team from UK Trade and Investment as well as from the Foreign Office in the Embassy and our two large consulates at São Paulo and Rio. Every year we had around 50 business delegations visiting from the UK. We also wanted to encourage more Brazilian investment in the UK.

We had plenty of interest from Scotland because of the links between Brazil's growing exploitation of deep-sea oil and gas and our experience in the North Sea. Aberdeen was a well-known destination for Brazilians in this field. The Scottish government decided to appoint a representative to work within our Consulate in Rio.

The Northern Irish, too, came to Brazil: First Minister Peter Robinson and Deputy First Minister Martin McGuinness. Their main success was a further investment by the Brazilian food company Marfrig in Northern Ireland.

Culture is as an important tool. We raised some money for a season of the UK in Brazil following the Olympics. The big London cultural organisations showed closer interest in Brazil. The Royal Opera House/Royal Ballet came to Rio as Lord Hall was stepping down and moving to the BBC – they featured two Brazilian dancers in their company. The V and A came to an agreement with the Ministry of Culture including helping over an exhibition in Brasilia. The Science Museum is collaborating with Rio's new Museum of Tomorrow. The Tate has a collaboration with São Paulo. The Natural History Museum and Tate have been active too.

Film plays its part promoting the British brand. I regret that we did not make more of the premiere of the Iron Lady in Rio. I did host a showing of Skyfall in Brasilia.

I learned in Brazil the power of Education and Culture in Diplomacy. We are still not good at exploiting the synergies between UK and Brazil in these areas – not least because responsibility in Whitehall falls between stools. I'd favour giving much more power to a beefed-up UK Trade and Investment.

★★★

Do you miss Brazil? That is the question I have often been asked since returning to the UK. On a cold and damp Winter's day sitting in front of a PC, the warmth of Brazil is an attractive memory! But the answer is: no. Diplomats get used to the idea of working a few years in one country, getting to know people and the issues there – and then moving back to your own country or to another foreign posting. Which was your favourite country? Again, no simple answer. There are wonderful memories of them all. As for Brazil, that having been my last posting and in the position of Ambassador, being the representative of the UK in the country, inevitably those memories are especially vivid.

Coming back to UK, I have been lecturing on Brazil while I still have some fairly current knowledge – in universities and on cruise ships – and helping UK institutions with their international work. I've started a bilateral forum, the Conversa, for private discussion between senior Brazilians and Brits involved in public policy, business and education/ science about how to make the most of synergies between the two countries.

We should remember our shared history, shared areas of culture and shared interests. Above all you have to take a long view. As Ambassador I woke up every morning enthused by the opportunities to make a difference and went to bed frustrated by the difficulty of getting things done.

PART VIII

WILL BRAZIL ALWAYS
BE THE COUNTRY OF
THE FUTURE?

Stefan Zweig was so impressed by Brazil during his short sojourn while in exile in World War 2 that he called it "a country of the future". Over the last two hundred years at least, many Brazilians have believed that. As the 21st century moves on that belief in the future is ever more tinged with disappointment that progress is so uneven.

Yes, the Brazilian economy has developed fast since World War 2. Poverty has been reduced. Democracy is well established, if not yet unassailable. This country, blessed with wonderful resources and – despite the joke at the beginning of this piece on Brazil – wonderful people too, is not yet the finished article.

Writing in 2015, Brazil's reputation is sinking in the backwash of the Petrobras scandal, the so-called "Petrolão" "the Big Oily" echoing the "Mensalão", "The Big Monthly Payment" scandal of 2006 onwards. The Mensalão was about the Ruling Workers' Party paying members of congress of other parties for their votes with cash creamed off from inflated government contracts. There was eventually a Supreme Court trial, broadcast live every evening on TV and remarkable for the persistent brilliance of Joaquim Barbosa, then Chief Justice, a black polymath whom the black staff at the Embassy saw as an inspiration. Some people were convicted and imprisoned including a former Chief of Staff to President Lula, but the episode did not end with a feeling that that high-level corruption had been dealt a mortal blow. The questions about links to the Presidency were not cleared up.

Petrobras has been a symbol of the economic rise of Brazil since it was founded in 1953. In 1997 it lost its monopoly on oil and gas business in Brazil. But it went on to become the largest company in South America and the 8th largest in the world in 2011 after a world-record selling of shares on the Brazilian stock exchange to the tune of US$72.2 billion. It has oil and energy assets in 18 countries as well as being at the heart of the development of Brazil's large off-shore oil finds.

Yet it had been apparent for some time that not all was well. Its debts increased from US$25 billion to US$ 170 billion from 2013 to 2014.

64 per cent of the shares are in the hands of the Brazilian government, its Sovereign Wealth Fund and its Development Bank BNDES. The President of the Republic appoints the CEO. Governments have advertised Petrobras as a symbol of national pride, developing "our" oil and gas in the interest of the nation. The amounts of money made available over the years to the company by the government for investment are staggering.

Petrobras became a symbol of what is wrong with Brazil. In February 2014 police began the so-called Operation Car Wash investigating kickbacks from the six big Brazilian construction firms and use of money from inflated contracts for the Workers' Party. Many people have been arrested. The CEO of the company has been replaced. There have been calls for the impeachment of President Dilma Rousseff. She – as

Energy Minister, Chief of Staff to President Lula and now President of the Republic herself – was seen by many either involved or incompetent.

Investors called Petrobras to account in the US Justice System too. This led to a sharp downgrade in the company's investment rating, which in turn hit Brazil's investment rating. The economy suffered too.

So here we have, 25 years after the resumption of democracy, corruption at the highest levels of business and politics tainting even the President of the Republic, and a political system where it is phenomenally difficult to meet public expectations that the guilty should be brought to justice and punished and it be made impossible for such things to happen again. Brazilian police investigators and the media are good at uncovering and publicising wrong-doing. But that is only the beginning of the story. Whereas in other western countries this would be the stage where many of the protagonists would resign, in Brazil there will be endless shananigans before anyone is brought before a court let alone a final judgement issued and sentences begun.

The fact is that the rewards of corruption are so great and the chances of punishment so slender that so far the balance of risk has been on the side of carrying on corruptly.

This is the way it has always been done – an unholy alliance between big business and the top levels of government and politics is necessary to get things done. Too many Brazilians in the past have shrugged their shoulders saying it was ever thus and nothing will ever change. But here are ever more people who say that is no longer acceptable. Brazil is at a stage where it needs to move on. .

On 21 June 2013, while I was still in Brazil as Ambassador, over a million Brazilians came out on to the streets in cities around the country. The catalyst was the amount of money spent on the FIFA World Cup, some of it in vanity projects like the Brasilia stadium, instead of on health and education. Corruption was one of the issues. The political elite was shaken but rode out the storm.

In March 2015 the streets of São Paulo saw more big demonstrations focussed on the Petrobras scandal and corruption with some people even calling for the return of military rule, harking back to the coup of 1964 interrupting democracy for 25 years but seen by some as necessary at that time to stop civilian misgovernance. This is not a widespread view and the military are not nowadays involved in political debate. I cannot see this happening.

But these are danger signs. The question before Brazil is whether the political class is capable of reforming itself. Not easy. Turkeys don't vote for Christmas. Being in Congress is a cushy number and makes it difficult for you to be prosecuted.

Even among those who want to reform there is no consensus on what to do. For a start, they could change the voting system for Congress. The Workers' Party argues that there should be public funding of political parties to avoid the need to rely on money from illicit sources. This is a debate in many countries, including the UK. In Brazil, many people would be loath to put more public money into the hands of those they believe are already misusing it.

Everything hangs on political reform. Only then will Brazil be able to tackle the raft of other reforms needed – health, education, pensions, cutting red tape, a more open economy, better justice system. The key is the system for electing Congress and the accountability of the Congress to their constituents. Elections for President, Governor and Mayor work better – a clear choice of personalities with their programmes. Perhaps smaller constituencies with many fewer members elected as individuals rather than on a party ticket?

I am an optimist. 2015 is a grim year shaking the confidence of Brazilians in their country's direction. Yet, I expect that looking back from 2030 we shall see a Brazil which has moved on even if it has not solved all the serious problems it faces. Just how much it will have moved on will depend on whether the hunger in civil society for reform can be translated through the political system. I believe that Dilma Rousseff means what

she says about tackling corruption. But she does not seem to know how to do this or have the power to do so. She was re-elected, just, in 2014 because so many Brazilians in the lower socio-economic classes saw her as the guarantor of their continued economic rise. Even this group now has its doubts. As I write her popularity is at an all-time low for any Brazilian President.

It may be for the next President of Brazil to make the step change Brazil is crying out for so that it is no longer seen as a country failing to fulfil its potential. Brazil will move forward and the UK should be its partner along the way.

Index of Names

Bibliography

Ever The Diplomat – Sir Sherard Cowper-Col Harperpress 2012

The Legal Status of Berlin – Ian Hendry and Michael Wood Grotius Publications 1987

Naturalists in Paradise: Wallace, Bates and Spruce in the Amazon – John Hemming Thames and Hudson 2015

Brazil The Troubled Rise of a Global Power – Michael Reid Yale University Press 2014

Spandauer Tagebücher – Albert Speer Propyläen 1975

Ingleses no Brasil – Gilberto Freyre – Gilbertiana Topbooks Third Edition 2000

DC Confidential – Sir Christopher Meyer, Weidenfield & Nicholson 2005

The Way Prepared – Leslie McLonghlan, Librairiee du Libon 1974

Dominion – CJ Samson, MacMillon, 2012.